HEAVEN FORBID

*To my mother and father, Virgilia and William Cotter,
my uncle, Theodore Mooney, my brothers and sisters, my husband Mark Badger and
my son, Bill and my daughter, Jill for their love and devotion*

Heaven Forbid
An International Legal Analysis of
Religious Discrimination

ANNE-MARIE MOONEY COTTER
Social Security Disability Law Firm, USA

Taylor & Francis Group

LONDON AND NEW YORK

First published 2009 by Ashgate Publishing

2 Park Square, Milton Park, Abingdon, Oxon OX14 4RN
711 Third Avenue, New York, NY 10017, USA

Routledge is an imprint of the Taylor & Francis Group, an informa business

First issued in paperback 2016

Copyright © 2009 Anne-Marie Mooney Cotter

Anne-Marie Mooney Cotter has asserted her right under the Copyright, Designs and Patents Act, 1988, to be identified as the author of this work.

All rights reserved. No part of this book may be reprinted or reproduced or utilised in any form or by any electronic, mechanical, or other means, now known or hereafter invented, including photocopying and recording, or in any information storage or retrieval system, without permission in writing from the publishers.

Notice:
Product or corporate names may be trademarks or registered trademarks, and are used only for identification and explanation without intent to infringe.

British Library Cataloguing in Publication Data
Cotter, Anne-Marie Mooney
   Heaven forbid : an international legal analysis of
   religious discrimination
   1. Religious minorities - Legal status, laws, etc.
   2. Discrimination - Law and legislation
   I. Title
   342'.0852

Library of Congress Cataloging-in-Publication Data
Cotter, Anne-Marie Mooney.
   Heaven forbid : an international legal analysis of religious discrimination / by Anne-Marie Mooney Cotter.
     p. cm.
   Includes bibliographical references and index.
   ISBN 978-0-7546-7385-9
   1. Religious minorities--Legal status, laws, etc. 2. Discrimination--Religious aspects. 3. Freedom of religion (International law) 4. Religion and law. I. Cotter, Anne-Marie Mooney. II. Title.

   K3280.C68 2009
   342.08'52--dc22

2008045368

ISBN 13: 978-0-7546-7385-9 (hbk)
ISBN 13: 978-1-138-26002-3 (pbk)

Contents

Biography		*vii*
1	Introduction to Heaven Forbid	1
2	Heaven Forbid in Religious Discrimination	7
3	Heaven Forbid in the United Nations	19
4	Heaven Forbid in Australia and New Zealand	65
5	Heaven Forbid in Africa and South Africa	93
6	Heaven Forbid in Canada, Mexico and the United States	131
7	Heaven Forbid in the North American Free Trade Agreement	169
8	Heaven Forbid in the United Kingdom and Ireland	221
9	Heaven Forbid in the European Union	265
10	Conclusion to Heaven Forbid	315
Bibliography		*319*
Index		*329*

Biography

Dr. Anne-Marie Mooney Cotter, Esq. is a Montrealer, fluent in both English and French. She earned her Bachelor's degree from McGill University at age 18; her Juris Doctor law degree from one of the leading civil rights institutions, Howard University School of Law; and her Doctorate degree (Ph.D.) from Concordia University, where she specialized in Political Economy International Law, particularly on the issue of equality. Her work experience has been extensive, Chief Advisor and later Administrative Law Judge appointed by the Prime Minister to the Veterans Review and Appeals Tribunal in Canada; Supervising Attorney and later Executive Director for the Legal Services Corporation in the United States; National Director for an environmental network in Canada; Faculty for Business Law at the Law School, Law Society of Ireland; Associate at the law firm of Blake Cassels and Graydon L.L.P. with a secondment as in-house counsel with Agrium Inc. in Canada; Attorney with the Disability Law Center of Alaska; and Solo Practitioner of the Social Security Disability Law Firm. She volunteers as arbitrator for the Annual International Commercial Arbitration Moot Competition. She is also a gold medalist in figure skating. Dr. Cotter is the wife of Mark Badger and the proud mother of Bill and Jill.

Chapter 1
Introduction to Heaven Forbid

So we come here today to dramatize a shameful condition. In a sense we've come to our nation's capital to cash a check. When the architects of our republic wrote the magnificent words of the Constitution and the Declaration of Independence, they were signing a promissory note to which every (human) was to fall heir. This note was the promise that all ... would be guaranteed the unalienable rights of life, liberty, and the pursuit of happiness ... A check which has come back marked insufficient funds. We refuse to believe that there are insufficient funds in the great vaults of opportunity of this nation. And so we've come to cash this check, a check that will give us upon demand the riches of freedom and the security of justice.[1]

In our universal quest for justice in general and religious tolerance in *Heaven Forbid*, we may learn from the immortal words of one of the greatest civil rights leaders and human rights activists, Dr. Martin Luther King Jr. This book, *Heaven Forbid*, focuses on the goal of religious equality and the importance of the law and legislation to combat religious discrimination in these troubling times. The aim of this book is to better understand the issue of inequality and to improve the likelihood of achieving religious equality in the future and ending religious inequality. *Heaven Forbid* examines the primary role of legislation, which has an impact on the court process, as well as the primary role of the judicial system, which has an impact on the fight for religious tolerance. This is the fifth book in a series of books on discrimination law. Other titles in the series are *Gender Injustice* dealing with gender discrimination, *Race Matters* dealing with race discrimination, *This Ability* dealing with disability discrimination, and *Just a Number* dealing with age discrimination. A similar approach and structure is used throughout the series to illustrate comparisons and contradictions in discrimination law.

Fundamental rights are rights which either are inherent in a person by natural law or are instituted in the citizen by the State. The ascending view of the natural law of divine origin over human law involves moral expectations in human beings through a social contract, which includes minimum moral rights of which one may not be deprived by government or society. The competing view is that courts operating under the Constitution can enforce only those guarantees which are expressed. Thus, legislation has an impact on the court system and on society as a whole. Internationally and nationally, attempts have been made to improve the situation of those who are members of religious minorities and outlaw religious discrimination through acceptance and accommodation.

In looking at the relationship between *Heaven Forbid* and the law, the book deals comprehensively with the issue of religious discrimination throughout its chapters: Chapter 1 introduces the reader to the core area of religious inequality; Chapter 2 covers religious inequality in human relations around the world; Chapter 3 looks at the United Nations; Chapters 4 and 5 examine religious inequality in Australia and New Zealand, and Africa and South Africa, respectively; Chapters 6 and 7 examine religious inequality in Canada, Mexico and the United States, and the North American situation with the North American Free Trade Agreement regarding religious discrimination, respectively; Chapters 8 and 9 examine religious inequality in the United Kingdom and Ireland, and the European situation with the European Union Treaty regarding religious discrimination, respectively; and Chapter 10 concludes this overview of religious inequality.

The globalization process and the various economic agreements have a direct impact on people's lives as key players in the labor market today. This study seeks to comparatively analyze legislation impacting religious equality in various countries internationally. It also examines the two most important trade agreements of our day, namely the North American Free Trade Agreement and the European Union Treaty in a historical and compelling analysis of equality. Although an important trade agreement with implications for labor, the North American Free Trade Agreement has a different system from the European system in that it has no overseeing court with jurisdiction over the respective countries. Further, the provisions for nondiscrimination in the labor process are contained in a separate document, the North American Agreement on Labor Cooperation. On the other hand, the European Union Treaty takes a different approach by directly providing for nondiscrimination, as well as an overseeing court, the European Court of Justice, and the treaty is made part of the domestic law of every Member State, weakening past discriminatory laws and judgments. Further, the European process actively implements religious equality by way of European Union legislation.

North America, as the new world with its image of freedom and equality, is considered to have made great strides in civil rights. However, the American philosophy of survival of the fittest, the pursuit of materialism and the search for the fountain of youth have slowed down the process. With the advent of the European Union, the coming together of nations has had a very positive influence on the enforcement of human rights, much more so than that of North America, because of the unique European approach.

All parties must cooperate, and governments need to work with businesses, trade unions and society as a whole, so together they can create an environment where all humans can participate at all levels of political life and decision making. Indeed, combating religious inequality and achieving religious equality requires a strong *Heaven Forbid* focus on religion in constitutional, legal, judicial and electoral frameworks for all humans to be actively involved at the national and international levels.

According to liberal democracy, the rule of law is the foundation stone for the conduct of institutions. *Heaven Forbid* offers a defense of the notion that social reform is possible and plausible through key institutions, which include the legal system and its use of the law. For liberal democracy, the legislative system is the core for the governance of society in the way it functions toward social equality of opportunity. It is clear that if we initially reform our legislation and our laws and in the end our way of thinking, then there will be a change in the institutions of society and their functioning, which will be a major step forward in societal reform.

The law is of central importance in the debate for change from religious inequality to religious equality. Actionable and enforceable rights are legal norms, which represent social facts demarcating areas of action linked with universalized freedom.[2] Law is a powerful tool, which can and must be used to better society. Associated with command, duty and sanction, and emanating from a determined source, law is a rule of conduct enforced by sanctions, and administered by a determinate locus of power concentrated in a sovereign or a surrogate, the court. Therefore, the justice system and the courts play a vital role in enforcing the law.

Legitimacy has subjective guarantees of internalization with the acceptance and belief in authority, and objective guarantees of enforcement with the expectation of reactions to the behavior.[3] Therefore, law must recognize equally all members of society, including those who belong to minority religions, in order for it to be effective. Further, in order for a law to be seen as legitimate from society's point of view and accepted by the people, in general to be followed, a process of inclusive interaction by all affected must first be realized. When creating laws, this means that input from various groups, including all humans and all religions, is critical.

Thus, laws have two components, namely, facts, which stabilize expectations and sustain the order of freedom; and norms, which provide a claim of approval by everyone. Law makes possible highly artificial communities whose integration is based simultaneously on the threat of internal sanctions and the supposition of a rationally motivated agreement.[4] Religious discrimination and injustice can be undercut through the effective use of both the law and the courts.

The facticity of the enforcement of law is intertwined with the legitimacy of a genesis of law that claims to be rational, because it guarantees liberty. Laws can go a long way in forbidding inequality and providing for equality; where one ends the other begins. There are two ranks of law, namely ordinary law of legislation, administration and adjudication; and higher constitutional law affecting rights and liberties, which government must respect and protect. The latter encompasses the constitutions of the various nations as interpreted by the supreme courts. Law holds its legitimacy and validity by virtue of its coercive potential, its rational claim of acceptance as right. It is procedurally constructed to claim agreement by all citizens in a discursive process purported to be open to all equally for legitimacy with a presumption of fair results. The legitimate legal order is found in its reflexive process. Therefore, we must all believe that equality is a good and necessary thing, which is essential to the very growth of society and to the ending of religious discrimination.

Thus, conflict resolution is a process of reasoned agreement where, firstly, members assume the same meanings by the same words; secondly, members are rationally accountable for their actions; and thirdly, mutually acceptable resolutions can be reached so that supporting arguments justify the confidence in the notion that the truth in justice will not be proven false.[5] Disenchantment with the law and the legal process only serves to undermine the stabilization of communities. By legitimizing the legal process and holding up the ideals of equality in the fight against religious discrimination, the law and the courts can bring about change.

All humans have had to fight in the formulation of laws and in the enforcement of equality in the courts. Religion like class rests on economic determination and historical change. Inequality in the distribution of private property among different classes of people has been a characteristic of society. The ruling class loathes that which it is not, that which is foreign to it, and this has traditionally been those who belong to minority religions. The patriarchal system has freely fashioned laws and adjusted society to suit those in power, and this has traditionally been young white Anglo-Saxon Protestant men.

Relationships, opportunities, attributes and preconceived notions are socially constructed and are learned through socialization processes. They are context and time-specific but changeable, since the physical and the mental determine what is expected, allowed and valued in a given situation. In most societies, there are differences and inequalities between humans in the decision-making opportunities, assignment of responsibilities, undertaking of activities and access to and control over resources with religion part of the broader sociocultural context. There are important criteria for analysis, including religion, race, gender, age, poverty and class, and hence all these can, alone or combined, amount to discrimination.

The concept of equality is the ignoring of difference between individuals for a particular purpose in a particular context, or the deliberate indifference to specified differences in the acknowledgement of the existence of difference. It is important to note that assimilation is not equality. The notion of rights and of equality should be bound to the notion of justice and fairness. Legal freedom and rights must be seen as relationships not possessions—as doing, not having. While injustice involves a constraint of freedom and a violation of human dignity through a process of oppression and domination, justice involves the institutional conditions necessary for the development and exercise of individual capacities for collective communication and cooperation.[6] Discrimination is the withholding from the oppressed and subordinated what enables them to exercise private and public autonomy. The struggle must be continued to bring about psychological, sociological and institutional changes to allow all members of the human race including those belonging to religious minorities to feel equal and to recognize all religions as being so. Solidarity and cooperation are required for universal and global equality.

Though humans are mortal and civilizations come and go, from Biblical times to our days, there has been a fixed pivot for the thoughts of all generations and for humans of all continents, namely the equal dignity inherent in the human personality.[7] Even Pope John XXIII described the United Nations Declaration of Human Rights in his 1963 Encyclical *Pacem in Terris*, as 'one of the most important acts of the United Nations' and as 'a step towards the politico-judicial organization of the world community'; 'In social life, every right conferred on man by nature creates in others (individuals and collectivities) a duty, that of recognizing and respecting that right'.[8] Further, Pope John Paul II described the importance of work and of just remuneration in his 1981 Encyclical *Laborem Exercens*:

> Work bears a particular mark of ... humanity, the mark of a person operating within a community of persons .... While work, in all its many senses, is an obligation, that is to say a duty, it is also a source of rights on the part of the worker. These rights must be examined in the broad context of human rights as a whole, which are connatural with man, and many of which are proclaimed by various international organisations and increasingly guaranteed by the individual States for their citizens. Respect for this broad range of human rights constitutes the fundamental condition for peace in the modern world: peace both within individual countries and societies and in international relations .... The human rights that flow from work are part of the broader context of those fundamental rights of the person .... The key problem of social ethic ... is that of just remuneration for work done .... Hence, in every case, a just wage is the concrete means of verifying the justice of the whole socio-economic system and, in any case, of checking that it is functioning justly.[9]

An improvement in equality of opportunity is sought for all rather than a utopian state of equality. No one should misunderstand this. Clearly, oppression exists. Rather, this book *Heaven Forbid* seeks to add to the list of inequalities to be considered, and does not rule out other forms of injustices besides religious inequality. Generalities are not presumed nor are they made here, for this would detract from the very purpose of this book, to bring to the forefront of discussion the reality of injustice, not to create further injustice, in the pursuit of *Heaven Forbid*.

Notes

1   King Jr., Dr. Martin Luther, *March on Washington*, United States, 1963.
2   Habermas, Jurgen, *Between Facts and Norms*, Massachusetts, 1998, p. xii.
3   Fried, Morton, *The Evolution of Political Society*, New York, 1967, p. 23.
4   Habermas, Jurgen, *Between Facts and Norms*, Massachusetts, 1998, p. 8.
5   *Ibid.*, at p. xv.
6   *Ibid.*, at p. 419.
7   Cassin, René, *From the Ten Commandments to the Rights of Man*, France, 1969.
8   Pope John XXIII, *Pacem in Terris*, Rome, 1963.
9   Pope John Paul II, *Laborem Exercens*, Rome, 1981.

References

Cassin, René (1969), *From the Ten Commandments to the Rights of Man*, France.
Fried, Morton (1967), *The Evolution of Political Society*, Random House, New York.

Habermas, Jurgen (1998), *Between Facts and Norms*, MIT Press, Massachusetts.
King Jr., Dr. Martin Luther (1963), *March on Washington*, United States.
Pope John XXIII (1963), *Pacem in Terris*, Rome.
Pope John Paul II (1981), *Laborem Exercens*, Rome.

Chapter 2
Heaven Forbid in Religious Discrimination

Introduction

In the quest for religious tolerance in *Heaven Forbid*, this chapter will examine religious discrimination particularly and religion generally. All human, civil, cultural, economic, political and social rights, including the right to development, are universal, indivisible, interdependent and interrelated. Governments and others must not only refrain from violating human rights, but must work actively to promote and protect these rights. Human rights issues of discrimination continue to mar progress towards empowerment where those who belong to minority religions continue to be stereotyped and discriminated against and face systemic barriers and prejudice that prevent them from accessing the opportunities created for the achievement of equality.

Oh! God

The word discrimination comes from the Latin 'discriminare', which means to 'distinguish between'. Discrimination is more than distinction, it is action based on prejudice resulting in unfair treatment of people. Social theories of egalitarianism claim that social equality regardless of religion should prevail. Unlawful discrimination can be characterized as direct or indirect. Direct discrimination involves treating someone less favorably, because of the possession of a prohibited attribute such as religion than they would treat someone without the prohibited attribute who was in the same circumstances. Indirect discrimination involves setting a condition or requirement that a smaller proportion of those with the prohibited attribute can comply with than those who do not have the prohibited attribute, without reasonable justification.

Within the equal opportunities/individual merit approach can be found a spectrum of tests for discrimination. At one end of the spectrum, there is the 'equality as mere rationality' approach, where arbitrary and unreasonable behavior is deemed discriminatory, but justifications for discrimination are accepted at face value. At the other end of the spectrum, there is the 'equality as fairness' approach, where justifications are examined critically, the possibility of indirect discrimination is recognized, and burdens of proof may be shifted. There is a third conception of equality which goes beyond the individual merit approach but avoids the explicitly redistributive language of equality of results, the 'radical equality of opportunity', which argues for institutional and structural changes to remove the barriers to equal participation of people belonging to religious minorities. It involves the creation of positive duties on employers to promote equality, by reviewing employment practices and workplace organization.

Building religious rights on the existing corpus of employee rights has the important limitation that the rights created are confined to those in employment. One purpose of a definition of religion is to establish a standard for specifying who has rights under antidiscrimination legislation, which is common to both existing and prospective employees, and avoids setting different standards for 'insiders' and 'outsiders'. This is a laudable ideal, but it comes up against a very basic problem about the fair allocation of costs across employers. The difficulty for a job-seeker is that no employer has any particular or special duty towards him relative to other employers.

Prejudice is, as the name implies, the process of pre-judging something. In general, it implies coming to a judgment on the subject before learning where the preponderance of the evidence actually lies, or formation of a judgment without direct experience. When applied to social groups, prejudice generally refers to existing biases toward the members of such groups, such as those belonging to minority religions, often based on social stereotypes, and at its most extreme, denying groups benefits and rights unjustly or, conversely, unfairly showing unwarranted favor towards others. It may be a matter of early education; those taught that certain attitudes are the correct ones may form opinions without weighing the evidence on both sides of a given question. Many prejudicial behaviors are picked up at a young age by children emulating their elders' way of thinking and speaking, with no malice intended on the child's part. Overall, prejudice has been termed an adaptive behavior by sociologists.

Discrimination is to make a distinction. Commonplace forms of invidious discrimination include distinctions by religion, race, skin color, ethnicity, nationality, gender, marital status, age and socio-economic class. Invidious discrimination classifies people into different groups in which group members receive distinct and typically unequal treatments and rights without rational justification. Expectations and obligations of group members are also biased by invidious discrimination. If the justification is rational, then the discrimination is not invidious. By virtue of establishing nationalism, as opposed to globalism, every government has formalized and supported discrimination. However, many governments have attempted to control discrimination through civil rights legislation, equal opportunity laws and institutionalized policies of affirmative action.

Affirmative action or positive discrimination is a policy or a program providing access to systems for people of a minority group, who have traditionally been discriminated against, with the aim of creating a more egalitarian society. This consists of access to education, employment, health care or social welfare. The terms 'affirmative action' and 'positive discrimination' originate in law, where it is common for lawyers to speak of affirmative or positive remedies that command the wrongdoer to do something. In contrast, negative remedies command the wrongdoer to not do something or to stop doing something. In employment, affirmative action may also be known as employment equity or preferential hiring. Affirmative action requires that institutions increase hiring and promotion of candidates of mandated groups. It originally began as a government remedy for past government and social injustices, and exists to change the distribution of such things as jobs, education or wealth based on certain characteristics.

Supporters of affirmative action argue that affirmative action policies counteract a systemic discrimination by providing a balancing force. A certain group may be less proportionately represented in an area, often employment or education, due, in the view of proponents, to past or ongoing discrimination against members of the group. The theory is that a simple adoption of meritocratic principles along the lines of religious-blindness would not suffice to change the situation: regardless of overt principles, people already in positions of power are likely to hire people they know, and people from similar backgrounds; also, ostensible measures of merit might well be biased toward the same groups who were already empowered. In such a circumstance, proponents believe government action giving members of the group preferential treatment is necessary in order to achieve a proportionate distribution. A written affirmative action plan must include goals and timetables for achieving full utilization of all people, especially those from minority religions, in quotas based on an analysis of the current workforce compared to the availability in the general labor pool. Supporters of affirmative action argue that it benefits society as a whole; given that affirmative action is effective, since creating a diverse culture increases the quality of the society.

From its outset, affirmative action was seen as a transitional strategy, with the intent that in a period, variously estimated from a generation to a century, the effects of past discrimination would be sufficiently countered that such a strategy would no longer be necessary: the power elite would reflect the demographics of society at large. Opponents of affirmative action regard it as demeaning to members of disadvantaged groups, in that affirmative action wrongly sends a condescending message that they are not capable enough to be considered on their own merits. Critics often object to the use of quotas in affirmative action. There is dispute over whether this *de jure* illegality prevents *de facto* quotas, and attempts have been made to show that these goals are not quotas. However, some believe eradicating affirmative action will further deepen economic disparity between groups.

Free market libertarians believe any form of unjustified discrimination is likely to lead to inefficiencies, and that a rational person would therefore be unlikely to seek to discriminate one way or another and should therefore be free to decide who to select. Therefore, libertarians generally do not advocate antidiscrimination laws, as they reportedly distort the situation. They believe that inefficient, overregulated, noncompetitive industries enable unjustified discrimination, as said industries need not compete and hire on credentials relevant to the job. In terms of policy, libertarians favor repealing all affirmative action legislation and regulation, so that the government has no official stance on the practice, leaving the decision to uphold and maintain such a policy up to the individual institutions.

Overall, equal opportunity refers to the idea that all people should start out in life from the same platform, in that all should have equal opportunities in life, regardless of where they were born or who their parents were. Egalitarianism is the moral doctrine that equality ought to prevail throughout society, and according to legal egalitarianism, everyone ought to be considered equal under the law.

It is important to note that policies, decisions and negotiations that fail to take into account the impact on all members of society may reflect systemic discrimination. Tokenism occurs when a small group is invited to participate in an initiative to demonstrate that a program is progressive or to show someone has consulted the constituency, but in fact has ignored their views, which is discriminatory in itself. Standards or rules of behavior are norms, which help us to predict the behavior of others and, in turn, allow others to know what to expect of us, with our culture defining what is proper and improper behavior, what is right and wrong, and what we are expected to do and not to do.[1]

The concept of the minority group has long provided a valuable frame of reference for understanding the experiences of groups of people in society who are singled out, based on some cultural or physical characteristic, for discriminatory treatment.[2] In terms of religion and culture, they are a cross-cutting determinant within the framework for understanding. Cultural values and traditions determine to a large extent how a given society views religion. Culture is a key factor in whether or not co-residency with other religions is the preferred way of living. There is enormous cultural diversity and complexity within countries, and among countries and regions of the world. Policies and programs need to respect current cultures and traditions, while de-bunking outdated stereotypes and misinformation. Moreover, there are critical universal values that transcend culture, such as ethics and human rights.

While the significance of national and regional particularities and various historical, cultural and religious backgrounds must be borne in mind, it is the duty of States, regardless of their political, economic and cultural systems, to promote and protect human rights and fundamental freedoms of all people. The implementation of these principles of equality, including through national laws, strategies, policies, programmes and development priorities, is the sovereign responsibility of each State, in conformity with human rights and fundamental freedoms. The significance of, and full respect for, various religious, philosophical and ethical values, and for cultural and racial backgrounds of individuals and communities should contribute to the full enjoyment of human rights, in order to achieve equality, development and peace.

There must be immediate and concerted action by all to create a peaceful, just and humane world based on human rights and fundamental freedoms, including the principle of equality for all religions and from all walks of life; and to this end, broad-based and sustained economic growth in the context of sustainable development is necessary to sustain social development and social justice. Success will require a strong commitment on the part of governments, international organizations and institutions at all levels. It will also require adequate mobilization of resources from multilateral, bilateral and private sources for the advancement of all humans for strengthening the capacity of national, sub-regional, regional and international institutions; a commitment to equal rights, equal responsibilities and equal opportunities for the equal participation of all regardless of religion, in all national, regional and international bodies in the policy-making processes; and the establishing or strengthening of mechanisms at all levels for accountability to the world's population in general.

As globalization continues to influence economic opportunities worldwide, its effects remain uneven, creating both risks and opportunities for different groups. For many, globalization has intensified existing inequalities and insecurities, often translating into the loss of livelihoods, labor rights and social benefits. Organizations and networks are taking on issues of social justice and equal rights to influence economic policies and decisions at the micro, meso and macro levels.

Even with economic growth, conditions can arise which can aggravate social inequality and marginalization. Hence, it is indispensable to search for new alternatives that ensure that all members of society benefit from economic growth based on a holistic approach to all aspects of development: equality between people, social justice, conservation and protection of the environment, sustainability, solidarity, participation and cooperation, peace and respect for human rights. The rapid process of adjustment due to downsizing in sectors has led to increased unemployment and underemployment. Structural adjustment programs have not been successfully designed to minimize their negative effects on vulnerable and disadvantaged groups, to assure positive effects on those groups by preventing their marginalization in society.

Multilateral trade negotiations underscore the increasing interdependence of national economies, as well as the importance of trade liberalization and access to open dynamic markets. Only a new era of international cooperation among peoples based on a spirit of partnership within an equitable international social and economic environment, along with a radical transformation of the relationship to one of full and equal partnership will enable the world to meet the challenges of the twenty-first century. Interestingly, the growing strength of the nongovernmental sector has become a driving force for change. Nongovernmental organizations (NGOs) have played an important advocacy role in advancing legislation or mechanisms to ensure the promotion of all people, and have become catalysts for new approaches to development.

Actions to be taken at the national and international levels by all governments, the United Nations' system, international and regional organizations, including international financial institutions, the private sector, nongovernmental organizations (NGOs) and other actors of civil society, include the creation and maintenance of a nondiscriminatory as well as religious-sensitive legal environment through review of legislation with a view to striving to remove discriminatory provisions. Problems continue to persist in addressing the challenges of equalities, empowerment, poverty eradication, and advancement of all. Political, economic and ecological crises, systematic or *de facto* discrimination, violations of and failure to protect human rights and fundamental freedoms, and ingrained prejudicial attitudes towards different groups are impediments to equality. It will be critical for the international community to demonstrate a new commitment for the future to inspire a new generation to work together for a more just society. The advancement of all and the achievement of religious equality are a matter of human rights and a condition for social justice.

The large majority of the world's people have religious beliefs.[3] Many regard religious freedom as the most important right, because religion is viewed by people as having such a central place in their lives that. At the same time, global trends, regional distinctions, local preferences, and personal histories often lead to significant overlap between religious identity and ethnicity, class, language group or political affiliation. The right to religious freedom can be abused in many ways both blatant and subtle, or in law *de jure* or *de facto*. There are many types of religious abuses impeding religious freedom, namely totalitarian/authoritarian regimes, state hostility toward minority religions, state neglect of societal discrimination, discriminatory legislation that favors majority religions, and denunciation of certain religions as cults:

1. The first and most stark category of abuses is seen in totalitarian and authoritarian regimes, which seek to control religious thought and expression, and regard some or all religious groups as enemies of the State because of their religious beliefs or their independence from central authority. Some governments are hostile and repressive towards particular groups, often identifying them as 'security threats'. It is important to distinguish between groups of religious believers who express legitimate political grievances, and those that misuse religion to advocate violence against other religious groups or the State. It is an abuse when a government broadly represses religious expression among a peacefully practicing population on the grounds of security concerns.
2. A second category of abuses occurs with State hostility toward minority or nonapproved religions. These governments implement policies designed to demand that adherents recant their faith, cause religious group members to flee the country, or intimidate and harass certain religious groups. This leads to State repression of religious groups linked to ethnic identity, with a government dominated by a majority ethnic group suppressing the faith of a minority group.
3. A third category of abuses stems from a State's failure to address either societal discrimination or societal abuses against religious groups. In these countries, legislation may discourage religious discrimination and persecution, but officials fail to prevent conflicts, harassment or other harmful acts against minority religious groups. Protecting religious freedom requires having good laws in writing, but also active work by a government at all levels to prevent abuses by governmental or private actors, to bring abusers to justice, and to provide redress to victims. Governments have the

responsibility to ensure that their agents do not commit abuses of religious freedom, and to protect religious freedom by rule of law in a way that ensures that private actors obey. In addition, governments must foster an environment of respect and tolerance for all people.
4. A fourth category of abuses is that which occurs when governments have enacted discriminatory legislation or policies that favor majority religions and disadvantage minority religions, which often results from historical dominance by the majority religion and a bias against new or minority religions. Governments have acted on a widely held ideology that links national identity with a particular religion by enacting legislation that favors the majority religion and discriminates against minority religions. Though the majority of the population in such a country may worship without harassment, such a situation cannot be characterized as true freedom to choose one's faith and worship freely. Furthermore, government backing of a religion can result in restrictions even on worshippers in the majority when the State enforces only one interpretation of that religion.
5. Finally, the practice of discriminating against certain religions by identifying them as dangerous cults or sects is a common type of abuse, even in countries where religious freedom is otherwise respected.[4]

The laws against religious discrimination present employers with a seeming contradiction: on the one hand, employers cannot make employment decisions based on a person's religion, while on the other hand, employers might have to take an employee's religion into account when making certain workplace decisions. In developing a framework for antidiscrimination legislation, an initial decision has to be made regarding the prohibited grounds, such as 'religion' only, 'religious belief', or 'religion or belief':

1. The first option is for the legislation to cover only 'religion' not 'beliefs'. Restricting the legislation to the protection of religion provides relatively greater certainty than the other options, since beliefs are a far broader category than religion. However, the restriction of the legislation to religion may exclude from its protection discrimination against those with ethical belief systems which fall outside traditional religions, and might also exclude atheists and agnostics.
2. The second option would be to prohibit discrimination on the grounds of 'religious belief'. Atheism and agnosticism would be protected by legislation that covers discrimination on the grounds of 'religious belief', since the principle of equality would require that they be protected by antidiscrimination legislation in the same way as belief in a religion is treated.[5]
3. The third option, a broader approach covering both 'religion or belief', is consistent with the Article 13 European employment directive which refers specifically to prohibiting discrimination in employment on the grounds of religion or belief. If the UK legislation were to cover 'religion

or belief' then the definition of religion would become less of an acute issue. In particular new religious movements would gain the protection of the legislation without the need for their recognition as religions, and it would be clear that nonreligious beliefs are covered.[6]

The difficulty of defining religion is regarded as a key obstacle to legislation prohibiting religious discrimination. For those framing legislation, there are three options:

1. The first option is to attempt a definition within the legislation or through a statutory code of practice. A starting point may be the classical sociological definition of religion set out by Durkheim: '[A] unified system of beliefs and practices relative to sacred things, that is to say, things set apart and forbidden – beliefs and practices which unite into one single moral community called a Church, all those who adhere to them'.[7] Alternatively, one could take the Oxford English Dictionary definition of religion as 'action or conduct indicating a belief in, reverence for, and desire to please, a divine ruling power; the exercise or practice of rites or observances implying this…a particular system of faith and worship'.[8] The advantage of utilizing a statutory code of practice, to which the courts must have regard, is that it provides guidance to users of the legislation on where to draw the line while leaving flexibility to deal sensitively with individual cases. However, any definition will inevitably exclude some groups and would require further interpretation.

2. The second option is to have a list of recognized religions with a process and criteria for such recognition, where certain religions are given the status of legal person in public law. The status of legal person gives rise to certain rights, in particular the right to levy church taxes through the services of the State, and the right to tax advantages and tax exemptions. A 'cult' is granted the status of a legal person in public law when, in light of its statute and its membership, it gives every indication of durability.[9] Recognition requires a 'measure of internal organisation, adequate financing, and a certain period of existence; in practice, existence for thirty or forty years is required before a religious community can be considered to have shown sufficient durability'.[10] The creation of lists of accepted religions raises the issue of the recognition of new religious movements. There are several advantages to an official list system of religions: it provides a system of executive supervision to prevent protection being given to fleeting beliefs, or ones which are believed to present a threat to other human rights and values; it also allows for a high degree of certainty as regards the scope of legislation for various purposes; and in the case of antidiscrimination legislation, it would reduce the need for litigation to decide whether a religious group came within the scope of the Act. There are also several disadvantages: it would require an administrative or judicial procedure in order to determine

the status of a particular religion; certainty may be outweighed by rigidity and the possibly unfair exclusion of new and unpopular beliefs, since a law against religious discrimination is primarily concerned with conferring protection on individuals in respect of their own sincerely held beliefs, rather than protecting or legitimating any particular religion.
3. The third option is to leave the definition of religion for the courts to develop, with guidance provided by the enforcement commission. Internationally, most antidiscrimination legislation, which prohibit discrimination on the grounds of religion, adopt this approach. The meaning of 'religion' may depend on the purposes of the statute or other legal instrument in which the word is used, with the main purpose of antidiscrimination legislation to protect the individual from arbitrary treatment based on stereotypes or unjustified practices. The courts will not be concerned with the legitimacy of a particular creed, but rather with whether or not there has been discrimination because an individual is believed, rightly or wrongly, to subscribe to those beliefs.[11]

In terms of a voluntary system of religious tolerance in the workplace, the main advantage of a non-statutory voluntary code of practice on religious discrimination is that it can be relatively easily introduced and updated and avoids imposing bureaucratic requirements on employers and service providers. The main disadvantage is that although a voluntary approach may succeed in influencing the behavior of some organizations, it will be disregarded by others who for economic or social reasons are resistant to change. The general conclusion is that voluntary self-regulation can work only if complemented by measures which are aimed at organizations which fail to comply voluntarily. Small and medium-sized employers are less likely to support legislation, and for this reason legislation needs to be clear and simple and sufficiently flexible to allow account to be taken of the size and administrative resources of those on whom duties are placed.

Among the tools available to employers to facilitate requests for religious accommodation are:

1. Voluntary Substitutes and 'Swaps': In order to promote an atmosphere in which such substitutions are favorably regarded, reasonable accommodation without undue hardship is generally possible where a voluntary substitute or swap with substantially similar qualifications is available. One means of substitution is the voluntary swap.
2. Flexible Scheduling: In order to provide reasonable accommodation for the religious practices of employees, the following list is an example of areas in which flexibility might be introduced: flexible arrival and departure times; floating or optional holidays; flexible work breaks; time off in lieu; unpaid leave; use of lunch time in exchange for early departure; staggered work hours; and permitting an employee to make up time lost due to the observance of religious practices.

3. Lateral Transfer and Change of Job Assignments: When an employee cannot be accommodated either as to his entire job or an assignment within the job, employers and labor organizations should consider whether or not it is possible to change the job assignment or give the employee a lateral transfer.[12]

In terms of reasonable accommodation, the most common areas in which employers may be required to accommodate religious observance and practice are:

1. Dress Codes: While health and safety considerations may be one of the factors in determining whether accommodation is reasonable, the Human Rights Equal Opportunity Commission (HREOC) guidelines suggest allowing employees to wear head coverings required by religious practice such as yarmulkes, turbans and hijabs, as well as allowing Christian employees to wear a cross around their neck or pinned on their clothes.
2. Break policies and observance of prayer times: While the Working Time Regulations 1998, S.I. 1998/1833 in respect of the maximum length of the working day and week, and for rest breaks and holidays is to be observed, there should be flexibility in relation to commencement and finishing times as well as the opportunity to work reduced lunch hours where an employee is observing a fast, or wishing to attend a prayer service.
3. Recruitment and job applications: Jobs should be advertised to a wide audience including minority media, and only essential job requirements should be used as selection criteria. The HREOC guidelines suggest that job application forms and interviews should not contain questions about availability for work that are asked in a manner that reveals the applicant's creed, nor should questions be designed to reveal that religious requirements might conflict with the prospective employer's work schedule or workplace routine, and therefore, there should not be inquiries as to religious affiliation, places of worship or customs observed.
4. Religious leave: In considering religious leave requests where Staff may sometimes wish to work public holidays in place of their own religious festivals, the following may be taken into consideration: The availability and access of the work location; the safety and security of the workplace; the ability to verify that work has been completed; and the financial viability.[13]

Conclusion

Fairness at work and good job performance go hand in hand. Tackling religious discrimination helps to attract, motivate, and retain staff and enhances an organization's reputation as an employer. Eliminating discrimination helps everyone to have an equal opportunity to work and to develop their skills. In order to protect human rights, it is necessary for States to avoid, as far as possible, resorting to reservations of international agreements, and to ensure that no reservation is incompatible with the object and purpose of the Convention or is otherwise incompatible with international treaty law. The full enjoyment of equal rights is undermined by the discrepancies between some national legislation, and international law and international instruments on human rights. Overly complex administrative procedures, lack of awareness within the judicial process and inadequate monitoring of the violation of human rights, coupled with the underrepresentation of disabled groups in justice systems, insufficient information on existing rights, and persistent attitudes and practices perpetuate *de facto* and *de jure* inequality, which is also exacerbated by the lack of enforcement of civil, penal, labor and commercial laws or codes, or administrative rules and regulations intended to ensure the full enjoyment of human rights and fundamental freedoms, in the pursuit of *Heaven Forbid*.

Notes

1 Harris, Diana K., 'Age Norms', in Erdman B. Palmore, Laurence Branch, Diana K. Harris, *Encyclopedia of Ageism*, The Haworth Press, Inc, New York, 2005.
2 Wirth, L., 'The Problem of Minority Groups', in R. Linton (Ed.), *The Science of Man in the World Crisis* (pp. 347-372), Columbia University Press, New York, 1945.
3 Bureau of Democracy, Human Rights and Labor, *International Religious Freedom Report*, 2006.
4 *Ibid.*
5 Greenwalt, K., *Diverse Perspectives and the Religion Clause: An Examination of Justification and Qualifying Beliefs*, 74(5) *Notre Dame Law Review* 1433, 1999, at p. 1463.
6 Hepple QC, Bob, Choudhury, Tufval, Home Office Research Study 221, *Tackling Religious Discrimination: Practical Implications for Policy-Makers and Legislators*, Home Office Research, Development and Statistics Directorate, 2001.
7 Durkheim, E. (1975), *The Elementary Forms of Religious Life*, 1915, trans. J.W. Swain, Free Press, New York, p. 62.
8 Oxford English Dictionary.
9 Amor, A., *Implementation of the Declaration on the Elimination of All Forms of Intolerance and Discrimination Based on Religion or Belief*, UN doc E/CN.4/1998/6/Add.2, at para 17.
10 Boyle, K. and Sheen, J., *Freedom of Religion and Belief - A World Report*, Routledge, London, 1997, p. 308.
11 Hepple QC, Bob, Choudhury, Tufval, Home Office Research Study 221, *Tackling Religious Discrimination: Practical Implications for Policy-Makers and Legislators*, Home Office Research, Development and Statistics Directorate, 2001.
12 *Ibid.*
13 *Ibid.*

References

Amor, A., Implementation of the Declaration on the Elimination of All Forms of Intolerance and Discrimination Based on Religion or Belief, UN doc E/CN.4/1998/6/Add.2.

Boyle, K. and Sheen, J. (1997), *Freedom of Religion and Belief - A World Report*, Routledge, London.

Bureau of Democracy, Human Rights and Labor (2006), *International Religious Freedom Report*.

Durkheim, E. (1975), *The Elementary Forms of Religious Life,* 1915, trans. J.W Swain, Free Press, New York.

Greenwalt, K. (1999), Diverse Perspectives and the Religion Clause: An Examination of Justification and Qualifying Beliefs, 74(5) *Notre Dame Law Review* 1433.

Harris, Diana K. (2005), 'Age Norms', in Erdman B. Palmore, Laurence Branch, Diana K. Harris, *Encyclopedia of Ageism*, The Haworth Press, Inc, New York.

Hepple QC, Bob, Choudhury, Tufval (2001), Home Office Research Study 221, *Tackling Religious Discrimination: Practical Implications for Policy-Makers and Legislators*, Home Office Research, Development and Statistics Directorate.

Oxford English Dictionary.

Wirth, L. (1945),' The Problem of Minority Groups', in R. Linton (Ed.), *The Science of Man in the World Crisis* (pp. 347-72), Columbia University Press, New York.

Chapter 3
Heaven Forbid in the United Nations

Introduction

In the quest for religious tolerance as *Heaven Forbid*, this chapter will examine efforts against religious discrimination in the United Nations. It will look at the important United Nations' legislation dealing with religious discrimination in the fight for religious equality, namely the Charter of the United Nations; the Statute of the International Court of Justice; the Universal Declaration of Human Rights; the International Covenant on Civil and Political Rights; the Optional Protocol to the International Covenant on Civil and Political Rights; the International Covenant on Economic, Social and Cultural Rights; for religious minorities, the International Convention on the Elimination of All Forms of Racial Discrimination; for religious women, the Convention on the Elimination of All Forms of Discrimination against Women and the Optional Protocol to the Convention on the Elimination of All Forms of Discrimination against Women; United Nations Principles for Older Persons; the Convention on the Rights of the Child; the Convention concerning Discrimination in respect of Employment and Occupation; the Equal Remuneration Convention (ILO No. 100); the Discrimination (Employment and Occupation) Convention (ILO No. 111); the Employment Policy Convention (ILO No. 122; and specifically, the Declaration on the Elimination of All Forms of Intolerance and of Discrimination Based on Religion or Belief; and the Resolution on the Elimination of All Forms of Religious Intolerance.

Through the work of the United Nations, international laws, called treaties or conventions, have been developed that require countries to work towards the elimination of all forms of discrimination, and they operate like a contract, as they apply throughout the world. When a country becomes a Party to a convention, it is bound to act in accordance with the rules contained in that convention. In addition to international treaties and conventions, there are several international declarations. The declarations are statements of principles, which are developed through the United Nations or other international bodies, and express the international community's aspirations to eliminate discrimination. These international declarations differ from treaties, because they do not always impose binding international legal obligations, but they are morally binding and have much influence over countries in setting acceptable standards of human rights protections. Internationally, the fundamental concept of human rights is one which human beings have striven both to suppress and promote.

Charter of the United Nations

The Preamble of the Charter of the United Nations, signed on 26 June 1945, states:

> WE THE PEOPLES OF THE UNITED NATIONS DETERMINED
> to save succeeding generations from the scourge of war, which twice in our lifetime has brought untold sorrow to mankind, and
> to reaffirm faith in fundamental human rights, in the dignity and worth of the human person, in the equal rights of men and women and of nations large and small, and
> to establish conditions under which justice and respect for the obligations arising from treaties and other sources of international law can be maintained, and
> to promote social progress and better standards of life in larger freedom,
>
> AND FOR THESE ENDS
>
> to practice tolerance and live together in peace with one another as good neighbours, and
> to unite our strength to maintain international peace and security, and
> to ensure, by the acceptance of principles and the institution of methods, that armed force shall not be used, save in the common interest, and
> to employ international machinery for the promotion of the economic and social advancement of all peoples,
>
> HAVE RESOLVED TO COMBINE OUR EFFORTS TO ACCOMPLISH THESE AIMS
>
> Accordingly, our respective Governments, through representatives assembled in the city of San Francisco, who have exhibited their full powers found to be in good and due form, have agreed to the present Charter of the United Nations and do hereby establish an international organization to be known as the United Nations.[1]

The purposes of the United Nations as outlined in Article 1 are to maintain international peace and security, and to that end to take effective collective measures for the prevention and removal of threats to the peace, and for the suppression of acts of aggression or other breaches of the peace, and to bring about by peaceful means, and in conformity with the principles of justice and international law, adjustment or settlement of international disputes or situations which might lead to a breach of the peace; to develop friendly relations among nations based on respect for the principle of equal rights and self-determination of peoples, and to take other appropriate measures to strengthen universal peace; to achieve international cooperation in solving international problems of an economic, social, cultural, or humanitarian character, and in promoting and encouraging respect for human rights and for fundamental freedoms for all without distinction; and to be a center for harmonizing the actions of nations in the attainment of these common ends.²

In terms of international economic and social cooperation, Article 55 guarantees equal rights in employment without distinction:

> 55. With a view to the creation of conditions of stability and well-being which are necessary for peaceful and friendly relations among nations based on respect for the principle of equal rights and self-determination of peoples, the United Nations shall promote:
> a. higher standards of living, full employment, and conditions of economic and social progress and development;
> b. solutions of international economic, social, health, and related problems; and international cultural and educational cooperation; and
> c. universal respect for, and observance of, human rights and fundamental freedoms for all without distinction as to race, sex, language, or religion.³

Importantly, the International Court of Justice (ICJ) is established under Article 92 as the principal judicial organ of the United Nations, functioning in accordance with the Statute of the Permanent Court of International Justice.⁴ By virtue of Article 96, the General Assembly, the Security Council, and other organs of the United Nations and specialized agencies may request the International Court of Justice to give an advisory opinion on any legal question.⁵ Further, Article 94 binds Member States in their compliance with the decisions of the ICJ in that each Member of the United Nations undertakes to comply with the decision of the International Court of Justice in any case to which it is a party; and if any party to a case fails to perform the obligations incumbent upon it under a judgment rendered by the Court, the other party may have recourse to the Security Council, which may, if it deems necessary, make recommendations or decide upon measures to be taken to give effect to the judgment.⁶ In addition, Article 95 holds that nothing in the present Charter shall prevent Members of the United Nations from entrusting the solution of their differences to other tribunals by virtue of agreements already in existence or which may be concluded in the future.⁷

Statute of the International Court of Justice

Article 1 of the Statute of the International Court of Justice, signed on 26 June 1945, holds that the International Court of Justice (ICJ), established by the Charter of the United Nations as the principal judicial organ of the United Nations, shall be constituted and shall function in accordance with the provisions of the present Statute.⁸ By virtue of Article 34, only States may be parties in cases before the Court which, subject to and in conformity with its Rules, may request of public international organizations information relevant to cases before it, and shall receive such information presented by such organizations on their own initiative.⁹

Jurisdiction of the Court is established under Article 36 as comprising all cases which the parties refer to it and all matters specially provided for in the Charter of the United Nations or in treaties and conventions in force. Further, the States Parties to the present Statute may at any time declare that they recognize as compulsory *ipso facto* and without special agreement, in relation to any other State accepting the same obligation, the jurisdiction of the Court in all legal disputes concerning the interpretation of a treaty; any question of international law; the existence of any fact which, if established, would constitute a breach of an international obligation; and the nature or extent of the reparation to be made for the breach of an international obligation.[10] As to the application of choice of law, Article 38 maintains that the Court, whose function is to decide in accordance with international law such disputes as are submitted to it, shall apply international conventions, whether general or particular, establishing rules expressly recognized by the contesting States; international custom, as evidence of a general practice accepted as law; the general principles of law recognized by civilized nations; and judicial decisions and the teachings of the most highly qualified publicists of the various nations, as subsidiary means for the determination of rules of law.[11]

Universal Declaration of Human Rights

The Universal Declaration of Human Rights was adopted by the United Nations on 10 December 1948. The Preamble of the Universal Declaration of Human Rights states:

> Whereas recognition of the inherent dignity and of the equal and inalienable rights of all members of the human family is the foundation of freedom, justice and peace in the world,
>
> Whereas disregard and contempt for human rights have resulted in barbarous acts which have outraged the conscience of mankind, and the advent of a world in which human beings shall enjoy freedom of speech and belief and freedom from fear and want has been proclaimed as the highest aspiration of the common people,
>
> Whereas it is essential, if man is not to be compelled to have recourse, as a last resort, to rebellion against tyranny and oppression, that human rights should be protected by the rule of law,
>
> Whereas it is essential to promote the development of friendly relations between nations,
>
> Whereas the peoples of the United Nations have in the Charter reaffirmed their faith in fundamental human rights, in the dignity and worth of the human person and in the

equal rights of men and women and have determined to promote social progress and better standards of life in larger freedom,

Whereas Member States have pledged themselves to achieve, in co-operation with the United Nations, the promotion of universal respect for and observance of human rights and fundamental freedoms,

Whereas a common understanding of these rights and freedoms is of the greatest importance for the full realization of this pledge.

The General Assembly of the United Nations proclaims:

THIS UNIVERSAL DECLARATION OF HUMAN RIGHTS as a common standard of achievement for all peoples and all nations, to the end that every individual and every organ of society, keeping this Declaration constantly in mind, shall strive by teaching and education to promote respect for these rights and freedoms and by progressive measures, national and international, to secure their universal and effective recognition and observance, both among the peoples of Member States themselves and among the peoples of territories under their jurisdiction.[12]

Article 1 recognizes human beings as free and equal:

> 1. All human beings are born free and equal in dignity and rights. They are endowed with reason and conscience and should act towards one another in a spirit of brotherhood.[13]

In the fight for equality, Article 2, which specifies religion, is a helpful tool, since it holds that:

> 2. Everyone is entitled to all the rights and freedoms set forth in this Declaration, without distinction of any kind, such as race, color, sex, language, religion, political or other opinion, national or social origin, property, birth or other status.[14]

Further, important in the fight against religious discrimination, Article 18 guarantees freedom of religion:

> 18. Everyone has the right to freedom of thought, conscience and religion; this right includes freedom to change his religion or belief, and freedom, either alone or in community with others and in public or private, to manifest his religion or belief in teaching, practice, worship and observance.[15]

Equality before the law without discrimination, important for religious discrimination cases, is guaranteed in Article 7:

7. All are equal before the law and are entitled without any discrimination to equal protection of the law. All are entitled to equal protection against any discrimination in violation of this Declaration and against any incitement to such discrimination.[16]

In the effort to redress discriminatory action, Article 8 establishes that everyone has the right to an effective remedy by competent national tribunals for acts violating the fundamental rights granted him by the constitution or by law.[17]

Importantly, employment rights, including equal pay for equal work, are protected under Article 23:

23.(1) Everyone has the right to work, to free choice of employment, to just and favorable conditions of work and to protection against unemployment.
(2) Everyone, without any discrimination, has the right to equal pay for equal work.
(3) Everyone who works has the right to just and favorable remuneration ensuring for himself and his family an existence worthy of human dignity, and supplemented, if necessary, by other means of social protection.
(4) Everyone has the right to form and to join trade unions for the protection of his interests.[18]

The right to education as a means of enhancement and advancement throughout one's life is established in Article 26, which holds that everyone has the right to education, in that education shall be free, at least in the elementary and fundamental stages, and elementary education shall be compulsory. Technical and professional education shall be made generally available and higher education shall be equally accessible to all on the basis of merit. Further, education shall be directed to the full development of the human personality and to the strengthening of respect for human rights and fundamental freedoms; it shall promote understanding, tolerance and friendship among all nations, racial or religious groups, and shall further the activities of the United Nations for the maintenance of peace.[19]

The Universal Declaration of Human Rights was codified into two Covenants, which the General Assembly adopted on 16 December 1966; these are the International Covenant on Civil and Political Rights and the International Covenant on Economic, Social and Cultural Rights. Described as the 'International Bill of Human Rights', the Covenants along with the Optional Protocols are landmarks in the efforts of the international community to promote human rights.

International Covenant on Civil and Political Rights (ICCPR)

The International Covenant on Civil and Political Rights was adopted and opened for signature, ratification and accession by the United Nations General Assembly in Resolution 2200A (XXI) of 16 December 1966, and entered into force on 23 March 1976.[20] The Covenant is divided into six parts: Part I reaffirms the right of self-determination; Part II formulates general obligations by States Parties, notably to implement the Covenant through legislative and other measures, to provide effective remedies to victims and to ensure equality, and it restricts the possibility of derogation; Part III outlines the general civil and political rights, including the right to life, the prohibition of torture, the right to liberty and security of person, the right to freedom of movement, the right to a fair hearing, the right to privacy, the right to freedom of religion, freedom of expression, freedom of peaceful assembly, the right to family life, the rights of children to special protection, the right to participate in the conduct of public affairs, the overarching right to equal treatment, and the special rights of persons belonging to ethnic, religious and linguistic minorities; Part IV regulates the election of members of the Human Rights Committee, the State reporting procedure and the interstate complaints mechanism; Part V stipulates that nothing in the Covenant shall be interpreted as impairing the inherent right of all peoples to fully enjoy and to utilize their natural resources; and Part VI provides that the Covenant shall extend to all parts of federal States and sets out the amendment procedure. Importantly, the Covenant is not subject to denunciation.

In the Preamble of the Covenant on Civil and Political Rights, the States Parties to the present Covenant undertake the agreement:

> Considering that, in accordance with the principles proclaimed in the Charter of the United Nations, recognition of the inherent dignity and of the equal and inalienable rights of all members of the human family is the foundation of freedom, justice and peace in the world,
>
> Recognizing that these rights derive from the inherent dignity of the human person,
>
> Recognizing that, in accordance with the Universal Declaration of Human Rights, the ideal of free human beings enjoying civil and political freedom and freedom from fear and want can only be achieved if conditions are created whereby everyone may enjoy his civil and political rights, as well as his economic, social and cultural rights,
>
> Considering the obligation of States under the Charter of the United Nations to promote universal respect for, and observance of, human rights and freedoms,
>
> Realizing that the individual, having duties to other individuals and to the community to which he belongs, is under a responsibility to strive for the promotion and observance of the rights recognized in the present Covenant.[21]

The obligations of Member States are established in Article 2, which specifically mentions religion in Article 2.1:

> 2.1. Each State Party to the present Covenant undertakes to respect and to ensure to all individuals within its territory and subject to its jurisdiction the rights recognized in the present Covenant, without distinction of any kind, such as race, color, sex, language,

religion, political or other opinion, national or social origin, property, birth or other status.

2. Where not already provided for by existing legislative or other measures, each State Party to the present Covenant undertakes to take the necessary steps, in accordance with its constitutional processes and with the provisions of the present Covenant, to adopt such laws or other measures as may be necessary to give effect to the rights recognized in the present Covenant.

3. Each State Party to the present Covenant undertakes:

(a) To ensure that any person whose rights or freedoms as herein recognized are violated shall have an effective remedy, notwithstanding that the violation has been committed by persons acting in an official capacity;

(b) To ensure that any person claiming such a remedy shall have his right thereto determined by competent judicial, administrative or legislative authorities, or by any other competent authority provided for by the legal system of the State, and to develop the possibilities of judicial remedy;

(c) To ensure that the competent authorities shall enforce such remedies when granted.[22]

Importantly, religious freedom is guaranteed in Article 18:

18.1. Everyone shall have the right to freedom of thought, conscience and religion. This right shall include freedom to have or to adopt a religion or belief of his choice, and freedom, either individually or in community with others and in public or private, to manifest his religion or belief in worship, observance, practice and teaching.

2. No one shall be subject to coercion which would impair his freedom to have or to adopt a religion or belief of his choice.

3. Freedom to manifest one's religion or beliefs may be subject only to such limitations as are prescribed by law and are necessary to protect public safety, order, health, or morals or the fundamental rights and freedoms of others.

4. The States Parties to the present Covenant undertake to have respect for the liberty of parents and, when applicable, legal guardians to ensure the religious and moral education of their children in conformity with their own convictions.[23]

Further, children's rights as to religion are guaranteed in Article 24:

24.1. Every child shall have, without any discrimination as to race, colour, sex, language, religion, national or social origin, property or birth, the right to such measures of protection as are required by his status as a minor, on the part of his family, society and the State.[24]

Finally, protection is afforded to religious minorities in Article 27:

27. In those States in which ethnic, religious or linguistic minorities exist, persons belonging to such minorities shall not be denied the right, in community with the other

members of their group, to enjoy their own culture, to profess and practise their own religion, or to use their own language.[25]

Equality before the law, important for religious discrimination cases, is guaranteed under Article 26, which specifically mentions religion:

> 26. All persons are equal before the law and are entitled without any discrimination to the equal protection of the law. In this respect, the law shall prohibit any discrimination and guarantee to all persons equal and effective protection against discrimination on any ground such as race, color, sex, language, religion, political or other opinion, national or social origin, property, birth or other status.[26]

It prohibits discrimination in law or in fact in any field regulated by public authorities and its scope is not limited to civil and political rights, so that it can be used to challenge discriminatory laws whether or not they relate to civil and political rights.

Importantly, the Human Rights Committee is established under Article 28 and consists of eighteen members, carrying out the functions provided.[27] Additionally, the submission of reports in compliance with the Covenant is required in Article 40 and Article 45. Under Article 40, the States Parties to the present Covenant undertake to submit reports on the measures they have adopted which give effect to the rights recognized herein and on the progress made in the enjoyment of those rights within one year of the entry into force of the present Covenant for the States Parties concerned; and thereafter whenever the Committee so requests. Reports shall indicate the factors and difficulties, if any, affecting the implementation of the present Covenant. The Committee shall study the reports submitted by the States Parties to the present Covenant, and shall transmit its reports, and such general comments as it may consider appropriate, to the States Parties.[28] Under Article 45, the Committee shall submit to the General Assembly of the United Nations, through the Economic and Social council, an annual report on its activities.[29] The Human Rights Committee monitors implementation by States Parties in a variety of ways, and initial and periodic reports are examined by the plenary, which formulates concluding observations with concrete recommendations.

Other procedures of recourse are permitted under Article 44, which states that the provisions for the implementation of the present Covenant shall apply without prejudice to the procedures prescribed in the field of human rights by or under the constituent instruments and the conventions of the United Nations and of the specialized agencies and shall not prevent the States Parties to the present Covenant from having recourse to other procedures for settling a dispute in accordance with general or special international agreements in force between them.[30]

Optional Protocol to the International Covenant on Civil and Political Rights

The Optional Protocol to the International Covenant on Civil and Political Rights (ICCPR) of 16 December 1966 allows individuals, whose countries are party to the ICCPR and the protocol, who claim their rights under the ICCPR have been violated, and who have exhausted all domestic remedies, to submit written communications to the United Nations Human Rights Committee. States Parties to the ICCPR undertake to ensure that all enjoy all the civil and political rights in the Covenant on a basis of equality.

The Preamble of the Optional Protocol to the International Covenant on Civil and Political Rights states:

> The States Parties to the present Protocol,
>
> Considering that in order further to achieve the purposes of the International Covenant on Civil and Political Rights (hereinafter referred to as the Covenant) and the implementation of its provisions it would be appropriate to enable the Human Rights Committee set up in part IV of the Covenant (hereinafter referred to as the Committee) to receive and consider, as provided in the present Protocol, communications from individuals claiming to be victims of violations of any of the rights set forth in the Covenant.[31]

Article 1 empowers the Committee to hear claims of violations:

> 1. A State Party to the Covenant that becomes a Party to the present Protocol recognizes the competence of the Committee to receive and consider communications from individuals subject to its jurisdiction who claim to be victims of a violation by that State Party of any of the rights set forth in the Covenant. No communication shall be received by the Committee if it concerns a State Party to the Covenant which is not a Party to the present Protocol.[32]

Finally, Article 2 preserves people's rights to redress:

> 2. Subject to the provisions of article 1, individuals who claim that any of their rights enumerated in the Covenant have been violated and who have exhausted all available domestic remedies may submit a written communication to the Committee for consideration.[33]

International Covenant on Economic, Social and Cultural Rights (ICESCR)

The International Covenant on Economic, Social and Cultural Rights was adopted and opened for signature, ratification and accession by General Assembly resolution

2200A (XXI) of 16 December 1966, and entered into force 16 January 1976.[34] In a world where, according to the United Nations Development Program (UNDP), 'a fifth of the developing world's population goes hungry every night, a quarter lacks access to even a basic necessity like safe drinking water, and a third lives in a state of abject poverty at such a margin of human existence that words simply fail to describe it',[35] the importance of renewed attention and commitment to the full realization of economic, social and cultural rights is self-evident with such marginalization. Despite significant progress since the establishment of the United Nations in addressing problems of human deprivation, well over 1 billion people live in circumstances of extreme poverty, homelessness, hunger and malnutrition, unemployment, illiteracy and chronic ill-health. More than 1.5 billion people lack access to clean drinking water and sanitation, and some 500 million children do not have access to even primary education, with more than 1 billion adults not able to read and write. Economic, social and cultural rights are designed to ensure the protection of people as full persons, based on a perspective in which people can enjoy rights, freedoms and social justice.

In the Preamble of the International Covenant on Economic, Social and Cultural Rights, the States Parties to the present Covenant undertake the agreement:

> Considering that, in accordance with the principles proclaimed in the Charter of the United Nations, recognition of the inherent dignity and of the equal and inalienable rights of all the members of the human family is the foundation of freedom, justice and peace in the world,
>
> Recognizing that these rights derive from the inherent dignity of the human person,
>
> Recognizing that, in accordance with the Universal Declaration of Human Rights, the ideal of free human beings enjoying freedom from fear and want can only be achieved if conditions are created whereby everyone may enjoy his economic, social and cultural rights, as well as his civil and political rights and freedom,
>
> Realizing that the individual, having duties to other individuals and to the community to which he belongs, is under a responsibility to strive for the promotion and observance of the rights recognized in the present Covenant.[36]

Article 2 specifically guarantees the right to freedom of religion without discrimination:

> 2.1. Each State Party to the present Covenant undertakes to take steps, individually and through international assistance and co-operation, especially economic and technical, to the maximum of its available resources, with a view to achieving progressively the full realization of the rights recognized in the present Covenant by all appropriate means, including particularly the adoption of legislative measures.

> 2. The States Parties to the present Covenant undertake to guarantee that the rights enunciated in the present Covenant will be exercised without discrimination of any kind as to race, colour, sex, language, religion, political or other opinion, national or social origin, property, birth or other status.
> 3. Developing countries, with due regard to human rights and their national economy, may determine to what extent they would guarantee the economic rights recognized in the present Covenant to non-nationals.[37]

Importantly, employment rights under Article 6 establish:

> 6.1. The States Parties to the present Covenant recognize the right to work, which includes the right of everyone to the opportunity to gain his living by work which he freely chooses or accepts, and will take appropriate steps to safeguard this right.
> 2. The steps to be taken by a State Party to the present Covenant to achieve the full realization of this right shall include technical and vocational guidance and training programmes, policies and techniques to achieve steady economic, social and cultural development and full and productive employment under conditions safeguarding fundamental political and economic freedoms to the individual.[38]

Further, Article 7 is a guarantee for equal rights in terms of equal pay and access to employment:

> 7. The States to the present Covenant recognize the right of everyone to the enjoyment of just and favorable conditions of work which ensure, in particular:
> (1) Remuneration which provides all workers, as a minimum, with:
>   1. Fair wages and equal remuneration for work of equal value without distinction of any kind, … with equal pay for equal work;
>   2. A decent living for themselves and their families in accordance with the provisions of the present Covenant;
> (2) Safe and healthy working conditions;
> (3) Equal opportunity for everyone to be promoted in his employment to an appropriate higher level, subject to no considerations other than those of seniority and competence;
> (4) Rest, leisure and reasonable limitation of working hours and periodic holidays with pay, as well as remuneration for public holidays.[39]

Article 13 guarantees the right to education for the enhancement of the person throughout one's life in that the State Parties to the Covenant recognize the right of everyone to education for the enhancement of the person, as guaranteed in Article 13. Education shall be directed to the full development of the human personality and the sense of its dignity, shall strengthen the respect for human rights and fundamental freedoms, shall enable all persons to participate effectively in a free society, promote understanding, tolerance and friendship among all nations and all racial, ethnic or religious groups, and further the activities of the United Nations for the maintenance of peace.[40]

Compliance by States Parties with their obligations under the Covenant and the level of implementation of the rights and duties in question is monitored by the Committee on Economic, Social and Cultural Rights, which submits annual reports on its activities to the Economic and Social Council. The Committee works on the basis of many sources of information, including reports submitted by States Parties and information from United Nations specialized agencies, including the International Labour Organization, the United Nations Educational, Scientific and Cultural Organization, the World Health Organization, the Food and Agriculture Organization of the United Nations, the World Bank and the International Monetary Fund, as well as the United Nations Development Program, the Office of the United Nations High Commissioner for Refugees and the United Nations Centre for Human Settlements (Habitat). It also makes use of information from other United Nations treaty bodies, from national nongovernmental and community-based organizations working in States which have ratified the Covenant, and from international human rights organizations.

Of all the basic human rights standards, the International Covenant on Economic, Social and Cultural Rights provides one of the most important international legal frameworks for protecting basic human rights. The Covenant contains significant international legal provisions establishing economic, social and cultural rights, including rights relating to work in just and favorable conditions, social protection, an adequate standard of living, the highest attainable standards of physical and mental health, education, and enjoyment of the benefits of cultural freedom and scientific progress. In the fight against discrimination, it also provides for the right of self-determination; the right to work; the right to just and favorable conditions of work; the right to form and join trade unions; the right to social security and social insurance; protection and assistance to the family; the right to adequate standard of living; the right to the highest attainable standard of physical and mental health; the right to education; the right to take part in cultural life; and the right to enjoy the benefits of scientific progress.

International Convention on the Elimination of All Forms of Racial Discrimination (ICEAFRD)

Important for religious minorities, the International Convention on the Elimination of All Forms of Racial Discrimination was adopted on 21 December 1965.[41] The Convention was the first human rights instrument to establish an international monitoring system and was also revolutionary in its provision of national measures toward the advancement of specific racial or ethnic groups. The Convention is especially important for older minorities, who can suffer several layers of discrimination due to race and religious intolerance. The Convention defines and condemns racial discrimination, and commits States to change national laws and policies, which create or perpetuate racial discrimination. One of the main objectives of the Convention is to promote racial equality, and as such, the Convention not only aims to achieve *de jure* racial equality but also *de facto* equality, which allows the various ethnic, racial and national groups to enjoy the same social development. Furthermore, the Convention recognizes that certain racial or ethnic groups may need special protection or may need to be assisted by special measures in order to achieve adequate development, and the Convention provides that such special measures shall not be considered racial discrimination as long as they are not continued after the objectives for which they were taken have been achieved.

The Preamble of the International Covenant on the Elimination of All Forms of Racial Discrimination states:

The States Parties to this Convention,

Considering that the Charter of the United Nations is based on the principles of the dignity and equality inherent in all human beings, and that all Member States have pledged themselves to take joint and separate action, in co-operation with the Organization, for the achievement of one of the purposes of the United Nations which is to promote and encourage universal respect for and observance of human rights and fundamental freedoms for all, without distinction as to race, sex, language or religion,

Considering that the Universal Declaration of Human Rights proclaims that all human beings are born free and equal in dignity and rights and that everyone is entitled to all the rights and freedoms set out therein, without distinction of any kind, in particular as to race, colour or national origin,

Considering that all human beings are equal before the law and are entitled to equal protection of the law against any discrimination and against any incitement to discrimination,

Considering that the United Nations has condemned colonialism and all practices of segregation and discrimination associated therewith, in whatever form and wherever they exist, and that the Declaration on the Granting of Independence to Colonial Countries and Peoples of 14 December 1960 (General Assembly resolution 1514 (XV)) has affirmed and solemnly proclaimed the necessity of bringing them to a speedy and unconditional end,

Considering that the United Nations Declaration on the Elimination of All Forms of Racial Discrimination of 20 November 1963 (General Assembly resolution 1904 (XVIII)) solemnly affirms the necessity of speedily eliminating racial discrimination throughout the world in all its forms and manifestations and of securing understanding of and respect for the dignity of the human person,

Convinced that any doctrine of superiority based on racial differentiation is scientifically false, morally condemnable, socially unjust and dangerous, and that there is no justification for racial discrimination, in theory or in practice, anywhere,

Reaffirming that discrimination between human beings on the grounds of race, colour or ethnic origin in an obstacle to friendly and peaceful relations among nations and is capable of disturbing peace and security among peoples and the harmony of persons living side by side even within one and the same State,

Convinced that the existence of racial barriers is repugnant to the ideals of any human society,

Alarmed by manifestations of racial discrimination still in evidence in some areas of the world and by governmental policies based on racial superiority or hatred, such as policies of apartheid, segregation or separation,

Resolved to adopt all necessary measures for speedily eliminating racial discrimination in all its forms and manifestations, and to prevent and combat racist doctrines and practices in order to promote understanding between races and to build an international community free from all forms of racial segregation and racial discrimination,

Bearing in mind the Convention concerning Discrimination in respect of Employment and Occupation adopted by the International Labour Organisation in 1958, and the Convention against Discrimination in Education adopted by the United Nations Educational, Scientific and Cultural Organization in 1960,

Desiring to implement the principles embodied in the United Nations Declaration on the Elimination of All Forms of Racial Discrimination and to secure the earliest adoption of practical measures to that end,

Have agreed as follows.[42]

Importantly, Article 5 guarantees certain freedoms, specifically freedom of religion under Article 5(d)(vii):

5. In compliance with the fundamental obligations laid down in article 2 of this Convention, States Parties undertake to prohibit and to eliminate racial discrimination in all its forms and to guarantee the right of everyone, without distinction as to race, colour, or national or ethnic origin, to equality before the law, notably in the enjoyment of the following rights:
(a) The right to equal treatment before the tribunals and all other organs administering justice;

(b) The right to security of person and protection by the State against violence or bodily harm, whether inflicted by government officials or by any individual, group or institution;
(c) Political rights, in particular the rights to participate in elections to vote and to stand for election on the basis of universal and equal suffrage, to take part in the Government as well as in the conduct of public affairs at any level and to have equal access to public service;
(d) Other civil rights, in particular:
   (i) The right to freedom of movement and residence within the border of the State;
   (ii) The right to leave any country, including one's own, and to return to one's country;
   (iii) The right to nationality;
   (iv) The right to marriage and choice of spouse;
   (v) The right to own property alone as well as in association with others;
   (vi) The right to inherit;
   (vii) The right to freedom of thought, conscience and religion;
   (viii) The right to freedom of opinion and expression;
   (ix) The right to freedom of peaceful assembly and association;
(e) Economic, social and cultural rights, in particular:
   (i) The rights to work, to free choice of employment, to just and favourable conditions of work, to protection against unemployment, to equal pay for equal work, to just and favourable remuneration;
   (ii) The right to form and join trade unions;
   (iii) The right to housing;
   (iv) The right to public health, medical care, social security and social services;
   (v) The right to education and training;
   (vi) The right to equal participation in cultural activities;
(f) The right of access to any place or service intended for use by the general public, such as transport, hotels, restaurants, cafes, theatres and parks.[43]

Article 1.1 defines racial discrimination:

> 1.1 In this Convention, the term 'racial discrimination' shall mean any distinction, exclusion, restriction or preference based on race, color, descent, or national or ethnic origin which has the purpose or effect of nullifying or impairing the recognition, enjoyment or exercise, on an equal footing, of human rights and fundamental freedoms in the political, economic, social, cultural or any other field of public life.[44]

Affirmative action programs by way of special measures are covered under Article 1.3:

> 1.3 Special measures taken for the sole purpose of securing adequate advancement of certain racial or ethnic groups or individuals requiring such protection as may be necessary in order to ensure such groups or individuals equal enjoyment or exercise

of human rights and fundamental freedoms shall not be deemed racial discrimination, provided, however, that such measures do not, as a consequence, lead to the maintenance of separate rights for different racial groups and that they shall not be continued after the objectives for which they were taken have been achieved.[45]

Convention on the Elimination of All Forms of Discrimination against Women (CEDAW)

Important for religious women, the Convention on the Elimination of All Forms of Discrimination against Women (CEDAW) was adopted on 18 December 1979.[46] It is the most comprehensive treaty specifically on the human rights of women, establishing legally binding obligations to end discrimination. The Convention is especially important for older women, who can suffer several layers of discrimination due to gender and religious intolerance. Described as the 'International Bill of Rights for Women', the Convention provides for equality between women and men in the enjoyment of civil, political, economic, social and cultural rights. Discrimination against women is to be eliminated through legal, policy and programmatic measures, and through temporary special measures to accelerate women's equality, which are defined as nondiscriminatory. States Parties are required to end all forms of discrimination against women and to ensure their equality with men in political and public life with regard to nationality, education, employment, health, and economic and social benefits. The Convention obliges States Parties to modify the social and cultural patterns of conduct of men and women, in order to eliminate prejudices and customs, which are based on the idea of the inferiority or superiority of either of the sexes or on stereotyped roles for men and women.

The Preamble to the Convention on the Elimination of All Forms of Discrimination against Women states:

The States Parties to the present Convention,

Noting that the Charter of the United Nations reaffirms faith in fundamental human rights, in the dignity and worth of the human person and in the equal rights of men and women,

Noting that the Universal Declaration of Human Rights affirms the principle of the inadmissibility of discrimination and proclaims that all human beings are born free and equal in dignity and rights and that everyone is entitled to all the rights and freedoms set forth therein, without distinction of any kind, including distinction based on sex,

Noting that the States Parties to the International Covenants on Human Rights have the obligation to ensure the equal rights of men and women to enjoy all economic, social, cultural, civil and political rights,

Considering the international conventions concluded under the auspices of the United Nations and the specialized agencies promoting equality of rights of men and women,

Noting also the resolutions, declarations and recommendations adopted by the United Nations and the specialized agencies promoting equality of rights of men and women,

Concerned, however, that despite these various instruments extensive discrimination against women continues to exist,

Recalling that discrimination against women violates the principles of equality of rights and respect for human dignity, is an obstacle to the participation of women, on equal terms with men, in the political, social, economic and cultural life of their countries, hampers the growth of the prosperity of society and the family and makes more difficult the full development of the potentialities of women in the service of their countries and of humanity,

Concerned that in situations of poverty women have the least access to food, health, education, training and opportunities for employment and other needs,

Convinced that the establishment of the new international economic order based on equity and justice will contribute significantly towards the promotion of equality between men and women,

Emphasizing that the eradication of apartheid, all forms of racism, racial discrimination, colonialism, neo-colonialism, aggression, foreign occupation and domination and interference in the internal affairs of States is essential to the full enjoyment of the rights of men and women,

Affirming that the strengthening of international peace and security, the relaxation of international tension, mutual co-operation among all States irrespective of their social and economic systems, general and complete disarmament, in particular nuclear disarmament under strict and effective international control, the affirmation of the principles of justice, equality and mutual benefit in relations among countries and the realization of the right of peoples under alien and colonial domination and foreign occupation to self-determination and independence, as well as respect for national sovereignty and territorial integrity, will promote social progress and development and as a consequence will contribute to the attainment of full equality between men and women,

Convinced that the full and complete development of a country, the welfare of the world and the cause of peace require the maximum participation of women on equal terms with men in all fields,

Bearing in mind the great contribution of women to the welfare of the family and to the development of society, so far not fully recognized, the social significance of maternity and the role of both parents in the family and in the upbringing of children, and aware that the role of women in procreation should not be a basis for discrimination but that the upbringing of children requires a sharing of responsibility between men and women and society as a whole,

Aware that a change in the traditional role of men as well as the role of women in society and in the family is needed to achieve full equality between men and women,

Determined to implement the principles set forth in the Declaration on the Elimination of Discrimination against Women and, for that purpose, to adopt the measures required for the elimination of such discrimination in all its forms and manifestations,

Have agreed on the following.[47]

Article 1 defines gender discrimination:

1. For the purposes of the present Convention, the term "discrimination against women" shall mean any distinction, exclusion or restriction made on the basis of sex which has the effect or purpose of impairing or nullifying the recognition, enjoyment or exercise by women, irrespective of their marital status, on a basis of equality of men and women, of human rights and fundamental freedoms in the political, economic, social, cultural, civil or any other field.[48]

Article 4 contains an affirmative action strategy:

4.1. Adoption by States Parties of temporary special measures aimed at accelerating de facto equality between men and women shall not be considered discrimination as defined in the present Convention, but shall in no way entail as a consequence the maintenance of unequal or separate standards; these measures shall be discontinued when the objectives of equality of opportunity and treatment have been achieved.
2. Adoption by States Parties of special measures, including those measures contained in the present Convention, aimed at protecting maternity shall not be considered discriminatory.[49]

Crucially, Article 11.1 guarantees employment rights for women in terms of access to employment and equal pay:

11.1. States Parties shall take all appropriate measures to eliminate discrimination against women in the field of employment in order to ensure, on a basis of equality of men and women, the same rights, in particular:
(a) The right to work as an inalienable right of all human beings;

(b) The right to the same employment opportunities, including the application of the same criteria for selection in matters of employment;
(c) The right to free choice of profession and employment, the right to promotion, job security and all benefits and conditions of service and the right to receive vocational training and retraining, including apprenticeships, advanced vocational training and recurrent training;
(d) The right to equal remuneration, including benefits, and to equal treatment in respect of work of equal value, as well as equality of treatment in the evaluation of the quality of work;
(e) The right to social security, particularly in cases of retirement, unemployment, sickness, invalidity and old age and other incapacity to work, as well as the right to paid leave;
(f) The right to protection of health and to safety in working conditions, including the safeguarding of the function of reproduction.[50]

Finally, the important concept of equality before the law is guaranteed in Article 15:

15.1 States Parties shall accord to women equality with men before the law.
2. States Parties shall accord to women, in civil matters, a legal capacity identical to that of men and the same opportunities to exercise that capacity. In particular, they shall give women equal rights to conclude contracts and to administer property and shall treat them equally in all stages of procedure in courts and tribunals.
3. States Parties agree that all contracts and all other private instruments of any kind with a legal effect which is directed at restricting the legal capacity of women shall be deemed null and void.[51]

Optional Protocol to the Convention on the Elimination of All Forms of Discrimination against Women

Also important for religious women, the Optional Protocol to the Convention on the Elimination of All Forms of Discrimination Against Women (CEDAW) was adopted by the United Nations Commission on the Status of Women on 10 December 1999.[52] Essentially, an optional protocol is an additional enforcement mechanism for the original convention. The motivation behind the development of an Optional Protocol for CEDAW was to bring CEDAW itself on an equal footing with other international human rights instruments, enhancing its enforcement mechanisms. However, the Optional Protocol has provided an opportunity to strengthen the weak enforcement ability of CEDAW. The objective of the Optional Protocol is to allow individuals or groups of individuals such as religious women who have exhausted national remedies to petition the Committee directly about alleged violations of the Convention by their governments. By the Optional Protocol, States Parties undertake to make the Convention and the Protocol widely known and to facilitate access to information about the views and recommendations of the Committee.

United Nations Principles for Older Persons

Important for older religious people, the United Nations Principles for Older Persons, adopted by the UN General Assembly on 16 December 1991 (resolution 46/91) can be divided into five different clusters of relevant issues: independence, participation, care, self-fulfillment and dignity. The Preamble of the Principles for Older Persons states:

The General Assembly:

Appreciating the contribution that older persons make to their societies,

Recognizing that, in the Charter of the United Nations, the peoples of the United Nations declare...their determination to reaffirm faith in fundamental human rights, in the dignity and worth of the human person, in the equal rights of men and women and of nations large and small and to promote social progress and better standards of life in larger freedom,

Noting the elaboration of those rights in the Universal Declaration of Human Rights, the International Covenant on Economic, Social and Cultural Rights and the International Covenant on Civil and Political Rights and other declarations to ensure the application of universal standards to particular groups,

In pursuance of the International Plan of Action on Ageing, adopted by the World Assembly on Ageing and endorsed by the General Assembly in its resolution 37/51 of 3 December 1982,

Appreciating the tremendous diversity in the situation of older persons, not only between countries but within countries and between individuals, which requires a variety of policy responses,

Aware that in all countries, individuals are reaching an advanced age in greater numbers and in better health than ever before,

Aware of the scientific research disproving many stereotypes about inevitable and irreversible declines with age,

Convinced that in a world characterized by an increasing number and proportion of older persons, opportunities must be provided for willing and capable older persons to participate in and contribute to the ongoing activities of society,

Mindful that the strains on family life in both developed and developing countries require support for those providing care to frail older persons,

Bearing in mind the standards already set by the International Plan of Action on Ageing and the conventions, recommendations and resolutions of the International Labour Organization, the World Health Organization and other United Nations entities,

Encourages Governments to incorporate the following principles into their national programmes whenever possible:.[53]

There are a number of central themes running through the International Plan of Action on Ageing 2002:

a. The full realization of all human rights and fundamental freedoms of all older persons;
b. The achievement of secure ageing, which involves reaffirming the goal of eradicating poverty in old age and building on the United Nations Principles for Older Persons;
c. The empowerment of older persons to fully and effectively participate in the economic, political and social lives of their societies, including through income-generating and voluntary work;
d. The provision of opportunities for individual development, self-fulfillment and well being throughout life as well as in late life, through such things as access to lifelong learning and participation in the community while recognizing that older persons are not one homogenous group;
e. The full enjoyment of economic, social and cultural rights, and civil and political rights of people, and the elimination of all forms of violence and discrimination against older persons;
f. The commitment to gender equality among older persons through the elimination of gender-based discrimination;
g. The recognition of the crucial importance of families, intergenerational interdependence, solidarity and reciprocity for social development;
h. The provision of health care, support and social protection for older persons, including preventive and rehabilitative health care;
i. A partnership between all levels of government, civil society, the private sector and older persons themselves in translating the International Plan of Action into practical action;
j. The harnessing of scientific research and expertise, and the realization of the potential of technology to focus on the individual, social and health implications of ageing, in particular in developing countries;
k. The recognition of the situation of ageing of indigenous people, their unique circumstances and the need to seek the means to give them an effective voice in decisions directly affecting them.[54]

Convention on the Rights of the Child

Important for children and their religious upbringing, the Convention on the Rights of the Child entered into force on 2 September 1990. The Preamble of the Convention on the Rights of the Child states:

The States Parties to the present Convention,

Considering that, in accordance with the principles proclaimed in the Charter of the United Nations, recognition of the inherent dignity and of the equal and inalienable rights of all members of the human family is the foundation of freedom, justice and peace in the world,

Bearing in mind that the peoples of the United Nations have, in the Charter, reaffirmed their faith in fundamental human rights and in the dignity and worth of the human person, and have determined to promote social progress and better standards of life in larger freedom,

Recognizing that the United Nations has, in the Universal Declaration of Human Rights and in the International Covenants on Human Rights, proclaimed and agreed that everyone is entitled to all the rights and freedoms set forth therein, without distinction of any kind, such as race, colour, sex, language, religion, political or other opinion, national or social origin, property, birth or other status,

Recalling that, in the Universal Declaration of Human Rights, the United Nations has proclaimed that childhood is entitled to special care and assistance,

Convinced that the family, as the fundamental group of society and the natural environment for the growth and well-being of all its members and particularly children, should be afforded the necessary protection and assistance so that it can fully assume its responsibilities within the community,

Recognizing that the child, for the full and harmonious development of his or her personality, should grow up in a family environment, in an atmosphere of happiness, love and understanding,

Considering that the child should be fully prepared to live an individual life in society, and brought up in the spirit of the ideals proclaimed in the Charter of the United Nations, and in particular in the spirit of peace, dignity, tolerance, freedom, equality and solidarity,

Bearing in mind that the need to extend particular care to the child has been stated in the Geneva Declaration of the Rights of the Child of 1924 and in the Declaration of the Rights of the Child adopted by the General Assembly on 20 November 1959 and recognized in the Universal Declaration of Human Rights, in the International Covenant on Civil and Political Rights (in particular in articles 23 and 24), in the International Covenant on Economic, Social and Cultural Rights (in particular in article 10) and in the statutes and relevant instruments of specialized agencies and international organizations concerned with the welfare of children,

Bearing in mind that, as indicated in the Declaration of the Rights of the Child, 'the child, by reason of his physical and mental immaturity, needs special safeguards and care, including appropriate legal protection, before as well as after birth',

Recalling the provisions of the Declaration on Social and Legal Principles relating to the Protection and Welfare of Children, with Special Reference to Foster Placement and Adoption Nationally and Internationally; the United Nations Standard Minimum Rules for the Administration of Juvenile Justice (The Beijing Rules); and the Declaration on the Protection of Women and Children in Emergency and Armed Conflict,

Recognizing that, in all countries in the world, there are children living in exceptionally difficult conditions, and that such children need special consideration,

Taking due account of the importance of the traditions and cultural values of each people for the protection and harmonious development of the child,

Recognizing the importance of international co-operation for improving the living conditions of children in every country, in particular in the developing countries.[55]

Article 1 defines a child:

> 1. For the purposes of the present Convention, a child means every human being below the age of eighteen years unless under the law applicable to the child, majority is attained earlier.[56]

Importantly, Article 2 guarantees freedom of religion:

> 2.1. States Parties shall respect and ensure the rights set forth in the present Convention to each child within their jurisdiction without discrimination of any kind, irrespective of the child's or his or her parent's or legal guardian's race, colour, sex, language, religion, political or other opinion, national, ethnic or social origin, property, disability, birth or other status.
> 2.2. States Parties shall take all appropriate measures to ensure that the child is protected against all forms of discrimination or punishment on the basis of the status, activities, expressed opinions, or beliefs of the child's parents, legal guardians, or family members.[57]

Finally, freedom of religion is guaranteed to children under Articles 14 and 30:

14.1. States Parties shall respect the right of the child to freedom of thought, conscience and religion.
2. States Parties shall respect the rights and duties of the parents and, when applicable, legal guardians, to provide direction to the child in the exercise of his or her right in a manner consistent with the evolving capacities of the child.
3. Freedom to manifest one's religion or beliefs may be subject only to such limitations as are prescribed by law and are necessary to protect public safety, order, health or morals, or the fundamental rights and freedoms of others.[58]
30. In those States in which ethnic, religious or linguistic minorities or persons of indigenous origin exist, a child belonging to such a minority or who is indigenous shall not be denied the right, in community with other members of his or her group, to enjoy his or her own culture, to profess and practise his or her own religion, or to use his or her own language.

Equal Remuneration Convention (ILO No. 100)

Important for religious workers, the General Conference of the International Labor Organization, convened at Geneva, adopted the Equal Remuneration Convention (ILO No. 100) of 9 June 1951. The Preamble of the Equal Remuneration Convention states:

> The General Conference of the International Labour Organisation,
>
> Having been convened at Geneva by the Governing Body of the International Labour Office, and having met in its thirty-fourth session on 6 June 1951, and
>
> Having decided upon the adoption of certain proposals with regard to the principle of equal remuneration for men and women workers for work of equal value, which is the seventh item on the agenda of the session, and
>
> Having determined that these proposals shall take the form of an international Convention, Adopts this twenty-ninth day of June of the year one thousand nine hundred and fifty-one the following Convention, which may be cited as the Equal Remuneration Convention, 1951.[59]

The term remuneration is defined in Article 1:

> 1. For the purpose of this Convention:
> (a) The term 'remuneration' includes the ordinary, basic or minimum wage or salary and any additional emoluments whatsoever payable directly or indirectly, whether in cash or in kind, by the employer to the worker and arising out of the worker's employment;
> (b) The term 'equal remuneration for men and women workers for work of equal value' refers to rates of remuneration established without discrimination based on sex.[60]

Different methods for equality are envisioned in Article 2

> 2.1. Each Member shall, by means appropriate to the methods in operation for determining rates of remuneration, promote and, in so far as is consistent with such methods, ensure the application to all workers of the principle of equal remuneration for... workers for work of equal value.
> 2. This principle may be applied by means of:
> (a) National laws or regulations;
> (b) Legally established or recognised machinery for wage determination;
> (c) Collective agreements between employers and workers; or
> (d) A combination of these various means.[61]

Further, objective methods of appraisal are ensured in Article 3:

> 3.1. Where such action will assist in giving effect to the provisions of this Convention, measures shall be taken to promote objective appraisal of jobs on the basis of the work to be performed.
> 2. The methods to be followed in this appraisal may be decided upon by the authorities responsible for the determination of rates of remuneration, or, where such rates are determined by collective agreements, by the parties thereto.[62]

Discrimination (Employment and Occupation) Convention (ILO No. 111)

Important for religious workers, the General Conference of the International Labour Organization, convened at Geneva, adopted on 5 July 1958 the Discrimination (Employment and Occupation) Convention (ILO No. 111), which entered into force on 15 June 1960. The Preamble of the Discrimination (Employment and Occupation) Convention states:

> Having decided upon the adoption of certain proposals with regard to discrimination in the field of employment and occupation, and

> Having determined that these proposals shall take the form of an international Convention, and Considering that the Declaration of Philadelphia affirms that all human beings, irrespective of race, creed or sex, have the right to pursue both their material well-being and their spiritual development in conditions of freedom and dignity, of economic security and equal opportunity, and

> Considering further that discrimination constitutes a violation of rights enunciated by the Universal Declaration of Human Rights.[63]

The word 'discrimination' is defined in Article 1, which specifically mentions religion:

1. For the purpose of this Convention the term 'discrimination' includes:
(a) any distinction, exclusion or preference made on the basis of race, color, sex, religion, political opinion, national extraction or social origin, which has the effect of nullifying or impairing equality of opportunity or treatment in employment or occupation;
(b) such other distinction, exclusion or preference which has the effect of nullifying or impairing equality of opportunity or treatment in employment or occupation as may be determined by the Member concerned after consultation with representative employer's and worker's organisations, where such exist, and with other appropriate bodies.
2. Any distinction, exclusion or preference in respect of a particular job based on the inherent requirements thereof shall not be deemed to be discrimination.
3. For the purpose of this Convention the terms 'employment' and 'occupation' include access to vocational training, access to employment and to particular occupations, and terms and conditions of employment.[64]

Member commitment to equality of opportunity and treatment is contained in Article 2:

2. Each Member for which this Convention is in force undertakes to declare and pursue a national policy designed to promote, by methods appropriate to national conditions and practice, equality of opportunity and treatment in respect of employment and occupation, with a view to eliminating any discrimination in respect thereof.[65]

Further, Article 3 specifically enunciates Member responsibilities:

3. Each Member for which this Convention is in force undertakes, by methods appropriate to national conditions and practice:
(a) To seek the co-operation of employers' and workers' organizations and other appropriate bodies in promoting the acceptance and observance of this policy;
(b) To enact such legislation and to promote such educational programs as may be calculated to secure the acceptance and observance of the policy;
(c) To repeal any statutory provisions and modify any administrative instructions or practices which are inconsistent with the policy;
(d) To pursue the policy in respect of employment under the direct control of a national authority;
(e) To ensure observance of the policy in activities of vocational guidance, vocational training and placement services under the direction of a national authority;
(f) To indicate in its annual reports on the application of the Convention the action taken in pursuance of the policy and the results secured by such action.[66]

Finally, special measures are provided for in Article 5:

5.1. Special measures of protection or assistance provided in other Conventions or Recommendations adopted by the International Labor Conference shall not be deemed to be discrimination.

> 2. Any Member may, after consultation with representative employers' and workers' organizations, where such exist, determine that other special measures designed to meet the particular requirements of persons who, for reasons such as sex, age, disablement, family responsibilities or social or cultural status, are generally recognized to require special protection or assistance, shall not be deemed to be discrimination.[67]

Employment Policy Convention (ILO No. 122)

Important for religious workers, the General Conference of the International Labor Organization, convened in Geneva, adopted on 9 July 1964 the Employment Policy Convention (ILO No. 122), which entered into force on 9 July 1965. The Preamble of the Employment Policy Convention (ILO No. 122) states:

> Considering that the Declaration of Philadelphia recognizes the solemn obligation of the International Labor Organization to further among the nations of the world programs which will achieve full employment and the raising of standards of living, and that the Preamble to the Constitution of the International Labor Organization provides for the prevention of unemployment and the provision of an adequate living wage, and
>
> Considering further that under the terms of the Declaration of Philadelphia it is the responsibility of the International Labor Organization to examine and consider the bearing of economic and financial policies upon employment policy in the light of the fundamental objective that 'all human beings, irrespective of race, creed or sex, have the right to pursue both their material well-being and their spiritual development in conditions of freedom and dignity, of economic security and equal opportunity', and
>
> Considering that the Universal Declaration of Human Rights provides that 'everyone has the right to work, to free choice of employment, to just and favorable conditions of work and to protection against unemployment'.[68]

A commitment to full, productive and freely chosen employment is envisioned in Article 1, which specifies religion under Article 1(2)(c):

> 1. With a view to stimulating economic growth and development, raising levels of living, meeting manpower requirements and overcoming unemployment and underemployment, each Member shall declare and pursue, as a major goal, an active policy designed to promote full, productive and freely chosen employment.
> 2. The said policy shall aim at ensuring that:
> (a) There is work for all who are available for and seeking work;
> (b) Such work is as productive as possible;
> (c) There is freedom of choice of employment and the fullest possible opportunity for each worker to qualify for, and to use his skills and endowments in, a job for which

he is well suited, irrespective of race, color, sex, religion, political opinion, national extraction or social origin.

3. The said policy shall take due account of the stage and level of economic development and the mutual relationships between employment objectives and other economic and social objectives, and shall be pursued by methods that are appropriate to national conditions and practices.[69]

Respectfully, national conditions are taken into account in the carrying out of the policy:

> 2. Each Member shall, by such methods and to such extent as may be appropriate under national conditions:
> (a) Decide on and keep under review, within the framework of a coordinated economic and social policy, the measures to be adopted for attaining the objectives specified in article 1;
> (b) Take such steps as may be needed, including when appropriate the establishment of programs, for the application of these measures.[70]

Finally, a consultation process is envisioned in Article 3 for the implementation of the Employment Policy Convention:

> 3. In the application of this Convention, representatives of the persons affected by the measures to be taken, and in particular representatives of employers and workers, shall be consulted concerning employment policies, with a view to taking fully into account their experience and views and securing their full co-operation in formulating and enlisting support for such policies.[71]

Declaration on the Elimination of All Forms of Intolerance and of Discrimination Based on Religion or Belief

The Declaration on the Elimination of All Forms of Intolerance and of Discrimination Based on Religion or Belief was proclaimed by General Assembly resolution 36/55 on 25 November 1981. The Preamble of the Declaration on the Elimination of All Forms of Intolerance and of Discrimination Based on Religion or Belief states

> The General Assembly,

> Considering that one of the basic principles of the Charter of the United Nations is that of the dignity and equality inherent in all human beings, and that all Member States have pledged themselves to take joint and separate action in co-operation with the Organization to promote and encourage universal respect for and observance of human

rights and fundamental freedoms for all, without distinction as to race, sex, language or religion,

Considering that the Universal Declaration of Human Rights and the International Covenants on Human Rights proclaim the principles of nondiscrimination and equality before the law and the right to freedom of thought, conscience, religion and belief,

Considering that the disregard and infringement of human rights and fundamental freedoms, in particular of the right to freedom of thought, conscience, religion or whatever belief, have brought, directly or indirectly, wars and great suffering to mankind, especially where they serve as a means of foreign interference in the internal affairs of other States and amount to kindling hatred between peoples and nations,

Considering that religion or belief, for anyone who professes either, is one of the fundamental elements in his conception of life and that freedom of religion or belief should be fully respected and guaranteed,

Considering that it is essential to promote understanding, tolerance and respect in matters relating to freedom of religion and belief and to ensure that the use of religion or belief for ends inconsistent with the Charter of the United Nations, other relevant instruments of the United Nations and the purposes and principles of the present Declaration is inadmissible,

Convinced that freedom of religion and belief should also contribute to the attainment of the goals of world peace, social justice and friendship among peoples and to the elimination of ideologies or practices of colonialism and racial discrimination,

Noting with satisfaction the adoption of several, and the coming into force of some, conventions, under the aegis of the United Nations and of the specialized agencies, for the elimination of various forms of discrimination,

Concerned by manifestations of intolerance and by the existence of discrimination in matters of religion or belief still in evidence in some areas of the world,

Resolved to adopt all necessary measures for the speedy elimination of such intolerance in all its forms and manifestations and to prevent and combat discrimination on the ground of religion or belief,

Proclaims this Declaration on the Elimination of All Forms of Intolerance and of Discrimination Based on Religion or Belief.[72]

Article 1 guarantees freedom of religion:

1.1. Everyone shall have the right to freedom of thought, conscience and religion. This right shall include freedom to have a religion or whatever belief of his choice, and freedom, either individually or in community with others and in public or private, to manifest his religion or belief in worship, observance, practice and teaching.
2. No one shall be subject to coercion which would impair his freedom to have a religion or belief of his choice.
3. Freedom to manifest one's religion or belief may be subject only to such limitations as are prescribed by law and are necessary to protect public safety, order, health or morals or the fundamental rights and freedoms of others.[73]

Religious discrimination is defined in Article 2:

2.1. No one shall be subject to discrimination by any State, institution, group of persons, or person on the grounds of religion or other belief.
2. For the purposes of the present Declaration, the expression 'intolerance and discrimination based on religion or belief' means any distinction, exclusion, restriction or preference based on religion or belief and having as its purpose or as its effect nullification or impairment of the recognition, enjoyment or exercise of human rights and fundamental freedoms on an equal basis.[74]

Article 6 further defines religion:

6. In accordance with article I of the present Declaration, and subject to the provisions of article 1, paragraph 3, the right to freedom of thought, conscience, religion or belief shall include, inter alia, the following freedoms:
(a) To worship or assemble in connection with a religion or belief, and to establish and maintain places for these purposes;
(b) To establish and maintain appropriate charitable or humanitarian institutions;
(c) To make, acquire and use to an adequate extent the necessary articles and materials related to the rites or customs of a religion or belief;
(d) To write, issue and disseminate relevant publications in these areas;
(e) To teach a religion or belief in places suitable for these purposes;
(f) To solicit and receive voluntary financial and other contributions from individuals and institutions;
(g) To train, appoint, elect or designate by succession appropriate leaders called for by the requirements and standards of any religion or belief;
(h) To observe days of rest and to celebrate holidays and ceremonies in accordance with the precepts of one's religion or belief;
(i) To establish and maintain communications with individuals and communities in matters of religion and belief at the national and international levels.[75]

Article 3 regards religious discrimination as a violation of human rights:

> 3. Discrimination between human being on the grounds of religion or belief constitutes an affront to human dignity and a disavowal of the principles of the Charter of the United Nations, and shall be condemned as a violation of the human rights and fundamental freedoms proclaimed in the Universal Declaration of Human Rights and enunciated in detail in the International Covenants on Human Rights, and as an obstacle to friendly and peaceful relations between nations.[76]

Effective measures to guard against religious discrimination are contained in Article 4:

> 4.1. All States shall take effective measures to prevent and eliminate discrimination on the grounds of religion or belief in the recognition, exercise and enjoyment of human rights and fundamental freedoms in all fields of civil, economic, political, social and cultural life.
> 2. All States shall make all efforts to enact or rescind legislation where necessary to prohibit any such discrimination, and to take all appropriate measures to combat intolerance on the grounds of religion or other beliefs in this matter.[77]

The rights of children as regards religion is recognized in Article 5:

> 5.1. The parents or, as the case may be, the legal guardians of the child have the right to organize the life within the family in accordance with their religion or belief and bearing in mind the moral education in which they believe the child should be brought up.
> 2. Every child shall enjoy the right to have access to education in the matter of religion or belief in accordance with the wishes of his parents or, as the case may be, legal guardians, and shall not be compelled to receive teaching on religion or belief against the wishes of his parents or legal guardians, the best interests of the child being the guiding principle.
> 3. The child shall be protected from any form of discrimination on the ground of religion or belief. He shall be brought up in a spirit of understanding, tolerance, friendship among peoples, peace and universal brotherhood, respect for freedom of religion or belief of others, and in full consciousness that his energy and talents should be devoted to the service of his fellow men.
> 4. In the case of a child who is not under the care either of his parents or of legal guardians, due account shall be taken of their expressed wishes or of any other proof of their wishes in the matter of religion or belief, the best interests of the child being the guiding principle. 5. Practices of a religion or belief in which a child is brought up must not be injurious to his physical or mental health or to his full development, taking into account article 1, paragraph 3, of the present Declaration.[78]

National legislation to safeguard religion is recognized in Article 7:

7. The rights and freedoms set forth in the present Declaration shall be accorded in national legislation in such a manner that everyone shall be able to avail himself of such rights and freedoms in practice.[79]

Finally, Article 8 values the International Covenants on Human Rights:

8. Nothing in the present Declaration shall be construed as restricting or derogating from any right defined in the Universal Declaration of Human Rights and the International Covenants on Human Rights.[80]

Now over 25 years old, the Declaration on the Elimination of All Forms of Intolerance and of Discrimination Based on Religion or Belief is still the only international human rights instrument exclusively focused on the matter of religion or belief.

Resolution on the Elimination of All Forms of Religious Intolerance

The Resolution on the Elimination of All Forms of Religious Intolerance 48/128 was adopted by the General Assembly in 1993. The Preamble of the Resolution on the Elimination of All Forms of Religious Intolerance states:

The General Assembly,

Recalling that all States have pledged themselves, under the Charter of the United Nations, to promote and encourage universal respect for and observance of human rights and fundamental freedoms for all without distinction as to race, sex, language or religion,

Recognizing that those rights derive from the inherent dignity of the human person,

Reaffirming that discrimination against human beings on the grounds of religion or belief constitutes an affront to human dignity and a disavowal of the principles of the Charter,

Reaffirming its resolution 36/55 of 25 November 1981, by which it proclaimed the Declaration on the Elimination of All Forms of Intolerance and of Discrimination Based on Religion or Belief,

Recalling its resolution 47/129 of 18 December 1992, in which it requested the *Commission on Human Rights* to continue its consideration of measures to implement the Declaration,

Taking note of *Commission on Human Rights* resolution 1993/25 of 5 March 1993,

Reaffirming the call of the *World Conference on Human Rights* for all Governments to take all appropriate measures in compliance with their international obligations and with due regard to their respective legal systems to counter intolerance and related violence based on religion or belief, including practices of discrimination against women and the desecration of religious sites, recognizing that every individual has the right to freedom of thought, conscience, expression and religion,

Recalling *Commission on Human Rights* resolution 1992/17 of 21 February 1992, in which the Commission decided to extend for three years the mandate of the Special Rapporteur appointed to examine incidents and governmental actions in all parts of the world that are incompatible with the provisions of the Declaration and to recommend remedial measures, as appropriate, and recalling also *Economic and Social Council* decision 1992/226 of 20 July 1992,

Welcoming the appointment of Mr. Abdelfattah Amor as Special Rapporteur of the *Commission on Human Rights*, and calling upon all Governments to cooperate with the Special Rapporteur to enable him to carry out his mandate fully,

Recognizing that it is desirable to enhance the promotional and public information activities of the *United Nations* in matters relating to freedom of religion or belief and that both Governments and non-governmental organizations have an important role to play in this domain,

Emphasizing that non-governmental organizations and religious bodies and groups at every level have an important role to play in the promotion of tolerance and the protection of freedom of religion or belief,

Conscious of the importance of education in ensuring tolerance of religion and belief,

Alarmed that serious instances, including acts of violence, of intolerance and discrimination on the grounds of religion or belief occur in many parts of the world, as evidenced in the report of the former Special Rapporteur of the *Commission on Human Rights*, Mr. Angelo Vidal d'Almeida Ribeiro,

Reaffirming the dismay and condemnation expressed by the *World Conference on Human Rights* at the continued occurrence of gross and systematic violations and situations that constitute serious obstacles to the full enjoyment of all human rights, including religious intolerance,

Believing that further efforts are therefore required to promote and protect the right to freedom of thought, conscience, religion and belief and to eliminate all forms of hatred, intolerance and discrimination based on religion or belief,[81]

Article 1 recognizes freedom of religion as a human right:

1. Reaffirms that freedom of thought, conscience, religion and belief is a human right derived from the inherent dignity of the human person and guaranteed to all without discrimination;[82]

The importance of the constitution to guarantee freedom of religion is stressed in Article 2:

2. Urges States to ensure that their constitutional and legal systems provide full guarantees of freedom of thought, conscience, religion and belief, including the provision of effective remedies where there is intolerance or discrimination based on religion or belief;[83]

Articles 3 and 4 encourage States to take appropriate measures to combat religious discrimination:

3. Recognizes that legislation alone is not enough to prevent violations of human rights, including the right to freedom of religion or belief;[84]
4. Urges all States therefore to take all appropriate measures to combat hatred, intolerance and acts of violence, including those motivated by religious extremism, and to encourage understanding, tolerance and respect in matters relating to freedom of religion or belief;[85]

The respect of religions is stressed in Article 5, as well as the right of religion in Article 6:

5. Urges States to ensure that, in the course of their official duties, members of law enforcement bodies, civil servants, educators and other public officials respect different religions and beliefs and do not discriminate against persons professing other religions or beliefs;[86]
6. Calls upon all States to recognize, as provided in the *Declaration on the Elimination of All Forms of Intolerance and of Discrimination Based on Religion or Belief*, the right of all persons to worship or assemble in connection with a religion or belief, and to establish and maintain places for those purposes;[87]

The need for special protection of religious sites is emphasized in Article 7:

7. Also calls upon all States in accordance with their national legislation to exert utmost efforts to ensure that religious places and shrines are fully respected and protected;[88]

Public education regarding religious tolerance is outlined in Articles 8, 9 and 16:

8. Considers it desirable to enhance the promotional and public information activities of the United Nations in matters relating to freedom of religion or belief and to ensure that

appropriate measures are taken to this end in the *World Public Information Campaign for Human Rights*;[89]

9. Invites the Secretary-General to continue to give high priority to the dissemination of the text of the Declaration, in all the official languages of the United Nations, and to take all appropriate measures to make the text available for use by the United Nations information centres, as well as by other interested bodies;[90]

16. Urges all States to consider disseminating the text of the Declaration in their respective national languages and to facilitate its dissemination in national and local languages;[91]

Articles 10 and 11 recognize the importance of the Special Rapporteur:

10. Encourages the continuing efforts on the part of the Special Rapporteur appointed to examine incidents and governmental actions in all parts of the world that are incompatible with the provisions of the Declaration and to recommend remedial measures as appropriate;[92]

11. Encourages Governments to give serious consideration to inviting the Special Rapporteur to visit their countries so as to enable him to fulfill his mandate even more effectively;[93]

The importance of the promotion of religious tolerance is stressed in Article 12:

12. Recommends that the promotion and protection of the right to freedom of thought, conscience and religion be given appropriate priority in the work of the United Nations program of advisory services in the field of human rights, including work on the drafting of basic legal texts in conformity with international instruments on human rights and taking into account the provisions of the Declaration;[94]

The work of Nongovernmental Organizations is recognized in Articles 14 and 15:

14. Welcomes the efforts of non-governmental organizations to promote the implementation of the Declaration;[95]

15. Requests the Secretary-General to invite interested non-governmental organizations to consider what further role they could envisage playing in the implementation of the Declaration and in its dissemination in national and local languages;[96]

Despite the proliferation of anti-terrorist policy, discrimination against religious groups, minorities and migrant populations is on the rise. The United Nations' Special Rapporteur of the Commission on Human Rights on racism and related intolerance noted that 'the General Assembly is invited to draw the attention of Member States to the alarming signs of a retreat in the struggle against racism, racial discrimination and xenophobia as a result of the growing number of counterterrorism policies that generate new forms of discrimination against groups and entire communities, religions and spiritual traditions'.[97] Discrimination against

Muslims in the form of 'Islamophobia' must be given special attention, as well as continued vigilance against anti-Semitism and 'Christianophobia'. With regard to contemporary manifestations of racism, racial discrimination, xenophobia and related intolerance, attention is drawn to two developments of particular concern: the rise in racism and xenophobia as a result of identity constructs, and the mistreatment, contrary to international standards, of aliens, asylum-seekers, refugees and immigrants by the official administrative services of many States, especially in reception and waiting areas at airports, ports and stations which are becoming so-called no rights zones.

The Special Rapporteur demonstrated that the existence of racism, racial discrimination, xenophobia and related intolerance was indicative of the following alarming trends: the growing importance of the identity factor in recent manifestations of racism, racial discrimination and xenophobia; the tendency to establish a hierarchy in racial discrimination; the increasingly overt intellectual legitimization of racism, racial discrimination and xenophobia; the rise in and increasing influence of parties and movements with racist and xenophobic platforms; and increased racism in sports. In conclusion, the Special Rapporteur has highlighted various courses of action:

a. The importance of conducting an in-depth debate on the link between racism, discrimination and identity. In that regard, the Special Rapporteur wishes to draw the attention of European Union member States to the urgency of giving special attention, in the building of the identity of the new Europe, to its ethnic, cultural and religious pluralism;
b. The growing importance of achieving intellectual and cultural unanimity in combating racism and xenophobia, and the need to draw up an intellectual strategy for the fight against racism to be applied in the area of ideas, concepts, images, representations, perceptions and value systems;
c. The need to give equal treatment to all forms of racism and discrimination, while recognizing the singularity and specificity of each form of discrimination and racism;
d. The importance of more effectively combating organizations that promote ideas based on racial superiority or hatred, commit or incite acts of violence and of prosecuting them;
e. The need to prevent acceptance of racism and discrimination as a result of the inclusion of racist and xenophobic political platforms in the programs of democratic parties under the guise of combating terrorism and illegal immigration or 'national preference' in a context of economic stagnation;
f. The need to address the rise of racism in sports by conducting preventive educational and awareness-raising activities and condemning the perpetrators of racist incidents, in cooperation with national and international sports organizations. The Special Rapporteur also recommended the establishment of formal and closer collaboration between the United Nations and international sports bodies. He also urged international sports

bodies to take tough and credible measures against the perpetrators of racist incidents, especially sports executives, and to focus on the national dimension of the fight against racism by requesting national federations to submit annual reports on racist incidents and the action taken in response to them; and
g. The need for a firmer commitment of civil society to the fight against racism through programs designed to improve knowledge and appreciation of others and their culture.

The Special Rapporteur's specific recommendations are:

a. The need to take greater account than in the past of two developments in measures to combat racism and discrimination: the increasing intertwining of race, ethnicity, culture and religion, and the rise of anti-Semitism, Christianophobia and Islamophobia, as well as the clash of cultures, civilizations and religions generated by these developments, in particular in the current context of overemphasis on the fight against terrorism;
b. The need to take into account the following principles in the strategies to combat anti-Semitism, Christianophobia and Islamophobia:
(i) The historical and cultural depth of these three phobias, and thus the need to complement legal strategies with an intellectual and ethical strategy relating to the processes, mechanisms and representations which constitute these phobias over time;
(ii) The close and fundamental link between the spiritual, historical and cultural singularity of each of these phobias and the universality of their underlying causes and of the efforts needed to combat them;
(iii) Equal treatment of these phobias and avoidance of any prioritization of efforts to combat all forms of discrimination;
(iv) Application of the principle of secularism must be subject to particular vigilance so as not to generate or legitimize new forms of discrimination and, above all, not to constitute an obstacle to full participation in public life by believers and practitioners of various religions; and
(v) Respect for and promotion of religious and spiritual pluralism.[98]

In its resolution 59/177 of 2 March 2005 on global efforts for the total elimination of racism, racial discrimination, xenophobia and related intolerance and the comprehensive implementation of and follow-up to the Durban Declaration and Programme of Action, the General Assembly condemned all forms of racism and racial discrimination, including related acts of racially motivated violence, xenophobia and intolerance, as well as propaganda activities and organizations that attempt to justify or promote racism, racial discrimination, xenophobia and related intolerance in any form. It also recognized the increase in anti-Semitism, Christianophobia and Islamophobia in various parts of the world, as well as the emergence of racial and violent movements based on racism and discriminatory ideas directed against Arab, Christian, Jewish and Muslim communities, communities of people of African descent, communities of people of Asian descent and other communities. The General Assembly emphasized that it was the responsibility of States to adopt effective measures to combat criminal acts motivated by racism, racial discrimination, xenophobia and related intolerance, including measures to ensure that such motivations are considered an aggravating factor for the purposes of sentencing, to prevent those crimes from going unpunished and to ensure the rule of law. It was conscious that any form of impunity for crimes motivated by racist and xenophobic attitudes played a role in weakening the rule of law and democracy, tended to encourage the recurrence of such crimes and required resolute action and cooperation for its eradication. It condemned the misuse of print, audiovisual and electronic media and new communication technologies, including the Internet, to incite violence motivated by racial hatred, and called upon States to take all necessary measures to combat this form of racism in accordance with the commitments that they had undertaken under the Durban Declaration and Programme of Action.

Further, in its resolution 59/175 of 2 March 2005 on measures to be taken against political platforms and activities based on doctrines of superiority and violent nationalist ideologies which are based on racial discrimination or ethnic exclusiveness and xenophobia, including neo-Nazism, the General Assembly expressed particular alarm at the persistence of such ideas in political circles, in the sphere of public opinion and in society at large, and noted its determination to resist such political platforms and activities which can undermine the enjoyment of human rights and fundamental freedoms and of equality of opportunity.

In addition, in its resolution 2005/3 of 12 April 2005 on combating defamation of religions, the Commission, alarmed at the negative projection of Islam in the media and at the introduction and enforcement of laws that specifically discriminate against and target Muslims, noted with deep concern the intensification of the campaign of defamation of religions in the aftermath of the tragic events of 11 September 2001. The Special Rapporteur noted that Islamophobia is a particularly alarming manifestation of discrimination, and looked to the dynamic of the clash of cultures, civilizations and religions arising from four aspects of Islamophobia: (a) the perception, in reaction to acts of violence perpetrated by individuals claiming to be Muslims, of all Muslims and of the Islamic community as a whole as a political problem; (b) official policies of monitoring the teaching and practice of Islam; (c) the general increase in acts of violence against Islamic places of worship and culture, and Muslim worshippers; and (d) the overt intellectual legitimization of Islamophobia by leading researchers and writers and by some media outlets.

Finally, and most importantly, the Special Rapporteur noted three main ways of protecting and promoting multiculturalism:

1. The State must recognize the specific features of each of its component groups while advocating national unity;
2. The State should promote interaction among the different communities and

ethnic groups in order to ensure that none are isolated; and
3. The fight against racism should be linked to the promotion of multiculturalism, since combating racism should not lead to the isolation of any community; rather, it should protect all communities by fostering interaction among them.[99]

Overall, the promotion and protection of all human rights and fundamental freedoms is essential for the creation of an inclusive society for all. Specifically, religious tolerance requires a political, economic, ethical and spiritual vision for social development based on human dignity, human rights, equality, respect, peace, democracy, mutual responsibility and cooperation, and full respect for the various religious and ethical values, and cultural backgrounds of people. On the national level, innovation, mobilization of financial resources and the development of necessary human resources should be undertaken simultaneously. Progress should be contingent upon effective partnership among governments, all parts of civil society and the private sector, as well as an enabling environment based on democracy, the rule of law, respect for all human rights, fundamental freedoms and good governance at all levels, including national and international levels. Other crucial elements include: effective organizations of all people; educational, training and research activities on religious tolerance; and national data collection and analysis, such as the compilation of specific information for policy planning, monitoring and evaluation. Independent impartial monitoring of progress in implementation is valuable. Governments, as well as civil society, can facilitate the mobilization of resources by organizations representing and supporting all people by increasing incentives. On the international level, globalization and interdependence are opening new opportunities through trade, investment and capital flows, and advances in technology, including information technology, for the growth of the world economy and the development.

However, there remain serious challenges, including serious financial crises, insecurity, poverty, exclusion and inequality within and among societies. Considerable obstacles to further integration and full participation in the global economy remain. Unless the benefits of social and economic development are extended to all countries, a growing number of people in all countries and even entire regions will remain marginalized from the global economy. Obstacles affecting peoples and countries must be overcome in order to realize the full potential of opportunities presented for the benefit of all. Thus, globalization offers opportunities and challenges, but the developing countries and countries with economies in transition face special difficulties in responding to those challenges and opportunities. Globalization should be fully inclusive and equitable, with a strong need for policies and measures at the national and international levels, formulated and implemented with the full and effective participation of developing countries and countries with economies in transition to help them respond effectively to those challenges and opportunities.

In order to complement national development efforts, enhanced international cooperation is essential:

a. Recognizing the urgent need to enhance coherence, governance and consistency in the international monetary, financial and trading systems to improve global economic governance and to strengthen the United Nations leadership role in promoting development. Efforts should be strengthened at the national and international levels to enhance coordination among all relevant ministries and institutions to encourage policy and program coordination of national and international institutions, as well as coherence at the operational and international levels to meet the Millennium Declaration development goals of sustained economic growth, poverty eradication and sustainable development;
b. Noting the important efforts under way to reform the international financial architecture, which need to be sustained with greater transparency, and the effective participation of developing countries and countries with economies in transition. Since one major objective of the reform is to enhance financing for development and poverty eradication, a commitment exists to sound domestic financial sectors, which make a vital contribution to national development efforts as an important component of an international financial architecture that is supportive of development;
c. Calling for speedy and concerted action to address effectively debt problems of least developed countries, low-income developing countries and middle-income developing countries in a comprehensive, equitable development-oriented and durable way through various national and international measures designed to make their debt sustainable in the long term, including existing orderly mechanisms for debt reduction such as debt swaps for projects; and
d. Recognizing that a substantial increase in official development assistance and other resources will be required if developing countries are to achieve the internationally agreed development goals and objectives, including those contained in the Millennium Declaration.

Conclusion

Much needs to be done inside and outside the United Nations. Awareness and information about the situation of religious minorities is critical if full participation and equality are to be achieved. The media is a key partner in the process of empowering religious minorities, in addressing discrimination, prejudice and ignorance, and in ending stereotypical portrayals of religions. Nongovernmental organizations also have a vital role to play in building understanding among society as a whole, with a need to utilize information and communications technologies to empower all people. On the international level, attempts have been made to provide legislatively for equality to end religious discrimination. In recycling discrimination, 'the stream always tries to return to its habitual course'.[100] However, international law has made great strides to work toward overcoming religious discrimination, in the pursuit of *Heaven Forbid*.

Notes

1. United Nations, Charter of the United Nations, at the Preamble.
2. *Ibid.*, at Article 1.
3. *Ibid.*, at Article 55.
4. *Ibid.*, at Article 92.
5. *Ibid.*, at Article 96.
6. *Ibid.*, at Article 94.
7. *Ibid.*, at Article 95.
8. United Nations, Statute of the International Court of Justice, at Article 1.
9. *Ibid.*, at Article 34.
10. *Ibid.*, at Article 36.
11. *Ibid.*, at Article 38.
12. United Nations, Universal Declaration of Human Rights, at the Preamble.
13. *Ibid.*, at Article 1.
14. *Ibid.*, at Article 3.
15. *Ibid.*, at Article 18.
16. *Ibid.*, at Article 7.
17. *Ibid.*, at Article 8.
18. *Ibid.*, at Article 23.
19. *Ibid.*, at Article 26.
20. United Nations, International Covenant on Civil and Political Rights.
21. *Ibid.*, at the Preamble.
22. *Ibid.*, at Article 2.
23. *Ibid.*, at Article 18.
24. *Ibid.*, at Article 24.
25. *Ibid.*, at Article 27.
26. *Ibid.*, at Article 26.
27. *Ibid.*, at Article 28.
28. *Ibid.*, at Article 40.
29. *Ibid.*, at Article 45.
30. *Ibid.*, at Article 44.
31. United Nations, Optional Protocol to the International Covenant on Civil and Political Rights, at the Preamble.
32. *Ibid.*, at Article 1.
33. *Ibid.*, at Article 2.
34. United Nations, International Covenant on Economic, Social and Cultural Rights.
35. United Nations Development Program, *Human Development Report*, Oxford University Press, Oxford, 1994, p. 2.

36 United Nations, International Covenant on Economic, Social and Cultural Rights, at the Preamble.
37 *Ibid.*, at Article 2.
38 *Ibid.*, at Article 6.
39 *Ibid.*, at Article 7.
40 *Ibid.*, at Article 13.
41 United Nations, International Convention on the Elimination of All Forms of Racial Discrimination.
42 *Ibid.*, at the Preamble.
43 *Ibid.*, at Article 5.
44 *Ibid.*, at Article 1(1).
45 *Ibid.*, at Article 1(3)
46 United Nations, Convention on the Elimination of All Forms of Discrimination against Women.
47 *Ibid.*, at the Preamble.
48 *Ibid.*, at Article 1.
49 *Ibid.*, at Article 4.
50 *Ibid.*, at Article 11(1).
51 *Ibid.*, at Article 15.
52 United Nations, Optional Protocol to the Convention on the Elimination of All Forms of Discrimination against Women.
53 United Nations, Principles for Older Persons, at the Preamble.
54 United Nations, Second World Assembly on Ageism, International Plan of Action on Ageing.
55 United Nations, Convention on the Rights of the Child, at the Preamble.
56 *Ibid.*, at Article 1.
57 *Ibid.*, at Article 2.
58 *Ibid.*, at Article 14.
59 United Nations, Equal Remuneration Convention (ILO No. 100), at the Preamble.
60 *Ibid.*, at Article 1.
61 *Ibid.*, at Article 2.
62 *Ibid.*, at Article 3.
63 United Nations, Discrimination (Employment and Occupation) Convention (ILO No. 111), at the Preamble.
64 *Ibid.*, at Article 1.
65 *Ibid.*, at Article 2.
66 *Ibid.*, at Article 3.
67 *Ibid.*, at Article 5.
68 United Nations, Employment Policy Convention (ILO No. 122), at the Preamble.
69 *Ibid.*, at Article 1.
70 *Ibid.*, at Article 2.
71 *Ibid.*, at Article 3.
72 United Nations, Declaration on the Elimination of All Forms of Intolerance and of Discrimination Based on Religion or Belief, at the Preamble.

73 *Ibid.*, at Article 1.
74 *Ibid.*, at Article 2.
75 *Ibid.*, at Article 6.
76 *Ibid.*, at Article 3.
77 *Ibid.*, at Article 4.
78 *Ibid.*, at Article 5.
79 *Ibid.*, at Article 7.
80 *Ibid.*, at Article 8.
81 United Nations, Resolution on the Elimination of All Forms of Religious Intolerance 48/128, at the Preamble.
82 *Ibid.*, at Article 1.
83 *Ibid.*, at Article 2.
84 *Ibid.*, at Article 3.
85 *Ibid.*, at Article 4.
86 *Ibid.*, at Article 5.
87 *Ibid.*, at Article 6.
88 *Ibid.*, at Article 7.
89 *Ibid.*, at Article 8.
90 *Ibid.*, at Article 9.
91 *Ibid.*, at Article 16.
92 *Ibid.*, at Article 10.
93 *Ibid.*, at Article 11.
94 *Ibid.*, at Article 12.
95 *Ibid.*, at Article 14.
96 *Ibid.*, at Article 15.
97 United Nations, *The Fight Against Racism, Racial Discrimination, Xenophobia and Related Intolerance and the Comprehensive Implementation of and Follow-Up to the Durban Declaration and Programme of Action*, (E/CN.4/2005/18), 2005.
98 *Ibid.*
99 *Ibid.*
100 Canadian Advisory Council on the Status of Women, *Feminist Guide to the Canadian Constitution*, Ottawa, 1992, at p. 57.

References

Canadian Advisory Council on the Status of Women (1992), *Feminist Guide to the Canadian Constitution*, Ottawa.
United Nations (1945), Charter of the United Nations.
United Nations (1979), Convention on the Elimination of all Forms of Discrimination Against Women.
United Nations (1989), Convention on the Rights of the Child.
United Nations (1981), Declaration on the Elimination of All Forms of Intolerance and of Discrimination Based on Religion or Belief.

United Nations Development Program (1994), *Human Development Report*, Oxford University Press, Oxford.
United Nations (1958), Discrimination (Employment and Occupation) Convention (ILO No. 111).
United Nations (1964), Employment Policy Convention (ILO No. 122).
United Nations (1951), Equal Remuneration Convention (ILO No. 100).
United Nations (1965), International Convention on the Elimination of All Forms of Racial Discrimination.
United Nations (1966), International Covenant on Civil and Political Rights.
United Nations (1966), International Covenant on Economic, Social and Cultural Rights.
United Nations (1999), Optional Protocol to the Convention on the Elimination of All Forms of Discrimination against Women.
United Nations (1966), Optional Protocol to the International Covenant on Civil and Political Rights.
United Nations (1991), Principles for Older Persons.
United Nations (1993), Resolution on the Elimination of All Forms of Religious Intolerance 48/128.
United Nations (2002), Second World Assembly on Ageism.
United Nations (1945), Statute of the International Court of Justice.
United Nations (2005), *The Fight Against Racism, Racial Discrimination, Xenophobia and Related Intolerance and the Comprehensive Implementation of and Follow-Up to the Durban Declaration and Programme of Action*, (E/CN.4/2005/18).
United Nations (1948), Universal Declaration of Human Rights.

Chapter 4
Heaven Forbid in Australia and New Zealand

Introduction

In the quest for religious tolerance in *Heaven Forbid*, this chapter will examine efforts against religious discrimination in Australia and New Zealand. It will examine important legislation impacting religious rights, first in Australia, namely the Discrimination Act and the Anti-Discrimination Act, the Human Rights and Equal Opportunity Commission Act, and the Workplace Relations Act, as well as for religious minorities the Racial Discrimination Act and the Racial Hatred Act, and for religious women the Sex Discrimination Act; and then in New Zealand, namely the Treaty of Waitangi, the Bill of Rights Act, the Human Rights Act and the Human Rights Amendment Act, and the Employment Contracts Act and the Employment Relations Act, as well as for religious minorities the Race Relations Act.

Australia

Australian laws do impose an obligation on everyone to be vigilant about religious discrimination and to take action when incidents of prejudice occur, particularly where those incidents might be unlawful. Australia is a party to a number of international conventions and declarations which impose obligations to eliminate religious discrimination when ratified in Australian law, including the Universal Declaration of Human Rights. When Australia becomes a party to an international convention, the terms of the convention create binding obligations in international law. However, international laws do not automatically become a part of Australian law. The Australian government can choose to give effect to its international obligations in various forms, legislative, policy or symbolic. In Australia, they are reflected in a range of government policies and programs, and some are also incorporated in law. Australia has taken practical steps to improve access to justice and protection under the law in the pursuit of equality, and is committed to providing more accessible, low-cost alternative dispute resolution options. Australia has a regime of legislation and institutional mechanisms to protect against religious discrimination, and is committed to promoting, supporting and protecting human rights.

The following legislative instruments may be relevant to religious discrimination.

Discrimination Act and Anti-Discrimination Act

Important for religious freedom and tolerance, the Australian Discrimination Act 1991 (Act No. 81 of 1991) provides against religious discrimination. Section 7 enumerates the grounds, which include religion under (i):

> 7(1) This Act applies to discrimination on the ground of any of the following attributes:
> (a) sex;
> (b) sexuality;
> (c) transsexuality;
> (d) relationship status;
> (e) status as a parent or carer;
> (f) pregnancy;
> (g) breastfeeding;
> (h) race;
> (i) religious or political conviction;
> (j) disability;
> (k) membership or nonmembership of an association or organisation of employers or employees;
> (l) age;
> (m) profession, trade, occupation or calling;
> (n) association (whether as a relative or otherwise) with a person identified by reference to an attribute referred to in another paragraph of this subsection;
> (o) spent conviction within the meaning of the *Spent Convictions Act 2000*.
> (2) In this Act, a reference to an attribute mentioned in subsection (1) includes
> (a) a characteristic that people with that attribute generally have; and
> (b) a characteristic that people with that attribute are generally presumed to have; and
> (c) such an attribute that a person is presumed to have; and
> (d) such an attribute that the person had in the past but no longer has.[1]

Discrimination is defined under Section 8:

> 8(1) For this Act, a person *discriminates* against another person if
> (a) the person treats or proposes to treat the other person unfavourably because the other person has an attribute referred to in section 7; or
> (b) the person imposes or proposes to impose a condition or requirement that has, or is likely to have, the effect of disadvantaging people because they have an attribute referred to in section 7.

(2) Subsection (1) (b) does not apply to a condition or requirement that is reasonable in the circumstances.
(3) In deciding whether a condition or requirement is reasonable in the circumstances, the matters to be taken into account include
   (a) the nature and extent of the resultant disadvantage; and
   (b) the feasibility of overcoming or mitigating the disadvantage; and
   (c) whether the disadvantage is disproportionate to the result sought by the person who imposes or proposes to impose the condition or requirement.[2]

With regard to employees, Section 10 states:

10(1) It is unlawful for an employer to discriminate against a person
   (a) in the arrangements made for the purpose of deciding who should be offered employment; or
   (b) in deciding who should be offered employment; or
   (c) in the terms or conditions on which employment is offered.
(2) It is unlawful for an employer to discriminate against an employee
   (a) in the terms or conditions of employment that the employer affords the employee; or
   (b) by denying the employee access, or limiting the employee's access, to opportunities for promotion, transfer or training or to any other benefit associated with employment; or
   (c) by dismissing the employee; or
   (d) by subjecting the employee to any other detriment.[3]

Further, specific reference is made to employees' religious practices under Section 11:

11. It is unlawful for an employer to discriminate against an employee on the ground of religious conviction by refusing the employee permission to carry out a religious practice during working hours, being a practice
   (a) of a kind recognised as necessary or desirable by people of the same religious conviction as that of the employee; and
   (b) the performance of which during working hours is reasonable having regard to the circumstances of the employment; and
   (c) that does not subject the employer to unreasonable detriment.[4]

Religious bodies are protected under Section 32:

32. Part 3 does not apply in relation to
   (a) the ordination or appointment of priests, ministers of religion or members of any religious order; or
   (b) the training or education of people seeking ordination or appointment as priests, ministers of religion or members of a religious order; or
   (c) the selection or appointment of people to exercise functions for the purposes of, or in connection with, any religious observance or practice; or

(d) any other act or practice of a body established for religious purposes, if the act or practice conforms to the doctrines, tenets or beliefs of that religion and is necessary to avoid injury to the religious susceptibilities of adherents of that religion.[5]

Further, educational institutions conducted for religious purposes are protected under Section 33:

33(1) Section 10 or 13 does not make it unlawful for a person (the *first person*) to discriminate against someone else in relation to
(a) employment as a member of the staff of an educational institution; or
(b) a position as a contract worker that involves doing work in an educational institution;
if the institution is conducted in accordance with the doctrines, tenets, beliefs or teachings of a particular religion or creed, and the first person so discriminates in good faith to avoid injury to the religious susceptibilities of adherents of that religion or creed.
(2) Section 18 does not make it unlawful for a person (the *first person*) to discriminate against someone else in relation to the provision of education or training by an educational institution that is conducted in accordance with the doctrines, tenets, beliefs or teachings of a particular religion or creed, if the first person so discriminates in good faith to avoid injury to the religious susceptibilities of adherents of that religion or creed.[6]

Further, religious workers are protected under Section 44:

44. Section 10 (1) (a) or (b), section 12 (1) (a) or (b), section 13 (b) or section 14 (1) (a) or (2) (a) does not make unlawful:
(a) discrimination on the ground of religious conviction by an educational authority in relation to employment or work in an educational institution conducted by the authority; or
(b) discrimination on the ground of religious conviction by a religious body in relation to employment or work in a hospital or other place conducted by the body in which health services are provided;
if the duties of the employment or work involve, or would involve, the participation by the employee or worker in the teaching, observance or practice of the relevant religion.[7]

Finally, in terms of religious educational institutions, Section 46 provides:

46. Section 18 does not make unlawful discrimination on the ground of religious conviction in relation to a failure to accept a person's application for admission as a student at an educational institution that is conducted solely for students having a religious conviction other than that of the applicant.[8]

The Australian Anti-Discrimination Act 1991 (Act No. 85 of 1991) provides for the protection of an employee's religious beliefs under Section 7(1), which mentions religion specifically under (i):

> 7.(1) The Act prohibits discrimination on the basis of the following attributes
> a. sex;
> b. marital status;
> c. pregnancy
> d. parental status
> e. breast feeding
> f. age
> g. race
> h. impairment;
> i. religion;
> j. political belief or activity;
> k. trade union activity;
> l. lawful sexual activity;
> m. association with, or relation to, a person identified on the basis of any of the above attributes.[9]

Human Rights and Equal Opportunity Commission Act (HREOCA)

Important for equal rights, the Human Rights and Equal Opportunity Commission Act 1986 (HREOCA) gives effect to such relevant international conventions and declarations as the International Covenant on Civil and Political Rights, for religious minorities the Declaration on the Rights of Persons Belonging to National or Ethnic, Religious or Linguistic Minorities, and the International Labor Organization Convention on Discrimination in Employment and Occupation. The Human Rights and Equal Opportunity Commission (HREOC) inquires into complaints under federal antidiscrimination law and educates the community about obligations under domestic legislation. The HREOCA enables the HREOC to investigate complaints of breaches of conventions by Commonwealth Government agencies and may also investigate complaints of discrimination in employment by any employer.

Discrimination is defined in Section 3, which specifically mentions religion in Section 3(a) and (d):

> 3. discrimination, except in Part IIB, means:
> (a) any distinction, exclusion or preference made on the basis of race, colour, sex, religion, political opinion, national extraction or social origin that has the effect of nullifying or impairing equality of opportunity or treatment in employment or occupation; and
> (b) any other distinction, exclusion or preference that:

(i) has the effect of nullifying or impairing equality of opportunity or treatment in employment or occupation; and
(ii) has been declared by the regulations to constitute discrimination for the purposes of this Act;
but does not include any distinction, exclusion or preference:
(c) in respect of a particular job based on the inherent requirements of the job; or
(d) in connection with employment as a member of the staff of an institution that is conducted in accordance with the doctrines, tenets, beliefs or teachings of a particular religion or creed, being a distinction, exclusion or preference made in good faith in order to avoid injury to the religious susceptibilities of adherents of that religion or that creed.[10]

Further, the duties of the Commission are outlined in Section 10A:

10A(1) It is the duty of the Commission to ensure that the functions of the Commission under this or any other Act are performed:
(a) with regard for:
(i) the indivisibility and universality of human rights; and
(ii) the principle that every person is free and equal in dignity and rights; and
(b) efficiently and with the greatest possible benefit to the people of Australia.
(2) Nothing in this section imposes a duty on the Commission that is enforceable by proceedings in a court.[11]

Finally, the functions of Commission are outlined in Section 11:

11(1) The functions of the Commission are:
(a) such functions as are conferred on the Commission by the *Age Discrimination Act 2004*, the *Racial Discrimination Act 1975*, the *Sex Discrimination Act 1984* or any other enactment;
(aa) to inquire into, and attempt to conciliate, complaints of unlawful discrimination.[12]

Written complaints are contained in Section 46P:

46P(1) A written complaint may be lodged with the Commission, alleging unlawful discrimination.
(2) The complaint may be lodged:
(a) by a person aggrieved by the alleged unlawful discrimination:
(i) on that person's own behalf; or
(ii) on behalf of that person and one or more other persons who are also aggrieved by the alleged unlawful discrimination; or
(b) by 2 or more persons aggrieved by the alleged unlawful discrimination:
(i) on their own behalf; or
(ii) on behalf of themselves and one or more other persons who are also aggrieved by the alleged unlawful discrimination; or

(c) by a person or trade union on behalf of one or more other persons aggrieved by the alleged unlawful discrimination.

(3) A person who is a class member for a representative complaint is not entitled to lodge a separate complaint in respect of the same subject matter.

(4) If it appears to the Commission that:
(a) a person wishes to make a complaint under subsection (1); and
(b) the person requires assistance to formulate the complaint or to reduce it to writing;
the Commission must take reasonable steps to provide appropriate assistance to the person.[13]

The Australian Human Rights and Equal Opportunity Commission argued that while, as a general rule, in their private lives people should be able to shape their actions on the basis of their religious and other beliefs, this was not appropriate in public life 'where the state has a much clearer role in ensuring that people do not exercise their rights in a manner that infringes, unduly upon the rights and freedoms of others and that all people have basic guarantees of physical integrity, equality of opportunity and freedom from discrimination and injustice.'[14] Employment clearly fell within the ambit of public life, thus justifying legislative guarantees by the State. It recommended a limited exemption for religious organizations, in that it should apply only to employment of people by religious institutions and should be limited to discrimination that is required by the tenets and doctrines of the religion, is not arbitrary and is consistently applied.[15]

Workplace Relations Act

Important for employment rights, the Workplace Relations Act 1996 has provisions to safeguard groups of workers.[16] The Act provides for equal remuneration for work of equal value without discrimination. Section 3 enunciates the principal objectives, which includes religion:

3. The principal object of this Act is to provide a framework for cooperative workplace relations which promotes the economic prosperity and welfare of the people of Australia by:
(m) respecting and valuing the diversity of the work force by helping to prevent and eliminate discrimination on the basis of race, colour, sex, sexual preference, age, physical or mental disability, marital status, family responsibilities, pregnancy, religion, political opinion, national extraction or social origin.[17]

Employment is not to be terminated on certain grounds, including religion:

659(2) Except as provided by subsection (3) or (4), an employer must not terminate an employee's employment for any one or more of the following reasons, or for reasons including any one or more of the following reasons:

(f) race, colour, sex, sexual preference, age, physical or mental disability, marital status, family responsibilities, pregnancy, religion, political opinion, national extraction or social origin

(4) Subsection (2) does not prevent a matter referred to in paragraph (2)(f) from being a reason for terminating a person's employment as a member of the staff of an institution that is conducted in accordance with the doctrines, tenets, beliefs or teachings of a particular religion or creed, if the employer terminates the employment in good faith to avoid injury to the religious susceptibilities of adherents of that religion or creed.[18]

The Commission is to take into account discrimination issues under Section 104, which specifically mentions religion:

104. In the performance of its functions, the Commission must take into account the following:
(a) the need to apply the principle of equal pay for work of equal value;
(b) the need to prevent and eliminate discrimination because of, or for reasons including, race, colour, sex, sexual preference, age, physical or mental disability, marital status, family responsibilities, pregnancy, religion, political opinion, national extraction or social origin.[19]

Finally, the functions of the Workplace Authority Director are enumerated under Section 150B, which include the need to prevent and eliminate religious discrimination:

150B(2) In performing his or her functions relating to workplace agreements, the Workplace Authority Director must have particular regard to:
(d) the need to prevent and eliminate discrimination because of, or for reasons including, race, colour, sex, sexual preference, age, physical or mental disability, marital status, family responsibilities, pregnancy, religion, political opinion, national extraction or social origin.[20]

Racial Discrimination Act (RDA) and Racial Hatred Act (RHA)

Important for religious minorities, the Racial Discrimination Act 1975 (RDA), also known as An Act relating to the Elimination of Racial and other Discrimination, prohibits discrimination on the grounds of race, color, descent and national or ethnic origin.[21] The RDA gives effect to Australia's obligations under the International Convention on the Elimination of All Forms of Racial Discrimination. The RDA aims to ensure that all Australians, including seniors, can enjoy their human rights and freedoms in full equality regardless of their race, color, descent, or national or ethnic origin. The RDA applies to everyone in Australia including businesses, schools, and local, State, Territory and Commonwealth governmental agencies and departments. It overrides racially discriminatory legislation, making it ineffective. However, Commonwealth legislation which is racially discriminatory is not necessarily overridden by the RDA. Under the RDA, racial discrimination is unlawful whenever it impairs a person's equal enjoyment of his human rights and fundamental freedoms. In addition, the RDA has specific provisions making it unlawful to discriminate in areas such as employment, land, housing and accommodation, provision of goods and services, access to places and facilities for use by the public, advertising and joining a trade union. The RDA also makes indirect racial discrimination unlawful. In some cases, the RDA will permit special measures, which are distinctions based on race where there might be more favorable treatment for one racial group over another. It does so as a form of affirmative action, so that a group which has been traditionally denied human rights and access to rights can receive special treatment to redress the situation and to allow that group to enjoy human rights on an equal footing with the rest of the community. This form of favorable treatment is not unlawful discrimination and the special measure will be removed when equality has been achieved. Government support for special measures is not discriminatory, because the aim is to enhance the access of certain groups to justice, cultural expression and other rights and freedoms. The RDA is administered by the Human Rights and Equal Opportunity Commission (HREOC). HREOC has the responsibility for investigating complaints.

Importantly, Section 9 prohibits racial discrimination:

9(1) It is unlawful for a person to do any act involving a distinction, exclusion, restriction or preference based on race, color, descent or national or ethnic origin which has the purpose or effect of nullifying or impairing the recognition, enjoyment or exercise, on an equal footing, of any human right or fundamental freedom in the political, economic, social, cultural or any other field of public life.

(1A) Where:
   (a) a person requires another person to comply with a term, condition or requirement which is not reasonable having regard to the circumstances of the case; and
   (b) the other person does not or cannot comply with the term, condition or requirement; and
   (c) the requirement to comply has the purpose or effect of nullifying or impairing the recognition, enjoyment or exercise, on an equal footing, by persons of the same race, color, descent or national or ethnic origin as the other person, of any human right or fundamental freedom in the political, economic, social, cultural or any other field of public life;
   the act of requiring such compliance is to be treated, for the purposes of this Part, as an act involving a distinction based on, or an act done by reason of, the other person's race, color, descent or national or ethnic origin.

(2) A reference in this section to a human right or fundamental freedom in the political, economic, social, cultural or any other field of public life includes any right of a kind referred to in Article 5 of the Convention.

(3) This section does not apply in respect of the employment, or an application for the employment, of a person on a ship or aircraft (not being an Australian ship or aircraft) if that person was engaged, or applied, for that employment outside Australia.[22]

In addition, Section 10 guarantees equality before the law:

10(1) If, by reason of, or of a provision of, a law of the Commonwealth or of a State or Territory, persons of a particular race, color or national or ethnic origin do not enjoy a right that is enjoyed by persons of another race, color or national or ethnic origin, or enjoy a right to a more limited extent than persons of another race, color or national or ethnic origin, then, notwithstanding anything in that law, persons of the first-mentioned race, color or national or ethnic origin shall, by force of this section, enjoy that right to the same extent as persons of that other race, color or national or ethnic origin.[23]

Also important for religious minorities, the Racial Hatred Act 1995 (RHA) amended the Racial Discrimination Act (RDA) by adding in new laws specifically dealing with racial vilification. In addition to the RHA extending the coverage of the RDA to allow people to complain about racially offensive or abusive behavior, it also gives effect to some of Australia's obligations under the International Covenant on Civil and Political Rights, and the International Convention on the Elimination of All Forms of Racial Discrimination. The RHA aims to strike a balance between two valued rights, namely the right to communicate freely and the right to live free from vilification. It covers public acts, which are done because of the race, color, or national or ethnic origin of a person or group and reasonably likely in all circumstances to offend, insult, humiliate or intimidate that person or group. In bringing a complaint under the RHA, the complainant is responsible for proving that the act was done in public, that it was because of his ethnicity and that it was reasonably likely to offend, insult, humiliate or intimidate a reasonable person of that ethnicity. In claiming an exception, the respondent is responsible for establishing that the act was a genuine exception and that it was done reasonably and in good faith.

Sex Discrimination Act (SDA)

Important for religious women, the Sex Discrimination Act 1984 (SDA) prohibits discrimination on the grounds of gender, marital status, pregnancy, and potential pregnancy and family responsibilities, and is administered by the Sex Discrimination Commissioner under the auspices of the Human Rights and Equal Opportunity Commission (HREOC)[24]

Particularly, Section 5 deals directly with the definition of gender discrimination:

5(1) For the purposes of this Act, a person (in this subsection referred to as the discriminator) discriminates against another person (in this subsection referred to as the aggrieved person) on the ground of the sex of the aggrieved person if, by reason of:
(a) the sex of the aggrieved person;
(b) a characteristic that appertains generally to persons of the sex of the aggrieved person; or
(c) a characteristic that is generally imputed to persons of the sex of the aggrieved person; the discriminator treats the aggrieved person less favourably than, in circumstances that are the same or are not materially different, the discriminator treats or would treat a person of the opposite sex.
(2) For the purposes of this Act, a person (the discriminator) discriminates against another person (the aggrieved person) on the ground of the sex of the aggrieved person if the discriminator imposes, or proposes to impose, a condition, requirement or practice that has, or is likely to have, the effect of disadvantaging persons of the same sex as the aggrieved person.[25]

In terms of affirmative action, Section 7D stipulates that a person may take special measures for the purpose of achieving substantive equality between men and women; or people of different marital status; or women who are pregnant and people who are not pregnant.[26] The Act provides an important role for the HREOC in addressing the issue of gender discrimination. Its functions are defined under Section 48, namely to promote an understanding and acceptance of, and compliance with, this Act; to undertake research and educational programs on behalf of the Commonwealth for the purpose of promoting the objects of this Act; to examine enactments for the purpose of ascertaining whether they are inconsistent with or contrary to the objects of this Act, and to report to the Minister the results of any such examination.[27]

Specifically, in terms of accommodation, Section 23 states:

23(3) Nothing in this section applies to or in respect of:
(b) accommodation provided by a religious body.[28]

Further, with regard to religious bodies, Section 37 states:

37. Nothing in Division 1 or 2 affects:
(a) the ordination or appointment of priests, ministers of religion or members of any religious order;
(b) the training or education of persons seeking ordination or appointment as priests, ministers of religion or members of a religious order;
(c) the selection or appointment of persons to perform duties or functions for the purposes of or in connection with, or otherwise to participate in, any religious observance or practice; or

(d) any other act or practice of a body established for religious purposes, being an act or practice that conforms to the doctrines, tenets or beliefs of that religion or is necessary to avoid injury to the religious susceptibilities of adherents of that religion.[29]

Finally, with regard to educational institutions established for religious purposes, Section 38 states:

> 38 (1) Nothing in paragraph 14(1)(a) or (b) or 14(2)(c) renders it unlawful for a person to discriminate against another person on the ground of the other person's sex, marital status or pregnancy in connection with employment as a member of the staff of an educational institution that is conducted in accordance with the doctrines, tenets, beliefs or teachings of a particular religion or creed, if the first-mentioned person so discriminates in good faith in order to avoid injury to the religious susceptibilities of adherents of that religion or creed.
> (2) Nothing in paragraph 16(b) renders it unlawful for a person to discriminate against another person on the ground of the other person's sex, marital status or pregnancy in connection with a position as a contract worker that involves the doing of work in an educational institution that is conducted in accordance with the doctrines, tenets, beliefs or teachings of a particular religion or creed, if the first-mentioned person so discriminates in good faith in order to avoid injury to the religious susceptibilities of adherents of that religion or creed.
> (3) Nothing in section 21 renders it unlawful for a person to discriminate against another person on the ground of the other person's marital status or pregnancy in connection with the provision of education or training by an educational institution that is conducted in accordance with the doctrines, tenets, beliefs or teachings of a particular religion or creed, if the first-mentioned person so discriminates in good faith in order to avoid injury to the religious susceptibilities of adherents of that religion or creed.[30]

Clearly, some forms of discrimination, such as racial discrimination, by a religious body would be unacceptable; however, the Sex Discrimination Act (SDA) contains an exemption for religious bodies, allowing them to 'discriminate in relation to sex where employment is limited to one sex so as to comply with doctrines of the religion or avoid offending the religious susceptibilities of a significant number of its followers'.

In terms of religious discrimination, in *Church of the New Faith v. Commissioner for Pay-Roll Tax (Vic)* (1983) 154 CLR 120, the Australian High Court was unable to reach a consensus on the precise definition of religion when it considered the application of the law on pay-roll taxes.[31] In its view, a religion requires a belief in a supernatural Being, Thing or Principle and the acceptance of canons of conduct to give effect to that belief.[32] Further, there could be no comprehensive definition of religion but held that it was possible to identify characteristics indicating towards the existence of a religion. Finally, there was 'no single acceptable criterion, no essence of religion' and that any organization which claims to be a religious organization and which offers a way to find meaning and purpose in life is a religious organization.[33]

Overall, Australia aims to bolster the efforts of all government agencies, the private sector, the community and individuals to achieve equality, through, namely advancing outcomes in areas where there is discrimination and inequality; improving outcomes for those with special needs, the Indigenous population and those from a non-English speaking background; encouraging increased efforts by State/Territory and Commonwealth agencies to develop inclusive policies, programs and services; encouraging and facilitating the increased involvement of the private sector and community groups in taking responsibility for addressing discrimination and inequality.[34]

In terms of power and decision making, the critical area of concern is inequality in the sharing of power and decision making at all levels, with corrective action to take measures to ensure equal access to and full participation in power structures; and increase the capacity of all humans to participate in decision making and leadership. All peoples have a right and a responsibility to participate in the decision-making processes that shape the nation. Unless human beings are full and active participants in all spheres of public and private life, across a wide range of decision-making positions, the future will not reflect the talents, experience and aspirations of all citizens. Overall, greater diversity including seniors should be encouraged among those occupying senior decision-making positions; and opportunities should be expanded to participate in high-level positions, in order to create or strengthen national machineries and other governmental bodies; integrate neutral perspectives in legislation, public policies, programs and projects; and generate and disseminate disaggregated data and information for planning and evaluation. The participation of all humans on equal terms in political, social, economic and cultural life is essential to the progress and the well-being of society in general.

In terms of human rights, the critical area of concern is the lack of respect for and adequate promotion and protection of human rights, with corrective action to fully implement all human rights instruments; ensure equality and nondiscrimination under the law and in practice; and achieve legal literacy. Of particular concern is the level of access to and participation in processes relating to Australia's obligations under international instruments on human rights, including reporting and monitoring of obligations. Human rights are an inalienable, integral and indivisible aspect of life, in the legislative protections and the existence of agencies to enable citizens to exercise their rights and responsibilities.[35]

Explicit recognition of a positive duty toward equal rights is balanced by expanding the operation of the unjustifiable hardship defense. Legal adjustments will produce net benefits for the community without imposing undue hardship on the organizations required to make them, and will benefit the whole community. Artificial and real barriers to all people's participation in economic and social life need to be removed, and this will require a different mind set about new infrastructures, which should be friendly for all members of society.

New Zealand

New Zealand is an island nation of 103,000 square miles and a population of 4,180,000.[36] The country is predominantly Christian, but is becoming more religiously diverse. According to the 2001 census, approximately 56 percent of citizens identified themselves as Christian or members of individual Christian denominations. While the Anglicans and Presbyterians experienced a decline in membership between 2001 and 2006, the Roman Catholic Church and Methodists showed a slight increase; the Maori Christian churches, which integrate Christian tenets with pre-colonial Maori beliefs and include Ratana and Ringatu, experienced significant growth, as did the number affiliated with 'Evangelical, Born Again, and Fundamentalist' Christian groups; and non-Christian religions continued to show strong growth rates, driven primarily by immigration. According to 2006 census data, percentages of religious affiliation were: Anglican, 14.8 percent; Roman Catholic, 13.6 percent; Presbyterian, 10.7 percent; Methodist, 3.3 percent; Baptist, 1.3 percent; Ratana (a Maori/Christian group with services in the Maori language), 1.3 percent; Buddhist, 1.7 percent; Church of Jesus Christ of Latter day Saints (Mormons), 1 percent; and Hindu, 1.7 percent; Muslim, 1 percent; more than ninety religious groups with each less than 1 percent of the population; and 34.7 percent with no religious affiliation. The indigenous Maori, estimated at 15 percent of the population, tended to be followers of Presbyterianism, the Church of Jesus Christ of Latter-day Saints (Mormons), or Maori Christian faiths such as Ratana and Ringatu. The Auckland statistical area, which accounts for approximately 30 percent of the country's population, exhibited the greatest religious diversity; farther south on the North Island and on the South Island, the percentage of citizens who identified themselves with Christian faiths increased, while those affiliated with non-Christian religions decreased.

The existing legal and policy framework guarantees equal treatment of all faiths before the State, the right to safety for religious individuals and communities, freedom of religious expression, the right to recognition and reasonable accommodation for religious groups, and the promotion of understanding in education. The Government at all levels seeks to protect this right in full and does not in essence tolerate its abuse, either by governmental or private actors. As well, the government-funded Human Rights Commission actively promotes tolerance on the issue of religious freedom. The Government does not require licensing or registration before it will recognize a religious group. However, if a religious group desires to collect money for the promotion of religion or charitable causes and wishes to be recognized by the Inland Revenue Department (IRD) to obtain tax benefits, then it must register with the IRD as a charitable trust. The country has two registered Christian-associated political parties. Government policy and practice contributed to the generally free practice of religion; however, some businesses were fined if they attempted to operate on the official holidays of Christmas Day, Good Friday or Easter Sunday. The growing non-Christian communities have called for the Government to take into account the country's increasingly diverse religious makeup and offer greater holiday flexibility. In response, the Government removed some constraints on trade associated with the Christian faith, and in 2001, it enacted legislation that permits several types of businesses to remain open on Good Friday and Easter Sunday. In May 2007, New Zealand hosted the third meeting of the Asia Pacific Interfaith Dialogue in Waitangi, New Zealand.

The Education Act of 1964 specifies in its 'secular clause' that teaching within public primary schools 'shall be entirely of a secular character', but it also permits religious instruction and observances in State primary schools within certain parameters. If the school committee in consultation with the principal or head teacher so determines, any class may be closed at any time of the school day within specified limits for the purposes of religious instruction given by voluntary instructors, but attendance at religious instruction or observances is not compulsory. Public secondary schools also may permit religious instruction at the discretion of individual school boards, but religious instruction, if provided at a school, usually was scheduled after normal school hours. Further, under the Private Schools Conditional Integration Act of 1975, the Government, in response to its burgeoning general primary school role and to financial difficulties experienced by a large group of Catholic parochial schools, permitted the incorporation of private schools into the public school system. Designated as 'integrated schools', they were deemed to be of a 'unique character' and were permitted to receive public funding provided that they also enrolled non-preference students, such as non-Catholic students who attended a Catholic school. In 2005, of the 2,607 schools, there were 239 Catholic schools, 75 schools with other religious affiliation and 13 schools with no religious affiliation integrated into the public school system. A student cannot be required to attend an integrated school and admission to such a school is based on a student's request.

In terms of religious discrimination in employment, in 2003, the Office of Human Rights Proceedings settled a case in which the employer of a complainant, a member of the Seventh-day Adventist Church, breached the Human Rights Act by requiring the latter to work on his Saturday Sabbath. The employer acknowledged breaching the Act, paid a fine of $25,000, awarded a one-time six-week leave benefit, and agreed to an alternative roster so that the complainant would not be required to work on Saturdays. For the year ended June 30, 2006, the Human Rights Commission received 2,058 complaints having an element of unlawful discrimination under the Human Rights Act, and of these complaints, 70 or 3.4 percent were classified as unlawful discrimination on grounds of religious belief.[37]

New Zealand has ratified several international covenants, which obligate governments to ensure equality to enjoy all economic, social, cultural, civil and political rights. Although international agreements do not automatically become part of New Zealand domestic law upon ratification but must be enacted into law by Parliament, jurisprudence has developed in New Zealand that recognizes the value of international agreements as tools for interpreting the legislative provisions which implement them into domestic law.

The following legislative instruments may be relevant to religious discrimination.

Treaty of Waitangi

In the late 1830s, there were approximately 125,000 Māori and about 2000 settlers in New Zealand. More immigrants were arriving all the time though, and Captain William Hobson was sent to act for the British Crown in the negotiation of a treaty between the Crown and Māori. The Colonial Secretary, Lord Normanby, instructed Hobson:

> All dealings with the Aborigines for their Lands must be conducted on the same principles of sincerity, justice, and good faith as must govern your transactions with them for the recognition of Her Majesty's Sovereignty in the Islands. Nor is this all. They must not be permitted to enter into any Contracts in which they might be the ignorant and unintentional authors of injuries to themselves. You will not, for example, purchase from them any Territory the retention of which by them would be essential, or highly conducive, to their own comfort, safety or subsistence. The acquisition of Land by the Crown for the future Settlement of British Subjects must be confined to such Districts as the Natives can alienate without distress or serious inconvenience to themselves. To secure the observance of this rule will be one of the first duties of their official protector.

The Treaty of Waitangi is an important legislative instrument. The Preamble of the English version of the Treaty of Waitangi, which came into effect on 6 February 1840, states:

> HER MAJESTY VICTORIA Queen of the United Kingdom of Great Britain and Ireland regarding with Her Royal favor the Native Chiefs and Tribes of New Zealand and anxious to protect their just Rights and Property and to secure to them the enjoyment of Peace and Good Order has deemed it necessary in consequence of the great number of Her Majesty's Subjects who have already settled in New Zealand and the rapid extension of Emigration both from Europe and Australia which is still in progress to constitute and appoint a functionary properly authorized to treat with the Aborigines of New Zealand for the recognition of Her Majesty's Sovereign authority over the whole or any part of those islands, Her Majesty therefore being desirous to establish a settled form of Civil Government with a view to avert the evil consequences which must result from the absence of the necessary Laws and Institutions alike to the native population and to Her subjects has been graciously pleased to empower and to authorize me William Hobson a Captain in Her Majesty's Royal Navy Consul and Lieutenant Governor of such parts of New Zealand as may be or hereafter shall be ceded to her Majesty to invite the confederated and independent Chiefs of New Zealand to concur in the following Articles and Conditions.[38]

In terms of the meaning of the Treaty, the Preamble of the English text states that the British intentions were to protect Māori interests from the encroaching British settlement, provide for British settlement and establish a government to maintain peace and order. The Māori text has a different emphasis, suggesting that the Queen's main promises to Māori were to secure tribal *rangatiratanga* and secure Māori land ownership.

Article 1 states:

> The Chiefs of the Confederation of the United Tribes of New Zealand and the separate and independent Chiefs who have not become members of the Confederation cede to Her Majesty the Queen of England absolutely and without reservation all the rights and powers of Sovereignty which the said Confederation or Individual Chiefs respectively exercise or possess, or may be supposed to exercise or to possess over their respective Territories as the sole Sovereigns thereof.[39]

In terms of the meaning of the Treaty, in the Māori text of Article 1, the Māori gave the British a right of governance, *kawanatanga,* whereas in the English text, the Māori ceded 'sovereignty'. One of the problems that faced the original translators of the English draft of the Treaty was that 'sovereignty' in the British understanding of the word had no direct translation in the context of Māori society. *Rangatira*, the chiefs, held *rangatiratanga,* the autonomy and authority, over their own domains but there was no supreme ruler of the whole country. In the Māori text, the translators used the inadequate term *kawanatanga,* a transliteration of the word 'governance', which was then in current use. The Māori understanding of this word came from familiar use in the New Testament of the Bible when referring to the likes of Pontius Pilate, and from their knowledge of the role of the *Kawana*, the Governor of New South Wales, whose jurisdiction then extended to British subjects in New Zealand. As a result, in Article 1, the Māori believe they ceded to the Queen a right of governance in return for the promise of protection, while retaining the authority to manage their own affairs.

Article 2 states:

> Her Majesty the Queen of England confirms and guarantees to the Chiefs and Tribes of New Zealand and to the respective families and individuals thereof the full exclusive and undisturbed possession of their Lands and Estates Forests Fisheries and other properties which they may collectively or individually possess so long as it is their wish and desire to retain the same in their possession; but the Chiefs of the United Tribes and the individual Chiefs yield to Her Majesty the exclusive right of Preemption over such lands as the proprietors thereof may be disposed to alienate at such prices as may be agreed upon between the respective Proprietors and persons appointed by Her Majesty to treat with them in that behalf.[40]

In terms of the meaning of the Treaty, the Māori text of Article 2 uses the word *rangatiratanga* in promising to uphold the authority that tribes had always had over their lands and taonga. This choice of wording emphasizes status and authority. In the English text, the Queen guaranteed to the Māori the undisturbed possession of their properties, including their lands, forests, and fisheries, for as long as they wished to retain them, emphasizing property and ownership rights. Article 2 provides for land sales to be effected through the Crown, giving the Crown the right of pre-emption in land sales. The Waitangi Tribunal, after reading the instructions for the Treaty provided by Lord Normanby, concluded that the purpose of this provision was not just to regulate settlement but to ensure that each tribe retained sufficient land for its own purposes and needs.

Article 3 states:

> In consideration thereof Her Majesty the Queen of England extends to the Natives of New Zealand Her royal protection and imparts to them all the Rights and Privileges of British Subjects.
> W HOBSON Lieutenant Governor.
> Now therefore We the Chiefs of the Confederation of the United Tribes of New Zealand being assembled in Congress at Victoria in Waitangi and We the Separate and Independent Chiefs of New Zealand claiming authority over the Tribes and Territories which are specified after our respective names, having been made fully to understand the Provisions of the foregoing Treaty, accept and enter into the same in the full spirit and meaning thereof: in witness of which we have attached our signatures or marks at the places and the dates respectively specified.[41]

In terms of the meaning of the Treaty, in Article 3, the Crown promised to the Māori the benefits of royal protection and full citizenship, emphasizing equality. Further, in the epilogue, the signatories acknowledge that they have entered into the full spirit of the Treaty. It is the principles of the Treaty, rather than the meaning of its strict terms, that is important and the Waitangi Tribunal must have regard for cultural meanings of words, the surrounding circumstances, comments made at the time, and the parties' objectives.

Bill of Rights Act

Important for equal rights, according to the Preamble of the Bill of Rights Act 1990, as amended by the Human Rights Act, the Bill of Rights aims to affirm, protect, and promote human rights and fundamental freedoms in New Zealand; and to affirm New Zealand's commitment to the International Covenant on Civil and Political Rights.[42] It applies to acts done by the legislative, executive and judicial branches of the Government, or by any person or body in the performance of any public function, power or duty conferred or imposed on that person or body by or pursuant to law.

Importantly in the fight against religious discrimination, in terms of freedom of thought, conscience and religion, Section 13 states:

13. Everyone has the right to freedom of thought, conscience, religion, and belief, including the right to adopt and hold opinions without interference.[43]

Further, in terms of religion and belief, Section 15 guarantees:

15. Every person has the right to manifest that person's religion or belief in worship, observance, practice, or teaching, either individually or in community with others, and either in public or in private.[44]

In addition, freedom from discrimination is guaranteed under Section 19, which specifically mentions religion:

19(1) Everyone has the right to freedom from discrimination on the grounds of colour, race, ethnic or national origins, sex, marital status, or religious or ethical belief.
(2) Measures taken in good faith for the purpose of assisting or advancing persons or groups of persons disadvantaged because of colour, race, ethnic or national origins, sex, marital status, or religious or ethical belief do not constitute discrimination.[45]

Finally, rights of minorities are guaranteed under Section 20, which specifically mentions freedom of religion:

20. A person who belongs to an ethnic, religious, or linguistic minority in New Zealand shall not be denied the right, in community with other members of that minority, to enjoy the culture, to profess and practise the religion, or to use the language, of that minority.[46]

Importantly, the right to justice and hence remedies are contained in Section 27:

27(1) Every person has the right to the observance of the principles of natural justice by any tribunal or other public authority which has the power to make a determination in respect of that person's right, obligations, or interests protected or recognized by law.
(2) Every person whose rights, obligations, or interests protected or recognized by law have been affected by a determination of any tribunal or other public authority has the right to apply, in accordance with law, for judicial review of that determination.
(3) Every person has the right to bring civil proceedings against, and to defend civil proceedings brought by, the Crown, and to have those proceedings heard, according to law, in the same way as civil proceedings between individuals.[47]

Human Rights Act (HRA) and Human Rights Amendment Act

Important for equal rights, the Human Rights Act 1993 (HRA) protects New Zealanders from unlawful discrimination in a number of areas of life. The Human Rights Commission (HRC) was established by the Human Rights Commission Act 1977 (HRCA), and is empowered under the HRA to protect human rights in accordance with United Nations Covenants and Conventions. The Human Rights Amendment Act 2001 (HRAA) made several significant changes to the HRA, and specifically to the functions and powers of the Commission, and specifically as to the way complaints of unlawful discrimination are received and resolved by the Commission. Some of the key changes to the Commission's functions and powers include: advocating and promoting respect for, and appreciation of, human rights in New Zealand society, and encouraging the maintenance and development of harmonious relations between individuals and the diverse groups in New Zealand society; advocating and promoting, by education and publicity, respect for, and observance of, human rights; making public statements promoting an understanding of, and compliance with, the New Zealand Bill of Rights Act 1990; developing a national plan of action, in consultation with interested parties, for the promotion and protection of human rights in New Zealand; promoting, by research, education and discussion, a better understanding of the human rights dimensions of the Treaty of Waitangi and their relationship with domestic and international human rights law; bringing civil proceedings for any breach of the Act arising out of any inquiry conducted by the Commission; and applying to a court or tribunal to be appointed as intervener or as counsel, assisting the Court or Tribunal, in facilitating the performance of the Commission's functions relating to advocacy for, or promotion of, human rights.

Further, the functions and powers of the HRC include to encourage, by education and publicity, respect for and observance of human rights; to encourage and coordinate programs and activities in the field of human rights; to make public statements in relation to any matter affecting human rights, including statements promoting an understanding of, and compliance with, the Act; to prepare and publish guidelines for the avoidance of acts or practices that may be inconsistent with the provisions of this Act; to receive representations from members of the public on any matter affecting human rights; to consult and cooperate with other people and bodies concerned with the protection of human rights; to inquire into any matter, including any enactment or law, or any practice, or any procedure, whether governmental or nongovernmental, if it appears to the Commission that human rights are, or may be, infringed thereby; and to report to the Prime Minister from time to time on any matter affecting human rights, including the desirability of legislative, administrative, or other action to give better protection to human rights and to ensure better compliance with standards laid down in international instruments on human rights, the desirability of New Zealand becoming bound by any international instrument on human rights, and the implications of any proposed legislation or proposed policy of the Government that the Commission considers may affect human rights.[48] Employment remains the largest area of complaints at about 60 percent.

Overall, the Act defines unlawful discrimination; prohibited grounds are personal characteristics and discrimination because of these characteristics is unlawful. Important for equal rights, Section 21 defines discrimination under prohibited grounds for discrimination, including religion:

21(1) For the purposes of this Act, the prohibited grounds of discrimination are:
(c) Religious belief;
(d) Ethical belief, which means the lack of a religious belief, whether in respect of a particular religion or religions or all religions.
(2) Each of the grounds specified in subsection (1) of this section is a prohibited ground of discrimination, for the purposes of this Act, if
(a) It pertains to a person or to a relative or associate of a person; and
(b) It either
(i) Currently exists or has in the past existed; or
(ii) Is suspected or assumed or believed to exist or to have existed by the person alleged to have discriminated.[49]

Further, indirect discrimination is defined in Section 65:

65. Where any conduct, practice, requirement, or condition that is not apparently in contravention of any provision of this Part of this Act has the effect of treating a person or group of persons differently on one of the prohibited grounds of discrimination in a situation where such treatment would be unlawful under any provision of this Part of this Act other than this section, that conduct, practice, condition, or requirement shall be unlawful under that provision unless the person whose conduct or practice is in issue, or who imposes the condition or requirement, establishes good reason for it.[50]

As regards discrimination in employment, Section 22(1) states:

22(1) Where an applicant for employment or an employee is qualified for work of any description, it shall be unlawful for an employer, or any person acting or purporting to act on behalf of an employer:
(a) to refuse or omit to employ the applicant on work of that description which is available; or
(b) to offer or afford the applicant or the employee less favourable terms of employment, conditions of work, superannuation or other fringe benefits, and opportunities for training, promotion, and transfer than are made available to applicants or employees of the same or substantially similar capabilities employed in the same or substantially similar circumstances on work of that description; or
(c) to terminate the employment of the employee, or subject the employee to any detriment, in circumstances in which the employment of other employees employed on work of that description would not be terminated, or in which other employees employed on work of that description would not be subjected to such detriment; or
(d) to retire the employee, or to require or cause the employee to retire or resign (applies to all (a), (b), (c) and (d)), by reason of any of the prohibited grounds of discrimination.[51]

In terms of exceptions for purposes of religion, Section 28 states:

> 28(1) Nothing in section 22 of this Act shall prevent different treatment based on sex where the position is for the purposes of an organised religion and is limited to one sex so as to comply with the doctrines or rules or established customs of the religion.
> (2) Nothing in section 22 of this Act shall prevent different treatment based on religious or ethical belief where
>> (a) That treatment is accorded under section 65 of the Private Schools Conditional Integration Act 1975; or
>> (b) The sole or principal duties of the position (not being a position to which section 65 of the Private Schools Conditional Integration Act 1975 applies)
>>> (i) Are, or are substantially the same as, those of a clergyman, priest, pastor, official, or teacher among adherents of that belief or otherwise involve the propagation of that belief; or
>>> (ii) Are those of a teacher in a private school; or
>>> (iii) Consist of acting as a social worker on behalf of an organisation whose members comprise solely or principally adherents of that belief.
>
> (3) Where a religious or ethical belief requires its adherents to follow a particular practice, an employer must accommodate the practice so long as any adjustment of the employer's activities required to accommodate the practice does not unreasonably disrupt the employer's activities.[52]

Section 39 provides for exceptions in relation to qualifying bodies, including the religious:

> 39(1) Nothing in section 38 of this Act shall apply where the authorisation or qualification is needed for, or facilitates engagement in, a profession or calling for the purposes of an organised religion and is limited to one sex or to persons of that religious belief so as to comply with the doctrines or rules or established customs of that religion.[53]

Further, Section 35 outlines the general qualification on exceptions:

> 35. No employer shall be entitled ... to accord to any person in respect of any position different treatment based on a prohibited ground of discrimination even though some of the duties of that position would fall within any of those exceptions if, with some adjustment of the activities of the employer (not being an adjustment involving unreasonable disruption of the activities of the employer), some other employee could carry out those particular duties.[54]

Finally, measures to ensure equality are established under Section 73:

> 73(1) Anything done or omitted which would otherwise constitute a breach of any of the provisions of this Part of this Act shall not constitute such a breach if:
> (a) it is done or omitted in good faith for the purpose of assisting or advancing persons or groups of persons, being in each case persons against whom discrimination is unlawful by virtue of this Part of this Act; and

(b) those persons or groups need or may reasonably be supposed to need assistance or advancement in order to achieve an equal place with other members of the community.[55]

Employment Contracts Act and Employment Relations Act

Important for employment rights, the Employment Contracts Act 1991[56] and the Employment Relations Act 2000[57] provide people with the right to take discrimination cases to the Employment Court as a personal grievance. Further, Section 3 of the Employment Relations Act establishes the objectives:

> 3. The object of this Act is
> (a) to build productive employment relationships through the promotion of mutual trust and confidence in all aspects of the employment environment and of the employment relationship
> (i) by recognising that employment relationships must be built on good faith behaviour; and
> (ii) by acknowledging and addressing the inherent inequality of bargaining power in employment relationships; and
> (iii) by promoting collective bargaining; and
> (iv) by protecting the integrity of individual choice; and
> (v) by promoting mediation as the primary problem-solving mechanism; and
> (vi) by reducing the need for judicial intervention; and
> (b) to promote observance in New Zealand of the principles underlying International Labour Organisation Convention 87 on Freedom of Association, and Convention 98 on the Right to Organise and Bargain Collectively.[58]

Finally, the jurisdiction of the Employment Court is established under Section 187 of the Employment Relations Act:

> 187(1) The Court has exclusive jurisdiction
> (a) to hear and determine elections under section 179 for a hearing of a matter previously determined by the Authority, whether under this Act or any other Act conferring jurisdiction on the Authority:
> (b) to hear and determine actions for the recovery of penalties under this Act for a breach of any provision of this Act (being a provision that provides for the penalty to be recovered in the Court):
> (c) to hear and determine questions of law referred to it by the Authority under section 177:
> (d) to hear and determine applications for leave to have matters before the Authority removed into the Court under section 178(3):
> (e) to hear and determine matters removed into the Court under section 178:
> (f) to hear and determine, under section 6(5), any question whether any person is to be declared to be

(i) an employee within the meaning of this Act; or

(ii) a worker or employee within the meaning of any of the Acts referred to in section 223(1):

(g) to order compliance under section 139:

(h) to hear and determine proceedings founded on tort and resulting from or related to a strike or lockout:

(i) to hear and determine any application for an injunction of a type specified in section 100:

(j) to hear and determine any application for review of the type referred to in section 194:

(k) to issue warrants under section 231:

(l) to exercise its powers in respect of any offence against this Act:

(m) to exercise such other functions and powers as are conferred on it by this or any other Act.

(2) The Court does not have jurisdiction to entertain an application for summary judgment.[59]

Race Relations Act

Important for religious minorities, the Race Relations Act 1971 guards against race discrimination in a number of areas, including employment, with Section 5 stating:

> 5(1) It shall be unlawful for any [person who is an] employer, or any person acting or purporting to act on behalf of any [person who is an] employer
> (a) To refuse or omit to employ any person on work of any description which is available and for which that person is qualified; or
> (b) To refuse or omit to offer or afford any person the same terms of employment, conditions of work, fringe benefits, and opportunities for training, promotion, and transfer as are made available for persons of the same or substantially similar qualifications employed in the same or substantially similar circumstances on work of that description; or
> (c) To dismiss any person, or subject any person to any detriment, in circumstances in which other persons employed by that employer on work of that description are not or would not be dismissed or are not or would not be subjected to such detriment
> by reason of the color, race, or ethnic or national origins of that person ....
> (3) Nothing in this section shall apply in respect of the employment of any person for any purpose for which persons of a particular ethnic or national origin have or are commonly found to have a particular qualification or aptitude.[60]

Importantly, in terms of measures to ensure equality, Section 9 states:

> 9. Anything done or omitted which would otherwise constitute a breach of any of the provisions of sections 4 to 7 of this Act shall not constitute such a breach if

(a) It is done or omitted in good faith for the purpose of assisting or advancing persons or groups of persons, being in each case persons of a particular color, race, or ethnic or national origin; and
(b) Those groups or persons need or may reasonably be supposed to need assistance or advancement in order to achieve an equal place with other members of the community.[61]

Finally, Section 9A provides for racial harmony:

9A. 1) It shall be unlawful for any person
(a) To publish or distribute written matter which is threatening, abusive, or insulting, or to broadcast by means of radio or television words which are threatening, abusive, or insulting;
or
(b) To use in any public place..., or within the hearing of persons in any such public place, or at any meeting to which the public are invited or have access, words which are threatening, abusive, or insulting,
being matter or words likely to excite hostility or ill-will against, or bring into contempt or ridicule, any group of persons in New Zealand on the ground of the colour, race, or ethnic or national origins of that group of persons.[62]

Conclusion

Despite strong legislative provisions both in Australia and New Zealand, there is still progress to be made to achieve equal outcomes and opportunities for all religions. Equality and the rights contained within legislation rely on the overall legal system, as well as cultural attitudes for implementation and enforcement. However, gaps do exist in the coverage of legislation, and in the manner by which it is enforced. Taking concrete action to advance human rights and support opportunity and choice require a concerted effort across the whole of government, in addition to the important ongoing role of specialist human rights monitoring and complaints mechanisms, in the pursuit of *Heaven Forbid*.

Notes

1 Discrimination Act, Australia, at Section 7.
2 *Ibid.*, at Section 8.
3 *Ibid.*, at Section 10.
4 *Ibid.*, at Section 11.
5 *Ibid.*, at Section 32.
6 *Ibid.*, at Section 33.
7 *Ibid.*, at Section 44.

8   *Ibid.*, at Section 46.
9   Anti-Discrimination Act, Australia, at Section 7.
10 Human Rights and Equal Opportunity Commission Act, Australia, at Section 3.
11 *Ibid.*, at Section 10A.
12 *Ibid.*, at Section 11.
13 *Ibid.*, at Section 46P.
14 Human Rights and Equal Opportunity Commission, *Article 18 – Freedom of Religion and Belief*, 1998, p. 108.
15 *Ibid.*, at p. 111.
16 Workplace Relations Act, Australia.
17 *Ibid.*, at Section 3.
18 *Ibid.*, at Section 659(2).
19 *Ibid.*, at Section 104.
20 *Ibid.*, at Section 150B.
21 Racial Discrimination Act, Australia.
22 *Ibid.*, at Section 9.
23 *Ibid.*, at Section 10.
24 Sex Discrimination Act, Australia, at Section 3.
25 *Ibid.*, at Section 5.
26 *Ibid.*, at Section 7D.
27 *Ibid.*, at Section 48.
28 *Ibid.*, at Section 23(3)(b).
29 *Ibid.*, at Section 37.
30 *Ibid.*, at Section 38.
31 *Church of the New Faith v. Commissioner for Pay-Roll Tax* (Vic) (1983) 154 CLR 120.
32 *Ibid.*, at 136.
33 *Ibid.*, at 150.
34 *Australia's Beijing Plus Five Action Plan 2001–2005*.
35 *Ibid.*
36 New Zealand Bureau of Democracy, Human Rights, and Labor, *International Religious Freedom Report*, 2007.
37 *Ibid.*
38 Treaty of Waitangi, New Zealand, at the Preamble.
39 *Ibid.*, at Article 1.
40 *Ibid.*, at Article 2.
41 *Ibid.*, at Article 3.
42 Bill of Rights Act, New Zealand, at the Preamble.
43 *Ibid.*, at Section 13.
44 *Ibid.*, at Section 15.
45 *Ibid.*, at Section 19.
46 *Ibid.*, at Section 20.
47 *Ibid.*, at Section 27.
48 Human Rights Act, New Zealand, at Section 5(1).

49 *Ibid.*, at Section 21.
50 *Ibid.*, at Section 65.
51 *Ibid.*, at Section 22(1).
52 *Ibid.*, at Section 28.
53 *Ibid.*, at Section 39.
54 *Ibid.*, at Section 35.
55 *Ibid.*, at Section 73.
56 Employment Contracts Act, New Zealand.
57 Employment Relations Act, New Zealand.
58 *Ibid.*, at Section 3.
59 *Ibid.*, at Section 187.
60 Race Relations Act, New Zealand., at Section 5.
61 *Ibid.*, at Section 9.
62 *Ibid.*, at Section 9A.

References

Anti-Discrimination Act, Australia, 1991.
Australia's Beijing Plus Five Action Plan 2001–2005.
Bill of Rights Act, New Zealand, 1990.
Church of the New Faith v. Commissioner for Pay-Roll Tax (Vic) (1983) 154 CLR 120.
Discrimination Act, Australia, 1991.
Employment Contracts Act, New Zealand, 1991.
Employment Relations Act, New Zealand, 2000.
Gething L. (1999), *We're Growing Old Too: Quality of Life and Service Provision Issues for People with Long Standing Disabilities who are Ageing*, Community Disability and Ageing Program, The University of Sydney.
Human Rights Act, New Zealand, 1993.
Human Rights and Equal Opportunity Commission Act, Australia, 1986.
Human Rights and Equal Opportunity Commission (1998), *Article 18 – Freedom of Religion and Belief.*
New Zealand Bureau of Democracy, Human Rights, and Labor, *International Religious Freedom Report*, 2007.
Race Relations Act, New Zealand, 1971.
Racial Discrimination Act, Australia, 1975.
Racial Hatred Act, Australia, 1995.
Sex Discrimination Act, Australia, 1984.
Treaty of Waitangi, New Zealand, 1840.
Workplace Relations Act, Australia, 1996.

Chapter 5
Heaven Forbid in Africa and South Africa

Introduction

In the quest for religious tolerance in *Heaven Forbid*, this chapter will examine efforts against religious discrimination on the continent of Africa, and in South Africa. It will examine important legislation impacting religious rights, first in Africa, namely the Charter of the Organization of African Unity, the African Charter on Human and Peoples' Rights and the Protocol of the African Charter on Human and Peoples' Rights, and for religious women, the Protocol on Rights of Women in Africa; and then in South Africa, namely the Interim Constitution Schedule 4 and the Constitution, the Employment Equity Act, and the Promotion of Equality and Prevention of Unfair Discrimination Act.

Africa

Africa is not a single uniform entity. Within Africa, there is much diversity, in terms of religion, age, disability, race, culture, gender relations, society, family, geography, economy, and natural resources. There is not one formula that can be applied in every case, and as such every community has to make its individual needs heard. In addition, Africa is not static. It is a continent in flux and is rapidly undergoing fundamental changes, namely the growth of urban populations, deterioration of the environment and increasing desertification, growing dependency on world markets, increasing numbers of young people and seniors, and civil strife and conflict. Development policies, plans and programs must be flexible to react and respond to these changes. The knowledge, attitudes and practices of the general African population have some components that are historically accumulated, based on the cultural and institutional heritage of the past. This is especially so among populations where a majority live in traditional ways, a lesser proportion are in transition, and a small, powerful minority are considered 'modern'. Citizen services during the past several decades seem to have been dominated by the disparate trends and methods of funding from various European countries. Such developments, imported from countries with much stronger economies and longer histories of universal primary and child-centered education, as well as educational research, have seldom been culturally or conceptually appropriate to the countries in which they have taken place. Setting current efforts against a century or more of antiquated foreign development is intended to bring more realistic perspectives.

The current emphases within South Africa on human rights and policy reform go hand in hand with greater empowerment of all people. In terms of international trade, African countries adopted the Dakar/Ngor Declaration in 1992 as the African common position to the International Conference on Population and Development (ICPD). It was recognized that population and development are inextricably linked, and that empowering and meeting people's needs for education and health are necessary for both individual advancement and balanced development. For population and sustainable development in Africa, a key measure must be the promotion of access to equitable distribution of resources. Further, there needs to be a mix of macroeconomic and structural policies and programs for enhancing investment, growth, poverty reduction and social development; infrastructure improvement and institutional support services policies; and policies aimed at strengthening grassroots institutions and local participation. The ICPD+5 Program of Action recommended a set of interdependent quantitative goals and objectives, which included universal access to primary education, with special attention to closing the gap in primary and secondary school education; universal access to primary health care; universal access to a full range of comprehensive reproductive health care services, including family planning; reductions in infant, child and maternal morbidity and mortality; and increased life expectancy impacting seniors.

Overall, in terms of trade and its impact on people in Africa, in 2000, the United States Congress passed the African Growth and Opportunity Act (AGOA), which eliminated American duties on textile imports from eligible sub-Saharan countries.[1] Further, a new round of global trade negotiations, dubbed the Doha Development Round, began in 2002. However, to ensure long-term benefits from better access to American markets, African countries must diversify their economies, investing in infrastructure and in education to attract higher-tech companies. Africa's main goals are to substantially reduce or eliminate all tariffs on agricultural products, including quota duties; substantially reduce or eliminate tariff escalation; simplify complex tariffs by converting all tariffs to an *ad valorem* or fixed percentage of a product's value; substantially reduce or eliminate market-distorting export subsidies and domestic support; and recognize and meet the special needs of the world's least developed countries.

Importantly, the New Partnership for Africa's Development (NEPAD) is a pledge by all of Africa's leaders to eradicate poverty in which many seniors live and move towards sustainable growth and development. The partnership focuses on African ownership of the development process and seeks to reinvigorate the continent in all areas of human activity. Through cooperation and partnership, African leaders have agreed to promote the role of different groups in social and economic development; promote and protect democracy and human rights by developing standards for accountability, transparency and participatory governance; restore and maintain macroeconomic stability; implement transparent legal and regulatory frameworks; revitalize and extend education, technical training and health care services; and promote the development of infrastructure, agriculture, agroprocessing, and manufacturing to meet the needs of export and domestic markets as well as local employment. NEPAD draws Africa's attention to the seriousness of the continent's economic challenges, the potential for addressing them and the challenge of mobilizing support. The main strategies proposed include pursuing equality in education, business, and public service; developing education and human resources at all levels, and in particular increasing the role of information and communication technology in education and training, inducing a 'brain gain' for Africa and eliminating disparities in education; and increasing domestic resource mobilization and accelerating foreign investment, creating a conducive environment for private sector activities, with an emphasis on domestic entrepreneurs.[2]

Charter of the Organization of African Unity

The heads of African states and governments signed the Charter of the Organization of African Unity on 25 May 1963 in Addis Ababa, Ethiopia, and it entered into force on 13 September 1963. The Preamble of the Charter of the Organization of African Unity states:

Convinced that it is the inalienable right of all people to control their own destiny,

Conscious of the fact that freedom, equality, justice and dignity are essential objectives for the achievement of the legitimate aspirations of the African peoples,

Conscious of our responsibility to harness the natural and human resources of our continent for the total advancement of our peoples in all spheres of human endeavor,

Inspired by a common determination to promote understanding among our peoples and cooperation among our states in response to the aspirations of our peoples for brotherhood and solidarity, in a larger unity transcending ethnic and national differences,

Convinced that, in order to translate this determination into a dynamic force in the cause of human progress, conditions for peace and security must be established and maintained,

Determined to safeguard and consolidate the hard-won independence as well as the sovereignty and territorial integrity of our states, and to fight against neo-colonialism in all its forms,

Dedicated to the general progress of Africa,

Persuaded that the Charter of the United Nations and the Universal Declaration of Human Rights, to the Principles of which we reaffirm our adherence, provide a solid foundation for peaceful and positive cooperation among States,

Desirous that all African States should henceforth unite so that the welfare and well-being of their peoples can be assured,

Resolved to reinforce the links between our states by establishing and strengthening common institutions.[3]

Article I establishes the Organization of African Unity:

I.1. The High Contracting Parties do by the present Charter establish an Organization to be known as the ORGANIZATION OF AFRICAN UNITY.

2. The Organization shall include the Continental African States, Madagascar and other Islands surrounding Africa.[4]

Its purposes are outlined in Article II:

II. 1. The Organization shall have the following purposes:

(a) To promote the unity and solidarity of the African States;
(b) To coordinate and intensify their cooperation and efforts to achieve a better life for the peoples of Africa;
(c) To defend their sovereignty, their territorial integrity and independence;
(d) To eradicate all forms of colonialism from Africa; and
(e) To promote international cooperation, having due regard to the Charter of the United Nations and the Universal Declaration of Human Rights.

2. To these ends, the Member States shall coordinate and harmonize their general policies, especially in the following fields:

(a) Political and diplomatic cooperation;
(b) Economic cooperation, including transport and communications;
(c) Educational and cultural cooperation;
(d) Health, sanitation and nutritional cooperation;
(e) Scientific and technical cooperation; and
(f) Cooperation for defense and security.[5]

The various institutions are outlined in Article VII:

VII. The Organization shall accomplish its purposes through the following principal institutions:

1. The Assembly of Heads of State and Government.
2. The Council of Ministers.
3. The General Secretariat.

4. The Commission of Mediation, Conciliation and Arbitration.[6]

The Assembly of Heads of State and Government is contained in Article VIII:

> VIII. The Assembly of Heads of State and Government shall be the supreme organ of the Organization. It shall, subject to the provisions of this Charter, discuss matters of common concern to Africa with a view to coordinating and harmonizing the general policy of the Organization. It may in addition review the structure, functions and acts of all the organs and any specialized agencies which may be created in accordance with the present Charter.[7]

The Council of Ministers is contained in Article XII:

> XII. 1. The Council of Ministers shall consist of Foreign Ministers or other Ministers as are designated by the Governments of Member States.
>
> 2. The Council of Ministers shall meet at least twice a year. When requested by any Member State and approved by two-thirds of all Member States, it shall meet in extraordinary session.[8]

The General Secretariat is contained in Article XVI:

> XVI. There shall be a Secretary-General of the Organization, who shall be appointed by the Assembly of Heads of State and Government. The Secretary-General shall direct the affairs of the Secretariat.[9]

The Commission of Mediation, Conciliation and Arbitration is contained in Article XIX:

> XIX. Member States pledge to settle all disputes among themselves by peaceful means and, to this end decide to establish a Commission of Mediation, Conciliation and Arbitration, the composition of which and condition of service shall be defined by a separate Protocol to be approved by the Assembly of Heads of State and Government. Said Protocol shall be regarded as forming an integral part of the present Charter.[10]

The Specialized Commission is contained in Article XX:

> XX. The Assembly shall establish such Specialized Commissions as it may, deem necessary, including the following:
>
> 1. Economic and Social Commission.
> 2. Educational, Scientific, Cultural and Health Commission.
> 3. Defense Commission.[11]

African Charter on Human and Peoples' Rights

The African Charter on Human and Peoples' Rights was adopted by the Eighteenth Assembly of Heads of State and Government on 27 June 1981 in Nairobi, Kenya. The Preamble of the African Charter on Human and Peoples' Rights, which specifically mentions religion, states:

> The African States members of the Organization of African Unity, parties to the present Convention entitled African Charter on Human and Peoples' Rights,
>
> Considering the Charter of the Organization of African Unity, which stipulates that 'freedom, equality, justice and dignity are essential objectives for the achievement of the legitimate aspirations of the African peoples';
>
> Reaffirming the pledge they solemnly made in Article 2 of the said Charter to eradicate all forms of colonialism from Africa, to coordinate and intensify their cooperation and efforts to achieve a better life for the peoples of Africa and to promote international cooperation having due regard to the Charter of the United Nations and the Universal Declaration of Human Rights;
>
> Taking into consideration the virtues of their historical tradition and the values of African civilization which should inspire and characterize their reflection on the concept of human and peoples' rights,
>
> Recognizing on the one hand, that fundamental human rights stem from the attitudes of human beings, which justifies their international protection, and on the other hand that the reality and respect of peoples' rights should necessarily guarantee human rights;
>
> Considering that the enjoyment of rights and freedoms also implies the performance of duties on the part of everyone;
>
> Convinced that it is henceforth essential to pay particular attention to the right to development and that civil and political rights cannot be dissociated from economic, social and cultural rights in their conception as well as universality and that the satisfaction of economic, social and cultural rights is a guarantee for the enjoyment of civil and political rights;
>
> Conscious of their duty to achieve the total liberation of Africa, the peoples of which are still struggling for their dignity and genuine independence, and undertaking to eliminate colonialism, neo-colonialism, apartheid, zionism and to dismantle aggressive foreign military bases and all forms of discrimination, language, religion or political opinions;
>
> Reaffirming their adherence to the principles of human and peoples' rights and freedoms contained in the declarations, conventions and other instruments adopted by

the Organization of African Unity, the Movement of Non-Aligned Countries and the United Nations;

Firmly convinced of their duty to promote and protect human and peoples' rights and freedoms and taking into account the importance traditionally attached to these rights and freedoms in Africa.[12]

In terms of rights and duties in general and human and peoples' rights, specifically, Article 1 states:

The Member States of the Organization of African Unity, parties to the present Charter shall recognize the rights, duties and freedoms enshrined in the Charter and shall undertake to adopt legislative or other measures to give effect to them.[13]

Article 5 upholds the dignity of the human person:

Every individual shall have the right to the respect of the dignity inherent in a human being and to the recognition of his legal status. All forms of exploitation and degradation of man, particularly slavery, slave trade, torture, cruel, inhuman or degrading punishment and treatment shall be prohibited.[14]

The concept of equality is guaranteed in Article 19:

All peoples shall be equal; they shall enjoy the same respect and shall have the same rights. Nothing shall justify the domination of a people by another.[15]

Further, important for equal rights and religious discrimination cases, Article 2, which specifically mentions religion, protects against discrimination:

Every individual shall be entitled to the enjoyment of the rights and freedoms recognized and guaranteed in the present Charter without distinction of any kind such as race, ethnic group, color, sex, language, religion, political or any other opinion, national and social origin, fortune, birth or any status.[16]

In addition, Article 8 provides for freedom of religion:

Freedom of conscience, the profession and free practice of religion shall be guaranteed. No one may, subject to law and order, be submitted to measures restricting the exercise of these freedoms.[17]

Finally, respect and religious tolerance without discrimination are espoused in Article 28:

> Every individual shall have the duty to respect and consider his fellow beings without discrimination, and to maintain relations aimed at promoting, safeguarding and reinforcing mutual respect and tolerance.[18]

Further, Article 3 guarantees equal protection of the law:

> Every individual shall be equal before the law.

> Every individual shall be entitled to equal protection of the law.[19]

Crucial for equal rights and religious discrimination cases, employment rights and equal pay for equal work are guaranteed in Article 15:

> Every individual shall have the right to work under equitable and satisfactory conditions, and shall receive equal pay for equal work.[20]

The right to education for advancement and the importance of community are recognized in Article 17:

> Every individual shall have the right to education.

> Every individual may freely take part in the cultural life of his community.

> The promotion and protection of morals and traditional values recognized by the community shall be the duty of the State.[21]

Article 20 upholds self-determination of people:

> All peoples shall have the right to existence. They shall have the unquestionable and inalienable right to self-determination. They shall freely determine their political status and shall pursue their economic and social development according to the policy they have freely chosen.

> Colonized or oppressed peoples shall have the right to free themselves from the bonds of domination by resorting to any means recognized by the international community.

> All peoples shall have the right to the assistance of the State Parties to the present Charter in their liberation struggle against foreign domination, be it political, economic or cultural.[22]

Cultural development of the heritage of mankind is recognized in Article 22:

> All peoples shall have the right to their economic, social and cultural development with due regard to their freedom and identity and in the equal enjoyment of the common heritage of mankind.
>
> States shall have the duty, individually or collectively, to ensure the exercise of the right to development.[23]

Duties of individuals towards one another are established in Article 27:

> Every individual shall have duties towards his family and society, the State and other legally recognized communities and the international community.
>
> The rights and freedoms of each individual shall be exercised with due regard to the rights of others, collective security, morality and common interest.[24]

In Article 29, the individual shall also have the duty, among other things:

> To serve his national community by placing his physical and intellectual abilities at its service;
>
> To preserve and strengthen positive African cultural values in his relations with other members of the society, in the spirit of tolerance, dialogue and consultation and, in general, to contribute to the promotion of the moral well being of society.[25]

Article 7 stresses the importance of the courts in safeguarding rights:

> 7.1. Every individual shall have the right to have his cause heard. This comprises: (a) the right to an appeal to competent national organs against acts of violating his fundamental rights as recognized and guaranteed by conventions, laws, regulations and customs in force; (b) the right to be presumed innocent until proved guilty by a competent court or tribunal; (c) the right to defence, including the right to be defended by counsel of his choice; (d) the right to be tried within a reasonable time by an impartial court or tribunal. 2. No one may be condemned for an act or omission which did not constitute a legally punishable offence at the time it was committed. No penalty may be inflicted for an offence for which no provision was made at the time it was committed. Punishment is personal and can be imposed only on the offender.[26]

The paramount role of the Courts is guaranteed in Article 26:

> State Parties to the present Charter shall have the duty to guarantee the independence of the Courts and shall allow the establishment and improvement of appropriate national institutions entrusted with the promotion and protection of the rights and freedoms guaranteed by the present Charter.[27]

The African Commission on Human and Peoples' Right is established under Article 30:

> An African Commission on Human and Peoples' Rights, hereinafter called 'the Commission', shall be established within the Organization of African Unity to promote human and peoples' rights and ensure their protection in Africa.[28]

The mandate of the Commission is contained in Article 45:

> The functions of the Commission shall be:
>
> > To promote human and peoples' rights and in particular:
> >
> > > to collect documents, undertake studies and researches on African problems in the field of human and peoples' rights, organize seminars, symposia and conferences, disseminate information, encourage national and local institutions concerned with human and peoples' rights and, should the case arise, give its views or make recommendations to Governments.
> > >
> > > to formulate and lay down principles and rules aimed at solving legal problems relating to human and peoples' rights and fundamental freedoms upon which African Governments may base their legislation.
> > >
> > > cooperate with other African and international institutions concerned with the promotion and protection of human and peoples' rights.
>
> Ensure the protection of human and peoples' rights under conditions laid down by the present Charter.
>
> Interpret all the provisions of the present Charter at the request of a State Party, an institution of the OAU or an African Organization recognized by the OAU.
>
> Perform any other tasks which may be entrusted to it by the Assembly of Heads of State and Government.[29]

The procedure of the Commission is contained in Article 46:

> The Commission may resort to any appropriate method of investigation; it may hear from the Secretary General of the Organization of African Unity or any other person capable of enlightening it.[30]

Communications from States are envisioned in Article 47:

> If a State Party to the present Charter has good reasons to believe that another State Party to this Charter has violated the provisions of the Charter, it may draw, by written communication, the attention of that State to the matter. This Communication shall also be addressed to the Secretary General of the OAU and to the Chairman of the Commission. Within three months of the receipt of the Communication, the State to which the Communication is addressed shall give the enquiring State, written explanation or statement elucidating the matter. This should include as much as possible, relevant information relating to the laws and rules of procedure applied and applicable and the redress already given or course of action available.[31]

Further, Article 48 provides for submissions to the Commission:

> If within three months from the date on which the original communication is received by the State to which it is addressed, the issue is not settled to the satisfaction of the two States involved through bilateral negotiation or by any other peaceful procedure, either State shall have the right to submit the matter to the Commission through the Chairman and shall notify the other States involved.[32]

So too under Article 49:

> Notwithstanding the provisions of Article 47, if a State Party to the present Charter considers that another State Party has violated the provisions of the Charter, it may refer the matter directly to the Commission by addressing a communication to the Chairman, to the Secretary General of the Organization of African unity and the State concerned.[33]

Exhaustion of remedies is recognized under Article 50:

> The Commission can only deal with a matter submitted to it after making sure that all local remedies, if they exist, have been exhausted, unless it is obvious to the Commission that the procedure of achieving these remedies would be unduly prolonged.[34]

A report issued by the Commission is entailed in Article 52:

> After having obtained from the States concerned and from other sources all the information it deems necessary and after having tried all appropriate means to reach an amicable solution based on the respect of human and peoples' rights, the Commission shall prepare, within a reasonable period of time from the notification referred to in Article 48, a report to the States concerned and communicated to the Assembly of Heads of State and Government.[35]

In terms of Applicable Principles, Article 60 states:

> The Commission shall draw inspiration from international law on human and peoples' rights, particularly from the provisions of various African instruments on Human and Peoples' Rights, the Charter of the United Nations, the Charter of the Organization of African Unity, the Universal Declaration of Human Rights, other instruments adopted by the United Nations and by African countries in the field of Human and Peoples' Rights, as well as from the provisions of various instruments adopted within the Specialized Agencies of the United Nations of which the Parties to the present Charter are members.[36]

Further, Article 61 holds:

> The Commission shall also take into consideration, as subsidiary measures to determine the principles of law, other general or special international conventions, laying down rules expressly recognized by Member States of the Organization of African Unity, African practices consistent with international norms on Human and Peoples' Rights, customs generally accepted as law, general principles of law recognized by African States as well as legal precedents and doctrine.[37]

Protocol to the African Charter on Human and Peoples' Rights on the Establishment of an African Court on Human and Peoples' Rights

The Preamble of the Protocol to the African Charter on Human and Peoples' Rights on the Establishment of an African Court on Human and Peoples' Rights 2003 states:

> The Member States of the Organization of African Unity hereinafter referred to as the OAU, States Parties to the African Charter on Human and Peoples' Rights,
>
> Considering that the Charter of the Organization of African Unity recognizes that freedom, equality, justice, peace and dignity are essential objectives for the achievement of the legitimate aspirations of the African Peoples;
>
> Noting that the African Charter on Human and Peoples' Rights reaffirms adherence to the principles of Human and Peoples' Rights, freedoms and duties contained in the declarations, conventions and other instruments adopted by the Organization of African Unity, and other international organizations;
>
> Recognizing that the two-fold objective of the African Commission on Human and Peoples' Rights is to ensure on the one hand promotion and on the other protection of Human and Peoples' Rights, freedom and duties;
>
> Recognizing further, the efforts of the African Charter on Human and Peoples' Rights in the promotion and protection of Human and Peoples' Rights since its inception in 1987;

Firmly convinced that the attainment of the objectives of the African Charter on Human and Peoples' Rights requires the establishment of an African Court on Human and Peoples' Rights to complement and reinforce the functions of the African Commission on Human and Peoples' Rights.[38]

Important for equal rights, an African Court of Human and Peoples' Rights, is established under Article 1:

There shall be established within the Organization of African Unity an African Court of Human and Peoples' Rights hereinafter referred to as 'the Court', the organization, jurisdiction and functioning of which shall be governed by the present Protocol.[39]

The relationship between the Court and the Commission is enunciated under Article 2:

The Court shall, bearing in mind the provisions of this Protocol, complement the protective mandate of the African Commission on Human and Peoples' Rights hereinafter referred to as 'the Commission', conferred upon it by the African Charter on Human and Peoples' Rights, hereinafter referred to as 'the Charter'.[40]

The Jurisdiction of the Court is established under Article 3:

The jurisdiction of the Court shall extend to all cases and disputes submitted to it concerning the interpretation and application of the Charter, this Protocol and any other relevant Human Rights instrument ratified by the States concerned. In the event of a dispute as to whether the Court has jurisdiction, the Court shall decide.[41]

The Court may issue advisory opinions as outlined under Article 4:

At the request of a Member State of the OAU, the OAU, any of its organs, or any African organization recognized by the OAU, the Court may provide an opinion on any legal matter relating to the Charter or any other relevant human rights instruments, provided that the subject matter of the opinion is not related to a matter being examined by the Commission. The Court shall give reasons for its advisory opinions provided that every judge shall be entitled to deliver a separate of dissenting decision.[42]

Access to the Court is established under Article 5:

The following are entitled to submit cases to the Court:

The Commission

The State Party, which had lodged a complaint to the Commission

The State Party against which the complaint has been lodged at the Commission

The State Party whose citizen is a victim of human rights violation

African intergovernmental organizations

When a State Party has an interest in a case, it may submit a request to the Court to be permitted to join.

The Court may entitle relevant non-governmental organizations (NGOs) with observer status before the Commission, and individuals to institute cases directly before it ....[43]

The issue of admissibility of cases is examined in Article 6:

The Court, when deciding on the admissibility of a case instituted under Article 5...of this Protocol, may request the opinion of the Commission which shall give it as soon as possible.

The Court shall rule on the admissibility of cases taking into account the provisions of Article 56 of the Charter.

The Court may consider cases or transfer them to the Commission.[44]

Article 7 establishes the Sources of Law:

The Court shall apply the provision of the Charter and any other relevant human rights instruments ratified by the States concerned.[45]

Importantly, the independence of the Court is underlined in Article 17:

The independence of the judges shall be fully ensured in accordance with international law.

No judge may hear any case in which the same judge has previously taken part as agent, counsel or advocate for one of the parties or as a member of a national or international court or a commission of enquiry or in any other capacity. Any doubt on this point shall be settled by decision of the Court.[46]

Evidence is stressed under Article 26:

The Court shall hear submissions by all parties and if deemed necessary, hold an enquiry. The States concerned shall assist by providing relevant facilities for the efficient handling of the case.

> The Court may receive written and oral evidence including expert testimony and shall make its decision on the basis of such evidence.[47]

Findings of the Court are provided for under Article 27:

> If the Court finds that there has been violation of a human or peoples' rights, it shall make appropriate orders to remedy the violation, including the payment of fair compensation or reparation.
>
> In cases of extreme gravity and urgency, and when necessary to avoid irreparable harm to persons, the Court shall adopt such provisional measures as it deems necessary.[48]

Finally, the Judgment of Court is underlined under Article 28:

> The Court shall render its judgment within ninety (90) days of having completed its deliberations.
>
> The judgment of the Court decided by majority shall be final and not subject to appeal.
>
> Without prejudice to sub-Article 2 …, the Court may review its decision in the light of new evidence under conditions to be set out in the Rules of Procedure.
>
> The Court may interpret its own decision.
>
> The judgment of the Court shall be read in open court, due notice having been given to the parties.
>
> Reasons shall be given for the judgment of the Court.
>
> If the judgment of the court does not represent, in whole or in part, the unanimous decision of the judges, any judge shall be entitled to deliver a separate or dissenting opinion.[49]

Importantly, Article 30 provides for the execution of judgment:

> The States Parties to the present Protocol undertake to comply with the judgment in any case to which they are parties within the time stipulated by the Court and to guarantee its execution.[50]

Protocol on Rights of Women in Africa

Important for religious women, in the Preamble to the Protocol on Rights of Women in Africa 2003, the State Parties to the Protocol on the Rights of Women in Africa undertake the agreement:

CONSIDERING that Article 66 of the African Charter on Human and Peoples' Rights provides for special protocols or agreements, if necessary, to supplement the provisions of the African Charter, and that the OAU Assembly of Heads of State and Government meeting in its Thirty-first Ordinary Session in Addis Ababa, Ethiopia, in June 1995, endorsed by resolution AHG/Res.240 (XXXI) the recommendation of the African Commission on Human and Peoples' Rights to elaborate a Protocol on the Rights of Women in Africa;

CONSIDERING that Article 2 of the African Charter on Human and Peoples' Rights enshrines the principle of non-discrimination on the grounds of race, ethnic group, color, sex, language, religion, political or any other opinion, national and social origin, fortune, birth or other status;

FURTHER CONSIDERING that Article 18 of the African Charter on Human and Peoples' Rights calls on all Member States to eliminate every discrimination against women and to ensure the protection of the rights of women as stipulated in international declarations and conventions;

NOTING that Articles 60 and 61 of the African Charter on Human and Peoples' Rights recognize regional and international human rights instruments and African practices consistent with international norms on human and peoples' rights as being important reference points for the application and interpretation of the African Charter;

RECALLING that women's rights have been recognized and guaranteed in all international human rights instruments, notably the Universal Declaration of Human Rights, the International Covenant on Civil and Political Rights, the International Covenant on Economic, Social and Cultural Rights, the Convention on the Elimination of All Forms of Discrimination Against Women and all other international conventions and covenants relating to the rights of women as being inalienable, interdependent and indivisible human rights;

NOTING that women's rights and women's essential role in development have been reaffirmed in the United Nations Plans of Action on the Environment and Development in 1992, on Human Rights in 1993, on Population and Development in 1994 and on Social Development in 1995;

FURTHER NOTING that the Plans of Action adopted in Dakar and in Beijing call on all Member States of the United Nations, which have made a solemn commitment to implement them, to take concrete steps to give greater attention to the human rights of women in order to eliminate all forms of discrimination and of gender-based violence against women;

BEARING IN MIND related Resolutions, Declarations, Recommendations, Decisions and other Conventions aimed at eliminating all forms of discrimination and at promoting equality between men and women;

CONCERNED that despite the ratification of the African Charter on Human and Peoples' Rights and other international human rights instruments by the majority of Member States, and their solemn commitment to eliminate all forms of discrimination and harmful practices against women, women in Africa still continue to be victims of discrimination and harmful practices;

FIRMLY CONVINCED that any practice that hinders or endangers the normal growth and affects the physical, emotional and psychological development of women and girls should be condemned and eliminated, and DETERMINED to ensure that the rights of women are protected in order to enable them to enjoy fully all their human rights.[51]

Under Article 1, 'Discrimination against women' is defined as any distinction, exclusion or restriction based on sex, or any differential treatment whose objective or effects compromise or destroy the recognition, enjoyment or the exercise by women, regardless of their marital status, of human rights and fundamental freedoms in all spheres of life.[52] Further, 'Harmful Practices' (HPs) is defined as all behavior, attitudes and practices which negatively affect the fundamental rights of women and girls, such as their right to life, health and bodily integrity.[53]

Importantly, Article 2(1) is paramount in the fight for the elimination of discrimination against women:

2(1) State Parties shall combat all forms of discrimination against women through appropriate legislative measures. In this regard they shall:
    i. include in their national constitutions and other legislative instruments the principle of equality between men and women and ensure its effective application;
    ii. enact and effectively implement appropriate national legislative measures to prohibit all forms of harmful practices which endanger the health and general well-being of women and girls;
    iii. integrate a gender perspective in their policy decisions, legislation, development plans, activities and all other spheres of life;
    iv. take positive action in those areas where discrimination against women in law and in fact continues to exist.[54]

In looking at the important concern of economic and social welfare rights, Article 13 is critical for equal rights:

13. State Parties shall guarantee women equal opportunities to work. In this respect, they shall:
    i. promote equality in access to employment;

ii. promote the right to equal remuneration for jobs of equal value for men and women;
iii. ensure transparency in employment and dismissal relating to women in order to address issues of sexual harassment in the workplace;
iv. allow women freedom to choose their occupation, and protect them from exploitation by their employers;
v. create conditions to promote and support the occupations and economic activities dominated by women, in particular, within the informal sector;
vi. encourage the establishment of a system of protection and social insurance for women working in the informal sector;
vii. introduce a minimum age of work and prohibit children below that age from working, and prohibit the exploitation of children, especially the girl-child;
viii. take the necessary measures to recognize the economic value of the work of women in the home;
ix. guarantee adequate pre and post-natal maternity leave;
x. ensure equality in taxation for men and women;
xi. recognize the right of salaried women to the same allowances and entitlements as those granted to salaried men for their spouses and children;
xii. recognize motherhood and the upbringing of children as a social function for which the State, the private sector and both parents must take responsibility.[55]

South Africa

In South Africa, the general amicable relationship among religious groups in society contributed to religious freedom.[56] South Africa has an area of 470,693 square miles, and its population is approximately 46.9 million. According to figures on religious demography from the 2001 census, approximately 80 percent of the population belonged to the Christian faith, and 4 percent to other religions, including Hinduism (1.2 percent), Islam (1.5 percent), Judaism (0.2 percent) and traditional African beliefs (0.3 percent), with approximately 15 percent of the population indicating that it belonged to no particular religion or declined to indicate an affiliation. The African Independent Churches were the largest group of Christian churches. There were more than 4,000 of these churches, with a total membership of more than ten million. Although these churches originally were founded as breakaways from various mission churches, the so-called Ethiopian churches, the African Independent Churches consisted mostly of Zionist or Apostolic churches and also included some Pentecostal branches. The Zionist Christian Church was the largest African Independent Church with 11.1 percent of the population. The African Independent Churches attracted persons in rural and urban areas. Other Christian churches included the Dutch Reformed family of churches, which consisted of approximately 6.7 percent of the population, and the Roman Catholic

Church, which consisted of approximately 7.1 percent. Protestant denominations include the Methodist (6.8 percent), Anglican (3.8 percent), Lutheran (2.5 percent), Presbyterian (1.9 percent), Baptist (1.5 percent) and Congregational (1.1 percent) churches. The largest traditional Pentecostal churches were the Apostolic Faith Mission, the Assemblies of God, and the Full Gospel Church. A number of charismatic churches have been established in recent years, with their subsidiary churches, together with those of the Hatfield Christian Church in Pretoria, grouped in the International Fellowship of Christian Churches. The Greek Orthodox and Seventh-day Adventist churches were also active. Approximately 15 percent of the population claimed no affiliation with any formal religious organization. It was believed that many of these persons adhered to traditional indigenous religions, with followers believing that certain practitioners may manipulate the power of the spirits using herbs, therapeutic techniques or supernatural powers. Many people combined Christian and traditional indigenous religious practices.

According to the latest available statistics from the 2001 census, an estimated 80 percent of Black Africans, who constitute the majority of the population, were Christian. Approximately 87 percent of whites were Christian and almost 1.4 percent Jewish. Nearly half (47.3 percent) of Indians were Hindu, 49 percent were either Muslim (24.6 percent) or Christian (24.4 percent) and 3.7 percent fell into other categories. The majority of Muslims was either of Indian origin, largely located in KwaZulu-Natal, or belonged to the multiethnic community in the Western Cape. A number of Christian organizations, including the Salvation Army, Promise Keepers, Operation Mobilization, Campus Crusade and the Church of Jesus Christ of Latter-day Saints (Mormons), operated in the country doing missionary work, giving aid, and providing training. The Muslim World League also was active, as was the Zionist International Federation. There are many ecumenical contacts among the various churches, with the largest of these being the South African Council of Churches, which represents the Methodist Church, the Church of the Province of South Africa (Anglican), various Lutheran and Presbyterian churches, and the Congregational Church. The major traditional indigenous religions, most of the Afrikaans-language churches, and the Pentecostal and charismatic churches are not members of the SACC and usually have their own coordinating and liaison bodies. The Catholic Church's relationship with other churches continued to become more open, and it worked closely with other churches on the socio-political front.

The South African Constitution provides for freedom of religion, and the government generally respected this right in practice, with the government at all levels seeking to protect this right in full not tolerating its abuse, either by governmental or private actors. The Bill of Rights prohibits the government from unfairly discriminating directly or indirectly against anyone based on religion, and persons belonging to a religious community may not be denied the right to practice their religion, and to form, join and maintain religious associations with other members of that community. Cases of discrimination against a person on the grounds of religious freedom may be taken to the constitutional court.

While Christianity is the dominant religion, the law does not recognize a State religion. Leading government officials and ruling party members adhere to a variety of faiths, including various Christian denominations, Islam, and Judaism. Only Christian holy days, such as Christmas and Good Friday, are recognized as national religious holidays; however, members of other religious groups are allowed to celebrate their religious holidays without government interference. The government allows, but does not require, 'religion education' in public schools; however, 'religious instruction' or the advocating of tenets of a particular faith is not permitted in public schools. Further, the government does not require religious groups to be licensed or registered.[57]

Interim Constitution Schedule 4

The Constitutional Principles for the Republic of South Africa are contained in Schedule 4 of the Interim Constitution. Important for equal rights, Principle I guarantees equality:

> I. The Constitution of South Africa shall provide for the establishment of one sovereign state, a common South African citizenship and a democratic system of government committed to achieving equality between men and women and people of all races.[58]

In addition, Principle II also guarantees fundamental rights, freedoms and civil liberties:

> II. Everyone shall enjoy all universally accepted fundamental rights, freedoms and civil liberties, which shall be provided for and protected by entrenched and justiciable provisions in the Constitution....[59]

Important for equal rights and religious discrimination cases, the prohibition against discrimination and the promotion of equality are contained within Principle III:

> III. The Constitution shall prohibit racial, gender and all other forms of discrimination and shall promote racial and gender equality and national unity.[60]

Further, the fundamental guarantee of equality of all before the law is contained in Principle V:

> V. The legal system shall ensure the equality of all before the law and an equitable legal process. Equality before the law includes laws, programs or activities that have as their object the amelioration of the conditions of the disadvantaged, including those disadvantaged on the grounds of race, color or gender.[61]

Importantly, freedom of religion and religious association is protected under Principle XI and XII respectively:

XI. The diversity of language and culture shall be acknowledged and protected, and conditions for their promotion shall be encouraged.[62]

XII. Collective rights of self-determination in forming, joining and maintaining organs of civil society, including linguistic, cultural and religious associations, shall, on the basis of non-discrimination and free association, be recognised and protected.[63]

The Supremacy clause is contained in Principle IV, which states that the Constitution shall be the supreme law of the land; it shall be binding on all organs of state at all levels of government.[64] In addition, the separation of powers for objectivity and accountability is contained in Principle VI, which establishes that there shall be a separation of powers between the legislature, executive and judiciary, with appropriate checks and balances to ensure accountability, responsiveness and openness.[65] Finally, the important role of the judiciary is outlined in Principle VII:

VII. The judiciary shall be appropriately qualified, independent and impartial and shall have the power and jurisdiction to safeguard and enforce the Constitution and all fundamental rights.[66]

Constitution of South Africa

The Constitution of the Republic of South Africa was first adopted by the Constitutional Assembly on 8 May 1996 (Act 108 of 1996), and was signed into law on 10 December 1996. As an integration of ideas from ordinary citizens, civil society and political parties represented in and outside of the Constitutional Assembly, the Constitution of South Africa represents the collective wisdom of the South African people and has been arrived at by general agreement. The objective in this process was to ensure that the final Constitution be legitimate, credible and accepted by all South Africans.

The Preamble of the Constitution of the Republic of South Africa reads:

We, the people of South Africa,
Recognize the injustices of our past;
Honour those who suffered for justice and freedom in our land;
Respect those who have worked to build and develop our country; and
Believe that South Africa belongs to all who live in it, united in our diversity.
We therefore, through our freely elected representatives, adopt this Constitution as the supreme law of the Republic so as to
Heal the divisions of the past and establish a society based on democratic values, social justice and fundamental human rights;
Lay the foundations for a democratic and open society in which government is based on the will of the people and every citizen is equally protected by law;
Improve the quality of life of all citizens and free the potential of each person; and

> Build a united and democratic South Africa able to take its rightful place as a sovereign state in the family of nations.
> May God protect our people.
> Nkosi Sikelel' iAfrika. Morena boloka setjhaba sa heso.
> God seën Suid-Afrika. God bless South Africa.
> Mudzimu fhatutshedza Afurika. Hosi katekisa Afrika.[67]

The Founding Provisions of the Republic of South Africa are found in Section 1 of the Constitution, which stresses equality and the advancement of human rights, by stating that the Republic of South Africa is one, sovereign, democratic state founded on the following values: human dignity, the achievement of equality and the advancement of human rights and freedoms; non-racialism and non-sexism; and the supremacy of the constitution and the rule of law.[68]

The Supremacy Clause is found in Section 2 of the Constitution, which holds that the Constitution is the supreme law of the Republic; law or conduct inconsistent with it is invalid, and the obligations imposed by it must be fulfilled.[69] Important for equal rights, the right to equality is espoused in Section 3, which states that all citizens are equally entitled to the rights, privileges and benefits of citizenship; and equally subject to the duties and responsibilities of citizenship.[70]

Chapter 2 of the Constitution enumerates the Bill of Rights for South Africa. Section 7 states:

> 7(1) This Bill of Rights is a cornerstone of democracy in South Africa. It enshrines the rights of all people in our country and affirms the democratic values of human dignity, equality and freedom.
> (2) The state must respect, protect, promote and fulfil the rights in the Bill of Rights.
> (3) The rights in the Bill of Rights are subject to the limitations contained or referred to in Section 36, or elsewhere in the Bill.[71]

Application and jurisdiction of the Bill of Rights are outlined in Section 8:

> 8(1) The Bill of Rights applies to all law, and binds the legislature, the executive, the judiciary and all organs of state.
> (2) A provision of the Bill of Rights binds a natural or a juristic person if, and to the extent that, it is applicable, taking into account the nature of the right and the nature of any duty imposed by the right.
> (3) When applying a provision of the Bill of Rights to a natural or juristic person in terms of subsection (2), a court:
>   a) in order to give effect to a right in the Bill, must apply, or if necessary develop, the common law to the extent that legislation does not give effect to that right; and
>   b) may develop rules of the common law to limit the right, provided that the limitation is in accordance with Section 36(1).
> (4) A juristic person is entitled to the rights in the Bill of Rights to the extent required by the nature of the rights and the nature of that juristic person.[72]

In terms of equality for all regardless of religion, Section 9 goes on to outline and guarantee the important concept of equal protection, including against religious discrimination in Section 9(3):

> 9(1) Everyone is equal before the law and has the right to equal protection and benefit of the law.
> (2) Equality includes the full and equal enjoyment of all rights and freedoms. To promote the achievement of equality, legislative and other measures designed to protect or advance persons, or categories of persons, disadvantaged by unfair discrimination may be taken.
> (3) The state may not unfairly discriminate directly or indirectly against anyone on one or more grounds, including race, gender, sex, pregnancy, marital status, ethnic or social origin, color, sexual orientation, age, disability, religion, conscience, belief, culture, language and birth.
> (4) No person may unfairly discriminate directly or indirectly against anyone on one or more grounds in terms of subsection (3). National legislation must be enacted to prevent or prohibit unfair discrimination.
> (5) Discrimination on one or more of the grounds listed in subsection (3) is unfair unless it is established that the discrimination is fair.[73]

On human dignity, Section 10 states that everyone has inherent dignity and the right to have their dignity respected and protected.[74]

Importantly, Section 15 provides for freedom of religion, belief and opinion:

> 15(1) Everyone has the right to freedom of conscience, religion, thought, belief and opinion.
> (2) Religious observances may be conducted at state or state-aided institutions, provided that:
> (a) those observances follow rules made by the appropriate public authorities;
> (b) they are conducted on an equitable basis; and
> (c) attendance at them is free and voluntary.
> (3) (a) This section does not prevent legislation recognizing:
> (i) marriages concluded under any tradition, or a system of religious, personal or family law; or
> (ii) systems of personal and family law under any tradition, or adhered to by persons professing a particular religion.
> (b) Recognition in terms of paragraph (a) must be consistent with this section and the other provisions of the Constitution.[75]

Further, Section 16 provides for freedom of expression, which does not extend to religious hatred:

> 16(1) Everyone has the right to freedom of expression, which includes:
> (a) freedom of the press and other media;

(b) freedom to receive or impart information or ideas;
(c) freedom of artistic creativity; and
(d) academic freedom and freedom of scientific research.
(2) The right in subsection (1) does not extend to
(a) propaganda for war;
(b) incitement of imminent violence; or
(c) advocacy of hatred that is based on race, ethnicity, gender or religion, and that constitutes incitement to cause harm.[76]

Finally, Section 31 protects cultural, religious and linguistic communities, and in particular with regard to their religion:

31(1) Persons belonging to a cultural, religious or linguistic community may not be denied the right, with other members of that community
(a) to enjoy their culture, practise their religion and use their language; and
(b) to form, join and maintain cultural, religious and linguistic associations and other organs of civil society.
(2) The rights in subsection (1) may not be exercised in a manner inconsistent with any provision of the Bill of Rights.[77]

In the interpretation of the Bill of Rights, Section 39 stresses the importance of human dignity and equality:

39(1) When interpreting the Bill of Rights, a court, tribunal or forum:
must promote the values that underlie an open and democratic society based on human dignity, equality and freedom;
must consider international law; and
may consider foreign law.
(2) When interpreting any legislation, and when developing the common law or customary law, every court, tribunal or forum must promote the spirit, purport and objects of the Bill of Rights.
(3) The Bill of Rights does not deny the existence of any other rights or freedoms that are recognized or conferred by common law, customary law or legislation, to the extent that they are consistent with the Bill.[78]

In safeguarding the right to employment under the principle of freedom of trade, occupation and profession, important for equal rights, Section 22 states that every citizen has the right to choose their trade, occupation or profession freely, and the practice of a trade, occupation or profession may be regulated by law.[79] In terms of labor relations, Section 23 establishes that everyone has the right to fair labor practices, and every worker has the right to form and join a trade union; to participate in the activities and programs of a trade union; and to strike.[80] Further, in looking at the important right to education as a way of betterment, Section 29 states that everyone has the right to a basic education, including adult basic education; and to further education, which the state, through reasonable measures, must make progressively available and accessible.[81]

The powers of the courts in constitutional matters are outlined in Section 172(1), which holds that when deciding a constitutional matter within its power, a court must declare that any law or conduct that is inconsistent with the Constitution is invalid to the extent of its inconsistency; and may make any order that is just and equitable, including an order limiting the retrospective effect of the declaration of invalidity; and an order suspending the declaration of invalidity for any period and on any conditions, to allow the competent authority to correct the defect.[82]

In guaranteeing the right to administrative action, Section 33 states that everyone has the right to administrative action that is lawful, reasonable and procedurally fair.[83] Importantly, the right to access to the courts is outlined in Section 34, which holds that everyone has the right to have any dispute that can be resolved by the application of law decided in a fair public hearing before a court or, where appropriate, another independent and impartial tribunal or forum.[84] In order to guarantee rights enumerated under the Constitution, Section 38 ensures the enforcement of such rights, by holding that anyone listed has the right to approach a competent court, alleging that a right in the Bill of Rights has been infringed or threatened, and the court may grant appropriate relief, including a declaration of rights. The persons who may approach a court are anyone acting in their own interest; anyone acting on behalf of another person who cannot act in their own name; anyone acting as a member of, or in the interest of, a group or class of persons; anyone acting in the public interest; and an association acting in the interest of its members.[85]

However, the Constitution provides for a limitation of rights under Section 36(1), which provides that the rights in the Bill of Rights may be limited only in terms of law of general application to the extent that the limitation is reasonable and justifiable in an open and democratic society based on human dignity, equality and freedom, taking into account all relevant factors, including the nature of the right; the importance of the purpose of the limitation; the nature and extent of the limitation; the relation between the limitation and its purpose; and less restrictive means to achieve the purpose.[86]

Under the establishment and governing principles, Section 181 lists several important institutions mandated to strengthen constitutional democracy, namely the Public Protector; the Human Rights Commission; the Commission for the Promotion and Protection of the Rights of Cultural, Religious and Linguistic Communities; the Auditor-General; and the Electoral Commission.[87] The functions of the Human Rights Commission, are listed under Section 184, which states that it must promote respect for human rights and a culture of human rights; promote the protection, development and attainment of human rights; and monitor and assess the observance of human rights in the Republic. Further, the Human Rights Commission has the powers, as regulated by national legislation, necessary to perform its functions, including the power to investigate and to report on the observance of human rights; to take steps to secure appropriate redress where human rights have been violated; and to carry out research; and to educate.[88]

Employment Equity Act

The Preamble of the Employment Equity Act 1998, an Act to provide for employment equity and to provide for matters incidental thereto, states:

> Recognizing
>
> > that as a result of apartheid and other discriminatory laws and practices, there are disparities in employment, occupation and income within the national labor market; and that those disparities create such pronounced disadvantages for certain categories of people that they cannot be redressed simply by repealing discriminatory laws,
>
> Therefore, in order to
>
> > promote the constitutional right of equality and the exercise of true democracy; eliminate unfair discrimination in employment; ensure the implementation of employment equity to redress the effects of discrimination; achieve a diverse workforce broadly representative of our people; promote economic development and efficiency in the workforce; and give effect to the obligations of the Republic as a member of the International Labor Organization.[89]

According to Section 3, the Act must be interpreted in compliance with the Constitution so as to give effect to its purpose; taking into account any relevant code of good practice issued in terms of this Act or any other employment law; and in compliance with the international law obligations of the Republic, in particular those contained in the Discrimination (Employment and Occupation) Convention (No. 111) 1958.[90]

Important for equal rights and religious discrimination cases, the purpose of the Act is defined in Section 2 as to achieve equity in the workplace by promoting equal opportunity and fair treatment in employment through the elimination of unfair discrimination; and implementing affirmative action measures to redress the disadvantages in employment experienced by designated groups, in order to ensure their equitable representation in all occupational categories and levels in the workforce.[91]

Crucially, the elimination and the prohibition of unfair discrimination for people regardless of religion are called for in Sections 5 and 6(1) respectively:

> 5. Every employer must take steps to promote equal opportunity in the workplace by eliminating unfair discrimination in any employment policy or practice.[92]

6(1) No person may unfairly discriminate, directly or indirectly, against an employee, in any employment policy or practice, on one or more grounds, including race, gender, sex, pregnancy, marital status, family responsibility, ethnic or social origin, color, sexual orientation, age, disability, religion, HIV status, conscience, belief, political opinion, culture, language and birth.[93]

Article 6(2) allows for affirmative action programs and bona fide occupational qualifications:

6(2) It is not unfair discrimination to:
  a. take affirmative action measures consistent with the purpose of this Act; or
  b. distinguish, exclude or prefer any person on the basis of an inherent requirement of a job.[94]

Further, Section 15 goes on to outline affirmative action measures which are permitted:

15(1) Affirmative action measures are measures designed to ensure that suitably qualified people from designated groups have equal employment opportunities and are equitably represented in all occupational categories and levels in the workforce of a designated employer.
(2) Affirmative action measures implemented by a designated employer must include:
  a. measures to identify and eliminate employment barriers, including unfair discrimination, which adversely affect people from designated groups;
  b. measures designed to further diversity in the workplace based on equal dignity and respect of all people;
  c. making reasonable accommodation for people from designated groups in order to ensure that they enjoy equal opportunities and are equitably represented in the workforce of a designated employer;
  d. subject to subsection (3), measures to:
    i. ensure the equitable representation of suitably qualified people from designated groups in all occupational categories and levels in the workforce; and
    ii. retain and develop people from designated groups and to implement appropriate training measures, including measures in terms of an Act of Parliament providing for skills development.
(3) The measures referred to in subsection (2)(d) include preferential treatment and numerical goals, but exclude quotas.[95]

According to the burden of proof outlined in Section 11, whenever unfair discrimination is alleged in terms of this Act, the employer against whom the allegation is made must establish that it is fair.[96]

To combat religious discrimination in the workplace, Section 20 outlines the requirement of an employment equity plan:

20(1) A designated employer must prepare and implement an employment equity plan which will achieve reasonable progress towards employment equity in that employer's workforce.
(2) An employment equity plan prepared in terms of subsection (1) must state:
   a. the objectives to be achieved for each year of the plan;
   b. the affirmative action measures to be implemented as required by subsection 15(2);
   c. where underrepresentation of people from designated groups has been identified by the analysis, the numerical goals to achieve the equitable representation of suitably qualified people from designated groups within each occupational category and level in the workforce, the timetable within which this is to be achieved, and the strategies intended to achieve those goals;
   d. the timetable for each year of the plan for the achievement of goals and objectives other than numerical goals;
   e. the duration of the plan, which may not be shorter than one year or longer than five years;
   f. the procedures that will be used to monitor and evaluate the implementation of the plan and whether reasonable progress is being made towards implementing employment equity;
   g. the internal procedures to resolve any dispute about the interpretation or implementation of the plan;
   h. the persons in the workforce, including senior managers, responsible for monitoring and implementing the plan; and
   i. any other prescribed matter.[97]

The functions of the Commission for Employment Equity are enumerated in Section 30:

30(1) The Commission advises the Minister on:
   a. codes of good practice issued by the Minister;
   b. regulations made by the Minister; and
   c. policy and any other matter concerning this Act.
(2) In addition to the functions in subsection (1) the Commission may:
   a. make awards recognizing achievements of employers in furthering the purpose of this Act;
   b. research and report to the Minister on any matter relating to the application of this Act, including appropriate and well-researched norms and benchmarks for the setting of numerical goals in various sectors; and
   c. perform any other prescribed function.[98]

Under Section 35, a labor inspector has the authority to enter, question and inspect as provided,[99] and under Section 36, he must request and obtain a written undertaking from a designated employer to comply within a specified period, if the inspector has reasonable grounds to believe that the employer has failed to consult with employees; conduct an analysis; prepare and implement an employment equity plan; submit and publish its annual report; prepare a successive employment equity plan; assign responsibility to a senior manager; inform its employees; or keep records.[100] Under Section 37, a labor inspector may issue a compliance order to a designated employer if that employer has failed to act,[101] and finally, under Section 40, a designated employer may appeal to the Labor Court against a compliance order of the Director-General within 21 days after receiving that order.[102]

In terms of a Code of Good Practice, the process of developing a plan has three sequential phases: planning, development, and implementation and monitoring, according to the Employment Equity Act. The planning phase of the process should include assignment of responsibility and accountability to managers from different faiths; a communication, awareness and training program; consultation with relevant stakeholders; an analysis of existing employment policies, procedures, and practices; an analysis of the existing workforce profile; an analysis of relevant demographic information; and the development of meaningful benchmark comparisons. The development phase should include objectives set; corrective measures formulated; time frames established; the plan drawn up; resources identified and allocated for the implementation of the plan; and the plan communicated. The implementation and monitoring phase should include implementation; monitoring and evaluating progress; reviewing the plan; and reporting on progress.

In order to identify any barriers that may be responsible for the underrepresentation or under-utilization of employees from designated groups, including workers from religious minorities, a review of all employment policies, practices and procedures specifically, as well as the working environment in general, should be undertaken of employment policy or practices, such as recruitment, selection, pre-employment testing and induction that could be biased, inappropriate or unaffirming; practices related to succession and experience planning, and related promotions and transfers to establish whether designated groups are excluded or adversely impacted; utilization and job assignments to establish whether designated groups are able to meaningfully participate and contribute; current training and development methodologies and strategies; remuneration structures and practices such as equal remuneration for work of equal value; employee benefits related to retirement, risk and medical aid to establish whether designated groups have equal access; disciplinary practices which may have a disproportionately adverse effect on designated groups that may not be justified; the number and nature of dismissals, voluntary terminations and retrenchments of employees from designated groups that may indicate internal or external equity-related factors contributing to such terminations; and corporate culture which may be characterized by exclusionary social and other practices. All practices should be assessed in terms of cross-group fairness, and the review should take into account more subtle or indirect forms of discrimination and stereotyping, which could result in certain groups of people not being employed in particular jobs, or which could preclude people from being promoted.

Finally, affirmative action measures should be developed in terms of appointing members from designated groups for transparent and unbiased recruitment strategies; increasing the pool of available candidates; training, promoting and retaining people from designated groups; ensuring that members of designated groups are appointed in such positions that they are able meaningfully to participate in corporate decision-making processes; and transforming the corporate culture of the past in a way that affirms diversity in the workplace and harnesses the potential of all employees, regardless of religion.

Promotion of Equality and Prevention of Unfair Discrimination Act

The Preamble of the Promotion of Equality and Prevention of Unfair Discrimination Act 2000 states:

> The consolidation of democracy in our country requires the eradication of social and economic inequalities, especially those that are systematic in nature, which were generated in our history by colonialism, apartheid and patriarchy, and which brought pain and suffering to the great majority of our people …;
>
> The Constitution provides for the enactment of national legislation to prevent or prohibit unfair discrimination and to promote the achievement of equality;
>
> This implies the advancement, special legal and other measures, of historically disadvantaged individuals, communities and social groups who were dispossessed of their land and resources, deprived of their human dignity and who continue to endure the consequences;
>
> This Act endeavours to facilitate the transition to a democratic society, united in its diversity, marked by human relations that are caring and compassionate, and guided by the principles of equality, fairness, equity, social progress, justice human dignity and freedom.[103]

'Prohibited grounds', including religion, are defined under Section 1 as:

> (a) race, gender, sex, pregnancy, marital status, ethnic or social origin, color, sexual orientation, age, disability, religion, conscience, belief, culture, language and birth; or
> (b) any other ground where discrimination based on that other ground:
>   i. causes or perpetuates systemic disadvantage;
>   ii. undermines human dignity; or
>   iii. adversely affects the equal enjoyment of a person's rights and freedoms in a serious manner that is comparable to discrimination on a ground in paragraph (a).[104]

The objects of the Act are enumerated in Section 2, specifically Section 2(b)(v) as to religion:

2. The objects of this Act are:
   a. to enact legislation required by section 9 of the Constitution;
   b. to give effect to the letter and spirit of the Constitution, in particular:
      i. the equal enjoyment of all rights and freedoms by every person;
      ii. the promotion of equality;
      iii. the values of non-racialism and non-sexism contained in section 1 of the Constitution;
      iv. the prevention of unfair discrimination and protection of human dignity as contemplated in sections 9 and 10 of the Constitution;
      v. the prohibition of advocacy of hatred, based on race, ethnicity, gender or religion, that constitutes incitement to cause harm as contemplated in section 16(2)*(c)* of the Constitution and section 12 of this Act;
   (c) to provide for measures to facilitate the eradication of unfair discrimination, hate speech and harassment, particularly on the grounds of race, gender and disability;
   (d) to provide for procedures for the determination of circumstances under which discrimination is unfair;
   (e) to provide for measures to educate the public and raise public awareness on the importance of promoting equality and overcoming unfair discrimination, hate speech and harassment;
   (f) to provide remedies for victims of unfair discrimination, hate speech and harassment and persons whose right to equality has been infringed;
   (g) to set out measures to advance persons disadvantaged by unfair discrimination;
   (h) to facilitate further compliance with international law obligations including treaty obligations in terms of, amongst others, the Convention on the Elimination of All Forms of Racial Discrimination and the Convention on the Elimination of All Forms of Discrimination against Women.[105]

Further, the guiding principles are contained in Section 4:

4. (1) In the adjudication of any proceedings which are instituted in terms of or under this Act, the following principles should apply:
   (a) The expeditious and informal processing of cases, which facilitate participation by the parties to the proceedings;
   (b) access to justice to all persons in relevant judicial and other dispute resolution forums;
   (c) the use of rules of procedure...and criteria to facilitate participation;
   (d) the use of corrective or restorative measures in conjunction with measures of a deterrent nature;
   (e) the development of special skills and capacity for persons applying this Act in order to ensure effective implementation and administration thereof.

(2) In the application of this Act the following should be recognised and taken into account:
- (a) The existence of systemic discrimination and inequalities, particularly in respect of race, gender and disability in all spheres of life as a result of past and present unfair discrimination, brought about by colonialism, the apartheid system and patriarchy; and
- (b) the need to take measures at all levels to eliminate such discrimination and inequalities.[106]

It is understood that by virtue of Section 5, the Act binds the State and all persons,[107] and by virtue of Section 6, neither the State nor any person may unfairly discriminate against any person.[108] In terms of the burden of proof in religious discrimination cases, Section 13 stipulates:

13(1) If the complainant makes out a prima facie case of discrimination:
- (a) the respondent must prove, in the facts before the court, that the discrimination did not take place as alleged; or
- (b) the respondent must prove that the conduct is not based on one or more of the prohibited grounds.

(2) If the discrimination did take place:
- (a) on a ground in paragraph (a) of the definition of 'prohibited grounds' … then it is unfair, unless the respondent proves that the discrimination is fair;
- (b) on a ground in paragraph (b) of the definition of 'prohibited grounds', then it is unfair:
  - i. if one or more of the conditions set out in paragraph (b) of the definition of 'prohibited grounds' is established; and
  - ii. unless the respondent proves that the discrimination is fair.[109]

Section 14 establishes the determination of fairness or unfairness:

14(1) It is not unfair discrimination to take measures designed to protect or advance persons or categories of persons disadvantaged by unfair discrimination or the members of such groups or categories of persons.

(2) In determining whether the respondent has proved that the discrimination is fair, the following must be taken into account:
- (a) The context;
- (b) the factors referred to in subsection (3);
- (c) whether the discrimination reasonably and justifiably differentiates between persons according to objectively determinable criteria, intrinsic to the activity concerned.

(3) The factors referred to in subsection (2)(b) include the following:
- (a) Whether the discrimination impairs or is likely to impair human dignity;
- (b) the impact or likely impact of the discrimination on the complainant;
- (c) the position of the complainant in society and whether he or she suffers from

patterns of disadvantage or belongs to a group that suffers from patterns of disadvantage;
(d) the nature and extent of the discrimination;
(e) whether the discrimination is systematic in nature;
(f) whether the discrimination has a legitimate purpose;
(g) whether and to what extent the discrimination achieves its purpose;
(h) whether there are less restrictive and less disadvantageous means to achieve the purpose;
   i. whether and to what extent the respondent has taken such steps as being reasonable in the circumstances to:
   ii. address the disadvantage which arises from or is related to one or more of the prohibited grounds; or
   iii. accommodate diversity.[110]

Importantly, under Section 25, the State has a duty to promote equality and, as such, the State must, where necessary with the assistance of the relevant constitutional institutions, develop awareness of fundamental rights in order to promote a climate of understanding, mutual respect and equality; take measures to develop and implement programs in order to promote equality; and where necessary or appropriate develop action plans to address any unfair discrimination, hate speech or harassment. It must also enact further legislation that seeks to promote equality and to establish a legislative framework in line with the objectives of the Act; develop codes of practice as contemplated in the Act in order to promote equality; develop guidelines, including codes in respect of reasonable accommodation; provide assistance, advice and training on issues of equality; develop appropriate internal mechanisms to deal with complaints of unfair discrimination, hate speech or harassment; and conduct information campaigns to popularize the Act.[111]

Finally, Section 28 provides for special measures to promote equality:

28. (1) If it is proved in the prosecution of any offence that unfair discrimination on the grounds of race, gender or disability played a part in the commission of the offence, this must be regarded as an aggravating circumstance for purposes of sentence.

(2) The South African Human Rights Commission must, in its report referred to in section 15 of the Human Rights Commission Act, 1994 (Act No. 54 of 1994), include an assessment on the extent to which unfair discrimination on the grounds of race, gender and disability persists in the Republic, the effects thereof and recommendations on how best to address the problems.

(3)(a) The State, institutions performing public functions and all persons have a duty and responsibility, in particular to:
   i. eliminate discrimination on the grounds of race, gender and disability;
   ii. promote equality in respect of race, gender and disability.

(b) In carrying out the duties and responsibilities referred to in paragraph (a), the State, institutions performing public functions and, where appropriate and relevant, juristic and non-juristic entities, must:

i. audit laws, policies and practices with a view to eliminating all discriminatory aspects thereof;
ii. enact appropriate laws, develop progressive policies and initiate codes of practice in order to eliminate discrimination on the grounds of race, gender and disability;
iii. adopt viable action plans for the promotion and achievement of equality in respect of race, gender and disability; and
iv. give priority to the elimination of unfair discrimination and the promotion of equality in respect of race, gender and disability.[112]

The way to combat religious discrimination is neither to deny its existence or its systemic roots, nor to trivialize its impact, and those who deny it must be challenged because it is such denial that potentially entrenches inherited inequalities. We need to strengthen and in some cases revolutionize the democratic institutions and their capacity to deal with the barriers that perpetuate social exclusion and discrimination on the grounds of religion. In order to change entrenched discriminatory perceptions and prejudices, educational programs that popularize a rights-based approach to addressing discrimination should be developed for civil society as a whole. It is necessary to address discrimination and inequality in its many institutional and social forms. This includes changing the skewed distribution of resources through the equitable distribution of State funds, a program of economic empowerment, including economic empowerment for those from religious minorities, affirmative action, land reform and social development. It requires the transformation, in terms of composition, culture and focus, of institutions such as the judiciary, public service, private sector and academia. Essential to this are programs to promote multi-religious, multi-ageism, multiculturalism, multilingualism and tolerance in all institutions of social development. It is clear that much needs to be done to ensure that all people, including those from religious minorities, rightfully enjoy their constitutional rights, for which they have worked so hard all of their lives.

Conclusion

African States should share experiences on best practices in order to complement each other so as to ensure effective religious mainstreaming in legislation and court cases; continue to ensure that equal rights issues are integrated in all development programs and plans; develop common indicators for monitoring equal rights issues at local, regional, national and international levels; and encourage and support the initiation and coordination of periodical conference/seminars on equal rights and development. Indeed, a renewal of commitment to religious equality is overdue in Africa, where there is a great disparity in the level of human rights protection available to its inhabitants. Almost all African countries have constitutions or civil codes that prohibit discrimination. However, the level of protection varies from nation to nation, and entrenched attitudes and practices, as well as limited resources, limit the practical effect, in the pursuit of *Heaven Forbid*.

Notes

1 Economic Commission for Africa, *Economic Report on Africa*, 2002.
2 *Ibid.*
3 Charter of the Organization of African Unity, at the Preamble.
4 *Ibid.*, at Article I.
5 *Ibid.*, at Article II.
6 *Ibid.*, at Article VII.
7 *Ibid.*, at Article VIII.
8 *Ibid.*, at Article XII.
9 *Ibid.*, at Article XVI.
10 *Ibid.*, at Article XIX.
11 *Ibid.*, at Article XX.
12 African Charter on Human and Peoples' Rights.
13 *Ibid.*, at Article 1.
14 *Ibid.*, at Article 5.
15 *Ibid.*, at Article 19.
16 *Ibid.*, at Article 2.
17 *Ibid.*, at Article 8.
18 *Ibid.*, at Article 28.
19 *Ibid.*, at Article 3.
20 *Ibid.*, at Article 15.
21 *Ibid.*, at Article 17.
22 *Ibid.*, at Article 20.
23 *Ibid.*, at Article 22.
24 *Ibid.*, at Article 27.
25 *Ibid.*, at Article 29.
26 *Ibid.*, at Article 7.
27 *Ibid.*, at Article 26.
28 *Ibid.*, at Article 30.
29 *Ibid.*, at Article 45.
30 *Ibid.*, at Article 46.
31 *Ibid.*, at Article 47.
32 *Ibid.*, at Article 48.
33 *Ibid.*, at Article 49.
34 *Ibid.*, at Article 50.
35 *Ibid.*, at Article 52.
36 *Ibid.*, at Article 60.
37 *Ibid.*, at Article 61.

38 Protocol to the African Charter on Human and Peoples' Rights on the Establishment of an African Court on Human and Peoples' Rights, at the Preamble.
39 *Ibid.*, at Article 1.
40 *Ibid.*, at Article 2.
41 *Ibid.*, at Article 3.
42 *Ibid.*, at Article 4.
43 *Ibid.*, at Article 5.
44 *Ibid.*, at Article 6.
45 *Ibid.*, at Article 7.
46 *Ibid.*, at Article 17.
47 *Ibid.*, at Article 26.
48 *Ibid.*, at Article 27.
49 *Ibid.*, at Article 28.
50 *Ibid.*, at Article 30.
51 Protocol on the Rights of Women in Africa, at the Preamble.
52 *Ibid.*, at Article 1.
53 *Ibid.*, at Article 1.
54 *Ibid.*, at Article 2(1).
55 *Ibid.*, at Article 13.
56 Bureau of Democracy, Human Rights and Labor, *International Religious Freedom Report*, 2006.
57 *Ibid.*
58 Interim Constitution of South Africa, Schedule 4, Principle I.
59 *Ibid.*, at Principle II.
60 *Ibid.*, at Principle III.
61 *Ibid.*, at Principle V.
62 *Ibid.*, at Principle XI.
63 *Ibid.*, at Principle XII.
64 *Ibid.*, at Principle IV.
65 *Ibid.*, at Principle VI.
66 *Ibid.*, at Principle VII.
67 Constitution of South Africa, at the Preamble.
68 *Ibid.*, at Section 1.
69 *Ibid.*, at Section 2.
70 *Ibid.*, at Section 3.
71 *Ibid.*, at Section 7.
72 *Ibid.*, at Section 8.
73 *Ibid.*, at Section 9.
74 *Ibid.*, at Section 10.
75 *Ibid.*, at Section 15.
76 *Ibid.*, at Section 16.
77 *Ibid.*, at Section 31.
78 *Ibid.*, at Section 39.
79 *Ibid.*, at Section 22.

80 *Ibid.*, at Section 23.
81 *Ibid.*, at Section 29.
82 *Ibid.*, at Section 172(1).
83 *Ibid.*, at Section 33.
84 *Ibid.*, at Section 34.
85 *Ibid.*, at Section 38.
86 *Ibid.*, at Section 36(1).
87 *Ibid.*, at Section 181.
88 *Ibid.*, at Section 184.
89 Employment Equity Act, South Africa, at the Preamble.
90 *Ibid.*, at Section 3.
91 *Ibid.*, at Section 2.
92 *Ibid.*, at Section 5.
93 *Ibid.*, at Section 6(1).
94 *Ibid.*, at Section 6(2).
95 *Ibid.*, at Section 15.
96 *Ibid.*, at Section 11.
97 *Ibid.*, at Section 20.
98 *Ibid.*, at Section 30.
99 *Ibid.*, at Section 35.
100 *Ibid.*, at Section 36.
101 *Ibid.*, at Section 37.
102 *Ibid.*, at Section 40.
103 Promotion of Equality and Prevention of Unfair Discrimination Act, South Africa, at the Preamble.
104 *Ibid.*, at Chapter 1, Section 1.
105 *Ibid.*, at Section 2.
106 *Ibid.*, at Section 4.
107 *Ibid.*, at Section 5.
108 *Ibid.*, at Section 6.
109 *Ibid.*, at Section 13.
110 *Ibid.*, at Section 14.
111 *Ibid.*, at Section 25.
112 *Ibid.*, at Section 28.

References

African Charter on Human and Peoples' Rights, 1981.
Bureau of Democracy, Human Rights and Labor (2006), *International Religious Freedom Report*.
Charter of the Organization of African Unity, 1963.
Constitution of South Africa, 1996.
Economic Commission for Africa (2002), *Economic Report on Africa*.

Employment Equity Act, South Africa, 1998.
Interim Constitution of South Africa, Schedule 4.
Promotion of Equality and Prevention of Unfair Discrimination Act, South Africa, South Africa, 2000.
Protocol on the Rights of Women in Africa, 2003.
Protocol to the African Charter on Human and Peoples' Rights on the Establishment of an African Court on Human and Peoples' Rights, 2003.

Chapter 6
Heaven Forbid in Canada, Mexico and the United States

Introduction

In the quest for religious tolerance in *Heaven Forbid*, this chapter will examine efforts against religious discrimination in North America. As well as examining religious discrimination court cases, it will review discrimination legislation, in Canada, namely the Canadian Constitution, the Canadian Bill of Rights, the Canadian Human Rights Act and the Canada Employment Equity Act; then minimally in Mexico, namely the Constitución Política de los Estados Unidos Mexicanos, Ley Federal de Trabajo and the Ley del Seguro Social; and finally in the United States, namely the Declaration of Independence, the Federalist Papers, the American Constitution, the Equal Pay Act and the Civil Rights Act. Although neighbors, Canada and the United States have had separate histories and thus have undergone very different paths, with some rights having more of an impact in one country than the other.

Canada

The British model of government, which has influenced greatly the Canadian structure, sees the legislature making the laws and the judiciary applying them, with parliamentary supremacy not founded on democratic ideals, but rather a narrow power struggle.[1] Canada is a relatively young nation, founded officially by Confederation in 1867. While present Canada endorses multiculturalism, it is a country founded on the tale of 'two solitudes', English and French or Anglophone and Francophone, which lies at the heart of many a legal debate. While Canada is an officially bilingual country composed of ten provinces and three territories, it is important to note that the province of Quebec now remains by contrast officially unilingually Francophone.

Canadian Constitution

The Canadian Constitution, which includes the Canadian Charter of Rights and Freedoms, was proclaimed into force and entrenched on 17 April 1982.[2] It is made up of three separate documents: the British North America Act and its various amendments, the Constitution Act and its amending formula, and the Canadian

Charter of Rights and Freedoms, encompassing Articles 1 to 34 inclusively. In terms of the Charter of Rights and Freedoms, its purpose is to protect and safeguard the rights and freedoms enumerated, and to contain governmental action within reasonable limits. The supremacy of the Constitution is contained in Section 52(1) of the Constitution Act:

> 52(1) The Constitution of Canada is the supreme law of Canada and any law that is inconsistent with the provisions of the Constitution is, to the extent of the inconsistency, of no force or effect.[3]

Section 32 provides for its application to the Parliament and government of Canada, as well as to the legislature and government of each province.[4]

Fundamental Freedoms Important for religious discrimination cases, religion is specifically protected under Section 2(a) of the Charter:

> 2. Everyone has the following fundamental freedoms:
>   (a) freedom of conscience and religion;
>   (b) freedom of thought, belief, opinion and expression, including freedom of the press and other means of communication;
>   (c) freedom of peaceful assembly; and
>   (d) freedom of association.[5]

Multiculturalism and Aboriginal Rights Multiculturalism is established in Section 27:

> 27. This Charter shall be interpreted in a manner consistent with the preservation and enhancement of the multicultural heritage of Canadians.[6]

The protection of native people's rights within the Constitution is included in Sections 35(1) and (2), entitled 'Rights of the Aboriginal Peoples of Canada':

> 35(1) The existing aboriginal and treaty rights of the aboriginal peoples of Canada are hereby recognized and affirmed.
> (2) In this Act, 'aboriginal peoples of Canada' includes the Indian, Inuit and Métis peoples of Canada.[7]

Civil Rights Important for people who belong to religious minorities, Section 15, which came into effect on 17 April 1985 after a three-year implemented delay, specifically mentions religion, guarantees equality of rights, and also deals with affirmative action programs to help reverse the discrimination process:

> 15(1) Every individual is equal before and under the law and has the right to the equal protection and equal benefit of the law without discrimination and, in particular, without

discrimination based on race, national or ethnic origin, colour, religion, sex, age or mental or physical disability.

(2) Subsection (1) does not preclude any law, program or activity that has as its object the amelioration of conditions of disadvantaged individuals or groups including those that are disadvantaged because of race, national or ethnic origin, colour, religion, sex, age or mental or physical disability.[8]

Further, the Charter implements equality through Section 28, which cannot be overridden by legislation or act of Parliament:

28. Notwithstanding anything in this Charter, the rights and freedoms referred to in it are guaranteed equally to male and female persons.[9]

Provisions in Denial of Right The infamous 'notwithstanding' clause is Section 33, allowing the Canadian provinces to opt out of the Constitution for successive and infinite five-year periods:

33(1) Parliament or the legislature of a province may expressly declare in an Act of Parliament or of the legislature...that the Act or a provision thereof shall operate notwithstanding a provision included in...Section...15 of this Charter[10]

The Canadian Constitution extends power to judges to review legislative action on the basis of congruence with protected values in the Charter, and treats the judicial branch of government as a partner with the legislative and executive branches, in determining the rights of citizens. However, Section 33, the overriding clause, will ensure that legislatures rather than judges have the final say on important matters of public policy, so that laws offensive to certain provisions of the Charter may be upheld.

Importantly, Section 1 of the Charter is also an overriding clause:

1. The Canadian Charter of Rights and Freedoms set out is subject only to such reasonable limits prescribed by law as can be demonstrably justified in a free and democratic society.[11]

Thus, fundamental freedoms, as well as legal and equality rights, can be subjected to this notwithstanding clause. Remarkably, the right against religious discrimination is not absolute, since the Canadian Charter of Rights and Freedoms may be used to strengthen inequalities, by weighing in on the side of power, and undermine popular movements.

In terms of the burden of proof, Section 1 of the Charter has two functions: first, it guarantees the rights and freedoms set out in the provisions which follow it; and second, it states explicitly the exclusive justificatory criteria, outside of Section 33 of the Charter, against which limitations on those rights and freedoms may be measured. The onus of proving that a limitation on any Charter right is reasonable and demonstrably justified in a free and democratic society rests upon the party seeking to uphold the limitation. Limits on constitutionally guaranteed rights are clearly exceptions to the general guarantee. The presumption is that Charter rights are guaranteed unless the party invoking Section 1 can bring itself within the exceptional criteria justifying their being limited. The standard of proof under Section 1 is a preponderance of probabilities. Proof beyond a reasonable doubt would be unduly onerous on the party seeking to limit the right, because concepts such as 'reasonableness', 'justifiability' and 'free and democratic society' are not amenable to such a standard. Nevertheless, the preponderance of probability test must be applied rigorously.

The Supreme Court of Canada uses the purposive approach to interpret the Charter, whereby the underlying purpose of the legislative provision and the nature of the interest are identified. A two-step procedure is utilized to see whether the limit of the Charter contained in Section 1 can uphold an infringement of a right. Two questions are asked: (1) has the right been violated?; and (2) can the violation be justified under Section 1? The burden of proof is such that the onus of establishing a prima facie infringement of the Charter is on the person alleging it, while the onus of justifying a reasonable limit on the protected right is on the party invoking Section 1. Two criteria must be satisfied in order to come within Section 1 of the Charter: (1) the objective of the limiting measure must be sufficiently important, and the concerns must be pressing and substantial to justify overriding a constitutionally protected right; and (2) the means must be reasonable and demonstrably justified according to a proportionality test, which balances the interests of society against those of individuals. There are three components to the test: (1) the measure must be carefully designed to achieve the stated objective, and must not be arbitrary, unfair or irrational; (2) the measure should impair the right as little as possible; and (3) proportionality must exist between the effect of the limiting measure and its objectives (*Regina v. Oakes*, [1986] 1 SCR 103).[12]

Canadian Bill of Rights

In addition to the Canadian Constitution, there is the Canadian Bill of Rights, enacted on 10 August 1960.

Fundamental Freedoms   Human rights and fundamental freedoms are guaranteed in Section 1, which specifically mentions religion in Section 1(c):

> 1. It is hereby recognized and declared that in Canada there have existed and shall continue to exist without discrimination by reason of race, national origin, colour, religion or sex, the following human rights and fundamental freedoms, namely,
>   (a) the right of the individual to life, liberty, security of the person and enjoyment of property and the right not to be deprived thereof except by due process of law;
>   (b) the right of the individual to equality before the law and the protection of the law;

(c) freedom of religion;
(d) freedom of speech;
(e) freedom of assembly and of association; and
(f) freedom of the press.[13]

Canadian Human Rights Act (CHRA)

The Canadian Human Rights Act (CHRA) was implemented and came into force on 1 March 1978, and prohibits discrimination on the grounds of religion in all federal and federally regulated organizations. The provinces and territories have similar laws forbidding discrimination in their areas of jurisdiction. Complaints are handled by the Canadian Human Rights Commission and a number of provincial commissions.

The CHRA has been very influential for those seeking relief from human rights abuses and discrimination through a channel other than the traditional court system, namely the Canadian Human Rights Tribunal (CHRT). It implements a complaint process through a commission, which assumes that systemic discrimination does not exist but for a few cases. This differs from a proactive approach, which places an obligation on the employer to determine if systemic wage discrimination exists and to remedy it within a time frame. The Canadian Human Rights Commission (CHRC) administers the CHRA, in trying to ensure the principles of equal opportunity and nondiscrimination within the federal jurisdiction, that is the federal public service and federally regulated employers. The CHRA features a 'duty of accommodation' which requires employers to address the needs of people who are protected under the CHRA, and creates a smaller permanent human rights tribunal, which will improve the ability to hear and make decisions about cases effectively and efficiently.

Important for people from religious minorities, the purpose of the CHRA is outlined in Section 2, which specifically mentions religion:

> 2. The purpose of this Act is to extend the laws in Canada to give effect, within the purview of matters coming within the legislative authority of Parliament, to the principle that all individuals should have an opportunity equal with other individuals to make for themselves the lives that they are able and wish to have and to have their needs accommodated, consistent with their duties and obligations as members of society, without being hindered in or prevented from doing so by discriminatory practices based on race, national or ethnic origin, colour, religion, age, sex, sexual orientation, marital status, family status, disability or conviction for an offence for which a pardon has been granted.[14]

Further, important for religious discrimination cases, Section 3(1), which specifically mentions religion, states:

3(1). For all purposes of this Act, race, national or ethnic origin, colour, religion, age, sex, marital status, family status, disability and conviction for which a pardon has been granted are prohibited grounds of discrimination.[15]

Sections 7 and 10 go on to enumerate what is considered to be discriminatory:

> 7. It is a discriminatory practice, directly or indirectly:
>   (a) to refuse to employ or continue to employ any individual, or
>   (b) in the course of employment, to differentiate adversely in relation to an employee, on a prohibited ground of discrimination. [1976~77, c.33, s.7.3][16]
> 10. It is a discriminatory practice for an employer, employee organization or organization of employers:
>   (a) to establish or pursue a policy or practice, or
>   (b) to enter into an agreement affecting recruitment, referral, hiring, promotion, training, apprenticeship, transfer or any other matter relating to employment or prospective employment, that deprives or tends to deprive an individual or class of individuals of any employment opportunities on a prohibited ground of discrimination. [1976~77, c.33, s.l0; 1980~81~82~83, c.143, s.5.][17]

Further, under Section 11, it is discriminatory directly or indirectly to refuse to employ or, in the course of employment, to differentiate adversely against an employee in recruitment, referral, hiring, promotion, training or transfer policies:

> 11(2) In assessing the value of work performed by employees employed in the same establishment, the criterion to be applied is the composite of the skill, effort and responsibility required in the performance of the work and the conditions under which the work is performed.[18]

However, Section 15(1) allows for a bona fide occupational exception:

> 15(1) It is not a discriminatory practice if
>
> (*a*) any refusal, exclusion, expulsion, suspension, limitation, specification or preference in relation to any employment is established by an employer to be based on a *bona fide* occupational requirement.[19]

Further, special programs, including for workers from religious minorities, are allowed under Section 16, which specifically mentions religion:

> 16. It is not a discriminatory practice for a person to adopt or carry out a special program, plan or arrangement designed to prevent disadvantages that are likely to be suffered by, or to eliminate or reduce disadvantages that are suffered by, any group of individuals when those disadvantages would be or are based on or related to the race, national or ethnic origin, colour, religion, age, sex, marital status, family status

or disability of members of that group, by improving opportunities respecting goods, services, facilities, accommodation or employment in relation to that group.[20]

The CHRA looks at comparable worth, applying the same wages where respective work is shown to be equal in value through a combination of skill, effort, responsibility and working conditions, and thereby makes comparisons between dissimilar jobs. It is a discriminatory practice to establish different wages, so that if people do work of equal value in the same establishment then they must be paid equally. Discriminatory practices for wage inequities include segregated employment, exclusion of those categorically from the existing evaluation system, undervaluation of certain positions, fewer promotion opportunities, senior rules disadvantaging some groups, and discriminatory transfers, promotion and layoffs.[21] Discrimination includes practices or attitudes, whether by design or impact, which have the effect of limiting the individual's right to the opportunities generally available, because of attributes such as religion rather than actual characteristics. There are, however, some reasonable factors to permit a pay difference, such as periodic pay increases for length of service or working in remote locations. The CHRC only has jurisdiction over the federal public service and federally regulated employers in the quest for equal pay for work of equal value, and one drawback to the federal law is that it is limited to comparisons within the same establishment.

In terms of the onus of proof with respect to a complaint under the Act, the evidentiary burden in discrimination cases involving the refusal of employment appears clear and constant through all Canadian jurisdictions: a complainant must first establish a *prima facie* case of discrimination, and once that is done the burden shifts to the respondent to provide a reasonable explanation for the otherwise discriminatory behavior. Thereafter, assuming the employer has provided an explanation, the complainant has the eventual burden of showing that the explanation provided was merely 'pretext' and that the true motivation behind the employer's actions was in fact discriminatory (*Basi v. Canadian National Railway* (1984), 9 CHRR 4. D/5029, 5037 (CHRTribunal)).[22]

Thus, in an employment complaint, the Commission usually establishes a *prima facie* case by proving that: (1) the complainant was qualified for the particular employment; (2) the complainant was not hired; and (3) someone no better qualified but lacking the distinguishing feature which is the gravamen of the human rights complaint subsequently obtained the position. If these elements are proved, there is an evidentiary onus on the respondent to provide an explanation of events equally consistent with the conclusion that discrimination on the basis prohibited by the Code is not the correct explanation of what occurred (*Shakes v. Rex Pak Ltd.* (1982), 3 CHRR D/1001, 1002).[23] Should the respondent provide evidence of a nondiscriminatory reason for refusing to employ the complainant, then the complainant and the Commission can still establish that the reason advanced for non-employment is in fact a pretext, and that discrimination on an unlawful ground was one of the operative reasons for the respondent's actions (*Blake v. Ministry of Correctional Services and Mimico Correctional Institute* (1984), 5 CHRR D/2417

(Ontario)).[24] The ultimate onus of proof to establish the complaint on a balance of probabilities lies with the complainant and the Commission. Discrimination can be established by direct evidence or by circumstantial evidence, which is evidence that is consistent with the fact that is sought to be proven and inconsistent with any other rational conclusion, since it is not necessary to find that the respondent intended to discriminate against the complainant, it is sufficient to establish the complaint if it is found, on the balance of probabilities, that the respondent in fact discriminated against the complainant on one of the grounds alleged in their complaint (*Ontario Human Rights Commission v. Simpsons-Sears Ltd.*, [1985] SCR 536, 547).[25]

There are three essential steps in developing a special program: to identify as problems, areas within the organization in which the labor force is unrepresentative; to determine how the problems relate to organization policies, practices and procedures, both formal and informal; and to formulate solutions that aim to remove existing barriers and to provide for equitable representation. The criteria that indicate the need for a special program are: observable absence of members of certain groups in particular job categories or in the organization as a whole; existence of particularly high unemployment rates among certain groups; internal complaints and grievances from employees; external complaints by individuals or groups; inability of the organization to recruit or retain employees in terms of high turnover; and complaints filed with the CHRC alleging discriminatory practices. The primary objective of a special program is to increase the overall representation of the organization's labor force in some specific way. In setting objectives specific to the organization, the following factors must be considered: objectives should be quantitative, namely targets or goals; objectives should aim to correct underutilization or overconcentration where they occur in an organization; objectives must be specific as to target group and should also specify job category and geographical area; and objectives must be attainable within specific and reasonable timeframes. A special program is intended to be a temporary measure that should not outlive the identified problem of disadvantage, although the achievement of objectives will result in permanent organizational changes; objectives should realistically reflect the ability of the organization to respond to change; objectives must take into consideration the continuing rights of individuals, especially employees, not belonging to designated target groups; and objectives should be framed with care to be sensitive to the feelings and expectations of staff, including members of the target groups.

Canada Employment Equity Act

Important for religious workers, the purpose of the Canada Employment Equity Act, assented to 15 December 1995, as outlined in Section 2, is to achieve equality in the workplace so that no person shall be denied employment opportunities or benefits for reasons unrelated to ability and, in the fulfilment of that goal, to correct the conditions of disadvantage in employment experienced by members of visible minorities, aboriginal peoples, women and persons with disabilities, and by giving effect to the principle that employment equity means more than treating persons in the same way but also requires special measures and the accommodation of differences.[26] It covers the federal government, including the public service and crown corporations, as well as federally-regulated private sector employers with 100 or more employees, and addresses four designated groups: persons with disabilities, women, Aboriginal peoples and visible minorities. The Canadian Human Rights Commission (CHRC) is responsible for enforcing the obligations of employers to implement employment equity.

Section 5 establishes a duty of employers:

> 5. Every employer shall implement employment equity by
> (*a*) identifying and eliminating employment barriers against persons in designated groups that result from the employer's employment systems, policies and practices that are not authorized by law; and
> (*b*) instituting such positive policies and practices and making such reasonable accommodations as will ensure that persons in designated groups achieve a degree of representation in each occupational group in the employer's workforce that reflects their representation in
>   i. the Canadian workforce, or
>   ii. those segments of the Canadian workforce that are identifiable by qualification, eligibility or geography and from which the employer may reasonably be expected to draw employees.[27]

Further, Section 6 states that the obligation to implement employment equity does not require an employer to take a particular measure to implement employment equity where the taking of that measure would cause undue hardship to the employer; to hire or promote unqualified persons; with respect to the public sector, to hire or promote persons without basing the hiring or promotion on selection according to merit in cases where the Public Service Employment Act requires that hiring or promotion be based on selection according to merit; or to create new positions in its workforce.[28]

Section 10 provides for the implementation of an employment equity plan:

> 10. (1) The employer shall prepare an employment equity plan that
> (*a*) specifies the positive policies and practices that are to be instituted by the employer in the short term for the hiring, training, promotion and retention of persons in designated groups and for the making of reasonable accommodations for those persons, to correct the underrepresentation of those persons identified by the analysis ...;
> (*b*) specifies the measures to be taken by the employer in the short term for the elimination of any employment barriers identified by the review ...;
> (*c*) establishes a timetable for the implementation of the matters referred to in paragraphs (*a*) and (*b*);
> (*d*) where underrepresentation has been identified by the analysis, establishes short

term numerical goals for the hiring and promotion of persons in designated groups in order to increase their representation in each occupational group in the workforce in which underrepresentation has been identified and sets out measures to be taken in each year to meet those goals;

(e) sets out the employer's longer term goals for increasing the representation of persons in designated groups in the employer's workforce and the employer's strategy for achieving those goals; and

(f) provides for any other matter that may be prescribed.[29]

Finally, under Section 29, a Tribunal may, in the same manner and to the same extent as a superior court of record, summon and enforce the attendance of witnesses and compel them to give oral and written evidence on oath and to produce such documents and things as the Tribunal considers necessary for a full review; administer oaths; and receive and accept such evidence and other information, whether on oath or by affidavit or otherwise, as the Tribunal sees fit, whether or not that evidence or information would be admissible in a court of law.[30]

Citizenship offers a sense of belonging in one's country and gives each individual the right to participate in society and in its economic and political systems. It confers the protection of the State within Canada and abroad, while requiring individuals to obey this country's laws. In terms of a more complete set of rights, popular conceptions of citizenship incorporate an increasingly complete set of rights. From 'civil rights' such as freedom of speech, thought and faith, citizenship came to include 'political rights' as expressed by the right to hold office or to vote. Most recently, twentieth century citizenship is understood to comprise not only these but also 'social and economic rights'. These are the level of well-being and security that are required to exist in a society. They represent a commitment that there will be no internal 'borders' and that all those who call a particular country home can participate fully in the life of the community. Section 15 of the Charter has become a touchstone for people's rights. However, as we have seen, the Charter has its limits.[31] In terms of the legislative review process, the Government needs to establish an ongoing strategy and process to review laws, regulations, policies, practices and rules to remove barriers to full participation and ensure the equality of all people. This process can be used to apply a religious-based analysis to new policy, program and legislative initiatives and to plan for a comprehensive review of existing ones. Canada's labor market is evolving. New types of jobs are appearing in the workplace as others disappear. Governments are trying to respond to these changes and are working to ensure that all Canadians can participate in the new economy.

An important example of religious discrimination and ultimately religious tolerance in Canada involved one of the country's international symbols, the Royal Canadian Mounted Police (RCMP) dress uniform, which has been in existence over a hundred years. In response to an officer who wanted to wear a turban as an expression of his religion, the RCMP commissioner recommended the prohibition against turbans be lifted in 1989, and in 1990, the Federal Government, under the

Solicitor General, finally removed the ban preventing Sikhs in the RCMP from wearing turbans.

The legal workplace duty to accommodate requires the elimination of employment standards, rules, practices or other requirements that discriminate on prohibited grounds, such as religion.[32] Two Supreme Court of Canada cases, *Meiorin: British Columbia (Public Service Employee Relations Commission) (BCPSERC) v. The British Columbia Government and Service Employees Union (BCGSEU)* [1999], 35 C.H.R.R. D/257 (S.C.C.)[33] (gender discrimination at the workplace) and *Grismer: Terry Grismer (Estate) v. The British Columbia Superintendent of Motor Vehicles et al.*, [1999] 3 S.C.R. 868[34] (service discrimination to a person with a disability), established that accommodation is to be the norm, in line with affirmative action and employment equity work.

The Supreme Court decision in *Meiorin: British Columbia (Public Service Employee Relations Commission) (BCPSERC) v. The British Columbia Government and Service Employees Union (BCGSEU)* [1999], 35 C.H.R.R. D/257 (S.C.C.) requires employers to design workplace standards that do not discriminate, and developed the three-step Meiorin Test to determine if the employer has established a standard that is a bona fide occupational requirement; the employer must: 1. Demonstrate the standard was adopted for a purpose rationally connected to the performance of the job; 2. Honestly believe the standard is necessary to fulfill the legitimate, work-related purpose; and 3. Show the standard is reasonably necessary to the accomplishment of the legitimate, work-related purpose, so that it is impossible to accommodate workers without undue hardship to the employer.[35] To deal with step 3, the following questions are asked: Have alternatives been considered?; If so, why were these alternatives not adopted?; Must all workers meet a single standard, or could different standards be adopted?; Does the standard treat some more harshly than others?; If so, was the standard designed to minimize this differential treatment?; What steps were taken to find accommodations?; Is there evidence of undue hardship if accommodation were to be provided?; Have all parties who are required to accommodate played their roles? The Court did say accommodation would be the norm 'in so far as is reasonably possible', and accommodation is not required if it causes undue hardship.[36]

In terms of undue hardship, the Canadian Human Rights Act identifies only cost, and health and safety. To be considered undue hardship, financial costs must be so great as to alter the essential nature of the enterprise or affect its viability, and may include: financial cost, health and safety, impact on the collective agreement, interference with other workers' rights, employee morale, the size of the operation and the adaptability of the workforce and facilities.[37] In *Central Alberta Dairy Pool v. Alberta (Human Rights Commission)* [1990] 2 S.C.R. 489, when a Worldwide Church of God member requested an unpaid leave of absence for Easter Monday which he had been granted in the past, but now was denied and fired, the Supreme Court, although it agreed the employer that the rule about being at work on Mondays was a bona fide occupational requirement, found that it was guilty of adverse affect discrimination, because the rule indirectly infringed on the employee's religious beliefs and accommodating him would not have constituted undue hardship.[38]

In *O'Malley: Ontario (Human Rights Commission) v. Simpson-Sears Ltd.* [1985] 2 S.C.R. 536, when an employee, a Seventh Day Adventist, requested Saturday shifts off to observe the Sabbath, which involved no work from sundown Friday to sundown Saturday, conflicting with the store's requirement of work, the Supreme Court found that an employment rule, even if made in good faith for sensible business reasons, could result in adverse affect discrimination, and that the employer could have accommodated the employee without undue hardship by changing her shift schedule, deciding an employment rule honestly made for sound economic or business reasons, equally applicable to all to whom it is intended to apply, may yet be discriminatory if it affects a person or group of persons differently from others to whom it may apply.[39] The Court established three rules for these situations: (1) In adverse affect discrimination cases, the employer must make reasonable efforts to accommodate, up to undue hardship; (2) The employer cannot be expected to do more, if the problem is not resolved after these reasonable efforts have been made; and (3) Complainants must show they are experiencing discrimination because of a rule, and if this *prima facie* case is made, the employer must show that reasonable attempts were made to accommodate up to undue hardship.[40]

In terms of religious accommodation, in *Andrews v. Law Society of British Columbia* 10 C.H.R.R. D/5719, the Canadian Supreme Court recognized that 'the accommodation of differences...is the essence of true equality'.[41] Religious accommodation may require changes to employment practices that have been agreed in the terms of a collective bargaining agreement, so that the duty to accommodate may fall both on the employer and on unions. In *Central Okanagan School District No. 23 v. Renaud* (1992), 16 CHRR D/425, the Supreme Court of Canada noted that although the principle of equal liability applies, the employer has charge of the workplace and will be in a better position to formulate measures of accommodation.[42] Nevertheless, the Court held that this does not absolve a union of its duty to put forward alternative measures that are available. In short, when a union is a co-discriminator with an employer, it shares the obligation to remove or alleviate the source of the discriminatory effect. Unions may be liable in two situations: First, the union may cause or contribute to the discrimination by participating in the formulation of the work rule that has a discriminatory effect on the complainant, and this will generally be the case if the rule is a provision in the collective agreement; and Second, a union may be liable if it impedes the reasonable efforts of an employer to accommodate.[43]

In *CUPW v. Canada Post Corporation: CUPW v. Canada Post Corporation* [2001] B.C.J. No. 680 (C.A.), when an employee, who was a Seventh Day Adventist, argued that his religious beliefs prevented him from working from sundown Friday evening to sundown Saturday, despite the collective agreement requiring that he work Friday from 3 pm to 11 pm., the Supreme Court of Canada ruled that the school board and union both had a duty to accommodate the employee and decided unanimously that the employer and the union had discriminated against the employee by failing to accommodate his religious beliefs.[44] While the school board argued that it had not accommodated the employee because it wanted to avoid violating the collective agreement and having a grievance filed against it, the Court said it is relevant to review a collective agreement, to see what hardship might be involved in violating its terms, but a grievance in this case would not constitute undue hardship and the most reasonable accommodation might be one that required union approval for a change in the collective agreement. However, worker objections could constitute undue hardship in that 'the objection of employees based on well-grounded concerns that their rights will be affected must be considered. On the other hand, objections based on attitudes inconsistent with human rights are an irrelevant consideration'.[45]

Further, in *Gohm v. Domtar Inc. and OPEIU, Local 267* [1990], 12 C.H.R.R. D/161 (Ont. Bd. Inq.); affirmed [1992], 89 D.L.R. (4th) 305 (Ont. Div. Ct.)., when the employer agreed to accommodate an employee by rescheduling her to work Sunday instead of Saturday, provided she agreed not to receive premium pay for Sunday work as required by the collective agreement, the union blocked the employer's attempt, and in finding that the union had discriminated against the complainant, the Ontario Divisional Court set out the concept of 'equal partnership': Discrimination in the workplace is everybody's business and there can be no hierarchy of responsibility so that companies, unions and persons are all in a primary and equal position in a single line of defense against all types of discrimination.[46] However, a union may be exonerated if it has tried to amend a discriminatory clause, and the Court can look to see: Does the procedure identify clearly what accommodation is required?; Identify positions that could be used for accommodation?; Include the possibility of training as part of accommodation?; Provide for permanent accommodation, temporary accommodation and work-hardening measures?; Provide for adequate severance provisions if accommodation cannot be provided short of undue hardship?

Further, internationally, the United Nations Human Rights Committee has recognized that the definition of 'religion or belief' should be subjected to certain limits. In the case of *M.A.B.; W.A.T. and A.Y.T. v. Canada,* Communication No. 570/1993,[47] the applicants, associated with the Assembly of the Church of the Universe, argued that the Canadian *Narcotics Control Act* violated their right to freedom of thought, conscience and religion under Article 18 of the International Covenant on Civil and Political Rights (ICCPR), because it prohibited the use of marijuana, with their beliefs and practices including the care, cultivation, possession, distribution, maintenance, integrity and worship of marijuana, which they referred to as the 'sacrament' of the Church. The Committee said that the expression 'religion or belief' does not encompass a belief which consists primarily or exclusively of the worship of and distribution of a narcotic drug; even where the religion or belief is protected, religious observances, such as the use of prohibited drugs, may be restricted if this is objectively justified and reasonable, such as due to the harm caused by drugs.

In terms of inclusion, the principle of inclusiveness implied in Canadian citizenship gives the Government a base for its approach to today's requirements. The federal government should promote the equality commitments contained in the international and national instruments that underpin full citizenship. It should also support programs and policies that help all Canadians participate effectively in the economic and social mainstream.

It is essential for the principles and values in the Charter be applied in a more effective way to new laws, regulations, policies, programs and procedures as they are developed; and existing laws, regulations, policies, programs and procedures that put Canadians from religious minorities at a disadvantage, before these are challenged in the courts. While the federal government aims for and expects that its laws will not discriminate in their intent or effect, the reality is that, while many laws do not actively discriminate against Canadians from religious minorities, their effects are discriminatory. In terms of an inclusive labor market, a vision of inclusion is one in which programs and services are designed in consultation with people from religious minorities, in which employers hire individuals on the basis of their skills and abilities, and accommodating different ways to get work done happens as a matter of course in the workplace. Inclusiveness should be a matter of 'business as usual'. The Government should put in place operational, administrative and evaluative mechanisms to ensure that the labor market needs of people from all religions are served by programs and services for which it retains or shares responsibility. It should provide appropriate supports to local managers to help them include people from religious minorities among their clients and ensure that local managers are aware that they will be measured or evaluated on their ability to serve all people. A secure income is fundamental to the ability to enjoy the rights of citizenship, since without a secure income, an individual cannot satisfy the most basic living needs.[48]

As used in human rights laws, discrimination means making a distinction between certain individuals or groups based on a prohibited ground of discrimination. The Canadian Human Rights Act and provincial human rights codes forbid religious discrimination in employment, with exceptions in some cases regarding mandatory retirement and bona fide occupational requirements. Roughly 17.9 percent of all antidiscrimination clauses found in major Canadian collective agreements specifically refer to the federal or provincial human rights code.[49] According to the Canadian Human Rights Commission, discrimination means treating people differently, negatively or adversely because of prohibited grounds of discrimination such as age, race, religion or gender.

Mexico

Constitución Política de los Estados Unidos Mexicanos

The equality of all persons before the law is guaranteed by the Constitución Política de los Estados Unidos Mexicanos, the Political Constitution of the United Mexican States.[50] Article 1 establishes that all individuals shall enjoy the guarantees set down by the Constitution, which may not be restricted or suspended, except in those cases and conditions established therein.[51] In terms of equality in employment, Article 123(7) establishes that equal work performed in the same post with the same hours worked and conditions of efficiency shall also be remunerated with the same salary.[52]

Ley Federal de Trabajo

The entitlement to equal opportunities is set down in Article 3 and Article 164 of the Ley Federal de Trabajo (LFT), the Federal Labor Law.[53] Article 1 provides that no discrimination may be established between workers.[54] Article 86 establishes that equal work performed in the same post with the same hours worked and conditions of efficiency shall also be remunerated with the same salary.[55] Although there is no unemployment insurance per se, Articles 50 and 52 of the LFT establish an obligation on the part of employers to pay compensation to unfairly dismissed workers, and they would also have the option to be reinstated to the same job.[56] If the worker is discharged without justification and his employment is for a specified period, the worker is entitled to receive a severance payment equal to the wages received for half of the time of work with the same employer. For those workers with more than one year of service, the severance payment is equal to six months' wages for the first year of service plus 20 days' wages for each additional year of service. For workers with labor contracts of unspecified duration, the severance payment is equal to three months' wages, and they would also have the right to receive wages for the period between the day of dismissal and the day the severance compensation is paid. If a worker asks to be reinstated and the employer refuses, he has the right to receive 20 days' wages for each year of service in addition to the above.

Ley del Seguro Social

In terms of retirement income and health benefits, the social security system covers a broad range of social insurance, including retirement and dismissal due to old age, work risks, illness and maternity, disability and life, and nursery facilities for children, as well as other social benefits. The system is financed by premiums paid by employers and employees, and by contributions from the federal government. Premiums paid by the employer are equal to 8.5 percent of insurable earnings plus 13.9 percent of the minimum wage in the Distrito Federal for illness insurance plus a variable portion for work risks insurance. Employees' premiums are equal to two percent of their insurable earnings. In the case of workers receiving the minimum wage, according to Article 36, employers are obliged to pay the entire premium.[57] Contributions to the retirement insurance scheme are administered by means of individual accounts handled by private companies known as Administradores de Fondos para el Retiro de los Trabajadores (AFORES), Worker Retirement Fund Administrators.

United States of America

In a recent survey on religion, the American religious marketplace was found to be very volatile, as nearly half of American adults left the faith tradition of their upbringing to either switch allegiances or abandon religious affiliation altogether.[58] However, Americans are still deeply religious, with 84 percent of adults claiming a religious affiliation. Specifically, mainline Protestant churches are in decline, non-denominational churches are gaining and the ranks of the unaffiliated are growing. More than one-quarter of American adults have left the faith of their childhood for another religion or no religion at all, with one in four adults ages 18 to 29 claiming no affiliation with a religious institution. The majority of the unaffiliated, 12 percent of the overall population, describe their religion as 'nothing in particular', and about half of those say faith is at least somewhat important to them, with atheists or agnostics accounting for 4 percent of the total population.

It is estimated that the United States is 78 percent Christian, but will eventually lose its status as a majority Protestant nation, currently at 51 percent. The Roman Catholic Church has lost more members than any faith tradition because of affiliation swapping. While nearly one in three Americans were raised Catholic, fewer than one in four say they are Catholic today, which means roughly 10 percent of all Americans are ex-Catholics. The share of the population that identifies as Catholic, however, has remained fairly stable in recent decades thanks to an influx of immigrant Catholics, mostly from Latin America, with nearly half of all Catholics under 30 are Hispanic. On the Protestant side, changes in affiliation are swelling the ranks of nondenominational churches, while Baptist and Methodist traditions are showing net losses. Many Americans have vague denominational ties at best. People who call themselves 'just a Protestant', in fact, account for nearly 10 percent of all Protestants. Hindus claimed the highest retention of childhood members, at 84 percent. The group with the worst retention is one of the fastest growing, Jehovah's Witnesses, with only 37 percent of those raised in the sect known for door-to-door proselytizing saying they remain members. Among other findings involving smaller religious groups, more than half of American Buddhists surveyed were white, and most Buddhists were converts. More people in the survey pool identified themselves as Buddhist than Muslim, although both populations were small, less than 1 percent of the total population. By contrast, Jews accounted for 1.7 percent of the overall population.

Overall, there is a loss of confidence in organized religion, especially in the traditional religious forms. This is in keeping with the high tolerance among Americans for change, with the United States being a very fluid society. The American religious economy is compared to a marketplace, being very dynamic, very competitive.[59]

The American model sees judicial activism and the judicial power as fundamentally legislative in character, with royal power displaced and overthrown, but class power remaining, with the upper class combining the popular republican form of government.

Declaration of Independence

The concepts of equality and good government, found in the American judicial system, were equally important principles to the Founding Fathers of the United States. The Declaration of Independence, the bedrock of the United States' jurisprudence system, was enshrined on 4 July 1776. It fundamentally states:

> We hold these truths to be self-evident, that all men are created equal; that they are endowed by their Creator with certain unalienable rights; that among these are life, liberty and the pursuit of happiness. That, to secure these rights, governments are instituted among men, deriving their just powers from the consent of the governed; that whenever any form of government becomes destructive of these ends, it is the right of the people to alter or to abolish it, and to institute a new government, laying its foundation on such principles, and organize its powers in such form, as to them shall seem most likely to effect their safety and happiness.[60]

Federalist Papers

Influential thinkers, such as Jefferson, Madison and Jay, believed in a national government and a Bill of Rights, which they outlined in the Federalist Papers 1787–88. Government is seen as essential to the security of liberty, with every citizen ceding some rights for the protection thereof. The diversities in the faculties of men are recognized as where property rights originate. The objective of government is to secure the public good and private rights against the danger of factions, with the most common source of faction being the unequal distribution of property. The purpose of the Union is the common defense of the members, so that the means are proportionate to the ends. Government must act before the public and must be derived from the body of society. The Constitution is founded on the assent and ratification of the people, and every man who values liberty must cherish the attachment to the Union and preserve it.

Among the three branches of government, the Judicial branch is considered the least dangerous to the political rights of the Constitution. The Executive branch dispenses the honors and holds the sword; the Legislative branch controls the purse and prescribes the rules to regulate duties and rights; and the Judiciary has no influence over the sword or the purse, needing the aid of the Executive for the efficacy of judgments. Oppression can proceed from the Courts, but liberty will not be endangered if the branches are separate. The Constitution is the fundamental law of the land. 'We, the people of the United States, to secure the blessings of liberty to ourselves and our prosperity, do ordain and establish this Constitution for the United States of America'. As a recognition of popular rights, the judgments of many unite into one, with the voluntary consent of a whole people.[61] The Federalist Papers give us an important insight into the making of the Constitution, showing us early on the concept of equality of man and the formation of one government out of many people. The importance of the Judiciary must not be overlooked, as it is a major contributor of policy through its judgments, often itself influencing the sword, the Executive, and the purse, the Legislative. American constitutionalism is the product of the revolutionary movement in political thought of Hobbes, the parent of the modern American political process.[62] The chief purpose of political institutions is the management of social conflict. According to Hobbes, the only source of public authority is the private need of independently situated political actors, with a prior right to act based on self-defined standards of conscience and interest. If used wisely, the Constitution can serve to remedy past injustices of religious discrimination.

United States Constitution

Fundamental Freedoms The First Amendment to the Constitution, enacted in 1791, guarantees the freedoms of religion and expression:

> Amendment I
> Congress shall make no law respecting an establishment of religion, or prohibiting the free exercise thereof; or abridging the freedom of speech, or of the press; or the right of the people peaceably to assemble, and to petition the government for a redress of grievances.[63]

The Supreme Court has held that, under the First Amendment's Establishment Clause, Federal, State and local governments may not, directly or indirectly, demonstrate any preference for any church or any religious belief.

Civil Rights Important for people from religious minorities, the Fifth and Fourteenth Amendments of the Constitution, ratified in 15 December 1791 and 9 July 1868 respectively, are of paramount importance in the fight for human rights. With the due process clause of the Fifth Amendment including an equal protection component, the Fifth and Fourteenth Amendments provide due process of law and equal protection to citizens from federal and state actions respectively. Thus, they prohibit government from invidious discrimination:

Amendment V
No person shall ... be deprived of life, liberty, or property, without due process of law ....[64]

Amendment XIV
1. No state shall make or enforce any law which shall abridge the privileges or immunities of citizens of the United States; nor shall any state deprive any person of life, liberty, or property, without due process of law; nor deny to any person within its jurisdiction the equal protection of the laws.[65]

The 39th Article of the Magna Carta of 1215 is a foundation for the Fifth and Fourteenth Amendments of the American Constitution regarding due process and the rights of life, liberty and property. The Magna Carta states:

No free man shall be taken or imprisoned or dispossessed, or outlawed or banished, or in any way destroyed, nor will we go upon him nor send upon him, except by the legal judgement of his peers or by the law of the land.[66]

Further, important for religious minorities, the Thirteenth Amendment, ratified 6 December 1865, was the initial step in ending a great injustice in the United States, which had lasted for centuries, namely slavery:

Amendment XIII
1. Neither slavery nor involuntary servitude, except as a punishment for crime whereof the party shall have been duly convicted, shall exist within the United States, or any place subject to their jurisdiction.[67]

In addition, important for religious women, the Nineteenth Amendment ratified 18 August 1920, was an initial step in granting equality for women:

Amendment XIX
The right of citizens of the United States to vote shall not be denied or abridged by the United States or by any State on account of sex.
Congress shall have power to enforce this article by appropriate legislation.[68]

Finally, Article VI of the Constitution prohibits any requirement for an office holder to belong to or adhere to any particular religious faith:

VI. The Senators and Representatives..., and the Members of the several State Legislatures, and all executive and judicial Officers, both of the United States and of the several States, shall be bound by Oath or Affirmation, to support this Constitution; but no religious Test shall ever be required as a Qualification to any Office or public Trust under the United States.[69]

The American Founding Fathers designed the United States Constitution to be a set of broad guidelines established by free and intelligent men for the government of free and intelligent people for successive generations. It has survived for over two hundred years due to the common sense of the American people, the prudence of their representatives, and the calculated wisdom of its judicial interpreters, the Supreme Court of the United States.[70] Chief Justice Marshall said of the Constitution: 'It was intended to endure for ages to come and consequentially to be adapted to the various crises of human affairs' (*McCullough v. Maryland*, 4 Wheaton 415 (1819)).[71] It was a common opinion that each branch of government in matters pertaining to itself be the final judge of its own powers. However, it was the function of the judiciary, and especially the Supreme Court, to construe in the last resort the meaning of the Constitution, with its opinion final and binding. Justice Hughes stated: 'We are under a Constitution but the Constitution is what the judges say it is'. The United States Constitution, through Article 6(2) known as the Supremacy Clause, is the supreme law of the land:

> 6(2) This Constitution, and the Laws of the United States which shall be made in Pursuance thereof; and all Treaties made, or which shall be made, under the Authority of the United States, shall be the supreme Law of the Land; and the Judges in every State shall be bound thereby, any Thing in the Constitution or Laws of any State to the Contrary notwithstanding.[72]

The seminal case of *Marbury v. Madison*, 1 Cranch 137 (1803), brought forth the important principles that (1) the Constitution is the supreme law of the land; (2) the powers granted to various branches of government are limited; and (3) the sole and essential function of the Court is to determine which law should prevail in conflict of laws.[73]

In a dynamic society, the creativity of judges is important for the development of law and the adaptability of the Constitution to the needs of modern society, according to the Realist Theory. Courts are the best means for recognizing social change, in order to focus social attitudes on unachieved goals and assist in their attainment through a decision-making process of judgments and thus policy-making, according to the Free Legal Decision Sociological Jurisprudence Theory.[74] History has a record of the past and provides the Court with a reservoir of social wisdom and political insight. It points out the evils against which the great constitutional clauses were designed as remedies. The adjudicative process depends on a delicate symbiotic relationship, whereby the Court must know us better than we know ourselves, acting as a voice of the spirit to remind us of our better selves.[75] It provides a stimulus and quickens moral education. However, the roots of the Supreme Court's decisions must be already in the nation. The aspirations voiced by the Court must be those the community is willing not only to avow but in the end to live by. For the power of the great constitutional decisions rests upon the accuracy of the Court's perceptions of this kind of common will and upon its ability ultimately to command a consensus. The rule of law, the capacity to command free assent, is the substitute for power.[76] Law is the fabric of a free society, organized with a minimum of force and a maximum of reason, in an ideal sense of right and justice. Thus, a neutral government, with its various branches, serves only as a participant in the inhumanities of its citizens.

In terms of the burden of proof in discrimination cases, the United States Supreme Court examines the cause of action to see whether a Plaintiff is a member of a class, which as a matter of law can invoke the power of the court, and thus, the equal protection clause and the due process clause of the Constitutional Amendments confer a constitutional right to be free from discrimination (*Davis v. Passman*, 442 US 228 (1979)).[77] Importantly, over the years, in examining court challenges, the United States Supreme Court has developed three different levels of review and accompanying burden of proof, depending upon the type of action brought in a legal proceeding. The Court will first examine the legislative purpose of the governmental action alleged to be contrary to the constitutional amendments, and the plaintiff's burden to prove his case will then come into play. The three levels of review are: (1) the minimum rationality level applied to see the rational basis for the means to the ends so that a law will survive as long as it does not serve an important government objective or is not substantially related to the achievement of the objective, applied in religious discrimination cases; (2) the heightened scrutiny level where the defendant government must show that the restriction has a substantial relationship to an important government interest, applied in quasi-suspect classifications, such as gender discrimination cases; and (3) most importantly, the strict scrutiny level where the defendant government must show a compelling interest for the restriction, a hard burden to meet, applied in suspect classifications affecting fundamental rights, such as racial discrimination cases. Thus, the concept of the burden of proof is an important element in court cases. In the fight for equal rights without regard to religion, some would say religion, like race, should be considered suspect and thus be subject to the highest level of review of strict scrutiny. Until such time, people from religious minorities may wish to argue cases not only on the basis of religious discrimination but more importantly on the basis of gender or, even more, race discrimination in order to fall under the highest level strict scrutiny standard.

In addition, although the American Constitution is the paramount tool for redressing wrongs, the judicial system in the United States has seen the use of two acts, the Equal Pay Act and the Civil Rights Act as alternatives to the Constitution, with the latter having been the most successful in guarding against discrimination.

Equal Pay Act

Important for religious women, the Equal Pay Act 1963 establishes that it is unlawful for an employer to pay unequal wages for equal work based on a discriminatory distinction.[78] An exception is made where there is a system of (1) seniority; (2) merit; (3) earnings based on quantity or quality of production; or (4) something other than gender. Section 16 of the Equal Pay Act states:

> 16. No employer having employees .... shall discriminate, within any establishment ... between employees on the basis of sex by paying wages to employees in such establishment at a rate less than the rate at which he pays wages to employees of the opposite sex in such establishment for equal work on jobs the performance of which requires equal skill, effort and responsibility, and which are performed under similar working conditions except where such payment is made pursuant to 1) a seniority system, 2) a merit system, 3) a system which measures earnings by quantity or quality of product or 4) a differential based on any other factor other than sex.[79]

The Equal Pay Act only includes jobs that are very much alike or closely related, considered virtually or substantially identical (*Brennan v. City Stores*, 479 F.2d. 235 (1973)).[80] Jobs though not identical can be considered equal for Equal Pay Act standards, if there is only an insubstantial difference in skill, effort and responsibility (*Murphy v. Miller Brewer Co.*, 307 F.Supp. 829 (1969)).[81] For the Equal Pay Act, there is discrimination when there is a different wage rate for equal work, that is, work which requires equal skill, effort and responsibility under similar working conditions (*Corning Glass v. Brennan*, 417 US 188 (1974)).[82] Equal protection is violated only by intentional discrimination, and a different impact standing alone is not enough. Further, there is no legal duty to undo the effects of previous discrimination (*American Nurses' Association v. State of Illinois*, 783 F.2d. 716 (1986)).[83] In terms of the burden of proof, the Plaintiff has the burden of establishing that equal pay for equal work was not received, and then the Defendant, in rebutting a prima facie case, must show the different wages were based on seniority, merit, a quantitative or qualitative system, or reasons other than sex (*Spaulding v. University of Washington*, 740 F.2d. 686 (1984)).[84] The court, however, is concerned with the actual job performance and content, not job description, titles or classifications, and the scrutiny is done on a case-by-case basis so that if skill is irrelevant to job requirements, it is not considered. Therefore, a non-job-related pretext can act as a shield for invidious discrimination.

Civil Rights Act

Important for religious discrimination, Title VII, the Civil Rights Act 1964, incorporating some of the provisions of the earlier Equal Pay Act with the Bennett Act Amendment, was implemented to safeguard important civil liberties, and serves to strengthen legislation, thereby helping the courts rule against discrimination. Section 701(j) defines religion:

> (j) The term 'religion' includes all aspects of religious observance and practice, as well as belief, unless an employer demonstrates that he is unable to reasonably accommodate

to an employee's or prospective employee's religious observance or practice without undue hardship on the conduct of the employer's business.[85]

Importantly, Section 703(a) guards against religious discrimination in employment:

> 703(a) It shall be an unlawful employment practice for an employer, (1) to fail or refuse to hire or to discharge any individual, or otherwise to discriminate against any individual with respect to his compensation, terms, conditions, or privilege of employment, because of such individual's race, color, religion, sex, or national origin, or (2) to limit, segregate, or classify his employees or applicants for employment in any way which would deprive or tend to deprive any individual of employment opportunities or otherwise adversely affect his status as an employee, because of such individual's race, color, religion, sex, or national origin.[86]

Further, employment agencies and labor organizations are covered under Section 703(b) and 703(c) respectively:

> 703(b) It shall be an unlawful employment practice for an employment agency to fail or refuse to refer for employment, or otherwise to discriminate against, any individual because of his race, color, religion, sex, or national origin, or to classify or refer for employment any individual on the basis of his race, color, religion, sex, or national origin.[87]

> 703(c) It shall be an unlawful employment practice for a labor organization
> (1) to exclude or to expel from its membership, or otherwise to discriminate against, any individual because of his race, color, religion, sex, or national origin;
> (2) to limit, segregate, or classify its membership or applicants for membership, or to classify or fail or refuse to refer for employment any individual, in any way which would deprive or tend to deprive any individual of employment opportunities, or would limit such employment opportunities or otherwise adversely affect his status as an employee or as an applicant for employment, because of such individual's race, color, religion, sex, or national origin.[88]

Finally, training programs are covered under Section 703(d):

> 703(d) It shall be an unlawful employment practice for any employer, labor organization, or joint labor management committee controlling apprenticeship or other training or retraining, including on the job training programs to discriminate against any individual because of his race, color, religion, sex, or national origin in admission to, or employment in, any program established to provide apprenticeship or other training.[89]

An exemption for religious organizations or educational institutions is provided for under Section 702(a):

702(a) This subchapter shall not apply to an employer with respect to the employment of aliens outside any State, or to a religious corporation, association, educational institution, or society with respect to the employment of individuals of a particular religion to perform work connected with the carrying on by such corporation, association, educational institution, or society of its activities.[90]

Further, a bona fide occupational qualification exception is outlined in Section 703(e):

703(e) Notwithstanding any other provision of this subchapter, (1) it shall not be an unlawful employment practice for an employer to hire and employ employees, for an employment agency to classify, or refer for employment any individual, for a labor organization to classify its membership or to classify or refer for employment any individual, or for an employer, labor organization, or joint labor management committee controlling apprenticeship or other training or retraining programs to admit or employ any individual in any such program, on the basis of his religion, sex, or national origin in those certain instances where religion, sex, or national origin is a bona fide occupational qualification reasonably necessary to the normal operation of that particular business or enterprise, and (2) it shall not be an unlawful employment practice for a school, college, university, or other educational institution or institution of learning to hire and employ employees of a particular religion if such school, college, university, or other educational institution or institution of learning is, in whole or in substantial part, owned, supported, controlled, or managed by a particular religion or by a particular religious corporation, association, or society, or if the curriculum of such school, college, university, or other educational institution or institution of learning is directed toward the propagation of a particular religion.[91]

Section 703(h) covers unequal pay:

703(h) Notwithstanding any other provision of this title, it shall be a lawful employment practice for an employer to apply different standards of compensation, or different terms, conditions, or privileges of employment pursuant to a bona fide seniority or merit system, or a system which measures earnings by quantity or quality of production or to employees who work different locations, provided that such are not the result of an intention to discriminate because of race, color, religion, sex, or national origin. It shall not be an unlawful employment practice under this title for any employer to differentiate upon the basis of sex in determining the amount of wages or compensation paid to employees of such employer if such differentiation is authorized by the provisions of Section 6(d) of the Fair Standards Act.[92]

Section 703(j) guards against preferential treatment:

703(j) Nothing contained in this subchapter shall be interpreted to require any employer, employment agency, labor organization, or joint labor management committee subject to this subchapter to grant preferential treatment to any individual or to any group because of the race, color, religion, sex, or national origin of such individual or group on account of an imbalance which may exist with respect to the total number or percentage of persons of any race, color, religion, sex, or national origin employed by any employer, referred or classified for employment by any employment agency or labor organization, admitted to membership or classified by any labor organization, or admitted to, or employed in, any apprenticeship or other training program, in comparison with the total number or percentage of persons of such race, color, religion, sex, or national origin in any community, State, section, or other area, or in the available work force in any community, State, section, or other area.[93]

In addition, discriminatory advertizing is outlawed under Section 704(b):

704(b) It shall be an unlawful employment practice for an employer, labor organization, employment agency, or joint labor management committee controlling apprenticeship or other training or retraining, including on the job training programs, to print or publish or cause to be printed or published any notice or advertisement relating to employment by such an employer or membership in or any classification or referral for employment by such a labor organization, or relating to any classification or referral for employment by such an employment agency, or relating to admission to, or employment in, any program established to provide apprenticeship or other training by such a joint labor management committee, indicating any preference, limitation, specification, or discrimination, based on race, color, religion, sex, or national origin, except that such a notice or advertisement may indicate a preference, limitation, specification, or discrimination based on religion, sex, or national origin when religion, sex, or national origin is a bona fide occupational qualification for employment.[94]

The establishment of a discriminatory employment practice based on disparate impact is noted in Section 703(k):

703(k)(1)(A) An unlawful employment practice based on disparate impact is established under this title only if:
    i. a complaining party demonstrates that a respondent uses a particular employment practice that causes a disparate impact on the basis of race, color, religion, sex, or national origin and the respondent fails to demonstrate that the challenged practice is job related for the position in question and consistent with business necessity.[95]

Further, the duty of a complainant party in a discrimination case is outlined in Section 703(m):

703(m) Except as otherwise provided in this title, an unlawful employment practice is established when the complaining party demonstrates that race, color, religion, sex, or national origin was a motivating factor for any employment practice, even though other factors also motivated the practice.[96]

Section 706(g) provides for adjudicative relief:

> 706(g) If the court finds that the respondent has intentionally engaged in or is intentionally engaging in an unlawful employment practice charged in the complaint, the court may enjoin the respondent from engaging in such unlawful employment practice, and order such affirmative action as may be appropriate, which may include, but is not limited to, reinstatement or hiring of employees, with or without back pay ..., or any other equitable relief as the court deems appropriate .... No order of the court shall require the admission or reinstatement of an individual as a member of a union, or the hiring, reinstatement, or promotion of an individual as an employee, or the payment to him of any back pay, if such individual was refused admission, suspended, or expelled, or was refused employment or advancement or was suspended or discharged for any reason other than discrimination on account of race, color, religion, sex, or national origin or in violation of section 704(a).[97]

Finally, opposition to a discriminatory practice is protected under Section 704(a):

> 704(a) It shall be an unlawful employment practice for an employer to discriminate against any of his employees or applicants for employment, for an employment agency, or joint labor management committee controlling apprenticeship or other training or retraining, including on the job training programs, to discriminate against any individual, or for a labor organization to discriminate against any member thereof or applicant for membership, because he has opposed any practice made an unlawful employment practice by this subchapter, or because he has made a charge, testified, assisted, or participated in any manner in an investigation, proceeding, or hearing under this subchapter.[98]

In general, the Civil Rights Act eliminates artificial, arbitrary and unnecessary barriers to employment in the form of invidious discrimination, unless there is a demonstrably reasonable measure of job performance (*Griggs v. Duke Power Co.*, 401 US 424 (1971)).[99] Title VII prohibits discrimination allowing for compensation, thus recognizing equal pay as a legal right (*American Federation of State, County and Municipal Employees v. Washington*, 770 F.2d. 1401 (1985)).[100] In terms of the burden of proof, the Plaintiff has the burden to show he belongs to a group, has applied for a job, was qualified for the job that the employer tried to fill but was rejected, and the employer continued to seek applicants (*McDonnell Douglas Corp. v. Green*, 411 U.S. 792 (1973)),[101] and then the Defendant, in rebutting a *prima facie* case, is required to show the absence of a discriminatory motive for his actions. However, this was later revised by the court, so that the Defendant is not required to show the absence, but must merely articulate a legitimate nondiscriminatory reason for the employee's rejection (*Board of Trustees of Keene State College v. Sweeney*, 439 US 24 (1978)).[102]

The Civil Rights Act is often used to fight discrimination in compensation, with a differentiation made between disparate treatment and disparate impact. Disparate treatment is concerned with direct or circumstantial discriminatory motives, which lack well-defined criteria (*Spaulding v. University of Washington*, 740 F.2d. 686 (1984)),[103] and involves intent or motive as an essential element of liability concerning the effects of a chosen policy, with awareness alone of adverse consequences on a group being insufficient (*American Federation of State, County and Municipal Employees v. Washington*, 770 F.2d. 1401 (1985)).[104] In a disparate treatment approach, the Plaintiff is required to show by a preponderance of the evidence the overt motive, and then the Defendant, in rebutting a *prima facie* case, must prove that it was nondiscriminatory either by the four exceptions, by necessity or by a bona fide occupational qualification. On the other hand, disparate impact is more than an inference of discriminatory impact of outwardly neutral employment practices and adversity (*Spaulding v. University of Washington*, 740 F.2d. 686 (1984)),[105] and does not need a profession of intent by the employer to discriminate, only a clearly delineated employment practice (*American Federation of State, County and Municipal Employees v. Washington*, 770 F.2d. 1401 (1985)).[106] In a disparate impact approach, the Plaintiff need only show the disproportionate impact, and then the Defendant, in rebutting a *prima facie* case, must show that it was nondiscriminatory.

Thus, the Civil Rights Act prohibits religious discrimination in employment, education and accommodation because of their religion in hiring, firing and other terms and conditions of employment. The Act also requires employers to reasonably accommodate the religious practices of an employee or prospective employee, unless to do so would create an undue hardship upon the employer, such as more than ordinary administrative costs or if changing a bona fide seniority system to accommodate one employee's religious practices denies another employee the job or shift preference guaranteed by the seniority system. Employers cannot schedule examinations or other selection activities in conflict with a current or prospective employee's religious needs, inquire about an applicant's future availability at certain times, maintain a restrictive dress code, or refuse to allow observance of a Sabbath or religious holiday, unless the employer can prove that not doing so would cause an undue hardship. Flexible scheduling, voluntary substitutions or swaps, job reassignments and lateral transfers are some of the many areas of accommodation of an employee's religious beliefs. Further, an employee whose religious practices prohibit payment of union dues to a labor organization cannot be required to pay the dues, but may pay an equal sum to a charitable organization.

Legislation has indeed made an impact on discrimination. However, while legislation has had a marked effect on some forms of direct discrimination, such as in advertising vacancies or in the process of selection for promotion; there is no clear evidence so far of a total shift in the attitude of employers and society to workers from religious minorities, since this is likely to be a long-term process.

Evidence shows that legislation can only help to change attitudes if it operates in conjunction with other policies to promote equal rights and educate employers and workers about their obligations and rights; experience has shown that changing hearts and minds on religious discrimination is far from easy, and that it is only through doing so that equal respect and treatment of all people will become possible.[107]

When an individual is required to engage in conduct violative of his religious beliefs and opinions, he can look to the First Amendment. The First Amendment guarantee of freedom of religion was adopted 'to curtail the power of Congress to interfere with the individual's freedom to believe, to worship, and to express himself in accordance with the dictates of his own conscience' (*Wallace v. Jaffree*, 472 U.S. 38 (1985)).[108] The two components of the freedom of religion guarantee under the Constitution are the Anti-Establishment Clause (*Everson v. Board of Education of Ewing*, 330 U.S. 1 (1947))[109] and the Free Exercise Clause (*Cantwell v. State of Connecticut*, 310 U.S. 296 (1940)).[110]

The First Amendment prohibits the making of laws 'respecting the establishment of religion', which is not simply a prohibition against a government-sponsored church or a demand of equal treatment of religions, but a broader prohibition against laws 'which aid one religion, aid all religions, or prefer one religion over another' (*Everson v. Board of Education of Ewing*, 330 U.S. 1 (1947)).[111] The Clause erects a 'wall of separation' between Church and State (*Reynolds v. United States*, 98 U.S. 145 (1878)).[112] In order to withstand an Establishment Clause challenge, a three-part test must be satisfied: (1) the law must have a secular legislative purpose; (2) the principal or primary effect of the law must neither advance nor inhibit religion; and (3) the law must not foster 'an excessive government entanglement with religion' (*Lemon v. Kurtzman*, 403 U.S. 602 (1971).[113]

In looking at the two-step approach, first, the Court determines if the law significantly burdens the free exercise of religion; then, it considers the extent to which the belief is sincerely held (*Thomas v. Review Board of the Indiana Employment Security Division*, 450 U.S. 707 (1981))[114] and the central importance of the practice or belief in the religion (*Wisconsin v. Yoder*, 406 U.S. 205 (1972)),[115] but it declines to consider the truth or falsity of the belief or doctrine (*United States v. Ballard*, 322 U.S. 78 (1944)[116] or choose between doctrinal viewpoints within a religion (*Thomas v. Review Board of the Indiana Employment Security Division*, 450 U.S. 707 (1981)).[117] Interestingly, in *Thomas v. Review Board of the Indiana Employment Security Decision,* 450 U.S. 707 (1981), the Supreme Court has held that it is not within the power of the judiciary to question a litigant's interpretation of their religious claim except where the claim 'is so bizarre, so clearly non-religious in motivation, as not to be entitled to protection under the Free Exercise Clause'.[118]

In *Lynch v. Donnelly*, 465 U.S. 668 (1984),[119] the municipality's erection of a Nativity scene as part of an annual Christmas display was permissible as any benefit to religion was 'indirect, remote and incidental'; 'government may celebrate Christmas in some manner and form, but not in a way that endorses

Christian doctrine'. Hence, in *County of Allegheny v. American Civil Liberties Union Greater Pittsburgh Chapter*, 492 U.S. 573 (1989),[120] a menorah display along with a Christmas tree and a sign celebrating liberty was permissible, because it was a recognition 'that both Christmas and Chanukah are part of the same winter-holiday season and is therefore a secular celebration of 'cultural diversity'.

In Title VII, the Civil Rights Act, Congress prohibited discrimination in employment but provided an exemption for religion, which does not violate the Establishment Clause because of a mere accommodation for religion. In terms of establishment of religion outside of schools, Sunday closing Laws have long been upheld. In *McGowan v. Maryland*, 366 U.S. 420 (1961),[121] it was found that such laws have a secular purpose and effect in promoting a common day of rest. However, in *Estate of Thornton v. Caldor, Inc.*, 472 U.S. 703 (1985),[122] a law affording an employee with an absolute unqualified right not to work on the Sabbath of their choice 'has a primary effect that impermissibly advances a particular religious practice' violative of the Establishment Clause, since 'the employer and others must adjust their affairs to the command of the State whenever the statute is invoked by an employee'.

In terms of the free exercise of religion, coercion of religious beliefs or conduct is the claim under the Free Exercise Clause. The 'freedom to hold religious beliefs and opinions is absolute' (*Braunfeld v. Brown*, 366 U.S. 599 (1961));[123] however, while to believe is absolute, the freedom to act pursuant to one's religion is not, and 'conduct remains subject to regulation for protection of society' (*Cantwell v. State of Connecticut*, 310 U.S. 296 (1940)).[124] In *Torcaso v. Watkins*, 367 U.S. 488 (1961),[125] a test oath requiring a profession in a belief in God for public employment was held violative of free exercise. In *West Virginia State Board of Education v. Barnette*, 319 U.S. 624 (1943),[126] a Jehovah Witness challenged a law requiring him to salute the flag, which he believed violated the Scriptures, and the Court declared that government may not prescribe what shall be orthodox in politics, nationalism, religion or other matters of opinion.

The Court has distinguished between direct and indirect burdens on religion, in that direct burdens are laws which make a religious practice unlawful while imposing an especially severe burden on freedom of religion. In *Braunfeld v. Brown*, 366 U.S. 599 (1961),[127] since the closing law imposed only an economic burden on Orthodox Jewish merchants who closed on Saturdays for religious reasons, the burden was indirect and constitutional. 'Unless the State may accomplish its purpose by means which do not impose such a burden', then granting an exemption to Sabbatarians could have undermined the State's religious-neutral purpose of promoting a uniform day of rest.

However, in *Sherbert v. Verner*, 374 U.S. 398 (1963),[128] the Court struck down the denial of State unemployment benefits to a Seventh Day Adventist for refusing to work on Saturdays, the Sabbath day of her faith; while the burden on her religion was indirect, the coercive effect of the law imposed a significant burden on her religious liberty as 'the ruling forces her to choose between following the precepts of her religion and forfeiting benefits on the one hand, and abandoning one of the precepts of her religion in order to accept work on the other'. The Government's imposition of such a choice could be justified only by showing a 'compelling state interest' and that 'no alternative form of regulation' would suffice. The two-step approach first measures the severity of the burden the law places on the individual's free exercise; if that burden is a significant one, then the Government must show that the law is narrowly tailored to achieve a compelling state interest. Therefore, the less burdensome alternatives or less restrictive means test will be applied. As such, an accommodation was not violative of establishment principles but an effort to maintain neutrality between Sunday and Saturday Sabbatarians.

Further, in *Thomas v. Review Board of the Indiana Employment Security Division*, 450 U.S. 707 (1981),[129] the Court struck down the denial of unemployment benefits to a Jehovah's Witness who quit his job producing armaments, because of a sincere belief that such work violated his religion, since the law coerced him in his religious beliefs, which constituted a substantial indirect burden in the free exercise of his religion. As such, the Court found that 'where the State conditions receipt of an important benefit upon conduct proscribed by a religious faith..., thereby putting substantial pressure on an adherent to modify his behavior and to violate his beliefs, a burden upon religion exists'. Further, in *Hobbie v. Unemployment Appeals Compensation Commission of Florida*, 480 U.S. 136 (1987),[130] the firing of a Seventh Day Adventist by her private employer for refusing to work on Friday evenings and Saturdays violated the Free Exercise Clause, since no compelling interest was served by this pressure on her religious beliefs.

While indirect burdens on religion are sufficient to invoke strict scrutiny review, laws which compel an individual 'to perform acts undeniably at odds with fundamental tenets of their religious beliefs' amounting to direct burdens are especially coercive or religious liberty. In *Wisconsin v. Yoder*, 406 U.S. 205 (1972),[131] the Court invalidated the application of a State law requiring compulsory school attendance until age 16 to Amish children, since the Amish refused to send their children to public schools beyond the eighth grade based on their 'deep religious convictions' about the way to live. The Court found that while 'only those interests of the highest order and those not otherwise served can overbalance legitimate claims to the free exercise of religion', the State's interests in promoting self-reliant and self-sufficient participants in society were not undermined by an exemption for the Amish.

In *Lyng v. Northwest Indian Cemetery Protection Association*, 485 U.S. 439 (1988),[132] when the Federal Government allowed a timber harvesting and road construction in a national forest, which had been used for religious purposes by Indian tribes, a free exercise challenge of the Government action was rejected, as the effect was incidental in nature, and even though the consequences of the government action might destroy the religious practice, the 'indirect coercion or penalties' on free exercise did not invoke the use of a strict scrutiny standard. Laws which are religiously neutral are presumptively valid, and a free exercise claim does not relieve an individual from compliance with a generally applicable religiously neutral law, which is otherwise valid, as incidental burdens on the free exercise of religion would be insufficient to trigger the strict scrutiny standard. In *Goldman v. Weinberger*, 475 U.S. 503 (1986),[133] the reasonable and even-handed application of the Air Force dress codes preventing an Orthodox Jew from wearing a yarmulke as required by his religion was held constitutional, with a 'far more deferential' standard level of review in military cases.

However, in the Religious Freedom Restoration Act 1993 (RFRA), Congress sought to restore the use of the compelling government interest test as set forth in *Sherbert v. Verner*, 374 U.S. 398 (1963)[134] and *Wisconsin v. Yoder*, 406 U.S. 205 (1972).[135] The RFRA provides that the Government is precluded from imposing substantial burdens on the free exercise of religion even if they result from laws of general applicability, unless such laws further a compelling government interest and are the least restrictive means of accomplishing that interest.

The law provides an exemption from military service for persons who by reason of their 'religious training and belief are conscientiously opposed to participation of wars of any form'.[136] In *United States v. Seeger,* 380 U.S. 163 (1965), the Supreme Court defined religious training and belief as 'an individual's belief in relation to a 'Supreme Being' involving duties superior to those arising from any human relation, but [not including] essentially political, sociological or philosophical views or a merely personal moral code'; the 'test of belief in a relation to a Supreme Being' is whether a given belief that is sincere and meaningful occupies a place in the life of its possessor parallel to that filled by the orthodox belief in God of one who clearly qualifies for the exemption. Where such beliefs have parallel positions in the lives of their respective holders [the Supreme Court] cannot say that one is 'in a relation to a Supreme Being' and the other is not.'[137]

In terms of what is 'religion', non-theistic beliefs can qualify for constitutional protection (*Torcaso v. Watkins*, 367 U.S. 488 (1961)).[138] In *Welsh v. United States*, 398 U.S. 333 (1970),[139] conscientious objector status was extended to those having strong moral or public policy objections. However, in *Gillette v. United States*, 401 U.S. 437 (1971),[140] it was rejected for those objecting to a particular war. In *Frazee v. Illinois Department of Employment Security*, 489 U.S. 829 (1989),[141] the Court held that a free exercise claim will be upheld even where the claimant is not a member of an organized religion or any particular sect, since all that is required is a 'sincerely held' religious belief'.

Conclusion

The keys to the future for equal rights and religious tolerance in North America are the implementation and development of the law, the deepening in understanding of specific legal issues relating to human rights in the courts, and the raising of the level of awareness of legal rights and obligations, in the pursuit of *Heaven Forbid*. Appropriate also for religious tolerance, Martin Luther King Jr. in his struggle for civil rights stated:

I have a dream that one day every valley shall be exalted, every hill and mountain shall be made plain, and the crooked places shall be made straight and the glory of the Lord will be revealed and all flesh shall see it together. This is our hope. And when we allow freedom to ring, when we let it ring from every village and hamlet, from every state and city, we will be able to join hands and to sing in the words of the old Negro spiritual, 'Free at last, free at last; thank God Almighty, we are free at last'.[142]

Notes

1. Mandel, Michael, *The Charter of Rights and the Legalization of Politics in Canada*, Wall & Thompson, Toronto, 1989, p. 4.
2. Canadian Constitution, Canada.
3. Canadian Constitution, the Canadian Charter of Rights and Freedoms, Canada, at Section 52(1).
4. Canadian Constitution, Canada, at Section 32.
5. *Ibid.*, at Section 2.
6. *Ibid.*, at Section 27.
7. Canadian Constitution, Canada, at Section 35.
8. Canadian Constitution, the Canadian Charter of Rights and Freedoms, Canada, at Section 15.
9. *Ibid.*, at Section 28.
10. *Ibid.*, at Section 33.
11. *Ibid.*, at Section 1.
12. *Regina v. Oakes*, [1986] 1 SCR 103.
13. Canadian Bill of Rights, Canada, at Section 1.
14. Canadian Human Rights Act, Canada, at Section 2.
15. *Ibid.*, at Section 3(1).
16. *Ibid.*, at Section 7.
17. *Ibid.*, at Section 10.
18. *Ibid.*, at Section 11.
19. *Ibid.*, at Section 15(1).
20. Canadian Human Rights Act, Canada, at Section 16.
21. Labor Canada, *Equal Pay for Work of Equal Value*, Ottawa, 1986, p. 21.
22. *Basi v. Canadian National Railway* (1984), 9 CHRR 4. D/5029, 5037 (CHR Tribunal).
23. *Shakes v. Rex Pak Ltd.* (1982), 3 CHRR D/1001, 1002.
24. *Blake v. Ministry of Correctional Services and Mimico Correctional Institute* (1984), 5 CHRR D/2417 (Ontario).
25. *Ontario Human Rights Commission v. Simpsons-Sears Ltd.*, [1985] SCR 536, 547.
26. Canada Employment Equity Act, Canada, at Section 2.
27. *Ibid.*, at Section 5.
28. *Ibid.*, at Section 6.
29. *Ibid.*, at Section 10.
30. *Ibid.*, at Article 29.

31 Federal Task Force on Disability Issues, *Equal Citizenship for Canadians with Disabilities: The Will to Act*, 1996.
32 Hatfield, Robert, Duty to Accommodate, *Just Labour*, vol. 5 (Winter 2005).
33 *Meiorin: British Columbia (Public Service Employee Relations Commission) (BCPSERC) v. The British Columbia Government and Service Employees Union (BCGSEU)* [1999], 35 C.H.R.R. D/257 (S.C.C.).
34 *Grismer: Terry Grismer (Estate) v. The British Columbia Superintendent of Motor Vehicles et al.* [1999] 3 S.C.R. 868.
35 *Meiorin: British Columbia (Public Service Employee Relations Commission) (BCPSERC) v. The British Columbia Government and Service Employees Union (BCGSEU)* [1999], 35 C.H.R.R. D/257 (S.C.C.).
36 *Ibid.*
37 *Central Alberta Dairy Pool v. Alberta (Human Rights Commission)* [1990] 2 S.C.R. 489.
38 *Ibid.*
39 *O'Malley: Ontario (Human Rights Commission) v. Simpson-Sears Ltd.* [1985] 2 S.C.R. 536.
40 *Ibid.*
41 *Andrews v. Law Society of British Columbia* 10 C.H.R.R. D/5719 at D/5742.
42 *Central Okanagan School District No. 23 v. Renaud* (1992), 16 CHRR D/425.
43 *Ibid.*, at D/436 - D/437.
44 *CUPW v. Canada Post Corporation: CUPW v. Canada Post Corporation* [2001] B.C.J. No. 680 (C.A.).
45 *Ibid.*
46 *Gohm v. Domtar Inc. and OPEIU, Local 267* [1990], 12 C.H.R.R. D/161 (Ont. Bd. Inq.); affirmed [1992], 89 D.L.R. (4th) 305 (Ont. Div. Ct.).
47 *M.A.B.; W.A.T. and A.Y.T. v. Canada*, Communication No. 570/1993, Inadmissibility Decision of April 8 1994, cited in *Article 18-Freedom of Religion and Belief* (Human Rights and Equal Opportunities Commission, 1998), at p. 11.
48 *Ibid.*
49 Human Resources and Social Development Canada.
50 Constitución Política de los Estados Unidos Mexicanos, Mexico.
51 *Ibid.*, at Article 1.
52 *Ibid.*, at Article 123(7).
53 Ley Federal de Trabajo, Mexico, at Articles 3 and 164.
54 *Ibid.*, at Article 1.
55 *Ibid.*, at Article 86.
56 *Ibid.*, at Articles 50 and 52.
57 Ley del Seguro Social, Mexico, at Article 36.
58 Pew Forum on Religion and Public Life, 2008.
59 *Ibid.*
60 United States Declaration of Independence, United States.
61 Federalist Papers, United States.
62 Coleman, Frank, *Hobbes and America*, University of Toronto, Toronto, 1977, p. 3.

63 United States Constitution, United States, at Amendment I.
64 *Ibid.*, at Amendment V.
65 *Ibid.*, at Amendment XIV.
66 Magna Carta, Great Britain.
67 United States Constitution, United States, at Amendment XIII.
68 *Ibid.*, at Amendment XIX.
69 *Ibid.*, at Article VI.
70 North, Arthur, *The Supreme Court, Judicial Process and Judicial Politics*, Appleton Century Crofts, New York, 1964, p. 2.
71 *McCullough v. Maryland*, 4 Wheaton 415 (1819).
72 United States Constitution, United States, at Article 6(2).
73 *Marbury v. Madison*, 1 Cranch 137 (1803).
74 North, Arthur, *The Supreme Court, Judicial Process and Judicial Politics*, Appleton Century Crofts, New York, 1964, p. 8.
75 Cox, Archibald, *The Role of the Supreme Court in American Government*, Oxford University Press, New York, 1976, p. 117.
76 Cox, Archibald, *Civil Rights, The Constitution and the Court*, Harvard University Press, Cambridge, 1967, p. 21.
77 *Davis v. Passman*, 442 US 228 (1979).
78 Equal Pay Act, United States.
79 *Ibid.*, at Section 16.
80 *Brennan v. City Stores*, 479 F.2d. 235 (1973).
81 *Murphy v. Miller Brewer Co.*, 307 F.Supp. 829 (1969).
82 *Corning Glass Works v. Brennan*, 417 US 188 (1974).
83 *American Nurses' Association v. State of Illinois*, 783 F.2d. 716 (1986).
84 *Spaulding v. University of Washington*, 740 F.2d. 686 (1984).
85 Civil Rights Act, United States, at Section 701(j).
86 *Ibid.*, Section 703(a).
87 *Ibid.*, at Section 703(b).
88 *Ibid.*, at Section 703(c).
89 *Ibid.*, at Section 703(d).
90 *Ibid.*, at Section 702(a).
91 *Ibid.*, at Section 703(e).
92 *Ibid.*, at Section 703(h).
93 *Ibid.* at Section 703(j).
94 *Ibid.*, at Section 704(b).
95 *Ibid.*, at Section 703(k).
96 *Ibid.*, at Section 703(m).
97 *Ibid.*, at Section 706(g).
98 *Ibid.*, at Section 704(a).
99 *Griggs v. Duke Power Co.*, 401 US 424 (1971).
100 *American Federation of State, County and Municipal Employees v. Washington*, 770 F.2d. 1401 (1985).
101 *McDonnell Douglas Corp. v. Green*, 411 US 792 (1973).

102 *Board of Trustees of Keene State College v. Sweeney*, 439 US 24 (1978).
103 *Spaulding v. University of Washington*, 740 F.2d. 686 (1984).
104 *American Federation of State, County and Municipal Employees v. Washington*, 770 F.2d. 1401 (1985).
105 *Spaulding v. University of Washington*, 740 F.2d. 686 (1984).
106 *American Federation of State, County and Municipal Employees v. Washington*, 770 F.2d. 1401 (1985).
107 Hornstein, Zmira, *Outlawing Age Discrimination: Foreign Lessons, UK Choices*, The Policy Press.
108 *Wallace v. Jaffree*, 472 U.S. 38 (1985).
109 *Everson v. Board of Education of Ewing*, 330 U.S. 1 (1947).
110 *Cantwell v. State of Connecticut*, 310 U.S. 296 (1940).
111 *Everson v. Board of Education of Ewing*, 330 U.S. 1 (1947).
112 *Reynolds v. United States*, 98 U.S. 145 (1878).
113 *Lemon v. Kurtzman*, 403 U.S. 602 (1971).
114 *Thomas v. Review Board of the Indiana Employment Security Division*, 450 U.S. 707 (1981).
115 *Wisconsin v. Yoder*, 406 U.S. 205 (1972).
116 *United States v. Ballard*, 322 U.S. 78 (1944).
117 *Thomas v. Review Board of the Indiana Employment Security Division*, 450 U.S. 707 (1981).
118 *Ibid.*
119 *Lynch v. Donnelly*, 465 U.S. 668 (1984).
120 *County of Allegheny v. American Civil Liberties Union Greater Pittsburgh Chapter*, 492 U.S. 573 (1989).
121 *McGowan v. Maryland*, 366 U.S. 420 (1961).
122 *Estate of Thornton v. Caldor, Inc.*, 472 U.S. 703 (1985).
123 *Braunfeld v. Brown*, 366 U.S. 599 (1961).
124 *Cantwell v. State of Connecticut*, 310 U.S. 296 (1940).
125 *Torcaso v. Watkins*, 367 U.S. 488 (1961).
126 *West Virginia State Board of Education v. Barnette*, 319 U.S. 624 (1943).
127 *Braunfeld v. Brown*, 366 U.S. 599 (1961).
128 *Sherbert v. Verner*, 374 U.S. 398 (1963).
129 *Thomas v. Review Board of the Indiana Employment Security Division*, 450 U.S. 707 (1981).
130 *Hobbie v. Unemployment Appeals Compensation Commission of Florida*, 480 U.S. 136 (1987).
131 *Wisconsin v. Yoder*, 406 U.S. 205 (1972).
132 *Lyng v. Northwest Indian Cemetery Protection Association*, 485 U.S. 439 (1988).
133 *Goldman v. Weinberger*, 475 U.S. 503 (1986).
134 *Sherbert v. Verner*, 374 U.S. 398 (1963).
135 *Wisconsin v. Yoder*, 406 U.S. 205 (1972).
136 Universal Military Training and Armed Services Act, United States, 50 USC (1958 ed.), s.456(j).

137 *United States v. Seeger* 380 US 163 at 166.
138 *Torcaso v. Watkins*, 367 U.S. 488 (1961).
139 *Welsh v. United States*, 398 U.S. 333 (1970).
140 *Gillette v. United States*, 401 U.S. 437 (1971).
141 *Frazee v. Illinois Department of Employment Security*, 489 U.S. 829 (1989).
142 Martin Luther King Jr., March on Washington, 1963.

References

American Federation of State, County and Municipal Employees v. Washington, 770 F.2d. 1401 (1985).
American Nurses Association v. State of Illinois, 783 F.2d. 716 (1985).
Basi v. Canadian National Railway (1984), 9 CHRR 4. D/5029 (CHRTribunal).
Blake v. Ministry of Correctional Services and Mimico Correctional Institute (1984), 5 CHRR D/2417 (Ontario).
Board of Trustees of Keene State College v. Sweeney, 439 US 24 (1978).
Braunfeld v. Brown, 366 U.S. 599 (1961).
Brennan v. City Stores, 479 F.2d. 235 (1973).
British North America Act, Canada, 1867.
Canada Employment Equity Act, Canada, 1995.
Canadian Bill of Rights, Canada, 1960.
Canadian Human Rights Act, Canada, 1978.
Canadian Constitution, Canada, 1982.
Canadian Constitution, Canadian Charter of Rights and Freedoms, Canada, 1982.
Cantwell v. State of Connecticut, 310 U.S. 296 (1940).
Civil Rights Act, United States, 1964.
Coleman, Frank (1977), *Hobbes and America*, University of Toronto, Toronto.
Constitución Política de los Estados Unidos Mexicanos, Mexico.
Corning Glass Works v. Brennan, 417 US 188 (1974).
County of Allegheny v. American Civil Liberties Union Greater Pittsburgh Chapter, 492 U.S. 573 (1989).
Cox, Archibald (1967), *Civil Rights, The Constitution and the Court*, Harvard University Press, Cambridge.
Cox, Archibald (1976), *The Role of the Supreme Court in American Government*, New York: Oxford University Press, New York.
Davis v. Passman, 442 US 228 (1979).
Declaration of Independence, United States, 1776.
Ely, J. (1980), *Democracy and Distrust*, Harvard University Press, Cambridge.
Equal Pay Act, United States, 1963.
Estate of Thornton v. Caldor, Inc., 472 U.S. 703 (1985).
Everson v. Board of Education of Ewing, 330 U.S. 1 (1947).
Federalist Papers, United States, 1787-1788.

Federal Task Force on Disability Issues, *Equal Citizenship for Canadians with Disabilities: The Will to Act*, 1996.
Frazee v. Illinois Department of Employment Security, 489 U.S. 829 (1989).
Gillette v. United States, 401 U.S. 437 (1971).
Goldman v. Weinberger, 475 U.S. 503 (1986).
Grant, Hugh M.K. and Gretta Wong Grant, Gretta, *Age Discrimination and the Employment Rights of Elderly Canadian Immigrants*, 2002.
Griggs v. Duke Power Co., 401 US 424 (1971).
Higher Education Amendments, United States, 1998.
Hobbie v. Unemployment Appeals Compensation Commission of Florida, 480 U.S. 136 (1987).
Hornstein, Zmira, *Outlawing Age Discrimination: Foreign Lessons, UK Choices*, The Policy Press.
Human Resources and Social Development Canada.
Kimel v. Florida Board of Regents, 528 U.S. 62 (2000).
King Jr., Martin Luther (1963), *March on Washington*.
Labor Canada (1986), *Equal Pay for Work of Equal Value*, Ottawa.
Lemon v. Kurtzman, 403 U.S. 602 (1971).
Ley del Seguro Social, Mexico.
Ley Federal de Trabajo, Mexico.
Lynch v. Donnelly, 465 U.S. 668 (1984).
Lyng v. Northwest Indian Cemetery Protection Association, 485 U.S. 439 (1988).
M.A.B.; W.A.T. and A.Y.T. v. Canada, Communication No. 570/1993, Inadmissibility Decision of April 8 1994, cited in *Article 18-Freedom of Religion and Belief*, (Human Rights and Equal Opportunities Commission, 1998), at p. 11.
Magna Carta, Great Britain, 1215.
Mandel, Michael (1989), *The Charter of Rights and the Legalization of Politics in Canada*, Wall & Thompson, Toronto.
Marbury v. Madison, 1 Cranch 137 (1803).
McCullough v. Maryland, 4 Wheaton 415 (1819).
McDonnell Douglas Corp. v. Green, 411 US 792 (1973).
McGowan v. Maryland, 366 U.S. 420 (1961).
Murphy v. Miller Brewer Co., 307 F.Supp. 829 (1969).
North, Arthur (1964), *The Supreme Court, Judicial Process and Judicial Politics*, Appleton Century Crofts, New York.
Ontario Human Rights Commission v. Simpsons-Sears Ltd. [1985] SCR 536.
Pew Forum on Religion and Public Life, 2008.
Public Employees Retirement System of Ohio v. Betts, 492 U.S. 158 (1989).
Regina v. Oakes, [1986] 1 S.C.R. 103.
Reynolds v. United States, 98 U.S. 145 (1878).
Shakes v. Rex Pak Ltd. (1982), 3 CHRR D/1001.
Sherbert v. Verner, 374 U.S. 398 (1963).
Spaulding v. University of Washington, 740 F.2d. 686 (1984).

Thomas v. Review Board of the Indiana Employment Security Division, 450 U.S. 7 (1981).
Torcaso v. Watkins, 367 U.S. 488 (1961).
United States Constitution, United States, 1776.
United States v. Ballard, 322 U.S. 78 (1944).
United States v. Seeger, 380 U.S. 163 (1965).
Universal Military Training and Armed Services Act, United States, 50 USC (1958 ed.), s.456(j).
Wallace v. Jaffree, 472 U.S. 38 (1985).
Welsh v. United States, 398 U.S. 333 (1970).
West Virginia State Board of Education v. Barnette, 319 U.S. 624 (1943).
Wisconsin v. Yoder, 406 U.S. 205 (1972).

Chapter 7

Heaven Forbid in the North American Free Trade Agreement

Introduction

In the quest for religious tolerance in *Heaven Forbid*, this chapter will examine efforts against religious discrimination in the area of the North American Free Trade Agreement (NAFTA), which at the time was the largest economic and legal undertaking ever attempted, having an important impact on those who are religious specifically and the labor force generally. It will look at NAFTA from its inception, examining first its benefits and then its drawbacks. It will also look at the North American Agreement on Labor Cooperation (NAALC) and the Free Trade Area of the Americas (FTAA), as well as legislation of the Americas, namely the American Declaration of the Rights and Duties of Man, the American Convention on Human Rights, the Statute of the Inter-American Court on Human Rights, and the Inter-American Democratic Charter.

Toward the North American Free Trade Agreement (NAFTA)

An economic association for 'free trade' was first brought about in North America in 1854. Prior to this, however, there were several developments in the relationship between the United States and British North America, what was to become Canada. The War of 1812 brought an end to the fear of American annexation of Canada, with a new view of commercial and economic rivalry between the two countries. The Canadian national sentiment favored trade with the United States through transportation via the railways and the waterways. With the industrial movement in the 1850s came the Grand Trunk Railway system, with an investment of $100 million in transportation and communication.[1] The construction of canals and railways were a move toward the avoidance of continental integration with the United States. However, the United States, with these developments, was not seen as the enemy but a concurrent competitor, with Canada furnishing natural resources. It was more economical for the United States to pass exports by Montreal through the St. Lawrence seaway in order to lower transportation costs, and to assist them, the British, who controlled Canada at the time, would exempt the American traders from duties, treating them like Canadians. Among the market terminals of North America, Mississippi, the Hudson, New Orleans, New York and Montreal, the latter two were rivals, with New York prevailing. North American seaboard centers participated actively in the prosperity brought about by commercialism.

The Elgin-Marcy Reciprocity Treaty of 1854 was the first major trade pact between the United States and Canada. Reciprocity was an attempt to create, in North America, a single market area covering several distinct political jurisdictions, where specified types of products were freely exchanged for a partial and limited economic union between British North America and the United States.[2] It was thought to be the only feasible alternative to annexation. However, the American Civil War influenced the economic development of British North America, with new markets in the United States opening for Canadian exports. At the end of the war, the removal of restraints on the expansion of American settlement west of the Mississippi jeopardized the security of the Canadian West and hastened Confederation.[3] However, the waterways were a uniting force. The businessmen from Upper Canada, what was to become the Canadian Province of Ontario, were the first to seize the idea of reciprocity. Nevertheless, immediate economic and political union with the United States would have sacrificed for Canada valued institutions, national identity and loyalty to Britain. In the United States, the South with its plantations wanted low tariffs to lower prices of imported goods and to reduce the costs of production for exports of raw materials. On the other hand, the North, with its small farms and factories, was protectionist with little enthusiasm for reciprocity. It was seen as simply a concession for the inclusion of fisheries, the immediate and urgent objective.

Thus, the Treaty was abrogated by the United States on 17 March 1866, due to several antagonizing factors for the United States, namely British support for the Confederacy during the Civil War, new Canadian tariffs, the disastrous effects on timber- and grain-growing regions of the United States, the resentment by farming and lumber interests to Canadian competition, the jealousy by shipping and forwarding interests in Buffalo and Philadelphia of the St. Lawrence Route and of the Grand Trunk Railway system with the Victoria Bridge completion in Montreal in 1860 furthering competition, and the manufacturing interests blaming Canadian tariffs for the decline of certain exports.[4] While Canada's policy in economic relations was to favor east-west relations, the natural tendencies were the opposite, north-south. Shortly after the death of the Reciprocity Treaty until the advent of the 1911 'free trade' election in Canada, free trade with the United States had been the central issue in Canadian politics. Canadian Prime Minister Laurier was the first continentalist Prime Minister to appreciate that Canada shares North America with the United States, which shapes the national destiny.

With the 1911 Free Trade Agreement, Canada built up its own manufacturing protection tariff. At the time, there was the sentiment in Canada of 'no truck or trade with the Yankees'.[5] However, with the exception of Britain, Canada was the chief trading partner of the United States, and in 1910 alone, Canada bought $242 million and sold $97 million to the United States.[6] American President Taft negotiated for full-scale reciprocity for better trade relations between the United States and Canada, since common interests called for special arrangements, and

Canadians and Americans were reminded that there were 3000 miles of joint border between the two countries. The 1911 Free Trade Agreement was similar to the 1854 pact, but was not a treaty, and thus did not require the two-thirds approval of the US Senate. Most American tariffs on manufacturing goods were reduced, while most Canadian manufacturing tariffs remained. It was passed by Congress and signed by US President Taft. However, Canadian Prime Minister Borden, who defeated Prime Minister Laurier in 1911, opposed the trade legislation and did not put the reciprocity agreement to a vote, with the United States rescinding its vote eight years later.

Other agreements were entered into over the years, one of which was the General Agreement on Tariffs and Trade (GATT) 1947, whose purpose was to promote global trade between members through a reduction in tariffs. Canada wished for trade on a liberalized basis, the first Article of GATT, and same treatment. GATT provided for an impressive reduction of tariffs, with some even impeding economic efficiency, production, competition and growth. It permitted the United States and Canada to enter into free trade, with an agreement to remove customs duties and other restrictions on substantially all bilateral trade.[7] Over the last years of GATT and the advent of the World Trade Organization (WTO), Canadian exports multiplied ten times, the national wealth more than tripled and the number of jobs doubled.[8] On the other hand, unemployment had also risen over this period, which raises important questions about the benefits of free trade. Wartime demands required greater cooperation on a continental basis, with Canada and Mexico being prime sources of raw materials for American factories. Private negotiations on free trade once again took place in 1947 between American President Truman and Canadian Prime Minister King, in an era of the Marshall Plan, and of US economic assistance to Western Europe and Japan post-World War II. King approved the agreement in October 1947, but it was later vetoed in May 1948, because he feared the Canadian public would label it continentalist and anti-British.[9]

Overall, by examining the years leading to the advent of the Free Trade Agreement of the 1980s, we can observe a number of characteristics of the trade relationship between the two countries are notable: (1) Canada has been the initiator in free trade on almost all the occasions; (2) the United States has been largely indifferent except for President Taft in 1911; (3) in the two most important negotiations of the twentieth century, 1911 and 1947, Canada had second thoughts and put an end to the agreement; (4) the United States has been a formidable obstacle to closer economic ties between the two nations; (5) the 1911 and 1947 deals provided for more US concessions; (6) statements made by the United States were cannon fodder for groups in Canada which were opposed to annexation; (7) Canadian opponents say that economic costs to free trade outweigh economic benefits, and react on an emotional, loyal, national, love of country level, branding those in favor as stooges of American financial interests; (8) while there is more emphasis today on business, commercial and economic issues, Canada has cultural, regional economic development, social welfare and sovereignty concerns; and (9) when times are tough, Canada wants improved access to United States' markets while the United States turns inward toward protectionism.[10]

There is a regional aspect to the overall economic evolution of the North American continent. Canada's industrial development has been North American, with its development based on its natural resources, and its expansion characterized by large-scale monopolistic industries. Over time, Canada's dealings with Britain and the United States changed. Canada once had an autonomous relationship with Britain, producing an un-American sentiment. Britain use to be the major investor in Canada. However, over the years, the United States has replaced it. Canada went from dependence on Britain to dependence on the United States, thus producing a foreign-controlled economy. In addition, the nature of foreign investment had changed, since the British invested indirectly through obligations and finance, while the Americans invested directly, usually as proprietors funding production. Tariffs and natural resources attracted US enterprises, and Canada benefited from their capital, technological advancement and mass production. The United States invested $168 billion in 1900 and $881 billion in 1914. The Canadian policy, interestingly, was to increase tariffs and oblige US companies wishing to do business to build factories in Canada. Therefore, the United States penetrated the Canadian economy by installing branch plants for American-made products. By 1932, the United States had dominated the industrial sector, accounting for 82 percent of car production, 68 percent of electricity, one third of pulp and paper, and was solidly ahead in petroleum, pharmaceuticals, rubber, machinery and non-metallic minerals. Of the US enterprises in Canada, 36 percent of them were established in the period between 1920 to 1929. Today, Canada sends more than three-quarters of all its exports to the United States, accounting for 25 percent of its annual gross national product.[11]

The policy process resulted in the overwhelming trade dependence of Canada on the United States over the years. American policies are destined to affect the policies of Canada and North America as a whole. Canada is carried into the whirlpool of common points of view, to the advantage of the United States, and its own point of view is easily overwhelmed. Approaches should be adopted by which cultural traits of civilization might persist, with the least possible depreciation of the national sensibility of Canadians upon the US. Canada's trade pattern from the outset was based on the importing of manufactured goods in return for the exporting of staples to more advanced industrialized economies as the engine of growth of the Canadian economy.[12] The commercial rather than industrial bias of the Canadian capitalist class, along with dependent branch plant industrialization, flowed from the unequal alliance with American foreign ownership and capital. Canada was within the tight embrace of the American empire, and occupied whatever room was left open by US capital, becoming the exemplary client State. Today, the United States takes up 70 percent of Canada's total exports, and Canada takes in over 20 percent of United States' exports, which has a direct investment of roughly $20 billion.[13] It is not a zero sum gain with one benefiting at the expense of the other. Canada's prosperity depends on trade with other countries, with one third of its jobs and one quarter of its wealth tied to international trade.[14] From the outset, Canada was torn between republicanism and conservatism, trying to forge a national identity. Canada has wished to be more independent in its foreign policy, while at the same time, it has had to guard against the departure of Canadian firms going south in search of cheaper labor and less regulation.

Free trade continentalism, according to its advocates, involves: (1) tariff liberalization; (2) a high volume of trade with the United States; (3) meager diversification; (4) some protectionism by the United States; (5) restructuring of the Canadian economy for a more competitive industrial society; and 6) transborder transregionalism between Provinces and States. Continentalism is a process of microregional (subcontinental) integration, which is transnational (multinational corporations, unions, economic elites) and transgovernmental (direct contacts between two central bureaucracies and relations between Provinces and States), with closer Canada United States transactional ties (diplomatic, administrative, commercial, cultural) and structural interpenetration (economic).[15] Thus, Canada and the United States are somewhat similar as societies with transnational and transgovernmental relationships, attitudes and values, strong social factors and a deep-rooted structural economic interpenetration, in a widespread integration pattern. Canada is strategically situated, with its border and large cities close to US development centers.

While the free trade zone has eliminated trade barriers as to goods. However, the movement of capital in production has caused negative integration generating disturbances and distortions in the economy. This occurs especially if there is asymmetry within the society, causing imbalances, both regionally and between partners in interactions. The freeing of circulation of goods creates initial imbalances and economic distortions. Before World War II, Canada's prosperity depended on resource industries, which required a high cost in order to protect the manufacturing sector serving the home market. However, in the 1980s, the prosperity of resource-based industries was seriously hurt by international development in the areas of new sources of supply and man-made substitutes for natural materials.[16] Export- and service-related products depended on hard pressed resource-based industries, and this created uncertainties in business and job dislocations.[17] Textile and clothing industries are vulnerable in trade liberalization. The clothing industry would be hard-pressed in lowering prices, except for high volume segments that are successful when moving into particular niches for export. Canada has specialized and expanded its primary and manufacturing sectors, which the proponents of free trade argue has afforded a net benefit through access to the vital US market that is less restrictive and more secure. However, free trade advocates argue that it is important to secure continued access to the United States' market and to work against protectionism, for benefits to producers in sales and to consumers in prices.[18]

Overall, greater specialization in North America brings greater international competition, encouraging more rapid diffusion of new technology, new management and organizational production. The tertiary service industries are more sharply differentiated among countries by the varied regulatory environments. In the goods-producing industries, tariffs or quotas have been the main barrier. The service industry has subtle impediments, with discrimination being a barrier because of immigration labor laws, which are most evident today with illegal immigration at an all time high. National treatment calls for no regulatory distinction between foreign and domestic firms, which is good if there are similar industries for reciprocity and market access.[19] These laws restrict one country's firms transferring staff to the other country. Trade in services encompasses a large number of areas, having different characteristics of trade and efforts for international rule-making.

Considering these factors, sectoral trade discussions in 1983 later gave way to a comprehensive free trade approach in 1985. US President Reagan and Canadian Prime Minister Mulroney launched an initiative for a bilateral trade agreement, with its goal to remove all or most remaining barriers to cross-border trade in goods and services, and to create an enlarged body of agreed rules to govern trade, which produced the 1989 Canada United States Free Trade Agreement (FTA). President Reagan called the document, signed on 2 January 1988, the most important bilateral trade negotiation ever undertaken by the United States. It was horizontal, not sectoral, for market access and called for mutual restraint on unilateral commercial policies. It was believed that there would be a direct link between productivity and jobs,[20] affording a longer cycle of production, investment and specialization. This Free Trade Agreement was the biggest trade agreement ever reached between two countries, in excess of $200 billion in trade of goods and services.[21] Canada exports more per citizen than any counterpart in any other industrial power. Thirty percent of its national income is generated by exports with more than three million jobs depending on these exports. The United States absorbs 80 percent of Canada's exports, in a southward flow,[22] has an economy ten times bigger than Canada's, affording the latter greater access to opportunities. The relationship encourages lower-cost production in factories, and more specialized and efficient industries, thereby strengthening the capacity to compete in the global market. The goal is to generate growth and production, in order to increase the standard of living for challenging and rewarding careers. The United States, thereby, consolidates access to the biggest export market.

North American Free Trade Agreement (NAFTA)

In 1991, Canada, the United States and Mexico began negotiations for the North American Free Trade Agreement (NAFTA). The free trade agenda shifted from a sectoral approach to a comprehensive accord among the three countries, because of a difficulty in matching sectors and in accommodating regional concerns. The 1989 Canada United States Free Trade Agreement laid the foundation for NAFTA, which secured Canada's economic relationship with the United States.

Prior to NAFTA coming into effect on 1 January 1994, trade between the United States and Canada had never been larger and was growing faster than the rest of the economy. In addition, the flow of trade and investment among the United States, Canada and Mexico was $500 billion per year. Mexico has a rapidly growing market of over 85 million people, which historically was hard to penetrate because of strict Mexican barriers to trade. Before NAFTA, Mexico was restrictive on foreign investment. However, with NAFTA, Mexican tariffs are phased out over time. Mexico's border is aligned with the United States and its coastline faces Europe and Asia. It has a key global strategic advantage with its unique geographic position, and is considered the gateway to Latin America, being ranked twelfth in area among the world's nations.[23] Regulations give legal security to market transactions, protect consumers and the environment, and safeguard intellectual property rights. Free trade promotes competition and provides adequate incentives for private decision-making in a free market. However, the regulatory environment must ensure the rules of the game are clear and uniformly applied, subject to monitoring.

NAFTA was the biggest trade agreement ever signed at the time, covering 360 million consumers and far-reaching to remove all tariffs and liberalize non-tariff barriers to trade. It regulates trade in services, liberalizes investment, promotes specialization and implements a mechanism for a binding resolution to disputes, which is unprecedented in free trade. The objectives of NAFTA are the removal of tariff and non-tariff barriers for goods and services, the neutralization of government policies, practices and procedures, and a consistency with the GATT agreement to cover all trade.[24] The long-term goals of free trade are the improvement of real income wages and production, an increase in the number of jobs, a reduction of protectionism, a decrease in competitive pressures from developing and newly industrialized countries, and the mitigation of pressures due to global imbalances.[25]

The United States had several objectives of its own, namely the elimination of tariffs, the reduction of non-tariff barriers, the development of rules governing trade in services, trucking and insurance, the improvement of protection to intellectual property, greater discipline over subsidies, and an open and secure environment for foreign investment. Canada had several goals of its own, as well, namely the improved access to the United States and Mexico for goods and services, the strengthening of the initial Canada United States Free Trade Agreement, and the guarantee of its position as a prime location for investors to serve all the North American Continent. Canada hoped that NAFTA would supply it with a sharper edge for international competitiveness, by widening trade horizons and providing a bigger stage on which to demonstrate and prove its economic expertize and leadership.

NAFTA provided that tariffs would be removed within 10 years in the traditional sectors, accounting for half of the trade, and removed either immediately, in five years or exceptionally in 20 years for the remainder, moving toward a harmonized system of tariff nomenclature. It has quantitative restrictions, which build on GATT, and has a sectoral perspective as to agriculture, foods, automotives and energy. There are new elements to the agreement, which include the restriction of investment, the freedom in the future to regulate in conformity with the basic principles of nondiscrimination, and the principles of national treatment, right of establishment and right of commercial presence. NAFTA sets out strict rules of origin to qualify for preferential duties, requiring that products originate in North America. For those not meeting this, larger quotas for preferential access to the American market have been included, with these new levels helping textile and apparel manufacturers expand their exports of products to the lucrative American market. Canadian and Mexican tariffs on apparel were eliminated within 10 years, and tariffs on textiles within eight years. Mexico has concentrated on less expensive lower-quality items, while Canada has moved toward higher-value textiles and quality designer fashions. Further, the financial industry was first included in the Canadian United States Free Trade Agreement, and it was believed that freer market access for financial services would help trade flow more easily. The United States agreed to national treatment, market access and most favored nation status being applied to financial services, fully subjecting the sector to dispute settlement.

The NAFTA Secretariat, comprising the Canadian, American and Mexican Sections, is an organization established by the Free Trade Commission, pursuant to the North American Free Trade Agreement. It is responsible for the administration of the dispute settlement provisions of the Agreement, and its mandate includes the provision of assistance to the Commission, and support for various non-dispute-related committees and working groups. Each national Section maintains a court-like registry relating to panel, committee and tribunal proceedings. A similar administrative body, the Binational Secretariat, existed under the Canada United States Free Trade Agreement (FTA). The Parties have established permanent national Section offices, which are 'mirror-images' of one another, and are located in Ottawa, Washington and Mexico City respectively.

Importantly, the principal dispute settlement mechanisms of NAFTA are found in Chapters 11, 14, 19 and 20 of the Agreement. NAFTA establishes a mechanism for the settlement of disputes that assures both equal treatment among Parties in accordance with the principle of international reciprocity and due process before an impartial tribunal. Alternatively, the investor may choose the remedies available in the host country's domestic courts. An important feature of the arbitral provisions is the enforceability in domestic courts of final awards by arbitration tribunals. NAFTA provides for a trade commission in charge of political management, which includes a dispute settlement mechanism in the form of a panel, with an important role of the Commission to consider matters relating to the Agreement which are under dispute. When general disputes concerning NAFTA are not resolved through consultation within a specified period of time, the matter may be referred at the request of either Party to a non-binding panel. Various third party provisions are necessarily included, as a third party that considers it has a substantial interest in a disputed matter is entitled to join consultations or a proceeding as a complaining Party on written notice, but it does not join as a complainant, upon written notice, it is entitled to attend hearings, make written and oral submissions and receive written submissions of the disputing Parties. There is also a provision for an advisory committee to be established to provide recommendations to the Commission on the use of arbitration and other procedures for the resolution of international private commercial disputes, and if nothing results from the notification of a consultation action, then a panel review ensues with recommendations that are binding if both sides agree. The dispute settlement is also binding when one side believes that a surge of imports is damaging to it, thereby receiving compensation while the other side is snapped back to a most-favored nation tariff. This procedure was in effect for the first ten years of the agreement, providing steps for negotiation, legislation specificity and panel review. The settlement mechanism calls for compulsory consultation on changes of law and an evaluation procedure by a panel, with the right to retaliate or withdraw if the panel so favors. NAFTA also provides, for the first time, a system of settling private investment disputes in that those between an investor from a NAFTA country and another NAFTA government can be settled at the investor's option by binding international arbitration, with all investors treated equally. The dispute settlement provisions call for the rapid and fair settlement of disputes, including the use of impartial panels, and there are three basic steps to the process: first, consultation among the three countries for a satisfactory settlement; second, if the first round fails, the NAFTA trade commission, comprised of cabinet-level representatives, will examine the case for interpretation of trade rules; and third, if the second round fails, in order to promote an impartial decision, the issue will be reviewed by a specially selected panel, which is composed of five members chosen from a trilaterally agreed roster, with two panelists from the complaining party selected by the defending party, two from the defending party nominated by the complainant and the panel's chair allowed to be a representative from the third NAFTA country or another neutral country chosen by mutual agreement or drawn by lot.

The elimination of tariffs is important for a reduction of protectionism and a climate of open investment. Cross-border trade in services was first included in the Canada United States Free Trade Agreement, and NAFTA has extended these codes of binding rules and principles with procedures to encourage the recognition of licenses and certificates through mutually acceptable professional standards and criteria, such as education, experience and professional development. It opens up temporary entry across the border for over 60 professions. Further, there is a provision as to access for temporary personnel in the service and manufacturing sectors, as well as business recognition of professional and sales services in the spirit of freedom of movement. This latter aspect, however, has not yet been extended to blue-collar workers. As such, Canada's service industry is the fastest growing sector of the economy, accounting for the employment of roughly ten million Canadians and two-thirds of the workforce, as well as providing 90 percent of all new jobs in Canada in the last several years. Canada's export of services around the world totals an average of $24 billion per year, with business and professional services accounting for 20 percent of these exports. NAFTA obliges one country's service providers to treat the other country's no less favorably than their own for domestic and cross-border sales, distribution and the right of establishment of facilities, providing for mutually acceptable professional licensing standards. However, this equal employment provision in the Member States must go further to protect against any form of discrimination, including religion.

While the Canada United States Free Trade Agreement established the first comprehensive set of principles governing trade in services, NAFTA broadens these protections and extends them to Mexico. Virtually all services are covered by NAFTA, with key sectors being: accounting, architecture, land transport, publishing, consulting, commercial education, environmental services, enhanced telecommunications, advertising, broadcasting, construction, tourism, engineering, health care, management and legal services. Each country has also excluded certain sensitive sectors from coverage, such that Mexico will not liberalize services of public notaries, which are specifically reserved to Mexicans by the Mexican Constitution, and Canada has retained its cultural exclusion, which affects the entertainment and publishing industries. NAFTA does not remove or weaken licensing and certification requirements but, consistent with the principle of nondiscrimination, licensing of professionals, such as lawyers, doctors and accountants, are based on objective criteria aimed at ensuring competence, not nationality so that NAFTA does not permit American, Mexican or Canadian professionals to practice in the other Member countries, unless they have undergone the same licensing and certification procedures as a National professional.

The Preamble of the North American Free Trade Agreement, important for religious minorities, states:

The Government of Canada, the Government of the United Mexican States and the Government of the United States of America, resolved to:

STRENGTHEN the special bonds of friendship and cooperation among their nations;

CONTRIBUTE to the harmonious development and expansion of world trade and provide a catalyst to broader international cooperation;

CREATE an expanded and secure market for the goods and services produced in their territories;

REDUCE distortions to trade;

ESTABLISH clear and mutually advantageous rules governing their trade;

ENSURE a predictable commercial framework for business planning and investment;

BUILD on their respective rights and obligations under the *General Agreement on Tariffs and Trade* and other multilateral and bilateral instruments of cooperation;

ENHANCE the competitiveness of their firms in global markets;

FOSTER creativity and innovation, and promote trade in goods and services that are the subject of intellectual property rights;

CREATE new employment opportunities and improve working conditions and living standards in their respective territories;

UNDERTAKE each of the preceding in a manner consistent with environmental protection and conservation;

PRESERVE their flexibility to safeguard the public welfare;

PROMOTE sustainable development;

STRENGTHEN the development and enforcement of environmental laws and regulations; and

PROTECT, enhance and enforce basic workers' rights.[26]

Under the agreement, in terms of service providers, Article 1201 applies to measures adopted or maintained by a Party relating to cross-border trade in services by service providers of another Party, including measures respecting the production, distribution, marketing, sale and delivery of a service; the purchase or use of, or payment for, a service; the access to and use of distribution and transportation systems in connection with the provision of a service; the presence in its territory of a service provider of another Party; and the provision of a bond or other form of financial security as a condition for the provision of a service.[27]

Articles 1202 and 1203 provide that each Party shall accord to service providers of another Party treatment no less favorable than that it accords, in like circumstances, to service providers of any other Party or of a non-Party.[28] Further, Article 1208 maintains that each Party shall set out in its Schedule to Annex VI its commitments to liberalize quantitative restrictions, licensing requirements, performance requirements or other nondiscriminatory measures.[29]

Professional services are defined in Article 1213 as services, the provision of which requires specialized post-secondary education, or equivalent training or experience, and for which the right to practice is granted or restricted by a Party, but does not include services provided by tradespersons or vessel and aircraft crew members.[30]

Important to all workers, Article 1210 provides for licensing and certification requirements:

1210.1. With a view to ensuring that any measure adopted or maintained by a Party relating to the licensing or certification of nationals of another Party does not constitute an unnecessary barrier to trade, each Party shall endeavor to ensure that any such measure:

(a) is based on objective and transparent criteria, such as competence and the ability to provide a service;

(b) is not more burdensome than necessary to ensure the quality of a service; and

(c) does not constitute a disguised restriction on the cross-border provision of a service.

2. ... a Party shall not be required to extend to a service provider of another Party the benefits of recognition of education, experience, licenses or certifications obtained in another country, whether such recognition was accorded unilaterally or by arrangement or agreement with that other country. The Party according such recognition shall afford any interested Party an adequate opportunity to demonstrate that education, experience, licenses or certifications obtained in that other Party's territory should also be recognized or to negotiate and enter into an agreement or arrangement of comparable effect.

3. ... a Party shall eliminate any citizenship or permanent residency requirement for the licensing and certification of professional service providers in its territory ....[31]

Further, licensing and certification standards for professionals are provided for in Annex 1210.A.2.:

Annex 1210.A.2. The Parties shall encourage the relevant bodies in their respective territories to develop mutually acceptable standards and criteria for licensing and certification of professional service providers and to provide recommendations on mutual recognition to the Commission.[32]

Additionally, Annex 1210.A.3. provides for standards and criteria to be developed:

Annex 1210.A.3. The standards and criteria referred to in paragraph 2 may be developed with regard to the following matters:

(a) education: accreditation of schools or academic programs;

(b) examinations: qualifying examinations for licensing, including alternative methods of assessment such as oral examinations and interviews;

(c) experience: length and nature of experience required for licensing;

(d) conduct and ethics: standards of professional conduct and the nature of disciplinary action for non-conformity with those standards;

(e) professional development and re-certification: continuing education and ongoing requirements to maintain professional certification;

(f) scope of practice: extent of, or limitations on, permissible activities;

(g) local knowledge: requirements for knowledge of such matters as local laws, regulations, language, geography or climate; and

(h) consumer protection: alternatives to residency requirements, including bonding, professional liability insurance and client restitution funds, to provide for the protection of consumers.[33]

Finally, Annex 1210.B.1. provides that each Party shall, in implementing its obligations and commitments regarding foreign legal consultants as set out in its relevant Schedules and subject to any reservations therein, ensure that a national of another Party is permitted to practise or advise on the law of any country in which that national is authorized to practise as a lawyer.[34]

In terms of the temporary entry for people to conduct business, Chapter 16 and specifically Article 1601 specify:

> 1601. This Chapter reflects the preferential trading relationship between the Parties, the desirability of facilitating temporary entry on a reciprocal basis and of establishing transparent criteria and procedures for temporary entry, and the need to ensure border security and to protect the domestic labor force and permanent employment in their respective territories.[35]

Article 1602 outlines the general obligations:

> 1602.1. Each Party shall apply its measures relating to the provisions of this Chapter in accordance with Article 1601 and, in particular, shall apply expeditiously those measures so as to avoid unduly impairing or delaying trade in goods or services or conduct of investment activities under this Agreement.
> 2. The Parties shall endeavor to develop and adopt common criteria, definitions and interpretations for the implementation of this Chapter.[36]

Additional requirements are noted in Annex 1603, in order to gain entry for different classes of individuals in employment situations. Section A provides for business visitors:

> Annex 1603.A.1. Each Party shall grant temporary entry to a business person seeking to engage in a business activity set out in Appendix 1603.A.1, without requiring that person to obtain an employment authorization, provided that the business person otherwise complies with existing immigration measures applicable to temporary entry, on presentation of:
> (a) proof of citizenship of a Party;
> (b) documentation demonstrating that the business person will be so engaged and describing the purpose of entry; and
> (c) evidence demonstrating that the proposed business activity is international in scope and that the business person is not seeking to enter the local labor market.
> 2. Each Party shall provide that a business person may satisfy the requirements of paragraph 1(c) by demonstrating that:
> (a) the primary source of remuneration for the proposed business activity is outside the territory of the Party granting temporary entry; and
> (b) the business person's principal place of business and the actual place of accrual of profits, at least predominantly, remain outside such territory.

A Party shall normally accept an oral declaration as to the principal place of business and the actual place of accrual of profits. Where the Party requires further proof, it shall normally consider a letter from the employer attesting to these matters as sufficient proof.

3. Each Party shall grant temporary entry to a business person seeking to engage in a business activity other than those set out in Appendix 1603.A.1, without requiring that person to obtain an employment authorization, on a basis no less favorable than that provided under the existing provisions of the measures set out in Appendix 1603. A.3, provided that the business person otherwise complies with existing immigration measures applicable to temporary entry.

4. No Party may:

(a) as a condition for temporary entry under paragraph 1 or 3, require prior approval procedures, petitions, labor certification tests or other procedures of similar effect; or

(b) impose or maintain any numerical restriction relating to temporary entry under paragraph 1 or 3.

5. Notwithstanding paragraph 4, a Party may require a business person seeking temporary entry under this Section to obtain a visa or its equivalent prior to entry. Before imposing a visa requirement, the Party shall consult with a Party whose business persons would be affected with a view to avoiding the imposition of the requirement. With respect to an existing visa requirement, a Party shall consult, on request, with a Party whose business persons are subject to the requirement with a view to its removal.[37]

Section B provides for traders and investors:

Annex 1603.B.1. Each Party shall grant temporary entry and provide confirming documentation to a business person seeking to:

(a) carry on substantial trade in goods or services principally between the territory of the Party of which the business person is a citizen and the territory of the Party into which entry is sought, or

(b) establish, develop, administer or provide advice or key technical services to the operation of an investment to which the business person or the business person's enterprise has committed, or is in the process of committing, a substantial amount of capital, in a capacity that is supervisory, executive or involves essential skills, provided that the business person otherwise complies with existing immigration measures applicable to temporary entry.

2. No Party may:

(a) as a condition for temporary entry under paragraph 1, require labor certification tests or other procedures of similar effect; or

(b) impose or maintain any numerical restriction relating to temporary entry under paragraph 1.

3. Notwithstanding paragraph 2, a Party may require a business person seeking temporary entry under this Section to obtain a visa or its equivalent prior to entry.[38]

Section C provides for intra-company transferees:

Annex 1603.C.1. Each Party shall grant temporary entry and provide confirming documentation to a business person employed by an enterprise who seeks to render services to that enterprise or a subsidiary or affiliate thereof, in a capacity that is managerial, executive or involves specialized knowledge, provided that the business person otherwise complies with existing immigration measures applicable to temporary entry. A Party may require the business person to have been employed continuously by the enterprise for one year within the three-year period immediately preceding the date of the application for admission.

2. No Party may:

(a) as a condition for temporary entry under paragraph 1, require labor certification tests or other procedures of similar effect; or

(b) impose or maintain any numerical restriction relating to temporary entry under paragraph 1.

3. Notwithstanding paragraph 2, a Party may require a business person seeking temporary entry under this Section to obtain a visa or its equivalent prior to entry. Before imposing a visa requirement, the Party shall consult with a Party whose business persons would be affected with a view to avoiding the imposition of the requirement. With respect to an existing visa requirement, a Party shall consult, on request, with a Party whose business persons are subject to the requirement with a view to its removal.[39]

Section D provides for professionals:

Annex 1603.D.1. Each Party shall grant temporary entry and provide confirming documentation to a business person seeking to engage in a business activity at a professional level in a profession set out in Appendix 1603.D.1, if the business person otherwise complies with existing immigration measures applicable to temporary entry, on presentation of:

(a) proof of citizenship of a Party; and

(b) documentation demonstrating that the business person will be so engaged and describing the purpose of entry.

2. No Party may:

(a) as a condition for temporary entry under paragraph 1, require prior approval procedures, petitions, labor certification tests or other procedures of similar effect; or

(b) impose or maintain any numerical restriction relating to temporary entry under paragraph 1.

3. Notwithstanding paragraph 2, a Party may require a business person seeking temporary entry under this Section to obtain a visa or its equivalent prior to entry. Before imposing a visa requirement, the Party shall consult with a Party whose business persons would be affected with a view to avoiding the imposition of the requirement. With respect to an existing visa requirement, a Party shall consult, on request, with a Party whose business persons are subject to the requirement with a view to its removal.

4. Notwithstanding paragraphs 1 and 2, a Party may establish an annual numerical limit, which shall be set out in Appendix 1603.D.4, regarding temporary entry of business persons of another Party seeking to engage in business activities at a professional level

in a profession set out in Appendix 1603.D.1, if the Parties concerned have not agreed otherwise prior to the date of entry into force of this Agreement for those Parties. In establishing such a limit, the Party shall consult with the other Party concerned.

5. A Party establishing a numerical limit pursuant to paragraph 4, unless the Parties concerned agree otherwise:

(a) shall, for each year after the first year after the date of entry into force of this Agreement, consider increasing the numerical limit set out in Appendix 1603.D.4 by an amount to be established in consultation with the other Party concerned, taking into account the demand for temporary entry under this Section;

(b) shall not apply its procedures established pursuant to paragraph 1 to the temporary entry of a business person subject to the numerical limit, but may require the business person to comply with its other procedures applicable to the temporary entry of professionals; and

(c) may, in consultation with the other Party concerned, grant temporary entry under paragraph 1 to a business person who practices in a profession where accreditation, licensing, and certification requirements are mutually recognized by those Parties.

6. Nothing in paragraph 4 or 5 shall be construed to limit the ability of a business person to seek temporary entry under a Party's applicable immigration measures relating to the entry of professionals other than those adopted or maintained pursuant to paragraph 1.[40]

Finally, Appendix 1603.D.1 outlines the different professions provided for under NAFTA, along with the minimum educational requirements and alternative credentials.[41]

There are a number of institutions that are part of NAFTA. Article 2001 provides for the Free Trade Commission:

2001. 1. The Parties hereby establish the Free Trade Commission, comprising cabinet-level representatives of the Parties or their designees.

2. The Commission shall:

(a) supervise the implementation of this Agreement;

(b) oversee its further elaboration;

(c) resolve disputes that may arise regarding its interpretation or application;

(d) supervise the work of all committees and working groups established under this Agreement, referred to in Annex 2001.2; and

(e) consider any other matter that may affect the operation of this Agreement.

3. The Commission may:

(a) establish, and delegate responsibilities to, ad hoc or standing committees, working groups or expert groups;

(b) seek the advice of nongovernmental persons or groups; and

(c) take such other action in the exercise of its functions as the Parties may agree.[42]

Further, Article 2002 provides for the Secretariat:

2002. 1. The Commission shall establish and oversee a Secretariat comprising national Sections.
2. Each Party shall:
(a) establish a permanent office of its Section;
(b) be responsible for
    i. the operation and costs of its Section, and
    ii. the remuneration and payment of expenses of panelists and members of committees and scientific review boards established under this Agreement, as set out in Annex 2002.2;
(c) designate an individual to serve as Secretary for its Section, who shall be responsible for its administration and management; and
(d) notify the Commission of the location of its Section's office.
3. The Secretariat shall:
(a) provide assistance to the Commission;
(b) provide administrative assistance to
    i. panels and committees established under Chapter Nineteen (Review and Dispute Settlement in Antidumping and Countervailing Duty Matters), in accordance with the procedures established pursuant to Article 1908, and
    ii. panels established under this Chapter, in accordance with procedures established pursuant to Article 2012; and
(c) as the Commission may direct
    i. support the work of other committees and groups established under this Agreement, and
    ii. otherwise facilitate the operation of this Agreement.[43]

Importantly, in terms of dispute settlement, cooperation is stressed under Article 2003:

> 2003. The Parties shall at all times endeavor to agree on the interpretation and application of this Agreement, and shall make every attempt through cooperation and consultations to arrive at a mutually satisfactory resolution of any matter that might affect its operation.[44]

Recourse to dispute settlement procedures is enunciated under Articles 1606 and 2004:

> 1606.1. A Party may not initiate proceedings under Article 2007 (Commission – Good Offices, Conciliation and Mediation) regarding a refusal to grant temporary entry under this Chapter or a particular case arising under Article 1602(1) unless:
> (a) the matter involves a pattern of practice; and
> (b) the business person has exhausted the available administrative remedies regarding the particular matter.

2. The remedies referred to in paragraph (1) (b) shall be deemed to be exhausted if a final determination in the matter has not been issued by the competent authority within one year of the institution of an administrative proceeding, and the failure to issue a determination is not attributable to delay caused by the business person.[45]

2004. Except for the matters covered in Chapter Nineteen (Review and Dispute Settlement in Antidumping and Countervailing Duty Matters) and as otherwise provided in this Agreement, the dispute settlement provisions of this Chapter shall apply with respect to the avoidance or settlement of all disputes between the Parties regarding the interpretation or application of this Agreement or wherever a Party considers that an actual or proposed measure of another Party is or would be inconsistent with the obligations of this Agreement or cause nullification or impairment in the sense of Annex 2004.[46]

Further, in terms of panel proceedings, a request for an arbitral panel is contained in Article 2008:

2008. 1. If the Commission has convened pursuant to Article 2007(4), and the matter has not been resolved within:
(a) 30 days thereafter,
(b) 30 days after the Commission has convened in respect of the matter most recently referred to it, where proceedings have been consolidated pursuant to Article 2007(6), or
(c) such other period as the consulting Parties may agree,
any consulting Party may request in writing the establishment of an arbitral panel. The requesting Party shall deliver the request to the other Parties and to its Section of the Secretariat.
2. On delivery of the request, the Commission shall establish an arbitral panel.
3. A third Party that considers it has a substantial interest in the matter shall be entitled to join as a complaining Party on delivery of written notice of its intention to participate to the disputing Parties and its Section of the Secretariat. The notice shall be delivered at the earliest possible time, and in any event no later than seven days after the date of delivery of a request by a Party for the establishment of a panel.
4. If a third Party does not join as a complaining Party in accordance with paragraph 3, it normally shall refrain thereafter from initiating or continuing:
(a) a dispute settlement procedure under this Agreement, or
(b) a dispute settlement proceeding in the GATT on grounds that are substantially equivalent to those available to that Party under this Agreement,
regarding the same matter in the absence of a significant change in economic or commercial circumstances.
5. Unless otherwise agreed by the disputing Parties, the panel shall be established and perform its functions in a manner consistent with the provisions of this Chapter.[47]

The rules of procedure are outlined in Article 2012:

2012. 1. The Commission shall establish by January 1, 1994, Model Rules of Procedure, in accordance with the following principles:
(a) the procedures shall assure a right to at least one hearing before the panel as well as the opportunity to provide initial and rebuttal written submissions; and
(b) the panel's hearings, deliberations and initial report, and all written submissions to and communications with the panel shall be confidential.
2. Unless the disputing Parties otherwise agree, the panel shall conduct its proceedings in accordance with the Model Rules of Procedure.
3. Unless the disputing Parties otherwise agree within 20 days from the date of the delivery of the request for the establishment of the panel, the terms of reference shall be:
'To examine, in the light of the relevant provisions of the Agreement, the matter referred to the Commission (as set out in the request for a Commission meeting) and to make findings, determinations and recommendations as provided in Article 2016(2)'.[48]

Third party participation is permitted under Article 2013:

2013. A Party that is not a disputing Party, on delivery of a written notice to the disputing Parties and to its Section of the Secretariat, shall be entitled to attend all hearings, to make written and oral submissions to the panel and to receive written submissions of the disputing Parties.

The panel's final report is contained in Article 2017:

2017. 1. The panel shall present to the disputing Parties a final report, including any separate opinions on matters not unanimously agreed, within 30 days of presentation of the initial report, unless the disputing Parties otherwise agree.[49]
Implementation of the final report is stressed under Article 2018:
2018. 1. On receipt of the final report of a panel, the disputing Parties shall agree on the resolution of the dispute, which normally shall conform with the determinations and recommendations of the panel, and shall notify their Sections of the Secretariat of any agreed resolution of any dispute.[50]

Importantly, non-implementation and the suspension of benefits are provided for under Article 2019:

2019. 1. If in its final report a panel has determined that a measure is inconsistent with the obligations of this Agreement or causes nullification or impairment in the sense of Annex 2004 and the Party complained against has not reached agreement with any complaining Party on a mutually satisfactory resolution pursuant to Article 2018(1) within 30 days of receiving the final report, such complaining Party may suspend the application to the Party complained against of benefits of equivalent effect until such time as they have reached agreement on a resolution of the dispute.

2. In considering what benefits to suspend pursuant to paragraph 1:

(a) a complaining Party should first seek to suspend benefits in the same sector or sectors as that affected by the measure or other matter that the panel has found to be inconsistent with the obligations of this Agreement or to have caused nullification or impairment in the sense of Annex 2004; and

(b) a complaining Party that considers it is not practicable or effective to suspend benefits in the same sector or sectors may suspend benefits in other sectors.[51]

In terms of domestic proceedings and private commercial dispute settlement, Article 2020 provides for referrals of matters from judicial or administrative proceedings:

2020. 1. If an issue of interpretation or application of this Agreement arises in any domestic judicial or administrative proceeding of a Party that any Party considers would merit its intervention, or if a court or administrative body solicits the views of a Party, that Party shall notify the other Parties and its Section of the Secretariat. The Commission shall endeavor to agree on an appropriate response as expeditiously as possible.

2. The Party in whose territory the court or administrative body is located shall submit any agreed interpretation of the Commission to the court or administrative body in accordance with the rules of that forum.

3. If the Commission is unable to agree, any Party may submit its own views to the court or administrative body in accordance with the rules of that forum.[52]

Further, private rights are guaranteed under Article 2021:

2021. No Party may provide for a right of action under its domestic law against any other Party on the ground that a measure of another Party is inconsistent with this Agreement.[53]

Finally, Article 2022 provides for alternative dispute resolution:

2022. 1. Each Party shall, to the maximum extent possible, encourage and facilitate the use of arbitration and other means of alternative dispute resolution for the settlement of international commercial disputes between private parties in the free trade area.

2. To this end, each Party shall provide appropriate procedures to ensure observance of agreements to arbitrate and for the recognition and enforcement of arbitral awards in such disputes.[54]

North American Agreement on Labor Cooperation (NAALC)

The North American Agreement on Labor Cooperation (NAALC) 1993, a side agreement to NAFTA, promotes the enforcement of national labor laws and transparency in their administration, important for equal rights. Through NAALC, the NAFTA partners seek to improve working conditions and living standards in all three countries, and commit themselves to promoting principles that protect, enhance and enforce basic workers' rights. To accomplish these goals, the NAALC creates mechanisms for cooperative activities and intergovernmental consultations, as well as for independent evaluations and dispute settlement related to the enforcement of labor laws. Public submissions made under the NAALC have led to public hearings, ministerial consultations and action plans to address concerns raised. In addition, the NAFTA partners have established cooperative programs and technical exchanges on a number of issues such as industrial relations, health and safety, child labor, gender equity and migrant worker issues.

The agreement reflects the shared recognition of the United States, Mexico, and Canada that their mutual prosperity depends on the promotion of fair and open competition based on innovation and rising levels of productivity and quality with due regard for the importance of labor laws and principles. The Agreement increases cooperation and promotes greater understanding among the Parties in a broad range of labor areas; establishes the obligation of each Party to ensure the enforcement of its domestic labor laws; provides mechanisms to permit problem-solving consultations; enables the Parties to initiate evaluations of patterns of practice by independent committees of experts; and allows for dispute settlement procedures.

The general obligation of each Party is to ensure the effective enforcement of its own labor law. Specific obligations refer to publication of labor laws and related regulations and procedures, and to promotion of awareness of and compliance with them. Other obligations include government enforcement actions for promoting compliance and effective enforcement of its labor law, covering such matters as: appointing and training of inspectors, monitoring compliance and examining suspected violations; carrying out inspections, mandatory reporting and record keeping; encouraging worker-management committees; providing mediation, conciliation, or arbitration services; and initiating in a timely manner enforcement actions seeking appropriate remedies. Each Party is committed to ensuring access by persons with a legally recognized interest to administrative, judicial and related tribunals, including recourse to procedures by which labor rights can be enforced in a binding fashion. The Agreement also provides that such tribunals and proceedings before them would be fair and comply with due process.

A trinational Labor Commission is created to facilitate the achievement of the objectives of the Agreement and to deal with labor issues in a cooperative, and consultative manner that duly respects the three nations' sovereignty. The Labor Commission consists of a Ministerial Council, an International Coordinating Secretariat (ICS), and three National Administrative Offices (NAOs). The Ministerial Council consists of the Labor Ministers from the three signatory countries, who supervise the implementation of the Agreement, including directing the work of the ICS, and promote cooperative activities. An ICS, under the direction of the Ministerial Council, carries out the day-to-day work of the Commission, and is responsible for assisting the Council in its work, for gathering and periodically publishing information on labor matters in Canada, the United

States and Mexico, for planning and coordinating cooperative activities, and for supporting any working groups or evaluation committees established by the Ministerial Council. The NAOs, established by each Party, serve as a point of contact for and facilitate the provision of information to other Parties on domestic law and practice, receive public communications, conduct preliminary reviews and promote the exchange of information relevant to the Agreement.

As to resolution of disputes, if the Council cannot resolve a dispute involving a Party's alleged persistent pattern of failure to effectively enforce labor laws with respect to health and safety, child labor and minimum wage, relating to a situation involving mutually recognized labor laws and the production of goods or services traded between the Parties, any Party may request an arbitral panel, which will be established on a two-thirds vote of the council, and panelists will normally be chosen from a previously agreed roster of experts, including experts on labor matters. With the approval of the disputing Parties, a panel may seek information and technical advice from any person or body that it deems appropriate, and the report of the panel will be made publicly available five days after it is transmitted to the Parties. If a panel makes a finding that a Party has engaged in a persistent pattern of failure to effectively enforce its labor laws, the Parties may, within 60 days, agree on a mutually satisfactory action plan to remedy the non-enforcement. If there is no agreed action plan, then between 60 and 120 days after the final panel report, the panel may be reconvened to evaluate an action plan proposed by the Party complained against or to set out an action plan in its stead. Further, the panel would also make a determination on the imposition of monetary enforcement assessments on the alleged offending Party. The panel may be reconvened at any time to determine if an action plan is being fully implemented, and if not, the panel is to impose a monetary enforcement assessment on the alleged offending Party. In the event that a Party complained against fails to pay a monetary enforcement assessment or continues in its failure to enforce its labor law and minimum wage, the Party is liable for ongoing enforcement actions. In the case of Canada, the Commission, on the request of a complaining Party, collects the monetary enforcement assessment and enforces an action plan in summary proceedings before a Canadian court of competent jurisdiction. In the case of Mexico and the United States, the complaining Party or Parties may suspend NAFTA benefits based on the amount of the assessment.

The Preamble to the North American Agreement on Labor Cooperation (NAALC) states that the Government of the United States of America, the Government of Canada and the Government of the United Mexican States undertake the agreement:

RECALLING their resolve in the North American Free Trade Agreement (NAFTA) to:

create an expanded and secure market for the goods and services produced in their territories, enhance the competitiveness of their firms in global markets,

create new employment opportunities and improve working conditions and living standards in their respective territories, and

protect, enhance and enforce basic workers' rights;

AFFIRMING their continuing respect for each Party's constitution and law;

DESIRING to build on their respective international commitments and to strengthen their cooperation on labor matters;

RECOGNIZING that their mutual prosperity depends on the promotion of competition based on innovation and rising levels of productivity and quality;

SEEKING to complement the economic opportunities created by the NAFTA with the human resource development, labor-management cooperation and continuous learning that characterize high-productivity economies;

ACKNOWLEDGING that protecting basic workers' rights will encourage firms to adopt high-productivity competitive strategies;

RESOLVED to promote, in accordance with their respective laws, high-skill, high-productivity economic development in North America by:

investing in continuous human resource development, including for entry into the workforce and during periods of unemployment;

promoting employment security and career opportunities for all workers through referral and other employment services;

strengthening labor-management cooperation to promote greater dialogue between worker organizations and employers and to foster creativity and productivity in the workplace;

promoting higher living standards as productivity increases;

encouraging consultation and dialogue between labor, business and government both in each country and in North America;

fostering investment with due regard for the importance of labor laws and principles;

encouraging employers and employees in each country to comply with labor laws and to work together in maintaining a progressive, fair, safe and healthy working environment;

BUILDING on existing institutions and mechanisms in Canada, Mexico and the United States to achieve the preceding economic and social goals; and

CONVINCED of the benefits to be gained from further cooperation between them on labor matters.[55]

The objectives of the agreement are outlined in Article 1:

1(a) improve working conditions and living standards in each Party's territory;
(b) promote, to the maximum extent possible, the labor principles set out in Annex 1;
(c) encourage cooperation to promote innovation and rising levels of productivity and quality;
(d) encourage publication and exchange of information, data development and coordination, and joint studies to enhance mutually beneficial understanding of the laws and institutions governing labor in each Party's territory;
(e) pursue cooperative labor-related activities on the basis of mutual benefit;
(f) promote compliance with, and effective enforcement by each Party of, its labor law; and
(g) foster transparency in the administration of labor law.[56]

As such, the Preamble to NAALC reaffirms relevant provisions of the Preamble to NAFTA and adds further shared goals related to labor matters. Importantly, each Party is committed, in accordance with its domestic laws, to promote equal pay and to eliminate employment discrimination, important for equal rights in employment. Further, each is committed to the following labor principles: the freedom of association, the right to bargain collectively, the right to strike, prohibition of forced labor, restrictions on labor by children and young people, minimum employment standards, prevention of occupational accidents and diseases, compensation in cases of work accidents or occupational diseases, and protection of migrant workers. The Agreement sets forth the following general objectives: improving working conditions and living standards, promoting compliance with and effective enforcement of labor laws, promoting the Agreement's principles through cooperation and coordination, and promoting the publication and exchange of information to enhance the mutual understanding of the Parties' laws, institutions and legal systems.

Specifically, in terms of Obligations of the Parties and the Levels of Protection, Article 2 holds:

2. Affirming full respect for each Party's constitution, and recognizing the right of each Party to establish its own domestic labor standards, and to adopt or modify accordingly

its labor laws and regulations, each Party shall ensure that its labor laws and regulations provide for high labor standards, consistent with high quality and productivity workplaces, and shall continue to strive to improve those standards in that light.[57]

Importantly, government enforcement action is established under Article 3, which states that each Party shall promote compliance with and effectively enforce its labor law through appropriate government action, such as:

3(a) appointing and training inspectors;
(b) monitoring compliance and investigating suspected violations, including through on-site inspections;
(c) seeking assurances of voluntary compliance;
(d) requiring record keeping and reporting;
(e) encouraging the establishment of worker-management committees to address labor regulation of the workplace;
(f) providing or encouraging mediation, conciliation and arbitration services; or
(g) initiating, in a timely manner, proceedings to seek appropriate sanctions or remedies for violations of its labor law.[58]

Critical for religious discrimination cases, the agreement safeguards private action in Article 4:

4.1. Each Party shall ensure that persons with a legally recognized interest under its law in a particular matter have appropriate access to administrative, quasijudicial, judicial or labor tribunals for the enforcement of the Party's labor law.
2. Each Party's law shall ensure that such persons may have recourse to, as appropriate, procedures by which rights arising under:
(a) its labor law, including in respect of occupational safety and health, employment standards, industrial relations and migrant workers, and
(b) collective agreements,
can be enforced.[59]

Further, under procedural guarantees, Article 5 establishes:

5.1. Each Party shall ensure that its administrative, quasijudicial, judicial and labor tribunal proceedings for the enforcement of its labor law are fair, equitable and transparent and, to this end, each Party shall provide that:
(a) such proceedings comply with due process of law;
(b) any hearings in such proceedings are open to the public, except where the administration of justice otherwise requires;
(c) the parties to such proceedings are entitled to support or defend their respective positions and to present information or evidence; and
(d) such proceedings are not unneccessarily complicated and do not entail unreasonable charges or time limits or unwarranted delays.

2. Each Party shall provide that final decisions on the merits of the case in such proceedings are:
(a) in writing and preferably state the reasons on which the decisions are based;
(b) made available without undue delay to the parties to the proceedings and, consistent with its law, to the public; and
(c) based on information or evidence in respect of which the parties were offered the opportunity to be heard.
3. Each Party shall provide, as appropriate, that parties to such proceedings have the right, in accordance with its law, to seek review and, where warranted, correction of final decisions issued in such proceedings.
4. Each Party shall ensure that tribunals that conduct or review such proceedings are impartial and independent and do not have any substantial interest in the outcome of the matter.
5. Each Party shall provide that the parties to administrative, quasijudicial, judicial or labor tribunal proceedings may seek remedies to ensure the enforcement of their labor rights. Such remedies may include, as appropriate, orders, compliance agreements, fines, penalties, imprisonment, injunctions or emergency workplace closures.
6. Each Party may, as appropriate, adopt or maintain labor defense offices to represent or advise workers or their organizations.
7. Nothing in this Article shall be construed to require a Party to establish, or to prevent a Party from establishing, a judicial system for the enforcement of its labor law distinct from its system for the enforcement of laws in general.
8. For greater certainty, decisions by each Party's administrative, quasijudicial, judicial or labor tribunals, or pending decisions, as well as related proceedings shall not be subject to revision or reopened under the provisions of this Agreement[60]

In terms of cooperation for religious tolerance in the workplace, Article 11 underlines the importance of labor practices and cooperative activities for equality:

11.1. The Council shall promote cooperative activities between the Parties, as appropriate, regarding:
    a. occupational safety and health;
    b. child labor;
    c. migrant workers of the Parties;
    d. human resource development;
    e. labor statistics;
    f. work benefits;
    g social programs for workers and their families;
    h. programs, methodologies and experiences regarding productivity improvement;
    i. labor-management relations and collective bargaining procedures;
    j. employment standards and their implementation;
    k. compensation for work-related injury or illness;
    l. legislation relating to the formation and operation of unions, collective

bargaining and the resolution of labor disputes, and its implementation;
m. the equality of women and men in the workplace;
n. forms of cooperation among workers, management and government;
o. the provision of technical assistance, at the request of a Party, for the development of its labor standards; and
p. such other matters as the Parties may agree.

2. In carrying out the activities referred to in paragraph 1, the Parties may, commensurate with the availability of resources in each Party, cooperate through:
   a. seminars, training sessions, working groups and conferences;
   b. joint research projects, including sectoral studies;
   c. technical assistance; and
   d. such other means as the Parties may agree.

3. The Parties shall carry out the cooperative activities referred to in paragraph 1 with due regard for the economic, social, cultural and legislative differences between them.[61]

Importantly, Article 49 defines labor law, which specifically mentions the elimination of discrimination based on religion in Article 49.1(g):

49.1. For purposes of this Agreement:
'labor law' means laws and regulations, or provisions thereof, that are directly related to:
(a) freedom of association and protection of the right to organize;
(b) the right to bargain collectively;
(c) the right to strike;
(d) prohibition of forced labor;
(e) labor protections for children and young persons;
(f) minimum employment standards, such as minimum wages and overtime pay, covering wage earners, including those not covered by collective agreements;
(g) elimination of employment discrimination on the basis of grounds such as race, religion, age, sex, or other grounds as determined by each Party's domestic laws;
(h) equal pay for men and women;
(i) prevention of occupational injuries and illnesses;
(j) compensation in cases of occupational injuries and illnesses;
(k) protection of migrant workers.[62]

Further, in Article 7 of Annex 1, labor principles are outlined, including the elimination of employment discrimination, which specifically mentions religion:

Annex 1. The following are guiding principles that the Parties are committed to promote, subject to each Party's domestic law, but do not establish common minimum standards for their domestic law. They indicate broad areas of concern where the Parties have developed, each in its own way, laws, regulations, procedures and practices that protect the rights and interests of their respective workforces.

7. Elimination of employment discrimination on such grounds as race, religion, age, sex or other grounds, subject to certain reasonable exceptions, such as, where applicable, *bona fide* occupational requirements or qualifications and established practices or rules governing retirement ages, and special measures of protection or assistance for particular groups designed to take into account the effects of discrimination.[63]

In terms of the benefits and concerns of NAFTA, the advocates argue, provides several benefits: (1) improved access to the North American market of 360 million consumers, as to manufactured goods, and business and professional services; (2) opportunities to export more products and services to Mexico, which needs capital goods, services and investment; (3) new export and investment opportunities for companies in different markets; (4) a more equitable trading relationship through the elimination of almost all Mexican tariffs and imports, with Mexico being the largest trading partner in Latin America; (5) strengthened and precise North American rules of origin to determine which goods qualify for duty free treatment in North America; (6) opportunities to bid on large government procurement contracts, with equal access to the bidding process in some sectors; (7) improved methods to settle trade disputes among Canada, Mexico and the United States; (8) protection of key domestic interests, including culture, education, water, health and social services, such as childcare, the environment and aboriginal people; (9) increased market opportunities in Latin America; and (10) enhancement of the area as a foreign investment destination through secure access to the North American market for foreign investors, with key selling points of strong transportation and telecommunication infrastructures, abundant energy resources, a highly educated and skilled workforce, comprehensive social and health services, and a stable political and economic environment.[64] Further, the benefits of free trade, according to its advocates, are: (1) increased specialization; (2) rationalization, eliminating some production and expanding in others while introducing new production techniques, entailing (a) a reduction in the number of manufacturing plants, (b) an increase in production runs, (c) an increase in trade among the Parties, and (d) a reduction in production costs;[65] (3) longer production runs in larger specialized plants; and (4) easier transfer of technology. The costs of free trade are (1) transition; and (2) harmonization requirements.[66] Therefore, those in favor of the North American Free Trade Agreement argue that free trade improves efficiency and competition, stimulates production and economic growth, and opens new opportunities, supplementing and broadening the General Agreement on Tariffs and Trade (GATT) out of which grew the World Trade Organization (WTO).[67]

Overall, NAFTA eliminates the majority of current tariffs and import licenses on all manufactured goods, provides greater access for service industries, permits more mobility for professional and business workers, and allows easier entry into the North American market. By lowering trade barriers, the agreement has expanded trade in all three countries. This, some argue, has led to increased employment, more choices for consumers at competitive prices, and rising prosperity. From 1993, the year preceding the start of NAFTA implementation, to 2001, trade among the NAFTA nations climbed 109 percent, from US$297 billion to US$622 billion, and each day the NAFTA parties conduct nearly US$1.7 billion in trilateral trade. Because of NAFTA, North America is one of the most competitive, prosperous and economically integrated regions in the world. Looking at the Canadian situation, Canada's merchandise exports to its NAFTA partners climbed 95 percent, from US$117 billion to US$229 billion, while such exports to the rest of the world in the period increased only five percent. Looking at the Mexican situation, Mexico exported US$139 billion to its NAFTA partners, an increase of 225 percent, while such exports to the rest of the world increased 93 percent, with growth in Mexican exports accounting for more than half of the increase in Mexico's real gross domestic product. In looking at the American situation, United States merchandise exports to NAFTA partners nearly doubled from US$142 billion to US$265 billion, which was significantly higher than the 44 percent growth in exports to the rest of the world.[68]

An increasingly integrated North American market has stimulated capital flows, promoted the spread of technology, and contributed to increasing productivity and higher wages. Between 1994 and 2000, foreign direct investment (FDI) inflows in the NAFTA countries reached US$1.3 trillion, or about 28 percent of the world total, spurring economic development and growth throughout North America. The dynamic performance of exports and investment in North America has boosted economic activity and production in the region, and some argue, has contributed to the creation of more and better paying jobs in all three countries. Looking at the Canadian situation, the hourly wage rate in export-supported jobs is 35 percent higher than in the non-export sector. Looking at the Mexican situation, Mexico's annual average capital inflow reached US$11.7 billion, three times the annual received in the seven years prior to the Agreement, and the export sector is the country's leading job creation engine, accounting for more than half of Mexican manufacturing jobs gained, with these jobs paying nearly 40 percent more than those in the rest of the manufacturing sector. Looking at the American situation, the United States received large flows of foreign capital, approximately US$110.2 billion per year, and employment supported by merchandise exports to NAFTA countries grew to an estimated 2.9 million jobs, with these paying between 13 and 18 percent more than the average American national wage.

NAFTA, according to its critics who paint a more realistic picture, is not free, since Canada has paid a high price to gain greater access to the American and Mexican markets. Canadian consumers have seen prices rise along with the advent of the Goods and Services Tax, and thousands of jobs have been lost, with unemployment hovering around the 9 percent level.[69] The structural adjustment costs, such as a rise in unemployment, tend to be underestimated by free trade advocates. Further, the agreement is also not about trade, and is more about the creation of a new continental model of development for the regulation of capitalism.[70] It serves more as a corporate bill of rights entrenching deregulation and market orientation in an international treaty, while at the same time eroding the national economic, as well as social and political institutions. Neo-conservatives in Canada and the Unites

States wanted a deregulated continental model of development to increase capital mobility in order to restore profitability. Unfortunately, corporate managers have worked in a continent-wide drive to bring down wages and welfare state spending, by playing communities off against one another, doing away with crucial social programs. The hidden goal is to harmonize and integrate Canadian standards and institutions with the United States, and as a result, Canada's economy, political system and labor practices have been significantly altered due to closer ties with the United States' economy. Canada has been forced to acquiesce to the continental model of development by continental market forces and American geopolitical pressures. Free trade is designed to restructure society to suit corporate needs, causing a threat to communities by capital-enhanced geographic mobility, which is not universally beneficial.

Many have benefited, but in the eyes of the critics, many more have been hurt. Sovereignty has been compromised, and the three most important industries for Canada, wood exports, agriculture and automobile manufacturing, have been hurt. 'The burden of Free Trade driven restructuring was shared unequally on a national, regional, class and gender basis'.[71] The critics argue that the new capital labor accord relies on domination instead of negotiation. Canadian workers are suffering from a 'whiplash process', being forced concessions on wage benefits and work rules, and failure to acquiesce has resulted in relocation out of Canada. Mergers, temporary and part-time workers, and cheap labor increase competitiveness at a cost, free-trade-generated jobs not materializing as promised by the advocates. The Continental Model has led to polarization and segmentation of the Canadian labor force, and the discourse of universality has ended, so that there is more social inequality across Canada. The Welfare State is viewed as an impediment to profit in the eyes of business, which has chipped away at it, giving way to a 'policy of stealth'; and with deregulation, budget cuts and privatization, importance is given to corporate profit at the expense of social equality.

'Continental free trade has helped to create a neo-conservative utopia where issues such as social justice and regional equality have become relics' of a bygone era.[72] While opponents of free trade are said to suffer from 'emporiophobia', a fear of free trade, the effects of free trade are something to fear, since hemispheric free trade is now a possibility. It was argued that there would be a 'sucking sound' of jobs going south of the border, ultimately to Mexico.[73] However, no tripartite treaty will disturb the overwhelming dominance that accrues to the United States, because of its geographic position, between Canada and Mexico. A borderland is a region jointly shared by two nations that houses people with common social characteristics in spite of the political boundaries between them, and thus the United States has a strong influence on the other two countries bordering it. The outflow of investment and the hemorrhaging of profits and service payments out of Canada is intrinsically intertwined with NAFTA.[74] According to the critics, the human and economic debris will be with us for as long as we can see into the future. The single most important impact of NAFTA is the decline in the overall standard of living of Canadians, which has coincided with the agreements. We must be careful to reform democracy and political institutions so citizens and not just corporate business benefit from change. There is presently more foreign ownership and control in Canada, with fewer and poorer jobs. More imports of goods and services should be sourced in Canada, but there is a failure to develop new competitive products while at the same time having less diversification of exports.

Northrop Frye pointed out long ago about Canada, 'Why go to the trouble of annexing a country that is so easy to exploit without taking any responsibility for it'.[75] Economic penetration has proven simpler than military force. NAFTA, according to its critics, is a neo-conservative Americanization of Canada.[76] The pre-agreement years saw trade on a multilateral level, without abandoning national control of the foreign market. However, the agreement itself is seen as a straightjacket, because it is difficult to introduce new measures to strengthen or expand national control of firms and industries. It can be argued that it is a dangerous and indefensible gamble for Canada to commit to a binding dispute settlement mechanism with a trading partner, the United States, which has such a disproportionate power. NAFTA has set up a trading bloc designed to fit Canada and Mexico into the American model of development, keeping Europe and Japan out. Mexico is an attractive site for low-wage production of standardized industrial goods, and with this comes Canadian and American job losses, with production shifts to Mexico and a downward pressure on wages. Workers have been displaced from industries and are vulnerable to competition from low-wage countries, with the loss especially to low-income jobs. While the job crisis existed before free trade and was not confined to Canada, NAFTA does nothing for basic labor.

There is a conflict between the profitability of individual corporations and the pressures of global capabilities against human needs for high employment levels, decent pay, healthy working conditions and job security. To serve the corporate profit, what has occurred is a decrease in full-time employment and an increase in part-time and temporary employment at the expense of benefits, as well as an increase in unemployment and in welfare levels. As such, this has been 'the longest and deepest unemployment crisis since the Great Depression', with inappropriate monetary policy playing a major role.[77]

There is a gap in the free trade effect between the top corporate executive and the average shop floor worker. Free trade encourages self-reinforcing cycles of destructive competition, exerting great pressure on the Continent. It has eliminated jobs, depressed incomes and standards. The effects of investment diversion and export harassment far outweigh the positive effects of tariff reductions. There is a one-sided advantage for a corporate elite that is globally competitive, increasing profits, surviving and growing unfettered by government controls, and securing the highest rate of return for the interests of financial capital. Decent jobs and decent living standards have become unimportant. However, employment needs of society must be paramount, and therefore, corporate interests must yield to broader public interests. NAFTA is tilted in the wrong direction. Multilateral trading arrangements with the European Community and Japan would be alternatives to NAFTA and its shortfalls. Canada's social programs are a contrast to those of the United States. Americanization is balkanizing Canada. Regional equality is promised, but individuals, families, communities and regions are being abandoned. Canada was founded on the national principle of building strong communities and regions to serve the needs of residents, not to deplete these areas in order to supply land and factories for economic interests. With lay-offs and closures, there is a bitter legacy of unemployment, poverty and inequality, with society becoming distinctly harsher. Those who are able to thrive are doing very well, but the societal gap is growing so that there is a chasm between rich and poor, young and old, black and white, men and women, non-disabled and disabled, with a disappearing middle class. There is a severe strain on the societal fabric, with a sacrificing of the needs of many for the demands of few.

Among those who were opposed to NAFTA, well-known Canadian Mitchell Sharp stated it best:

> From the very beginnings of our country, we have sought to preserve a separate identity, to live in harmony with our next door neighbour but as an independent country. By entering into this . preferential agreement, we would be deciding no longer to resist the continental pull. On the contrary, we would be accelerating the process of the Americanisation of Canada.[78]

Many believe that free trade challenges the fundamentals of Canada's nationhood, with its powers limited by interdependence and domination from foreign multinationals. The benefits of free trade do not fall equally. Free trade serves to undermine full employment,[79] but the first essential ingredient for free trade should be a commitment to full employment. Sufficient independence for blueprint choices and for flexible alternatives for long-term planning is needed, looking away from integration.

By operating under the deceptive banner of 'free' trade, multinational corporations are working hard to expand their control over the international economy, and to dismantle vital health, safety and environmental protections, which in recent decades have been won by citizens' movements across the globe. According to consumer advocate Ralph Nader, this serves to devalue jobs, depress wage levels, make workplaces less safe, destroy family farms and undermine consumer protections.[80] Because of NAFTA, large global companies have capitalized on poverty in the Third World, by lowering safety and wages in employment. As such, workers, consumers and communities will continue to lose, while short-term profits soar and big business wins, in a threat to move South. Thus the centralization of commercial power is unsound, as the allocation of power to lower levels of government bodies tends to increase citizen power. There is a need for community-oriented production in smaller-scale operations, along with more flexibility and adaptability to local needs for sustainable production methods and democratic controls. There is a race 'to the bottom', pitting State against State, for the lowest wage levels, lowest environmental policies and lowest consumer safety standards.[81]

NAFTA has forced Canada to harmonize its social and economic policies to conform to the United States at the expense of its citizens. Free trade calls for privatization and deregulation, but policy intervention is needed to reduce unemployment and raise wage rates. There has been a shift away from service-type jobs, with pressure to decrease wages and provide fewer benefits for the sake of the almighty American dollar. There has been major job loss by sourcing services outside Canada but also outside the United States.[82] It is important to negotiate over the right of establishment and the right to national treatment. Manufacturing is vulnerable to trade liberalization, which will lead to an increase in unemployment and adverse working conditions, and the United States has an advantage over Canada, because of cheap material, capital intensiveness and technological advancement. As well, in the food industry, Canada is again at a disadvantage due to its size and climate. So too in the electrical field where the United States is again favored, because of a rationalization of production for specializations. Overall, there is a 'going South' policy, since Canadian firms want to locate elsewhere, while still having access to the Canadian market, but at the same time, by phasing out import restrictions, the domestic sector is not protected.

American legislation for North American realignment, it is argued, will curtail equal rights legislation, since equal pay is too costly for the industry. Free trade erodes the domestic service economy.[83] Of the three major categories of sectors, the primary (agriculture and resource extracting), the secondary (construction and manufacturing) and the tertiary (service), the service sector accounts for two-thirds of the national income and 70 percent of jobs in Canada. Foreign service industry activity is limited by non-tariff barriers, through control over investment, ownership and trade levels. The United States, however, believes that government intervention as a matter of security and sovereignty is an unfair practice. Since, the United States accounts for roughly 80 percent of Canada's trade, the Canadian market is vulnerable, because of the large percentage of US-owned businesses, which causes an indirect pressure to conform to United States policy. Interestingly, the United States has easier access to Canada than Canada to the United States, and the American trade remedy legislation imposes pressure upon Canada to harmonize, which impacts social services, availability of and types of employment, job loss, wages, and working conditions. Because of all of these factors, it is found that trade-led growth is not always an adequate economic policy. Free trade is a means not an end.

American Declaration of the Rights and Duties of Man

The Preamble of the American Declaration of the Rights and Duties of Man 1948, important for religious minorities, states:

All men are born free and equal, in dignity and in rights, and, being endowed by nature with reason and conscience, they should conduct themselves as brothers one to another.

The fulfilment of duty by each individual is a prerequisite to the rights of all. Rights and duties are interrelated in every social and political activity of man. While rights exalt individual liberty, duties express the dignity of that liberty.

Duties of a juridical nature presuppose others of a moral nature which support them in principle and constitute their basis.

In as much as spiritual development is the supreme end of human existence and the highest expression thereof, it is the duty of man to serve that end with all his strength and resources.

Since culture is the highest social and historical expression of that spiritual development, it is the duty of man to preserve, practice and foster culture by every means within his power.

And, since moral conduct constitutes the noblest flowering of culture, it is the duty of every man always to hold it in high respect.

WHEREAS:

The American peoples have acknowledged the dignity of the individual, and their national constitutions recognize that juridical and political institutions, which regulate life in human society, have as their principal aim the protection of the essential rights of man and the creation of circumstances that will permit him to achieve spiritual and material progress and attain happiness;

The American States have on repeated occasions recognized that the essential rights of man are not derived from the fact that he is a national of a certain state, but are based upon attributes of his human personality;

The international protection of the rights of man should be the principal guide of an evolving American law;

The affirmation of essential human rights by the American States together with the guarantees given by the internal regimes of the states establish the initial system of protection considered by the American States as being suited to the present social and juridical conditions, not without a recognition on their part that they should increasingly strengthen that system in the international field as conditions become more favourable.[84]

In terms of equal rights and religious equality, Article II, which specifically mentions creed, guarantees the right to equality before the law:

> II. All persons are equal before the law and have the rights and duties established in this Declaration, without distinction as to race, sex, language, creed or any other factor.[85]

Further, important for advancement, the right to education is guaranteed under Article XII:

> XII. Every person has the right to an education, which should be based on the principles of liberty, morality and human solidarity.
>
> Likewise every person has the right to an education that will prepare him to attain a decent life, to raise his standard of living, and to be a useful member of society. The right to an education includes the right to equality of opportunity in every case, in accordance with natural talents, merit and the desire to utilize the resources that the state or the community is in a position to provide. Every person has the right to receive, free, at least a primary education.[86]

In addition, important in the fight against religious discrimination, the right to work and to fair remuneration are contained in Article XIV:

> XIV. Every person has the right to work, under proper conditions, and to follow his vocation freely, in so far as existing conditions of employment permit. Every person who works has the right to receive such remuneration as will, in proportion to his capacity and skill, assure him a standard of living suitable for himself and for his family.[87]

The scope of the rights of man is outlined in Article XXVIII:

> XXVIII. The rights of man are limited by the rights of others, by the security of all, and by the just demands of the general welfare and the advancement of democracy.[88]

In terms of duties, the duty to obey the law is contained in Article XXXIII:

> XXXIII. It is the duty of every person to obey the law and other legitimate commands of the authorities of his country and those of the country in which he may be.[89]

Further, the duty to work is contained in Article XXXVII:

> XXXVII. It is the duty of every person to work, as far as his capacity and possibilities permit, in order to obtain the means of livelihood or to benefit his community.[90]

American Convention on Human Rights

The Preamble of the American Convention on Human Rights 1978, which entered into force on 18 July 1978, states:

> The American states signatory to the present Convention,
>
> *Reaffirming* their intention to consolidate in this hemisphere, within the framework of democratic institutions, a system of personal liberty and social justice based on respect for the essential rights of man;
>
> *Recognizing* that the essential rights of man are not derived from one's being a national of a certain state, but are based upon attributes of the human personality, and that they therefore justify international protection in the form of a convention reinforcing or complementing the protection provided by the domestic law of the American states;
>
> *Considering* that these principles have been set forth in the Charter of the Organization of American States, in the American Declaration of the Rights and Duties of Man, and in the Universal Declaration of Human Rights, and that they have been reaffirmed and refined in other international instruments, worldwide as well as regional in scope;
>
> *Reiterating* that, in accordance with the Universal Declaration of Human Rights, the Ideal of free men enjoying freedom from fear and want can be achieved only if conditions are created whereby everyone may enjoy his economic, social, and cultural rights, as well as his civil and political rights.[91]

Important for equal rights, Article 1, which specifically mentions religion, stresses the obligation to respect rights:

> 1. 1. The States Parties to this Convention undertake to respect the rights and freedoms recognized herein and to ensure to all persons subject to their jurisdiction the free and full exercise of those rights and freedoms, without any discrimination for reasons of race, color, sex, language, religion, political or other opinion, national or social origin, economic status, birth, or any other social condition.
> 2. For the purposes of this Convention, 'person' means every human being.[92]

Further, freedom of Conscience and Religion is guaranteed in Article 12:

> 12.1. Everyone has the right to freedom of conscience and of religion. This right includes freedom to maintain or to change one's religion or beliefs, and freedom to profess or disseminate one's religion or beliefs, either individually or together with others, in public or in private.
> 2. No one shall be subject to restrictions that might impair his freedom to maintain or to change his religion or beliefs.

3. Freedom to manifest one's religion and beliefs may be subject only to the limitations prescribed by law that are necessary to protect public safety, order, health, or morals, or the rights or freedoms of others.
4. Parents or guardians, as the case may be, have the right to provide for the religious and moral education of their children or wards that is in accord with their own convictions.[93]

Further, freedom of thought and expression are safeguarded as pertaining to religion in Article 13.5:

13.5. Any propaganda for war and any advocacy of national, racial, or religious hatred that constitute incitements to lawless violence or to any other similar action against any person or group of persons on any grounds including those of race, color, religion, language, or national origin shall be considered as offenses punishable by law.[94]

Important for religious discrimination cases, the right to equal protection is guaranteed under Article 24:

24. All persons are equal before the law. Consequently, they are entitled, without discrimination, to equal protection of the law.[95]

Further, freedom of movement and residence, critical for employment opportunities, is guaranteed under Article 22:

22. 1. Every person lawfully in the territory of a State Party has the right to move about in it, and to reside in it subject to the provisions of the law.
2. Every person has the right to leave any country freely, including his own.
3. The exercise of the foregoing rights may be restricted only pursuant to a law to the extent necessary in a democratic society to prevent crime or to protect national security, public safety, public order, public morals, public health, or the rights or freedoms of others.
4. The exercise of the rights recognized in paragraph 1 may also be restricted by law in designated zones for reasons of public interest.
5. No one can be expelled from the territory of the state of which he is a national or be deprived of the right to enter it.
6. An alien lawfully in the territory of a State Party to this Convention may be expelled from it only pursuant to a decision reached in accordance with law.
7. Every person has the right to seek and be granted asylum in a foreign territory, in accordance with the legislation of the state and international conventions, in the event he is being pursued for political offenses or related common crimes.
8. In no case may an alien be deported or returned to a country, regardless of whether or not it is his country of origin, if in that country his right to life or personal freedom is in danger of being violated because of his race, nationality, religion, social status, or political opinions.
9. The collective expulsion of aliens is prohibited.[96]

In terms of civil and political rights, the right to Juridical Personality is contained in Article 3:

> 3. Every person has the right to recognition as a person before the law.[97]
> Further, domestic legal effects are outlined in Article 2:
> 2. Where the exercise of any of the rights or freedoms referred to in Article 1 is not already ensured by legislative or other provisions, the States Parties undertake to adopt, in accordance with their constitutional processes and the provisions of this Convention, such legislative or other measures as may be necessary to give effect to those rights or freedoms.[98]

Crucially, the right to judicial protection is guaranteed under Article 25:

> 25. 1. Everyone has the right to simple and prompt recourse, or any other effective recourse, to a competent court or tribunal for protection against acts that violate his fundamental rights recognized by the constitution or laws of the state concerned or by this Convention, even though such violation may have been committed by persons acting in the course of their official duties.
> 2. The States Parties undertake:
> a. to ensure that any person claiming such remedy shall have his rights determined by the competent authority provided for by the legal system of the state;
> b. to develop the possibilities of judicial remedy; and
> c. to ensure that the competent authorities shall enforce such remedies when granted.[99]

In addition, Article 28 contains a federal clause:

> 28. 1. Where a State Party is constituted as a federal state, the national government of such State Party shall implement all the provisions of the Convention over whose subject matter it exercises legislative and judicial jurisdiction.[100]

As well, in terms of economic, social and cultural rights, Article 26 provides for progressive development:

> 26. The States Parties undertake to adopt measures, both internally and through international cooperation, especially those of an economic and technical nature, with a view to achieving progressively, by legislation or other appropriate means, the full realization of the rights implicit in the economic, social, educational, scientific, and cultural standards set forth in the Charter of the Organization of American States ....[101]

There are a number of competent organs involved as outlined in Article 33:

> 33. The following organs shall have competence with respect to matters relating to the fulfilment of the commitments made by the States Parties to this Convention:

a. the Inter-American Commission on Human Rights, referred to as 'The Commission'; and
b. the Inter-American Court of Human Rights, referred to as 'The Court'.[102]

In terms of the Inter-American Commission on Human Rights, Article 35 outlines the organization:

> 35. The Commission shall represent all the member countries of the Organization of American States.[103]

The functions of the Inter-American Commission on Human Rights are outlined in Article 41:

> 41. The main function of the Commission shall be to promote respect for and defense of human rights. In the exercise of its mandate, it shall have the following functions and powers:
> a. to develop an awareness of human rights among the peoples of America;
> b. to make recommendations to the governments of the member states, when it considers such action advisable, for the adoption of progressive measures in favor of human rights within the framework of their domestic law and constitutional provisions as well as appropriate measures to further the observance of those rights;
> c. to prepare such studies or reports as it considers advisable in the performance of its duties;
> d. to request the governments of the member states to supply it with information on the measures adopted by them in matters of human rights;
> e. to respond, through the General Secretariat of the Organization of American States, to inquiries made by the member states on matters related to human rights and, within the limits of its possibilities, to provide those states with the advisory services they request;
> f. to take action on petitions and other communications pursuant to its authority under the provisions of Articles 44 through 51 of this Convention; and
> g. to submit an annual report to the General Assembly of the Organization of American States.[104]

The competency to lodge petitions is outlined in Article 44:

> 44. Any person or group of persons, or any nongovernmental entity legally recognized in one or more member states of the Organization, may lodge petitions with the Commission containing denunciations or complaints of violation of this Convention by a State Party.[105]

Admissibility of petitions is outlined in Article 46:

> 46. 1. Admission by the Commission of a petition or communication ... shall be subject to the following requirements:

a. that the remedies under domestic law have been pursued and exhausted in accordance with generally recognized principles of international law;
b. that the petition or communication is lodged within a period of six months from the date on which the party alleging violation of his rights was notified of the final judgment;
c. that the subject of the petition or communication is not pending in another international proceeding for settlement.
2. The provisions of paragraphs 1.a and 1.b of this article shall not be applicable when:
a. the domestic legislation of the state concerned does not afford due process of law for the protection of the right or rights that have allegedly been violated;
b. the party alleging violation of his rights has been denied access to the remedies under domestic law or has been prevented from exhausting them; or
c. there has been unwarranted delay in rendering a final judgment under the aforementioned remedies.[106]

The procedure is outlined in Article 48:

48. 1. When the Commission receives a petition or communication alleging violation of any of the rights protected by this Convention, it shall proceed as follows:
a. If it considers the petition or communication admissible, it shall request information from the government of the state indicated as being responsible for the alleged violations and shall furnish that government a transcript of the pertinent portions of the petition or communication. This information shall be submitted within a reasonable period to be determined by the Commission in accordance with the circumstances of each case.
b. After the information has been received, or after the period established has elapsed and the information has not been received, the Commission shall ascertain whether the grounds for the petition or communication still exist. If they do not, the Commission shall order the record to be closed.
c. The Commission may also declare the petition or communication inadmissible or out of order on the basis of information or evidence subsequently received.
d. If the record has not been closed, the Commission shall, with the knowledge of the parties, examine the matter set forth in the petition or communication in order to verify the facts. If necessary and advisable, the Commission shall carry out an investigation, for the effective conduct of which it shall request, and the states concerned shall furnish to it, all necessary facilities.
e. The Commission may request the states concerned to furnish any pertinent information and, if so requested, shall hear oral statements or receive written statements from the parties concerned.
f. The Commission shall place itself at the disposal of the parties concerned with a view to reaching a friendly settlement of the matter on the basis of respect for the human rights recognized in this Convention.
2. However, in serious and urgent cases, only the presentation of a petition or communication that fulfils all the formal requirements of admissibility shall be necessary in order for the Commission to conduct an investigation with the prior consent of the state in whose territory a violation has allegedly been committed.[107]

In terms of the Inter-American Court of Human Rights, the right of submission is outlined in Article 61:

> 61.1. Only the States Parties and the Commission shall have the right to submit a case to the Court.[108]

The safeguarding of rights and the provision of measures are contained in Article 63:

> 63. 1. If the Court finds that there has been a violation of a right or freedom protected by this Convention, the Court shall rule that the injured party be ensured the enjoyment of his right or freedom that was violated. It shall also rule, if appropriate, that the consequences of the measure or situation that constituted the breach of such right or freedom be remedied and that fair compensation be paid to the injured party.
> 2. In cases of extreme gravity and urgency, and when necessary to avoid irreparable damage to persons, the Court shall adopt such provisional measures as it deems pertinent in matters it has under consideration. With respect to a case not yet submitted to the Court, it may act at the request of the Commission.[109]

In terms of procedure, Article 66 calls for reasons for judgments:

> 66. 1. Reasons shall be given for the judgment of the Court.[110]

Further, finality of judgment is contained in Article 67:

> 67. The judgment of the Court shall be final and not subject to appeal. In case of disagreement as to the meaning or scope of the judgment, the Court shall interpret it at the request of any of the parties, provided the request is made within ninety days from the date of notification of the judgment.[111]

Finally, compliance with the judgment is underlined in Article 68:

> 68. 1. The States Parties to the Convention undertake to comply with the judgment of the Court in any case to which they are parties.
> 2. That part of a judgment that stipulates compensatory damages may be executed in the country concerned in accordance with domestic procedure governing the execution of judgments against the state.[112]

Statute of the Inter-American Court on Human Rights

More specifically and carrying on from the American Convention on Human Rights, Article 1 of the Statute of the Inter-American Court on Human Rights 1980, which entered into force on 1 January 1980, outlines the nature of the legal organization:

1. The Inter-American Court of Human Rights is an autonomous judicial institution whose purpose is the application and interpretation of the American Convention on Human Rights. The Court exercises its functions in accordance with the provisions of the aforementioned Convention and the present Statute.[113]

The jurisdiction of the Court is contained in Article 2:

2. The Court shall exercise adjudicatory and advisory jurisdiction:
1. Its adjudicatory jurisdiction shall be governed by the provisions of Articles 61, 62 and 63 of the Convention, and
2. Its advisory jurisdiction shall be governed by the provisions of Article 64 of the Convention.[114]

The seat of the Court is contained in Article 3:

3. 1. The seat of the Court shall be San Jose, Costa Rica; however, the Court may convene in any member state of the Organization of American States (OAS) when a majority of the Court considers it desirable, and with the prior consent of the State concerned.[115]

Further, the composition of the Court is contained in Article 4:

4. 1. The Court shall consist of seven judges, nationals of the member states of the OAS, elected in an individual capacity from among jurists of the highest moral authority and of recognized competence in the field of human rights, who possess the qualifications required for the exercise of the highest judicial functions under the law of the State of which they are nationals or of the State that proposes them as candidates.
2. No two judges may be nationals of the same State.[116]

The structure of the Court includes the Presidency as outlined in Article 12 and the Secretariat as outlined in Article 14:

12. 1. The Court shall elect from among its members a President and Vice-President who shall serve for a period of two years; they may be reelected.
2. The President shall direct the work of the Court, represent it, regulate the disposition of matters brought before the Court, and preside over its sessions.[117]
14. 1. The Secretariat of the Court shall function under the immediate authority of the Secretary, in accordance with the administrative standards of the OAS General Secretariat, in all matters that are not incompatible with the independence of the Court.
2. The Secretary shall be appointed by the Court. He shall be a full-time employee serving in a position of trust to the Court, shall have his office at the seat of the Court and shall attend any meetings that the Court holds away from its seat.

> 3. There shall be an Assistant Secretary who shall assist the Secretary in his duties and shall replace him in his temporary absence.
> 4. The Staff of the Secretariat shall be appointed by the Secretary General of the OAS, in consultation with the Secretary of the Court. [118]

In terms of the workings of the Court, Article 24 outlines the hearings, deliberations and decisions:

> 24. 1. The hearings shall be public, unless the Court, in exceptional circumstances, decides otherwise.
> 2. The Court shall deliberate in private. Its deliberations shall remain secret, unless the Court decides otherwise.
> 3. The decisions, judgments and opinions of the Court shall be delivered in public session, and the parties shall be given written notification thereof. In addition, the decisions, judgments and opinions shall be published, along with judges' individual votes and opinions and with such other data or background information that the Court may deem appropriate.[119]

Article 27 stresses the importance of relations with the host country, governments and organizations:

> 27. 1. The relations of the Court with the host country shall be governed through a headquarters agreement. The seat of the Court shall be international in nature.
> 2. The relations of the Court with governments, with the OAS and its organs, agencies and entities and with other international governmental organizations involved in promoting and defending human rights shall be governed through special agreements.[120]

Finally, Article 28 stresses the importance of the relations with the Inter-American Commission on Human Rights:

> 28. The Inter-American Commission on Human Rights shall appear as a party before the Court in all cases within the adjudicatory jurisdiction of the Court, pursuant to Article 2(1) of the present Statute.[121]

Inter-American Democratic Charter

The Preamble of the Inter-American Democratic Charter 2001, which came into force on 11 September 2001, states:

> THE GENERAL ASSEMBLY,
>
> CONSIDERING that the Charter of the Organization of American States recognizes that representative democracy is indispensable for the stability, peace, and development

of the region, and that one of the purposes of the OAS is to promote and consolidate representative democracy, with due respect for the principle of nonintervention;

RECALLING that the Heads of State and Government of the Americas, gathered at the Third Summit of the Americas, held from April 20 to 22, 2001 in Quebec City, adopted a democracy clause which establishes that any unconstitutional alteration or interruption of the democratic order in a state of the Hemisphere constitutes an insurmountable obstacle to the participation of that state's government in the Summits of the Americas process;

REAFFIRMING that the participatory nature of democracy in our countries in different aspects of public life contributes to the consolidation of democratic values and to freedom and solidarity in the Hemisphere;

CONSIDERING that solidarity among and cooperation between American states require the political organization of those states based on the effective exercise of representative democracy, and that economic growth and social development based on justice and equity, and democracy are interdependent and mutually reinforcing;

BEARING IN MIND that the American Declaration on the Rights and Duties of Man and the American Convention on Human Rights contain the values and principles of liberty, equality, and social justice that are intrinsic to democracy;

REAFFIRMING that the promotion and protection of human rights is a basic prerequisite for the existence of a democratic society, and recognizing the importance of the continuous development and strengthening of the inter-American human rights system for the consolidation of democracy;

CONSIDERING that education is an effective way to promote citizens' awareness concerning their own countries and thereby achieve meaningful participation in the decision-making process, and reaffirming the importance of human resource development for a sound democratic system;

RECOGNIZING that the right of workers to associate themselves freely for the defense and promotion of their interests is fundamental to the fulfillment of democratic ideals.[122]

The anti-discrimination provision, important for religious minorities, is contained in Article 9, which specifically mentions religion:

The elimination of all forms of discrimination, especially gender, ethnic and race discrimination, as well as diverse forms of intolerance, the promotion and protection of human rights of indigenous peoples and migrants, and respect for ethnic, cultural and religious diversity in the Americas contribute to strengthening democracy and citizen participation.[123]

Workers' rights and labor standards are emphasized in Article 10:

> The promotion and strengthening of democracy requires the full and effective exercise of workers' rights and the application of core labor standards, as recognized in the International Labour Organization (ILO) Declaration on Fundamental Principles and Rights at Work ..., adopted in 1998, as well as other related fundamental ILO conventions. Democracy is strengthened by improving standards in the workplace and enhancing the quality of life for workers in the Hemisphere.[124]

The importance of claims and redress for grievances is outlined in Article 8:

> Any person or group of persons who consider that their human rights have been violated may present claims or petitions to the inter-American system for the promotion and protection of human rights in accordance with its established procedures.
>
> Member states reaffirm their intention to strengthen the inter-American system for the protection of human rights for the consolidation of democracy in the Hemisphere.[125]

Further, in terms of democracy and the inter-American system, Article 4 espouses the importance of transparency:

> Transparency in government activities, probity, responsible public administration on the part of governments, respect for social rights, and freedom of expression and of the press are essential components of the exercise of democracy.
>
> The constitutional subordination of all state institutions to the legally constituted civilian authority and respect for the rule of law on the part of all institutions and sectors of society are equally essential to democracy.[126]

Finally, in terms of human rights, Article 7 stresses the importance of democracy:

> Democracy is indispensable for the effective exercise of fundamental freedoms and human rights in their universality, indivisibility and interdependence, embodied in the respective constitutions of states and in inter-American and international human rights instruments.[127]

Conclusion

By recognizing that we share a hemisphere, NAFTA sets an important precedent for north-south continental trade, and looks toward the future by allowing for participation by other countries, if they meet the membership criteria set by the three founding nations. Latin American countries have expressed an interest in becoming signatory members of the Free Trade Agreement. In addition, the

Canadian Province of Quebec has already given thought to joining as a separate member in the event it becomes a separate nation., but wishes to maintain the current division of legislative powers, respect fully its unique social policy, language and culture, maintain a leeway to modernize and develop its economy, provide for transitional periods for businesses in less competitive sectors, adopt a dispute settlement mechanism, maintain its special status for agriculture and fisheries, and protect its right to decide on the Agreement in light of its interests. The Parties to the North American Free Trade Agreement (NAFTA) are cooperating to advance trade liberalization not only within North America with the NAFTA Superhighway, but also in the negotiations for the Free Trade Area of the Americas (FTAA). Recognizing their shared interests, the NAFTA partners have worked together to advance trade liberalization. In 2001, Canada hosted the Summit of the Americas, a gathering of the 34 democratically elected Heads of State of the Western Hemisphere. The FTAA would eliminate trade and investment barriers on virtually all goods and services traded by member countries, reduce prices for consumers and create new markets for producers throughout the hemisphere.

However, more needs to be done to legislate for equal rights and religious freedom for workers. President John F. Kennedy, who himself asked to be judged not by his religion but by his skills and experience, stated with regard to the relationship between Canada and the United States: 'Geography has made us neighbors, history has made us friends, the economy has made us partners and necessity has made us allies'.[128] In this spirit, important in the fight against religious discrimination, we need to work together to bring about full equality in the Americas, in the pursuit of *Heaven Forbid*.

Notes

1 Hamelin, Jean, *Histoire du Québec*, Edisem, St. Hyacinthe, 1976, p. 371.
2 Easterbrook, W.T. and Aitken, Hugh, *Canadian Economic History*, Macmillan, Toronto, 1976, p. 362.
3 *Ibid.*, at p. 361.
4 Fry, Earl, 'Trends in Canada-U.S. Free Trade Discussions', in A.R. Riggs and Tom Welk, *Canadian-American Free Trade: Historical, Political and Economic Dimensions*, The Institute for Research in Public Policy, Montreal, 1987, p. 28.
5 d'Aquino, Thomas, 'Truck and Trade with the Yankees, The Case for a Canada-U.S. Comprehensive Trade Agreement', in A.R. Riggs and Tom Velk, *Canadian-American Free Trade: Historical, Political and Economic Dimensions*, The Institute for Research on Public Policy, Montreal, 1987, p. 74.
6 Velk, Tom, and Riggs, A.R., 'The Ongoing Debate Over Free Trade', in A.R. Riggs and Tom Velk, *Canadian-American Free Trade: (The Sequel) Historical, Political and Economic Dimensions*, The Institute for Research on Public Policy, Montreal, 1988, p. 93.
7 General Agreement on Tariffs and Trade, at Article 24.

8   Laun, Louis, 'U.S.-Canada Free Trade Negotiations: Historical Opportunities', in A.R. Riggs and Tom Velk, *Canadian-American Free Trade: Historical, Political and Economic Dimensions*, The Institute for Research in Public Policy, Montreal, 1987, p. 205.
9   Fry, Earl, 'Trends in Canada-U.S. Free Trade Discussions', in A.R., Riggs and Tom Welk, *Canadian-American Free Trade: Historical, Political and Economic Dimensions*, The Institute for Research in Public Policy, Montreal, 1987, p. 9.
10 *Ibid.*, at p. 34.
11 *Ibid.*, at p. 27.
12 Watkins, Mel, 'The Political Economy of Growth', in Wallace Clement and Glen Williams, *The New Canadian Political Economy*, McGill-Queen's University Press, Kingston, 1989, p. 17.
13 Laun, Louis, 'U.S.-Canada Free Trade Negotiations: Historical Opportunities', in A.R. Riggs and Tom Velk, *Canadian-American Free Trade: Historical, Political and Economic Dimensions*, The Institute for Research in Public Policy, Montreal, 1987 p. 205.
14 Government of Canada, *The North American Free Trade Agreement At A Glance*, Ottawa, p. 1.
15 Soldatos, P., 'Canada's Foreign Policy in Search of a Fourth Option: Continuity and Change in Orientation Towards the U.S.', in A.R. Riggs and Tom Velk, *Canadian-American Free Trade: (The Sequel) Historical, Political and Economic Dimensions*, The Institute for Research on Public Policy, Montreal, 1988, p. 41.
16 Lipsey, Richard, 'Canada's Trade Options', in A.R. Riggs and TomVelk, *Canadian-American Free Trade: Historical, Political and Economic Dimensions*, The Institute for Research on Public Policy, Montreal, 1987, p. 59.
17 Brecher, Irving, 'The Free Trade Initiative, On Course or Off', in A.R. Riggs and Tom Velk, *Canadian-American Free Trade: Historical, Political and Economic Dimensions*, The Institute for Research in Public Policy, Montreal, 1987, p. 67.
18 Neufeld, E.P, 'Financial and Economic Dimensions of Free Trade', in A.R. Riggs and Tom Velk, *Canadian-American Free Trade: Historical, Political and Economic Dimensions*, The Institute for Research on Public Policy, Montreal, 1987, p. 152.
19 *Ibid.*, at p. 155.
20 Layton, Robert, 'Why Canada Needs Free Trade', in A.R. Riggs and Tom Velk, *Canadian-American Free Trade: Historical, Political and Economic Dimensions*, The Institute for Research in Public Policy, Montreal, 1987, p. 200.
21 Velk, Tom, and Riggs, A.R., 'The Ongoing Debate Over Free Trade', in A.R. Riggs and Tom Velk, *Canadian-American Free Trade: (The Sequel) Historical, Political and Economic Dimensions*, The Institute for Research on Public Policy, Montreal, 1988, p. 3.
22 d'Aquino, Thomas, 'Truck and Trade with the Yankees, The Case for a Canada-U.S. Comprehensive Trade Agreement', in A.R. Riggs and Tom Velk, *Canadian-American Free Trade: Historical, Political and Economic Dimensions*, The Institute for Research on Public Policy, Montreal, 1987, p. 74.

23 Mexican Investment Board, *Mexico Your Partner for Growth, Regulatory Reform and Competition Policy, Setting the Incentives for an Efficient Economy*, Mexico, 1994, p. 1.
24 Laun, Louis, 'U.S.-Canada Free Trade Negotiations: Historical Opportunities', in A.R. Riggs and Tom Velk, *Canadian-American Free Trade: Historical, Political and Economic Dimensions*, The Institute for Research in Public Policy, Montreal, 1987, p. 208.
25 Harris, Richard, 'Some Observations on the Canada-U.S. Free Trade Deal', in A.R. Riggs and Tom Velk, *Canadian-American Free Trade: (The Sequel) Historical, Political and Economic Dimensions*, The Institute for Research on Public Policy, Montreal 1988, p. 52.
26 North American Free Trade Agreement, at the Preamble.
27 *Ibid.*, at Article 1201.
28 *Ibid.*, at Article 1202, 1203.
29 *Ibid.*, at Article 1208.
30 *Ibid.*, at Article 1213.
31 *Ibid.*, at Article 1210.
32 *Ibid.*, at Annex 1210.A.2.
33 *Ibid.*, at Annex 1210.A.3.
34 *Ibid.*, at Annex 1210.B.1.
35 *Ibid.*, at Article 1601.
36 *Ibid.*, at Article 1602.
37 *Ibid.*, at Annex 1603.A.
38 *Ibid.*, at Annex 1603.B.
39 *Ibid.*, at Annex 1603.C.
40 *Ibid.*, at Annex 1603.D.
41 *Ibid.*, at Appendix 1603.D.1.
42 *Ibid.*, at Article 2001.
43 *Ibid.*, at Article 2002.
44 *Ibid.*, at Article 2003.
45 *Ibid.*, at Article 1606.
46 *Ibid.*, at Article 2004.
47 *Ibid.*, at Article 2008.
48 *Ibid.*, at Article 2012.
49 *Ibid.*, at Article 2017.
50 *Ibid.*, at Article 2018.
51 *Ibid.*, at Article 2019.
52 *Ibid.*, at Article 2020.
53 *Ibid.*, at Article 2021.
54 *Ibid.*, at Article 2022.
55 North American Agreement on Labor Cooperation (NAALC), at the Preamble.
56 *Ibid.*, at Article 1.
57 *Ibid.*, at Article 2.
58 *Ibid.*, at Article 3.

59 *Ibid.*, at Article 4.
60 *Ibid.*, at Article 5.
61 *Ibid.*, at Article 11.
62 *Ibid.*, at Article 49.
63 *Ibid.*, at Annex 1, Article 7.
64 Government of Canada, *The North American Free Trade Agreement At A Glance*, Ottawa, p. 3.
65 Wigle, Randall, 'The Received Wisdom of the Canada-U.S. Free Trade Qualifications', in A.R. Riggs and Tom Velk, *Canadian-American Free Trade: Historical, Political and Economic Dimensions*, The Institute for Research in Public Policy, Montreal, 1987, p. 92.
66 Raynauld, Andre, 'Looking Outward Again', in A.R. Riggs and Tom Velk, *Canadian American Free Trade: Historical, Political and Economic Dimensions*, The Institute for Research on Public Policy, Montreal, 1987, p. 86.
67 Stone, Frank, 'Removing Barriers to Canada', in A.R. Riggs and Tom Velk, *Canadian-American Free Trade: Historical, Political and Economic Dimensions*, The Institute for Research in Public Policy, Montreal, 1987, p. 183.
68 Government of Canada, *NAFTA at Eight*, Ottawa, 2002.
69 Merrett, Christopher, *Free Trade, Neither Free Nor About Trade*, Black Rose Books, New York, 1996, p. 270.
70 *Ibid.*, at p. 95.
71 *Ibid.*, at p. 271.
72 *Ibid.*, at p. 279.
73 McPhail, Brenda, *NAFTA Now*, University Press of America, Lanham, 1985, p. 44.
74 Hurtig, Mel, *The Betrayal of Canada*, Stoddart Publishing, Toronto, 1991, p. 303.
75 *Ibid.*, at p. 89.
76 Watkins, Mel, 'The Political Economy of Growth', in Wallace Clement and Glen Williams, *The New Canadian Political Economy*, McGill-Queen's University Press, Kingston, 1989, p. 3.
77 Campbell, Bruce, *Free Trade, Destroyer of Jobs*, Canadian Centre for Policy Alternatives, Ottawa. 1993, p. 2.
78 Axworthy, Lloyd, 'Free Trade, The Costs for Canada', in A.R. Riggs and Tom Velk, *Canadian-American Free Trade: (The Sequel) Historical, Political and Economic Dimensions*, The Institute for Research on Public Policy, Montreal, 1988, p. 38.
79 *Ibid.*, at p. 39.
80 Nader, Ralph, *The Case Against Free Trade*, Earth Island Press, San Francisco, 1993, p. 1.
81 *Ibid.*, at p. 6.
82 Griffin Cohen, Marjorie, *Free Trade and the Future of Women's Work, Manufacturing and Service Industries*, Garamond Press, Toronto, 1987, p. 16.
83 *Ibid.*, at p. 49.
84 American Declaration of the Rights and Duties of Man, at the Preamble.
85 *Ibid.*, at Article II.
86 *Ibid.*, at Article XII.

87 *Ibid.*, at Article XIV.
88 *Ibid.*, at Article XXVIII.
89 *Ibid.*, at Article XXXIII.
90 *Ibid.*, at Article XXXVII.
91 American Convention on Human Rights, at the Preamble.
92 *Ibid.*, at Article 1.
93 *Ibid.*, at Article 12.
94 *Ibid.*, at Article 13.5.
95 *Ibid.*, at Article 24.
96 *Ibid.*, at Article 22.
97 *Ibid.*, at Article 3.
98 *Ibid.*, at Article 2.
99 *Ibid.*, at Article 25.
100 *Ibid.*, at Article 28.
101 *Ibid.*, at Article 26.
102 *Ibid.*, at Article 33.
103 *Ibid.*, at Article 35.
104 *Ibid.*, at Article 41.
105 *Ibid.*, at Article 44.
106 *Ibid.*, at Article 46.
107 *Ibid.*, at Article 48.
108 *Ibid.*, at Article 61.
109 *Ibid.*, at Article 63.
110 *Ibid.*, at Article 66.
111 *Ibid.*, at Article 67.
112 *Ibid.*, at Article 68.
113 Statute of the Inter-American Court on Human Rights, at Article 1.
114 *Ibid.*, at Article 2.
115 *Ibid.*, at Article 3.
116 *Ibid.*, at Article 4.
117 *Ibid.*, at Article 12.
118 *Ibid.*, at Article 14.
119 *Ibid.*, at Article 24.
120 *Ibid.*, at Article 27.
121 *Ibid.*, at Article 28.
122 Inter-American Democratic Charter, at the Preamble.
123 *Ibid.*, at Article 9.
124 *Ibid.*, at Article 10.
125 *Ibid.*, at Article 8.
126 *Ibid.*, at Article 4.
127 *Ibid.*, at Article 7.
128 President John F. Kennedy.

References

American Convention on Human Rights, 1978.
American Declaration of the Rights and Duties of Man, 1948.
Axworthy, Lloyd (1988), 'Free Trade, The Costs for Canada', in A.R. Riggs and Tom Velk, *Canadian-American Free Trade: (The Sequel) Historical, Political and Economic Dimensions*, The Institute for Research on Public Policy, Montreal.
Brecher, Irving (1987), 'The Free Trade Initiative, On Course or Off', in A.R. Riggs and Tom Velk, *Canadian-American Free Trade: Historical, Political and Economic Dimensions*, The Institute for Research in Public Policy, Montreal.
Campbell, Bruce (1993), *Free Trade, Destroyer of Jobs*, Canadian Centre for Policy Alternatives, Ottawa.
Canada-United States Free Trade Agreement, 1989.
d'Aquino, Thomas (1987), 'Truck and Trade with the Yankees, The Case for a Canada-U.S. Comprehensive Trade Agreement', in A.R. Riggs and Tom Velk, *Canadian-American Free Trade: Historical, Political and Economic Dimensions*, The Institute for Research on Public Policy, Montreal.
Easterbrook, W.T. and Aitken, Hugh (1976), *Canadian Economic History*, Macmillan, Toronto.
Fry, Earl (1987), 'Trends in Canada-U.S. Free Trade Discussions', in A.R. Riggs and Tom Welk, *Canadian-American Free Trade: Historical, Political and Economic Dimensions*, The Institute for Research in Public Policy, Montreal.
General Agreement on Tariffs and Trade, 1947.
Government of Canada (2002), *NAFTA at Eight*, Ottawa.
Government of Canada (1993), *The North American Free Trade Agreement At A Glance*, Ottawa.
Griffin Cohen, Marjorie (1987), *Free Trade and the Future of Women's Work, Manufacturing and Service Industries*, Garamond Press, Toronto.
Hamelin, Jean (1976), *Histoire du Québec*, Edisem, St. Hyacinthe.
Harris, Richard (1988), 'Some Observations on the Canada-U.S. Free Trade Deal', in A.R. Riggs and Tom Velk, *Canadian-American Free Trade: (The Sequel) Historical, Political and Economic Dimensions*, The Institute for Research on Public Policy, Montreal.
Hurtig, Mel (1991), *The Betrayal of Canada*, Stoddart Publishing, Toronto.
Inter-American Democratic Charter, 2001.
Laun, Louis (1987), 'U.S.-Canada Free Trade Negotiations: Historical Opportunities', in A.R. Riggs and Tom Velk, *Canadian-American Free Trade: Historical, Political and Economic Dimensions*, The Institute for Research in Public Policy, Montreal.
Layton, Robert (1987), 'Why Canada Needs Free Trade', in A.R. Riggs and Tom Velk, *Canadian-American Free Trade: Historical, Political and Economic Dimensions*, The Institute for Research in Public Policy, Montreal.

Lipsey, Richard (1987), 'Canada's Trade Options', in A.R. Riggs and Tom Velk, *Canadian-American Free Trade: Historical, Political and Economic Dimensions*, The Institute for Research in Public Policy, Montreal.

McPhail, Brenda (1985), *NAFTA Now*, University Press of America, Lanham.

Merrett, Christopher (1996), *Free Trade, Neither Free Nor About Trade*, Black Rose Books, New York.

Mexican Investment Board (1994), *Mexico Your Partner for Growth, Regulatory Reform and Competition Policy, Setting the Incentives for an Efficient Economy*, Mexico.

Nader, Ralph (1993), *The Case Against Free Trade*, Earth Island Press, San Francisco.

Neufeld, E.P. (1987), 'Financial and Economic Dimensions of Free Trade', in A.R. Riggs and Tom Velk, *Canadian-American Free Trade: Historical, Political and Economic Dimensions*, The Institute for Research on Public Policy, Montreal.

North American Agreement on Labor Cooperation, 1993.

North American Free Trade Agreement, 1994.

President John F. Kennedy.

Raynauld, Andre (1987), 'Looking Outward Again', in A.R. Riggs and Tom Velk, *Canadian-American Free Trade: Historical, Political and Economic Dimensions*, The Institute for Research on Public Policy, Montreal.

Soldatos, P (1988), 'Canada's Foreign Policy in Search of a Fourth Option: Continuity and Change in Orientation Towards the U.S.', in A.R. Riggs and Tom Velk, *Canadian-American Free Trade: (The Sequel) Historical, Political and Economic Dimensions*, The Institute for Research on Public Policy, Montreal.

Statute of the Inter-American Court on Human Rights, 1980.

Stone, Frank (1987), 'Removing Barriers to Canada', in A.R. Riggs and Tom Velk, *Canadian-American Free Trade: Historical, Political and Economic Dimensions*, The Institute for Research on Public Policy, Montreal.

Velk, Tom and Riggs, A.R. (1987), 'The Ongoing Debate Over Free Trade', in A.R. Riggs and Tom Velk, *Canadian-American Free Trade: Historical, Political and Economic Dimensions*, The Institute for Research on Public Policy, Montreal.

Watkins, Mel (1989), 'The Political Economy of Growth', in Wallace Clement and Glen Williams, *The New Canadian Political Economy*, McGill-Queen's University Press, Kingston.

Wigle, Randall (1987), 'The Received Wisdom of the Canada-U.S. Free Trade Qualifications', in A.R. Riggs and Tom Welk, *Canadian-American Free Trade: Historical, Political and Economic Dimensions*, The Institute for Research in Public Policy, Montreal.

Chapter 8
Heaven Forbid in the United Kingdom and Ireland

Introduction

In the quest for religious tolerance in *Heaven Forbid*, this chapter will examine efforts against religious discrimination in the United Kingdom and Ireland. As well as examining religious discrimination court cases, it will review important legislation impacting equal rights, first in the United Kingdom, which encompasses England, Scotland, Wales and Northern Ireland, namely for religious minorities in general the Racial Relations Act and for religious women the Sexual Discrimination Act, and in particular the Equal Pay Act, the Equal Opportunities Commission (EOC) and the Code of Practice on Equal Pay, the Human Rights Act, the Employment Equality (Religion or Belief) Regulations and the Equality Act; and then in the Republic of Ireland, namely the Constitution, the Employment Equality Act and the Equal Status Act. There is a need for intervention in the application of human rights law to religious minorities.

United Kingdom

At the outset, if a court determines that it is impossible to interpret an Act of Parliament in a way which is compatible with European convention rights, a formal declaration of incompatibility may be made, and it is then for the Government and Parliament to decide whether or not to amend it. The European Convention on Human Rights upholds freedom of thought, conscience and religion, and the manifestation of religion and belief. This was included in the Human Rights Act (1998), but only applies directly to public bodies. The Employment Equality (Religion or Belief) Regulations 2003 makes it illegal to discriminate against people in employment or vocational training on the basis of their religion or beliefs. In addition, the Equality Act 2006 widened the scope to include the provision of goods, facilities and services, education, the use and disposal of premises, and the exercise of public functions. The religious discrimination regulations give protection against discrimination on the grounds of 'any religion, religious belief or philosophical belief' in a similar way to the existing race discrimination and sex discrimination laws, and the Equality Act 2006 widened this to specifically protect 'lack of belief' as well.

Race Relations Act (RRA)

Important for religious minorities, the Race Relations Act 1976 (RRA) defines direct and indirect discrimination, and victimization. The Act outlaws racial discrimination in employment, training, education, housing, public appointments, and the provision of goods, facilities and services. The Commission for Racial Equality (CRE) has the power to enforce the duties specified in the Act, as it will issue a compliance notice and if necessary seek a court order to enforce the notice. It places a general duty on a range of public authorities to promote race equality, with the duty's aim to make the promotion of race equality central to the work of the listed public authorities, which includes public functions carried out by private sector organizations and has only limited exemption. The public duty requires public bodies to implement race equality in all aspects of employment matters, such as recruitment and selection, training, promotion, discipline and dismissal. In relation to policy development and service delivery, the duty will encourage policy-makers to be more aware of possible problems; contribute to more informed decision making; make sure that policies are properly targeted; improve the authority's ability to deliver suitable and accessible services that meet varied needs; encourage greater openness about policy making; increase confidence in public services, especially among ethnic minority communities; help to develop good practice; and help to avoid claims of unlawful racial discrimination. Four principles should govern public authorities' efforts to meet their duty to promote race equality: promoting race equality is obligatory for all public authorities listed; public authorities must meet the duty to promote race equality in all relevant functions; the weight given to race equality should be proportionate to its relevance; and the elements of the duty are complementary, which means they are all necessary to meet the whole duty. The general duty has three parts: eliminating unlawful racial discrimination; promoting equality of opportunity; and promoting good relations between people of different racial groups.[1]

In terms of a General Statutory duty, Section 71(1) of the Race Relations Act states:

> 71(1) Every body or other person specified in Schedule 1A or a description falling within that Schedule shall, in carrying out its functions, have due regard to the need
> (a) to eliminate unlawful racial discrimination; and
> (b) to promote equality of opportunity and good relations between persons of different racial groups.[2]

In terms of the Employment Duty, Section 5 of the Race Relations Act 1976 (Statutory Duties) Order 2001 or Section 4 of the Race Relations Act 1976 (Statutory Duties) Order 2003 state:

> (a) A person...shall:
> i. Before 31 May 2002 (2001 Order) or 31 May 2004 (2003 Order) or 31 May 2005 (2004 Order) ..., have in place arrangements for fulfilling, as soon as

is reasonably practicable, its duties ..., and fulfil those duties in accordance with such arrangements.

ii. It shall be the duty of such a person to monitor, by reference to the racial groups to which they belong, the numbers of:

Staff in post.

Applicants for employment, training and promotion from each such group, and where that person has 150 or more full-time staff, the numbers of staff from each such group who:

— Receive training.

— Benefit or suffer detriment as a result of its performance assessment procedures.

— Are involved in grievance procedures.

— Are the subject of disciplinary procedures.

— Cease employment with that person.[3]

The divisions between religious discrimination and race discrimination are sometimes blurred, and some aspects of religious discrimination are covered by existing race relations legislation. The Race Relations Act (RRA), which prohibits discrimination on 'racial grounds', defined as 'colour, race, nationality, or ethnic or national origins', makes no express reference to religious discrimination. However, ways have been found to provide limited protection under the RRA to some religious groups which have the characteristics of an ethnic group, such as to Sikhs[4] and Jews.[5] The recognition of a religious community as an ethnic group provides them with protection from both direct and indirect discrimination. In *Mandla v. Dowell Lee* [1983] 2 AC 548, the House of Lords accepted that ethnic origin is a wider concept than race and identified several characteristics relevant to identifying an ethnic group; the two essential characteristics are: a long shared history, which the group is conscious of as distinguishing it from other groups; and a cultural tradition of its own, including family and social customs and manners, often but not necessarily associated with religious observance. Other characteristics were identified as relevant but not essential: a common geographical origin or descent from a small number of common ancestors; a common language, not necessarily peculiar to the group; a common religion different from that of neighboring groups or from the general community around it; and being a minority or being an oppressed or a dominant group within a larger community.[6] Under these criteria, Gypsies have been found to constitute a racial group by virtue of their shared history, geographical origins, distinct customs, a language derived from Romany and a common culture.[7] On the other hand Muslims,[8] Rastafarians[9] and Jehovah's Witnesses[10] have been held not to constitute racial or ethnic groups.

Another way of bringing religious groups within the ambit of the RRA has been through the concept of indirect discrimination. In *J H Walker Ltd v. Hussain* [1996] IRLR 11 EAT, it was decided that actions taken by an employer causing detriment to Muslims as a class, such as refusal to allow time off work for religious holidays, might be held to constitute indirect racial discrimination against those from an ethnic or national origin that is predominantly Muslim.[11] There is a limitation of using indirect race discrimination to tackle religious discrimination. In *Safouane & Bouterfas v. Joseph Ltd and Hannah* [1996] Case No. 12506/95/LS & 12569/95, when two Muslim complainants were dismissed for doing prayers during their breaks, the tribunal held that the acts did not constitute indirect racial discrimination, because the applicants belonged to the same North African ethnic Arab minority as the respondents and that they had a good record of employing staff from a diversity of backgrounds.[12]

Sex Discrimination Act (SDA)

Important for religious women, the Sex Discrimination Act 1975 (SDA) defines direct and indirect discrimination. Further, under the SDA, it is first up to the applicant to establish facts, which constitute a *prima facie* case of discrimination, as the burden of proof is initially on the employee to show on the balance of probabilities that her male comparator is doing the same or broadly similar work, or that her work has been rated as equivalent to his, or that her work is of equal value, and that his contract contains a more favorable term. The burden of proof then shifts from the applicant to the employer to show that there is a nondiscriminatory reason for their actions, that is the difference between the contracts is genuinely due to a material factor which is not the difference of gender. The material factor defense is the reason put forward by the employer to explain why the comparator, although doing equal work, is paid more than the applicant; to succeed in a defense, this factor must be significant and relevant; that is, it must be an important cause of the difference and apply to the jobs in question. The difference in pay must be genuinely due to the material factor which must not be tainted by gender discrimination. If the reason given for paying the comparator more is that he has certain skills which the applicant does not have, then the employer would have to demonstrate that these skills are necessary for the job, and genuinely applied during the performance of the job, and are not simply rewarded because past pay agreements recognized and rewarded skills which are no longer applicable; to succeed in a defense, the employer needs to show that the material factor accounts for the whole of the difference in pay.

Direct and indirect discrimination are defined in Section 1:

1(1) In any circumstances relevant for the purposes of any provision of this Act ..., a person discriminates against a woman if:
(a) on the ground of her sex he treats her less favourably than he treats or would treat a man, or
(b) he applies to her a requirement or condition which he applies or would apply equally to a man but:
    i. which is such that the proportion of women who can comply with it is considerably smaller than the proportion of men who can comply with it, and

ii. which he cannot show to be justifiable irrespective of the sex of the person to whom it is applied, and
iii. which is to her detriment because she cannot comply with it.[13]

In looking at discrimination in the employment stage, Section 6(2) states:

6(2) It is unlawful for a person, in the case of a woman employed by him at an establishment in Great Britain, to discriminate against her:
(a) in the way he affords her access to opportunities for promotion, transfer or training, or to any other benefits, facilities or services, or by refusing or deliberately omitting to afford her access to them, or
(b) by dismissing her, or subjecting her to any other detriment.[14]

There is an exception to the rule where sex is a genuine occupational qualification, which is contained in Section 7:

7(1) In relation to sex discrimination:
(a) section 6(1)(a) or (c) does not apply to any employment where being a man is a genuine occupational qualification for the job.
7(2) Being a man is a genuine occupational qualification for a job only where:
(a) the essential nature of the job calls for a man for reasons of physiology (excluding physical strength or stamina) or, in dramatic performances or other entertainment, for reasons of authenticity, so that the essential nature of the job would be materially different if carried out by a woman; or
(b) the job needs to be held by a man to preserve decency or privacy ...; or
(c) the nature or location of the establishment makes it impracticable for the holder of the job to live elsewhere than in premises provided by the employer ...;
(d) the nature of the establishment, or of the part of it within which the work is done, requires it to be held by a man ...; or
(e) the job needs to be held by a man because of restrictions imposed by the laws regulating the employment of women, or
(f) the holder of the job provides individuals with personal services promoting their welfare or education, or similar personal services, and those services can most effectively be provided by a man, or
(g) the job needs to be held by a man because it is likely to involve the performance of duties outside the United Kingdom in a country whose laws or customs are such that the duties could not, or could not effectively, be performed by a woman, or
(h) the job is one of two to be held by a married couple.[15]

Further, an exception is provided for religious organizations under Sections 19 and 35:

19(1) Nothing in this Part applies to employment for purposes of an organised religion where the employment is limited to one sex so as to comply with the doctrines of the

religion or avoid offending the religious susceptibilities of a significant number of its followers.
(2) Nothing in section 13 applies to an authorisation or qualification (as defined in that section) for purposes of an organised religion where the authorisation or qualification is limited to one sex so as to comply with the doctrines of the religion or avoid offending the religious susceptibilities of a significant number of its followers.[16]
35(1) A person who provides at any place facilities or services restricted to men does not for that reason contravene section 29(1) if
(a) the place is, or is part of, a hospital, reception centre provided by the Supplementary Benefits Commission or other establishment for persons requiring special care, supervision or attention, or
(b) the place is (permanently or for the time being) occupied or used for the purposes of an organised religion, and the facilities or services are restricted to men so as to comply with the doctrines of that religion or avoid offending the religious susceptibilities of a significant number of its followers, or
(c) the facilities or services are provided for, or are likely to be used by, two or more persons at the same time, and
(i) the facilities or services are such, or those persons are such, that male users are likely to suffer serious embarrassment at the presence of a woman, or
(ii) the facilities or services are such that a user is likely to be in a state of undress and a male user might reasonably object to the presence of a female user.[17]

Attempts have been made to use the Sex Discrimination Act 1975 (SDA) to provide protection against some aspects of religious discrimination. In the case of *Sardar v. McDonalds* (1998), a Muslim female complainant was successful in a claim of indirect sex discrimination after she was dismissed for wearing a scarf to cover her hair.[18]

Equal Pay Act (EPA), Equal Opportunities Commission (EOC) and the Code of Practice on Equal Pay

Important for equal rights in employment and in particular religious women, under the Equal Pay Act 1970 (EPA), genuine occupational qualification is recognized in Section 1(3):

1(3) An equality clause shall not operate in relation to a variation between the woman's contract and the man's contract if the employer proves that the variation is genuinely due to a material factor which is not the difference of sex … and that factor…must be a material difference between the woman's case and the man's ….[19]

Section 2(1) guarantees the important right of tribunal recourse for redress:

2(1) Any claim in respect of the contravention of a term modified or included by virtue of an equality clause, including a claim for arrears of remuneration or damages in respect of the contravention, may be presented by way of a complaint to an employment tribunal.[20]

The EPA covers all contractual terms and not simply those relating to pay, with claims taken initially to an Industrial Tribunal.

In terms of religious discrimination cases, the Code of Practice on Equal Pay is the main source of advice on implementing equal pay in the workplace and was issued by the Equal Opportunities Commission (EOC) in 1997. Employers must include an equality clause into individual contracts of employment. The EOC issued a Code of Practice for the purposes of the elimination of discrimination in employment; for guidance to employers, trade unions and employment agencies on measures that can be taken to achieve equality, and on what steps it is reasonably practicable for employers to take to ensure that their employees do not in the course of their employment act contrary to the law; and for the promotion of equality of opportunity in employment. The primary responsibility at law rests with each employer to ensure that there is no unlawful discrimination. The Code recommends the establishment and use of consistent criteria for selection, training, promotion, redundancy and dismissal that are made known to all employees, as part of good employment practices in eliminating disability discrimination. It is recommended that each individual should be assessed according to his personal capability to carry out a given job not on his religion.

The EOC recommends that a pay systems review should involve the following stages. Stage 1: undertake a thorough analysis of the pay system to produce a breakdown of all employees, which covers job title, grade, whether part-time or full-time, with basic pay, performance ratings and all other elements of remuneration; stage 2: examine each element of the pay system against the data obtained in stage 1; stage 3: identify any elements of the pay system that the review indicates may be the source of any discrimination; stage 4: change any rules or practices, including those in collective agreements, which stages 1 to 3 have identified as likely to give rise to discrimination in pay, in consultation with employees, trade unions or staff representatives where appropriate. Stages 1 to 3 may reveal that practices and procedures in relation to recruitment, selection and access to training have contributed to discrimination in pay, and these should be addressed; stage 5: analyze the likely effects of any proposed changes in practice to the pay system before implementation, in order to identify and rectify any discrimination that could be caused; stage 6: give equal pay to current employees. Where the review shows that some employees are not receiving equal pay for equal work and the reasons cannot be shown to be free of bias, then a plan must be developed for dealing with this; stage 7: set up a system of regular monitoring to allow checks to be made to pay practices; and stage 8: draw up and publish an equal pay policy with provision for assessing the new pay system or modification to a system in terms of discrimination.[21]

Human Rights Act (HRA)

Importantly, freedom of thought, conscience and religion is protected under Section 13 of the Human Rights Act (HRA):

(1) If a court's determination of any question arising under this Act might affect the exercise by a religious organisation (itself or its members collectively) of the Convention right to freedom of thought, conscience and religion, it must have particular regard to the importance of that right.
(2) In this section "court" includes a tribunal.[22]

The Home Secretary explained, at the Committee stage of the Bill, that the purpose of this clause was to reassure religious organizations 'against the Bill being used to intrude upon genuinely religious beliefs or practices based on their beliefs'. Further, 'the intention is to focus the courts' attention in any proceedings on the view generally held by the Church in question, and on its interest in protecting the integrity of the common faith of its members against attack, whether by outsiders or by individual dissidents. That is a significant protection.' The term 'religious organization' is not defined in the HRA, is flexible enough to cover cases involving religious charities where Church issues form a backdrop of the case, and is not tied to circumstances in which a religious organization is directly involved, as a body, in the court proceedings.

The HRA provides legal remedies for religious discrimination in connection with any convention right, which will provide an important avenue for challenging primary and secondary legislation, and the acts or omissions of public authorities, where religions or beliefs are treated unequally without objective and reasonable justification. There are several advantages to the HRA. The first is its open-ended nature, enabling the courts to develop religious discrimination law in a sensitive and flexible way in accordance with convention rights. The second advantage, from the viewpoint of Churches, is Section 13 of the HRA, which expressly emphasises that while religious organizations are not exempt, their position is not to be undermined. Any new UK legislation would have to take a very broad approach, such as on the definition of 'religion or belief' so that a declaration of compatibility with convention rights could be made by a Minister. There are, however, several disadvantages in relying on the HRA on its own. The first is that the courts will have no guidelines from Parliament on a number of difficult and controversial issues, such as the definition of religion or belief and on the limitations which should be imposed on the manifestation of religion or belief. Since these are generally matters of political judgment, Parliament should deal with them in the first instance. The courts will still retain the right to scrutinize legislation and the acts and omissions of public authorities so as to ensure that they are compatible with the convention, but this will then be a residuary rather than a primary role. The second disadvantage is that there is no free-standing right to complain of religious discrimination. This would be remedied if the Government was to ratify Protocol No.12 and the Secretary of State then made an Order under section 1(4) of the HRA to implement it. The third disadvantage is that the HRA applies only to public authorities. Although 'public authority' is defined broadly to include 'any person whose functions are functions of a public nature', it does not place obligations on private individuals or corporations. Borderline cases will arise where authorities have a mixture of public and private functions as a result of privatization or local partnership arrangements. These important issues could be more closely defined in domestic legislation, creating greater certainty and also consistency with other parts of antidiscrimination law.[23]

Employment Equality (Religion or Belief) Regulations

From 2 December 2003, when the Employment Equality (Religion or Belief) Regulations came into force, it became unlawful to discriminate against workers, because of religion or similar belief.[24] Religion or belief is defined as being any religion, religious belief or similar philosophical belief, but does not include any philosophical or political belief, unless it is similar to religious belief. The Regulations also cover those without religious or similar beliefs. In addition, discrimination on the grounds of religion or belief is illegal if carried out by institutes of further and higher education; employment agencies; providers of vocational training; qualifications bodies; trade organizations including trade unions; or by barristers or advocates taking pupils or partnerships within firms. These Regulations apply to all facets of employment, including recruitment, terms and conditions, promotions, transfers, dismissals and training. They make it unlawful on the grounds of religion or belief to:

- discriminate directly against anyone, that is, to treat them less favorably than others because of their religion or belief;
- discriminate indirectly against anyone, that is, to apply a criterion, provision or practice which disadvantages people of a particular religion or belief unless it can be objectively justified;
- subject someone to harassment, which is unwanted conduct that violates a person's dignity or creates an intimidating, hostile, degrading, humiliating or offensive environment having regard to all the circumstances and the perception of the victim;
- victimize someone, because they have made or intend to make a complaint or allegation or have given or intend to give evidence in relation to a complaint of discrimination on the grounds of religion or belief;
- discriminate or harass someone in certain circumstances after the working relationship has ended.

Exceptions may be made in very limited circumstances if there is a genuine occupational requirement for the worker to be of a particular religion or belief in order to do the job or to comply with the religious or belief ethos of the organization.

In terms of the Employment Equality (Religion or Belief) Regulations 2003, discrimination on grounds of religion or belief is defined under Regulation 3:

3(1) For the purposes of these Regulations, a person ('A') discriminates against another person ('B') if
(a) on grounds of religion or belief, A treats B less favourably than he treats or would treat other persons; or
(b) A applies to B a provision, criterion or practice which he applies or would apply equally to persons not of the same religion or belief as B, but
(i) which puts or would put persons of the same religion or belief as B at a particular disadvantage when compared with other persons,
(ii) which puts B at that disadvantage, and
(iii) which A cannot show to be a proportionate means of achieving a legitimate aim.
(3) A comparison of B's case with that of another person under paragraph (1) must be such that the relevant circumstances in the one case are the same, or not materially different, in the other.[25]

Further, discrimination by way of victimization is defined under Regulation 4:

4(1) For the purposes of these Regulations, a person ('A') discriminates against another person ('B') if he treats B less favourably than he treats or would treat other persons in the same circumstances, and does so by reason that B has
(a) brought proceedings against A or any other person under these Regulations;
(b) given evidence or information in connection with proceedings brought by any person against A or any other person under these Regulations;
(c) otherwise done anything under or by reference to these Regulations in relation to A or any other person; or
(d) alleged that A or any other person has committed an act which (whether or not the allegation so states) would amount to a contravention of these Regulations, or by reason that A knows that B intends to do any of those things, or suspects that B has done or intends to do any of them.
(2) Paragraph (1) does not apply to treatment of B by reason of any allegation made by him, or evidence or information given by him, if the allegation, evidence or information was false and not made (or, as the case may be, given) in good faith.[26]

Finally, harassment on grounds of religion or belief is defined under Regulation 5:

5(1) For the purposes of these Regulations, a person ('A') subjects another person ('B') to harassment where, on grounds of religion or belief, A engages in unwanted conduct which has the purpose or effect of
(a) violating B's dignity; or
(b) creating an intimidating, hostile, degrading, humiliating or offensive environment for B.
(2) Conduct shall be regarded as having the effect specified in paragraph (1)(a) or (b) only if, having regard to all the circumstances, including in particular the perception of B, it should reasonably be considered as having that effect.[27]

In terms of discrimination in employment and vocational training, Regulation 6 pertains to applicants and employees:

> 6(1) It is unlawful for an employer, in relation to employment by him at an establishment in Great Britain, to discriminate against a person
> (a) in the arrangements he makes for the purpose of determining to whom he should offer employment;
> (b) the terms on which he offers that person employment; or
> (c) by refusing to offer, or deliberately not offering, him employment.
> (2) It is unlawful for an employer, in relation to a person whom he employs at an establishment in Great Britain, to discriminate against that person
> (a) in the terms of employment which he affords him;
> (b) in the opportunities which he affords him for promotion, a transfer, training, or receiving any other benefit;
> (c) by refusing to afford him, or deliberately not affording him, any such opportunity; or
> (d) by dismissing him, or subjecting him to any other detriment.
> (3) It is unlawful for an employer, in relation to employment by him at an establishment in Great Britain, to subject to harassment a person whom he employs or who has applied to him for employment.[28]

However, Regulation 7 allows for exceptions for a genuine occupational requirement:

> 7(1) In relation to discrimination falling within regulation 3 (discrimination on grounds of religion or belief)
> (a) regulation 6(1)(a) or (c) does not apply to any employment;
> (b) regulation 6(2)(b) or (c) does not apply to promotion or transfer to, or training for, any employment; and
> (c) regulation 6(2)(d) does not apply to dismissal from any employment, where paragraph (2) or (3) applies.
> (2) This paragraph applies where, having regard to the nature of the employment or the context in which it is carried out
> (a) being of a particular religion or belief is a genuine and determining occupational requirement;
> (b) it is proportionate to apply that requirement in the particular case; and
> (c) either
>   i. the person to whom that requirement is applied does not meet it, or
>   ii. the employer is not satisfied, and in all the circumstances it is reasonable for him not to be satisfied, that that person meets it,
> and this paragraph applies whether or not the employer has an ethos based on religion or belief.

(3) This paragraph applies where an employer has an ethos based on religion or belief and, having regard to that ethos and to the nature of the employment or the context in which it is carried out
(a) being of a particular religion or belief is a genuine occupational requirement for the job;
(b) it is proportionate to apply that requirement in the particular case; and
(c) either
    i. the person to whom that requirement is applied does not meet it, or
    ii. the employer is not satisfied, and in all the circumstances it is reasonable for him not to be satisfied, that that person meets it.[29]

The liability of employers and principals is stressed in Regulation 22:

22(1) Anything done by a person in the course of his employment shall be treated for the purposes of these Regulations as done by his employer as well as by him, whether or not it was done with the employer's knowledge or approval.
(2) Anything done by a person as agent for another person with the authority (whether express or implied, and whether precedent or subsequent) of that other person shall be treated for the purposes of these Regulations as done by that other person as well as by him.
(3) In proceedings brought under these Regulations against any person in respect of an act alleged to have been done by an employee of his it shall be a defence for that person to prove that he took such steps as were reasonably practicable to prevent the employee from doing that act, or from doing in the course of his employment acts of that description.[30]

There is an exception for positive action under Regulation 25:

25(1) Nothing in Part II or III shall render unlawful any act done in or in connection with -
(a) affording persons of a particular religion or belief access to facilities for training which would help fit them for particular work; or
(b) encouraging persons of a particular religion or belief to take advantage of opportunities for doing particular work,
where it reasonably appears to the person doing the act that it prevents or compensates for disadvantages linked to religion or belief suffered by persons of that religion or belief doing that work or likely to take up that work.[31]

The burden of proof required is outlined in Regulation 29:

29 (2) Where, on the hearing of the complaint, the complainant proves facts from which the tribunal could, apart from this regulation, conclude in the absence of an adequate explanation that the respondent

(b) is by virtue of regulation 22 (liability of employers and principals)...to be treated as having committed against the complainant such an act,
the tribunal shall uphold the complaint unless the respondent proves that he did not commit, or as the case may be, is not to be treated as having committed, that act.[32]

Finally, remedies on complaints in employment tribunals are contained in Regulation 30:

> 30(1) Where an employment tribunal finds that a complaint presented to it under regulation 28 is well-founded, the tribunal shall make such of the following as it considers just and equitable
> (a) an order declaring the rights of the complainant and the respondent in relation to the act to which the complaint relates;
> (b) an order requiring the respondent to pay to the complainant compensation of an amount corresponding to any damages he could have been ordered by a county court or by a sheriff court to pay to the complainant if the complaint had fallen to be dealt with under regulation 31 (jurisdiction of county and sheriff courts);
> (c) a recommendation that the respondent take within a specified period action appearing to the tribunal to be practicable for the purpose of obviating or reducing the adverse effect on the complainant of any act of discrimination or harassment to which the complaint relates.
> (2) As respects an unlawful act of discrimination falling within regulation 3(1)(b), if the respondent proves that the provision, criterion or practice was not applied with the intention of treating the complainant unfavourably on grounds of religion or belief, an order may be made under paragraph (1)(b) only if the employment tribunal -
> (a) makes such order under paragraph (1)(a) (if any) and such recommendation under paragraph (1)(c) (if any) as it would have made if it had no power to make an order under paragraph (1)(b); and
> (b) (where it makes an order under paragraph (1)(a) or a recommendation under paragraph (1)(c) or both) considers that it is just and equitable to make an order under paragraph (1)(b) as well.
> (3) If without reasonable justification the respondent to a complaint fails to comply with a recommendation made by an employment tribunal under paragraph (1)(c), then, if it thinks it just and equitable to do so
> (a) the tribunal may increase the amount of compensation required to be paid to the complainant in respect of the complaint by an order made under paragraph (1)(b); or
> (b) if an order under paragraph (1)(b) was not made, the tribunal may make such an order.
> (4) Where an amount of compensation falls to be awarded under paragraph (1)(b), the tribunal may include in the award interest on that amount subject to, and in accordance with, the provisions of the Employment Tribunals (Interest on Awards in Discrimination Cases) Regulations 1996.[33]

Equality Act

In terms of the Equality Act 2006, the general duty of the Commission is outlined in Section 3:

> 3. The Commission shall exercise its functions under this Part with a view to encouraging and supporting the development of a society in which
> (a) people's ability to achieve their potential is not limited by prejudice or discrimination,
> (b) there is respect for and protection of each individual's human rights,
> (c) there is respect for the dignity and worth of each individual,
> (d) each individual has an equal opportunity to participate in society, and
> (e) there is mutual respect between groups based on understanding and valuing of diversity and on shared respect for equality and human rights.[34]

Further, equality and diversity are to be promoted under Section 8:

> 8(1) The Commission shall, by exercising the powers conferred by this Part
> (a) promote understanding of the importance of equality and diversity,
> (b) encourage good practice in relation to equality and diversity,
> (c) promote equality of opportunity,
> (d) promote awareness and understanding of rights under the equality enactments,
> (e) enforce the equality enactments,
> (f) work towards the elimination of unlawful discrimination, and
> (g) work towards the elimination of unlawful harassment.[35]

Finally, human rights are to be promoted under Section 9:

> 9(1) The Commission shall, by exercising the powers conferred by this Part
> (a) promote understanding of the importance of human rights,
> (b) encourage good practice in relation to human rights,
> (c) promote awareness, understanding and protection of human rights, and
> (d) encourage public authorities to comply with section 6 of the Human Rights Act (compliance with Convention rights).[36]

Importantly, religion and belief are defined under Section 44:

> 44 (a) 'religion' means any religion,
> (b) 'belief' means any religious or philosophical belief,
> (c) a reference to religion includes a reference to lack of religion, and
> (d) a reference to belief includes a reference to lack of belief.[37]

Further, discrimination is defined under Section 45:

> 45(1) A person ('A') discriminates against another ('B') for the purposes of this Part if on grounds of the religion or belief of B or of any other person except A (whether or not

it is also A's religion or belief) A treats B less favourably than he treats or would treat others (in cases where there is no material difference in the relevant circumstances).

(2) In subsection (1) a reference to a person's religion or belief includes a reference to a religion or belief to which he is thought to belong or subscribe.
(3) A person ('A') discriminates against another ('B') for the purposes of this Part if A applies to B a provision, criterion or practice
(a) which he applies or would apply equally to persons not of B's religion or belief,
(b) which puts persons of B's religion or belief at a disadvantage compared to some or all others (where there is no material difference in the relevant circumstances),
(c) which puts B at a disadvantage compared to some or all persons who are not of his religion or belief (where there is no material difference in the relevant circumstances), and
(d) which A cannot reasonably justify by reference to matters other than B's religion or belief.
(4) A person ('A') discriminates against another ('B') if A treats B less favourably than he treats or would treat another and does so by reason of the fact that, or by reason of A's knowledge or suspicion that, B
(a) has brought or intended to bring, or intends to bring, proceedings under this Part,
(b) has given or intended to give, or intends to give, evidence in proceedings under this Part,
(c) has provided or intended to provide, or intends to provide, information in connection with proceedings under this Part,
(d) has done or intended to do, or intends to do, any other thing under or in connection with this Part, or
(e) has alleged or intended to allege, or intends to allege, that a person contravened this Part.[38]

Discriminatory practices are outlawed under Section 53:

53(1) It is unlawful for a person to operate a practice which would be likely to result in unlawful discrimination if applied to persons of any religion or belief.[39]
Further, discriminatory advertisements are outlawed under Section 54:
54(1) It is unlawful to publish an advertisement, or to cause an advertisement to be published, if it indicates (expressly or impliedly) an intention by any person to discriminate unlawfully.
(4) A person who publishes an advertisement shall not be liable in proceedings under that section in respect of the publication of the advertisement if he proves that
(a) he published in reliance on a statement, made by a person causing the advertisement to be published, that subsection (1) would not apply, and
(b) that it was reasonable to rely on that statement.
(5) A person commits an offence if he knowingly or recklessly makes a false statement of the kind mentioned in subsection (4)(a).
(6) A person guilty of an offence under subsection (5) shall be liable on summary conviction to a fine not exceeding level 5 on the standard scale.[40]

Finally, employers' and principals' liability is outlined under Section 74:

> 74(1) Anything done by a person in the course of his employment shall be treated for the purposes of this Part as done by the employer as well as by the person.
> (2) Anything done by a person as agent for another shall be treated for the purposes of this Part as done by the principal as well as by the agent.
> (3) It is immaterial for the purposes of this section whether an employer or principal knows about or approves of an act.
> (4) In proceedings under this Part against a person in respect of an act alleged to have been done by his employee it shall be a defence for the employer to provide that he took such steps as were reasonably practicable to prevent the employee
> (a) from doing the act, or
> (b) from doing acts of that kind in the course of his employment.[41]

In *Saggers v. British Railways Board* [1977] IRLR 266, the Employment Appeal Tribunal held that the belief which falls to be considered is that which is held by the person whose belief is under consideration, rather than an established body of creed or dogma appertaining to the individual as well as a number of other persons.[42] Further, the definition of religion by charitable trusts has been considered more recently by the Charity Commissioners in the light of the HRA. In determining an application by the Church of Scientology, the Commissioners reviewed the existing case law and concluded that the 'English authorities were neither clear nor unambiguous as to the definition of religion in English charity law, and at best the cases are of persuasive value with the result that a positive and constructive approach and one which conforms to the ECHR principle, to identifying what is a religion in charity law could and should be adopted'.[43] They concluded that while belief in a supreme being was a necessary characteristic of religion for the purposes of English charity law it would not 'be proper to specify the nature of that supreme being or to require it to be analogous to the deity or supreme being of a particular religion'.[44] The Commissioners concluded that the Church of Scientology did claim to profess a belief in a supreme being; however the Church of Scientology was not recognized as a religion, because their core religious service of 'auditing and training' was not sufficient for the 'reverence and veneration for a supreme being', which the Commissioners considered 'necessary to constitute worship in English charity law'.[45]

In the context of religious discrimination in the United Kingdom, there is a need to accommodate diversity because our society is already structured around basic Christian assumptions and therefore already accommodates the needs of Christians in terms of Christmas and Easter holidays and Sunday closings. In a multifaith, multicultural society, the needs of individuals with different religious faiths should be met. The Employment Rights Act 1996 provides for those working in the retail or betting trades to opt out of Sunday working by giving their employer three months notice of their intention to stop working on Sundays.[46] Where employees request cessation of Sunday working on the grounds of their religion or belief, employers should consider whether Sunday working can be justified as a legitimate business need and whether it is proportionate to apply that justification to the individual, but refusal to adjust the individual's working patterns may be indirect discrimination if adequate justification cannot be shown. Further, in *Ahmad v. Inner London Education Authority* [1978] 1 All ER 574, a case involving a dispute between a Muslim teacher who requested time to attend Friday prayers and the local education authority, the court found that 'room has to be found for teachers and pupils of the new religions in the educational system, if discrimination is to be avoided. This calls not for a policy of the blind eye but for one of understanding. The system must be made flexible to accommodate their beliefs and their observances. Otherwise they will suffer discrimination'.[47]

Particular issues arise in relation to exemptions from the legislation for religious schools. In terms of employment in religious schools in England and Wales which is regulated by the *School Standards Framework Act 1998*, Section 59 provides that, in community, secular foundation or voluntary or special schools, no one can be disqualified from employment by reasons of his religious opinions, or of attending or omitting to attend religious worship,[48] but Section 60 provides that foundation or voluntary schools that have a 'religious character' can give preference in employment, remuneration and promotion to teachers 'whose religious beliefs are in accordance with the tenets' of that religion, and 'regard may be had, in connection with the termination of the employment of any teacher at that school, to any conduct on his part which is incompatible with the precepts, or with the upholding of the tenets, of the religion or religious denomination so specified'.[49]

Religion has long been a major issue in Northern Ireland, but mainland Britain has become increasingly secular. Despite the last census in England and Wales recording 85 percent of people as having a religious affiliation and the Anglican church controlling nearly one-in-five schools, many believers are non-practising. In a recent survey, ignorance and indifference towards religion were of widespread concern amongst all faith groups, which in organizational settings can contribute towards an environment in which discrimination of all kinds is able to thrive.[50] Those who actively practised their religion often thought that they were made to feel awkward and experienced pressure to conform. They thought that other people based their views on preconceived ideas and stereotypes, and seemed to neither know nor care about the things that were central to the experience of those for whom religious identity constituted an important, or the key, aspect of their lives. Hostility and violence were very real concerns for organizations representing Muslims, Sikhs and Hindus. The majority of Muslims thought that hostility, verbal abuse and unfair media coverage had become more frequent. Most Christians and Jews thought that things had stayed much the same, but a substantial number of Christians thought that ignorance, indifference and unfair media coverage had become more frequent. Some religious groups perceived improvements over the last five years, but the majority of Buddhist and Bahá'í organizations thought that ignorance was now less frequent.

Many tended to feel that some progress was being made in reducing unfair treatment and that a degree of religious pluralism was beginning to develop, although much remained to be done. A higher level of unfair treatment, which was characterized as frequent, was reported by Muslim organizations than by most other religious groups in every aspect of education, employment, housing, and law and order. Hindu, and especially Sikh, organizations also reported a relatively high level of unfair treatment and tended to highlight the same areas of concern. Christian organizations were generally much less likely to report unfair treatment, which was characterized as occasional rather than frequent. However, black-led Christian organizations and those representing groups such as Mormons and Jehovah's Witnesses were much more likely to report unfair treatment, which was characterized as overt hostility similar to that experienced by some of the non-Christian minorities, in nearly all walks of life than organizations in what are often seen as the 'mainstream' Christian traditions. Pagans and people from 'New Religious Movements' also reported open hostility and discrimination, and of being labeled as 'child abusers' and 'cults', particularly by the media.

For organizations from most religious traditions, employment was one of the three areas of life, along with education and the media, where their members were most likely to experience unfair treatment. The majority of Muslim, Sikh, and Hindu organizations, as well as the 'New Religious Movements' and Pagan organizations reported unfair treatment in almost every aspect of employment, and Muslim organizations were more likely than Sikh or Hindu organizations to indicate that this unfair treatment was frequent. In almost all traditions, fewer organizations reported unfair treatment in the voluntary sector than in the private or public sectors. Two or three times as many Christian organizations reported unfairness in the behavior of managers and colleagues than unfairness in the policies and practices of employers, while this distinction was much less marked for the other faith groups, which were more likely to detect unfairness in policy and practice, as well as in behavior. The small number of black-led groups were more likely to report unfair treatment than other Christian organizations.

In terms of the private sector, around three quarters or more of the Sikh, Muslim and Hindu organizations said their members experienced unfair treatment from private sector managers or colleagues, compared with just over 40 percent of the Christian organizations, and lower proportions in some of the other religions, such as Buddhists and Bahá'ís. In terms of the public sector, some religious traditions reported marginally less unfair treatment in the public sector than in the private sector. Organizations from some religions, such Muslim, Sikh, Christian, reported slightly more unfairness in public sector employment practices than in policies. In terms of the voluntary sector, fewer organizations indicated unfairness from either individuals or employers, and Muslim organizations were much more likely to indicate that unfairness in this sector was occasional than was the case with public and private sector employers.

The media was identified as the most frequent source of unfairness by people from all religious traditions, and the attitudes and behavior of journalists and presenters, and the coverage given to their religious community were both seen as relatively frequent sources of unfairness from all religions. Most traditions were more likely to report unfair treatment from the national media than the local, and from television and newspapers as opposed to radio. Many reported feeling that social stigma and perceptions of antisocial behavior were associated with difference, particularly around the need to abstain from common social practices on the grounds of religious convictions and traditions, particularly a concern for Bahá'ís, Jehovah's Witnesses, Muslims and Quakers. A number felt that others assumed that, in following their religious beliefs and practices, they were 'being awkward' or were troublemakers as they try to find ways to 'to fit in' or 'try not to be difficult'. Overall, in employment, people do not want to be seen as different, but they would like to have an environment that is appropriate, sensitive and acceptable to their religious needs, so that they do not constantly have to experience these tensions.[51]

Legislation in Northern Ireland reflects the particular sectarian issues in that jurisdiction famously known as the 'troubles', directed primarily at relations between the established Protestant and Roman Catholic communities.[52] In the case of discrimination on the grounds of religion or political opinion, the duty to promote equality of opportunity includes affirmative action defined in terms of steps to increase fair participation and fair access. The Northern Ireland Act 1998 prohibits discrimination by the government and public bodies on the grounds of religious belief or political opinion:

> 76(1) It shall be unlawful for a public authority carrying out functions relating to Northern Ireland to discriminate, or to aid or incite another person to discriminate, against a person or class of person on the ground of religious belief or political opinion.
>
> (2) An act which contravenes this section is actionable in Northern Ireland at the instance of any person adversely affected by it; and the court may
> (a) grant damages;
> (b) ... grant an injunction restraining the defendant from committing, causing or permitting further contraventions of this section.[53]

The statutory duty on public authorities is outlined in Article 75:

> 75(1) A public authority shall in carrying out its functions relating to Northern Ireland have due regard to the need to promote equality of opportunity
> (a) between persons of different religious belief, political opinion, racial group, age, marital status or sexual orientation;
> (2) Without prejudice to its obligations under subsection (1), a public authority shall in carrying out its functions relating to Northern Ireland have regard to the desirability of promoting good relations between persons of different religious belief, political opinion or racial group.[54]

Specifically, discrimination on religious grounds in employment is prohibited by the Fair Employment and Treatment (Northern Ireland) Order 1998 (FETO), which replaces the Fair Employment (Northern Ireland) Acts 1976 and 1989, and extends the protection to cover the provision of goods, services and facilities.[55] The regulations prohibit less favorable treatment in employment and training based on: a person's religion or belief; the perception of a person's religion or belief; a person's association with someone of a particular religion or belief; or a refusal by a person to comply with a discriminatory instruction. This does not cover discrimination based on something other than a religion or a similar philosophical belief, but it is unlawful to discriminate against someone of the same religion, or against someone for not belonging to a certain religion. Introducing the idea of reasonable adjustment or accommodation signifies an important shift in the understanding of equality.

With FETO prohibiting religious discrimination, employers have to ensure the active practice of fair employment and monitor the religious composition of their workforce regularly reviewing their recruitment, training and promotion practices.[56] Further, FETO requires private sector employers with more than ten full-time employees in Northern Ireland to register with the Equality Commission of Northern Ireland (ECNI).[57] Registered employers and public authorities are required to prepare and serve each year on the Commission a monitoring return to enable the composition of the work force and the composition of applications for employment, including part-time employees, in terms of membership of the Catholic and Protestant communities, to be ascertained.[58] The legislation allows affirmative action policies to be followed in relation to access to training, in the practice relating to the selection of workers for redundancy, and in measures taken to encourage applications from under-represented communities.

Importantly, discrimination is defined under Article 3:

3(1) In this Order 'discrimination' means
(a) discrimination on the ground of religious belief or political opinion; or
(b) discrimination by way of victimisation;
and 'discriminate' shall be construed accordingly
(2) A person discriminates against another person on the ground of religious belief or political opinion in any circumstances relevant for the purposes of this Order if
(a) on either of those grounds he treats that other less favourably than he treats or would treat other persons; or
(b) he applies to that other a requirement or condition which he applies or would apply equally to persons not of the same religious belief or political opinion as that other but
    i. which is such that the proportion of persons of the same religious belief or of the same political opinion as that other who can comply with it is considerably smaller than the proportion of persons not of that religious belief or, as the case requires, not of that political opinion who can comply with it; and
    ii. which he cannot show to be justifiable irrespective of the religious belief or political opinion of the person to whom it is applied; and
    iii. which is to the detriment of that other because he cannot comply with it.

(3) A comparison of the cases of persons of different religious belief or political opinion under paragraph (2) must be such that the relevant circumstances in the one case are the same, or not materially different, in the other.
(4) A person ('A') discriminates by way of victimisation against another person ('B') in any circumstances relevant for the purposes of this Order if
(a) he treats B less favourably than he treats or would treat other persons in those circumstances; and
(b) he does so for a reason mentioned in paragraph (5).
(5) The reasons are that
(a) B has
    i. brought proceedings against A or any other person under this Order; or
    ii. given evidence or information in connection with such proceedings brought by any person or any investigation under this Order; or
    iii. alleged that A or any other person has (whether or not the allegation so states) contravened this Order; or
    iv. otherwise done anything under or by reference to this Order in relation to A or any other person; or
(b) A knows that B intends to do any of those things or suspects that B has done, or intends to do, any of those things.[59]

Further, discrimination in employment is defined under Article 19:

19(1) It is unlawful for an employer to discriminate against a person, in relation to employment in Northern Ireland,
(a) where that person is seeking employment
    i. in the arrangements the employer makes for the purpose of determining who should be offered employment; or
    ii. in the terms on which he offers him employment; or
    iii. by refusing or deliberately omitting to offer that person employment for which he applies; or
(b) where that person is employed by him
    i. in the terms of employment which he affords him; or
    ii. in the way he affords him access to benefits or by refusing or deliberately omitting to afford him access to them; or
    iii. by dismissing him or by subjecting him to any other detriment.[60]

Finally, Article 70 provides for certain exceptions on religious grounds:

70(1) This Order does not apply to or in relation to
(a) any employment or occupation as a clergyman or minister of a religious denomination; or (b) employment for the purposes of a private household.
(2) Part VII does not apply to or in relation to any employment or occupation where the essential nature of the job requires it to be done by a person holding, or not holding, a particular religious belief.

(3) So far as they relate to discrimination on the ground of religious belief, Parts III and V do not apply to or in relation to any employment or occupation where the essential nature of the job requires it to be done by a person holding, or not holding, a particular religious belief.[61]

Affirmative action is defined in Article 4 as:

4(1)…action designed to secure fair participation in employment by members of the Protestant, or members of the Roman Catholic community, in Northern Ireland by means including
(a) the adoption of practices encouraging such participation; and
(b) the modification of practices that have or may have the effect of restricting or discouraging such participation.[62]

Equality of opportunity is defined in Article 5 as:

5(1)…equality of opportunity between persons of different religious beliefs.
(2) For the purposes of this Order a person of any religious belief has equality of opportunity with a person of any other religious belief if, being
(a) a person who is seeking employment or is in employment; or
(b) a person who is seeking to become engaged in, or is engaged in, any occupation,
he has in any circumstances the same opportunity of a kind mentioned in paragraph (4) as that other person has or would have in those circumstances, due allowance being made for any material difference in their suitability. (4) The kinds of opportunity referred to in paragraph (2) are
(a) in relation to an employment, the opportunity to be considered, and to be submitted for consideration, for the employment and to have and to hold it on any terms, with access to all benefits connected with it and without being subjected to any detriment; and
(b) in relation to an employment or an occupation
    i. the opportunity to become, and remain, on any terms a member of any vocational organisation which exists for purposes of the employment or the occupation (or for purposes of employments or occupations of any class which includes the employment or occupation), with access to all benefits of membership and without being subjected to any detriment; and
    ii. where services in connection with training for the employment are provided by a person other than the employer, or where services in connection with training for the occupation are provided by any person, the opportunity to have those services on any terms, with access to all benefits connected with them; and
    iii. the opportunity to have conferred on him, and to hold, on any terms any qualification which is needed for, or facilitates, his engagement in the employment or the occupation.[63]

Finally, Article 7 places a duty on the Equality Commission to promote equality of opportunity in Northern Ireland; to promote affirmative action; and to work for the elimination of unlawful discrimination promote affirmative action,[64] and Article 81 provides for the establishment of the Fair Employment Tribunal of Northern Ireland.[65]

Ireland

In looking at religious discrimination in the Republic of Ireland, religion is protected under the Constitution. Further, the two main pieces of legislation guarding against discrimination are the Employment Equality Act and the Equal Status Act.

Constitution of Ireland

The Constitution of Ireland (Bunreacht Na hEireann) was enacted by the People on 1st July, 1937 and came into operation from 29th December, 1937. The Preamble of the Constitution of Ireland states:

> In the Name of the Most Holy Trinity, from Whom is all authority and to Whom, as our final end, all actions both of men and States must be referred,
>
> We, the people of Éire,
>
> Humbly acknowledging all our obligations to our Divine Lord, Jesus Christ, Who sustained our fathers through centuries of trial,
>
> Gratefully remembering their heroic and unremitting struggle to regain the rightful independence of our Nation,
>
> And seeking to promote the common good, with due observance of Prudence, Justice and Charity, so that the dignity and freedom of the individual may be assured, true social order attained, the unity of our country restored, and concord established with other nations,
>
> Do hereby adopt, enact, and give to ourselves this Constitution[66]

Fundamental freedoms are guaranteed as personal rights under Article 40:

> 40. 1. All citizens shall, as human persons, be held equal before the law.
> This shall not be held to mean that the State shall not in its enactments have due regard to differences of capacity, physical and moral, and of social function.

2. (1) Titles of nobility shall not be conferred by the State.

(2) No title of nobility or of honour may be accepted by any citizen except with the prior approval of the Government.

3. (1) The State guarantees in its laws to respect, and, as far as practicable, by its laws to defend and vindicate the personal rights of the citizen.

(2) The State shall, in particular, by its laws protect as best it may from unjust attack and, in the case of injustice done, vindicate the life, person, good name, and property rights of every citizen.

(3) The State acknowledges the right to life of the unborn and, with due regard to the equal right to life of the mother, guarantees in its laws to respect, and, as far as practicable, by its laws to defend and vindicate that right.

This subsection shall not limit freedom to travel between the State and another state.

This subsection shall not limit freedom to obtain or make available, in the State, subject to such conditions as may be laid down by law, information relating to services lawfully available in another state.

4. (1) No citizen shall be deprived of his personal liberty save in accordance with law.

(2) Upon complaint being made by or on behalf of any person to the High Court or any judge thereof alleging that such person is being unlawfully detained, the High Court and any and every judge thereof to whom such complaint is made shall forthwith enquire into the said complaint and may order the person in whose custody such person is detained to produce the body of such person before the High Court on a named day and to certify in writing the grounds of his detention, and the High Court shall, upon the body of such person being produced before that Court and after giving the person in whose custody he is detained an opportunity of justifying the detention, order the release of such person from such detention unless satisfied that he is being detained in accordance with the law.

(3) Where the body of a person alleged to be unlawfully detained is produced before the High Court in pursuance of an order in that behalf made under this section and that Court is satisfied that such person is being detained in accordance with a law but that such law is invalid having regard to the provisions of this Constitution, the High Court shall refer the question of the validity of such law to the Supreme Court by way of case stated and may, at the time of such reference or at any time thereafter, allow the said person to be at liberty on such bail and subject to such conditions as the High Court shall fix until the Supreme Court has determined the question so referred to it.

(4) The High Court before which the body of a person alleged to be unlawfully detained is to be produced in pursuance of an order in that behalf made under this section shall, if the President of the High Court or, if he is not available, the senior judge of that Court who is available so directs in respect of any particular case, consist of three judges and shall, in every other case, consist of one judge only.

(5) Nothing in this section, however, shall be invoked to prohibit, control, or interfere with any act of the Defence Forces during the existence of a state of war or armed rebellion.

(6) Provision may be made by law for the refusal of bail by a court to a person charged with a serious offence where it is reasonably considered necessary to prevent the commission of a serious offence by that person.

5. The dwelling of every citizen is inviolable and shall not be forcibly entered save in accordance with law.

6. (1) The State guarantees liberty for the exercise of the following rights, subject to public order and morality:

    i. The right of the citizens to express freely their convictions and opinions.

    The education of public opinion being, however, a matter of such grave import to the common good, the State shall endeavour to ensure that organs of public opinion, such as the radio, the press, the cinema, while preserving their rightful liberty of expression, including criticism of Government policy, shall not be used to undermine public order or morality or the authority of the State.

    The publication or utterance of blasphemous, seditious, or indecent matter is an offence which shall be punishable in accordance with law.

    ii. The right of the citizens to assemble peaceably and without arms.

    Provision may be made by law to prevent or control meetings which are determined in accordance with law to be calculated to cause a breach of the peace or to be a danger or nuisance to the general public and to prevent or control meetings in the vicinity of either House of the Oireachtas.

    iii. The right of the citizens to form associations and unions.

    Laws, however, may be enacted for the regulation and control in the public interest of the exercise of the foregoing right.

(2) Laws regulating the manner in which the right of forming associations and unions and the right of free assembly may be exercised shall contain no political, religious or class discrimination.[67]

Fundamental rights pertaining to religion are contained in Article 44:

44.1. The State acknowledges that the homage of public worship is due to Almighty God. It shall hold His Name in reverence, and shall respect and honour religion.

2. 1. Freedom of conscience and the free profession and practice of religion are, subject to public order and morality, guaranteed to every citizen.

2. The State guarantees not to endow any religion.

3. The State shall not impose any disabilities or make any discrimination on the ground of religious profession, belief or status.

4. Legislation providing State aid for schools shall not discriminate between schools under the management of different religious denominations, nor be such as to affect prejudicially the right of any child to attend a school receiving public money without attending religious instruction at that school.

5. Every religious denomination shall have the right to manage its own affairs, own, acquire and administer property, movable and immovable, and maintain institutions for religious or charitable purposes.

6. The property of any religious denomination or any educational institution shall not be diverted save for necessary works of public utility and on payment of compensation.[68]

Employment Equality Act

In Ireland, the Employment Equality Act (1998) prohibits discrimination in employment and in other spheres of life on a number of grounds, including religion. The conception of equality in the EEA is based on individual merit, and moves towards the 'equality as rationality' end of the spectrum, addressing discrimination based on prejudice or stereotypes. The Act creates some positive duties to promote equality, despite the limits to positive action in favor of individuals. In addition, it established an Equality Authority with powers to develop codes of practice that have enhanced legal standing, and to promote equality through Equality Reviews and Action Plans. Positive measures are permitted under the Employment Equality Act, where the measures are 'intended to reduce or eliminate the effects of discrimination', and various provisions prevent challenges to measures targeted to disadvantaged groups, including seniors.

Important for equal rights, under the Employment Equality Act 1998, discrimination is outlined in Section 6, and in particular Sections 6(2)(e) as to religion:

> 6(1) For the purposes of this Act, discrimination shall be taken to occur where, on any of the grounds in *subsection (2)* (in this Act referred to as 'the discriminatory grounds'), one person is treated less favorably than another is, has been or would be treated.
> (2) As between any 2 persons, the discriminatory grounds (and the descriptions of those grounds for the purposes of this Act) are:
> (*a*) that one is a woman and the other is a man (in this Act referred to as 'the gender ground'),
> (*b*) that they are of different marital status (in this Act referred to as 'the marital status ground'),
> (*c*) that one has family status and the other does not (in this Act referred to as 'the family status ground'),
> (*d*) that they are of different sexual orientation (in this Act referred to as 'the sexual orientation ground'),
> (*e*) that one has a different religious belief from the other, or that one has a religious belief and the other has not (in this Act referred to as 'the religion ground'),
> (*f*) that they are of different ages, but subject to *subsection (3)* (in this Act referred to as 'the age ground'),
> (*g*) that one is a person with a disability and the other either is not or is a person with a different disability (in this Act referred to as 'the disability ground'),
> (*h*) that they are of different race, color, nationality or ethnic or national origins (in this Act referred to as 'the ground of race'),
> (*i*) that one is a member of the traveller community and the other is not (in this Act referred to as 'the traveller community ground').[69]

In terms of religious comparators, Section 28 states:

> 28(1) For the purpose of this Part, 'C' and 'D' represent 2 persons who differ as follows:
> (*d*) in relation to the religion ground, C and D have different religious beliefs or C has a religious belief and D does not, or *vice versa*.[70]

In addition, indirect discrimination is covered in Section 31:

> 31(1) Where a provision (whether in the nature of a requirement, practice or otherwise) relating to employment:
> (*a*) applies to all the employees or prospective employees of a particular employer who include C and D or, as the case may be, to a particular class of those employees or prospective employees which includes C and D,
> (*b*) operates to the disadvantage of C, as compared with D, in relation to any of the matters specified in *paragraphs (a) to (e) of section 8(1)*,
> (*c*) in practice can be complied with by a substantially smaller proportion of the employees or prospective employees having the same relevant characteristic as C when compared with the employees or prospective employees having the same relevant characteristic as D, and
> (*d*) cannot be justified as being reasonable in all the circumstances of the case,
> then ... for the purposes of this Act the employer shall be regarded as discriminating against C, contrary to *section 8*, on whichever of the discriminatory grounds gives rise to the relevant characteristics referred to in *paragraph (c)*.[71]

Further, discrimination by employers is outlined under Section 8:

> 8(1) In relation to:
> (*a*) access to employment,
> (*b*) conditions of employment,
> (*c*) training or experience for or in relation to employment,
> (*d*) promotion or re-grading, or
> (*e*) classification of posts,
> an employer shall not discriminate against an employee or prospective employee and a provider of agency work shall not discriminate against an agency worker.
> (5) Without prejudice to the generality of *subsection (1)*, an employer shall be taken to discriminate against an employee or prospective employee in relation to access to employment if the employer discriminates against the employee or prospective employee:
> (*a*) in any arrangements the employer makes for the purpose of deciding to whom employment should be offered, or
> (*b*) by specifying, in respect of one person or class of persons, entry requirements for employment which are not specified in respect of other persons or classes of

persons, where the circumstances in which both such persons or classes would be employed are not materially different.

(6) Without prejudice to the generality of *subsection (1)*, an employer shall be taken to discriminate against an employee or prospective employee in relation to conditions of employment if, on any of the discriminatory grounds, the employer does not offer or afford to that employee or prospective employee or to a class of persons of whom he or she is one:
> (*a*) the same terms of employment (other than remuneration and pension rights),
> (*b*) the same working conditions, and
> (*c*) the same treatment in relation to overtime, shift work, short time, transfers, lay-offs, redundancies, dismissals and disciplinary measures,

as the employer offers or affords to another person or class of persons, where the circumstances in which both such persons or classes are or would be employed are not materially different.

(7) Without prejudice to the generality of *subsection (1)*, an employer shall be taken to discriminate against an employee in relation to training or experience for, or in relation to, employment if, on any of the discriminatory grounds, the employer refuses to offer or afford to that employee the same opportunities or facilities for employment counseling, training (whether on or off the job) and work experience as the employer offers or affords to other employees, where the circumstances in which that employee and those other employees are employed are not materially different.

(8) Without prejudice to the generality of *subsection (1)*, an employer shall be taken to discriminate against an employee in relation to promotion if, on any of the discriminatory grounds:
> (*a*) the employer refuses or deliberately omits to offer or afford the employee access to opportunities for promotion in circumstances in which another eligible and qualified person is offered or afforded such access, or
> (*b*) the employer does not in those circumstances offer or afford the employee access in the same way to those opportunities.[72]

As well, discrimination as to bodies is covered under Section 13:

> 13. A body which
> (*a*) is an organisation of workers or of employers,
> (*b*) is a professional or trade organisation, or
> (*c*) controls entry to, or the carrying on of, a profession, vocation or occupation,
> shall not discriminate against a person in relation to membership of that body or any benefits, other than pension rights, provided by it or in relation to entry to, or the carrying on of, that profession, vocation or occupation.[73]

Further, the Employment Equality Act makes the principle of 'equal pay for like work' a term of every employment contract. Proving 'like work' means showing that the work of the person claiming equal pay, the claimant, is the same, similar or equal in value to the work of the appropriate comparator, the person with whom the claimant is comparing himself. The comparator must, among other things, be employed by the same or an associated employer, at the same time or during the previous or following three years. Section 7(1) establishes like work:

> 7(1) Subject to *subsection (2)*, for the purposes of this Act, in relation to the work which one person is employed to do, another person shall be regarded as employed to do like work if:
> (*a*) both perform the same work under the same or similar conditions, or each is interchangeable with the other in relation to the work,
> (*b*) the work performed by one is of a similar nature to that performed by the other and any differences between the work performed or the conditions under which it is performed by each either are of small importance in relation to the work as a whole or occur with such irregularity as not to be significant to the work as a whole, or
> (*c*) the work performed by one is equal in value to the work performed by the other, having regard to such matters as skill, physical or mental requirements, responsibility and working conditions.
> (3) In any case where:
> (*a*) the remuneration received by one person ('the primary worker') is less than the remuneration received by another ('the comparator'), and
> (*b*) the work performed by the primary worker is greater in value than the work performed by the comparator, having regard to the matters mentioned in *subsection (1)(c)*,
> then, for the purposes of *subsection (1)(c)*, the work performed by the primary worker shall be regarded as equal in value to the work performed by the comparator.[74]

In addition, entitlement to equal remuneration is covered under Section 29:

> 29(1) It shall be a term of the contract under which C is employed that, subject to this Act, C shall at any time be entitled to the same rate of remuneration for the work which C is employed to do as D who, at that or any other relevant time, is employed to do like work by the same or an associated employer.
> (3) For the purposes of this Part, where D's employer is an associated employer of C's employer, C and D shall not be regarded as employed to do like work unless they both have the same or reasonably comparable terms and conditions of employment.
> (4) Where a term of a contract of employment or a criterion applied to employees (including C and D):
> (*a*) applies to all employees of a particular employer or to a particular class of such employees (including C and D),
> (*b*) is such that the remuneration of those who fulfil the term or criterion is different from that of those who do not,
> (*c*) is such that the proportion of employees who can fulfil the term or criterion is substantially smaller in the case of the employees having the same relevant characteristic as C when compared with the employees having the same relevant characteristic as D, and

(*d*) cannot be justified as being reasonable in all the circumstances of the case,

then, for the purposes of *subsection (1)*, C and D shall each be treated as fulfilling or, as the case may be, as not fulfilling the term or criterion, whichever results in the higher remuneration.

(5) Subject to *subsection (4)*, nothing in this Part shall prevent an employer from paying, on grounds other than the discriminatory grounds, different rates of remuneration to different employees.[75]

Important for equal rights, an equality clause is outlined under Section 30:

30(1) If and so far as the terms of a contract of employment do not include (expressly or by reference to a collective agreement or otherwise) a non-discriminatory equality clause, they shall be taken to include one.

(2) A non-discriminatory equality clause is a provision relating to the terms of a contract of employment, other than a term relating to remuneration or pension rights, which has the effect that if:

(*a*) C is employed in circumstances where the work done by C is not materially different from that done by D in the same employment, and

(*b*) at any time C's contract of employment would (but for the non-discriminatory equality clause):

(i) contain a term which is or becomes less favorable to C than a term of a similar kind in D's contract of employment, or

(ii) not include a term corresponding to a term in D's contract of employment which benefits D,

then the terms of C's contract of employment shall be treated as modified so that the term in question is not less favorable to C or, as the case may be, so that they include a similar term benefiting C.

(3) A non-discriminatory equality clause shall not operate in relation to a difference between C's contract of employment and D's contract of employment if the employer proves that the difference is genuinely based on grounds which are not among those specified in *paragraphs (a) to (h) of section 28(1)*.[76]

Harassment in the workplace is covered under Section 32:

32(1) If, at a place where C is employed (in this section referred to as 'the workplace'), or otherwise in the course of C's employment, another individual ('E') harasses C by reference to the relevant characteristic of C and:

(*a*) C and E are both employed at that place or by the same employer,

(*b*) E is C's employer, or

(*c*) E is a client, customer or other business contact of C's employer and the circumstances of the harassment are such that C's employer ought reasonably to have taken steps to prevent it, then, for the purposes of this Act, the harassment constitutes discrimination by C's employer, in relation to C's conditions of employment, on whichever discriminatory ground is relevant to persons having the same relevant characteristic as C.

(6) If, as a result of any act or conduct of E another person ('F') who is C's employer would, apart from this subsection, be regarded...as discriminating against C, it shall be a defence for F to prove that F took such steps as are reasonably practicable:

> (*a*) ... to prevent C being treated differently in the workplace or otherwise in the course of C's employment and, if and so far as any such treatment has occurred, to reverse the effects of it, and
>
> (*b*) ... to prevent E from harassing C (or any class of persons of whom C is one).[77]

Importantly, positive action for workers from religious minorities is permitted as contained in Section 33, and in particular Section 33(1)(*a*):

> 33(1) Nothing in this Part or *Part II* shall prevent the taking of such measures...in order to facilitate the integration into employment, either generally or in particular areas or a particular workplace.
>
> (3) Nothing in this Part or *Part II* shall render unlawful the provision, by or on behalf of the State, of training or work experience for a disadvantaged group of persons if the Minister certifies that, in the absence of the provision in question, it is unlikely that that disadvantaged group would receive similar training or work experience.[78]

Further, special protection is afforded religious institutions by way of an exclusion under Section 37:

> 37(1) A religious, educational or medical institution which is under the direction or control of a body established for religious purposes or whose objectives include the provision of services in an environment which promotes certain religious values shall not be taken to discriminate against a person for the purposes of this Part or *Part II* if
>
> > (*a*) it gives more favourable treatment, on the religion ground, to an employee or a prospective employee over that person where it is reasonable to do so in order to maintain the religious ethos of the institution, or
> >
> > (*b*) it takes action which is reasonably necessary to prevent an employee or a prospective an employee undermining the religious ethos of the institution.
>
> (2) Nothing in this Part or *Part II* applies to discrimination against C in respect of employment in a particular post if the discrimination results from preferring D on the ground that the relevant characteristic of D is or amounts to an occupational qualification for the post in question.
>
> (4) Without prejudice to the generality of *subsection (2)*, in relation to discrimination on the religion ground or the ground of race, the relevant characteristic of D shall be taken to be an occupational qualification for a post where it is necessary that the post should be held by D because it is likely to involve the performance of duties outside the State in a place where the laws or customs are such that those duties could not reasonably be performed by a person who does

not have that relevant characteristic or, as the case may require, by a person who has a relevant characteristic of C.[79]

The Equality Authority has important legal powers, not to decide on disputes but to work generally for the elimination of discrimination and the promotion of equal opportunities. It can develop Codes of Practice, carry out equality reviews in particular employment, draw up Equality Action Plans, and serve Substantive Notices. The Authority has broad powers to ensure the development of a proactive equality-conscious approach to equal opportunities in the workplace. The functions of the Equality Authority are outlined under Section 39:

> 39. The Authority shall have, in addition to the functions assigned to it by any other provision of this Act or of any other Act, the following general functions:
> (*a*) to work towards the elimination of discrimination in relation to employment;
> (*b*) to promote equality of opportunity in relation to the matters to which this Act applies.[80]

The forum for seeking redress is covered under Section 77:

> 77(1) A person who claims:
> (*a*) to have been discriminated against by another in contravention of this Act,
> (*b*) not to be receiving remuneration in accordance with an equal remuneration term,
> (*c*) not to be receiving a benefit under an equality clause, or
> (*d*) to have been penalized in circumstances amounting to victimization,
> may, subject to *subsections (2) to (8)*, seek redress by referring the case to the Director.
> (2) If a person claims to have been dismissed:
> (*a*) in circumstances amounting to discrimination by another in contravention of this Act, or
> (*b*) in circumstances amounting to victimization,
> then, subject to *subsection (3)*, a claim for redress for the dismissal may be brought to the Labor Court and shall not be brought to the Director.
> (3) If the grounds for such a claim as is referred to in *subsection (1) or (2)* arise:
> (*a*) under *Part III*, or
> (*b*) in any other circumstances (including circumstances amounting to victimization) to which the Equal Pay Directive or the Equal Treatment Directive is relevant,
> then … the person making the claim may seek redress by referring the case to the Circuit Court, instead of referring it to the Director under *subsection (1)* or, as the case may be, to the Labor Court under *subsection (2)*.
> (4) In this Part, in relation to a case referred under any provision of this section:
> (*a*) 'the complainant' means the person by whom it is referred, and
> (*b*) 'the respondent' means the person who is alleged to have discriminated against the complainant or, as the case may be, who is responsible for providing the

remuneration to which the equal remuneration term relates or who is responsible for providing the benefit under the equality clause or who is alleged to be responsible for the victimization.[81]

Crucially, enforcement of determinations, decisions and mediated settlements is outlined under Section 91:

> 91(1) If an employer or any other person who is bound by the terms of:
> (a) a final determination of the Labor Court under this Part, or
> (b) a final decision of the Director under this Part,
> fails to comply with the terms of the determination or decision then, on an application under this section, the Circuit Court shall make, subject to *section 93*, an order directing the person affected (that is to say, the employer or other person concerned) to carry out the determination or decision in accordance with its terms.
> (2) If an employer or the person who is a party to a settlement ... fails to give effect, in whole or in part, to the terms of the settlement, then, on an application under this section, the Circuit Court may make an order directing the person affected (that is to say, the employer or the person who is a party to the settlement) to carry out those terms or, as the case may be, the part of those terms to which the application relates; but the Circuit Court shall not, by virtue of this subsection, direct any person to pay any sum or do any other thing which (had the matter been dealt with otherwise than by mediation) could not have been provided for by way of redress ....
> (3) An application under this section may not be made before the expiry of:
> (a) in the case of a determination or decision, the period within which an appeal might be brought against the determination or decision, and
> (b) in the case of a settlement reached as a result of mediation, 42 days from the date of the written record of the settlement.
> (4) An application under this section may be made:
> (a) by the complainant, or
> (b) in a case where the Authority is not the complainant, then, by the Authority with the consent of the complainant if the Authority considers that the determination, decision or settlement is unlikely to be implemented without its intervention.
> (5) On an application under this section, the Circuit Court shall exercise its functions under *subsection (1) or (2)* on being satisfied:
> (a) of the existence and terms of the determination, decision or settlement, and
> (b) of the failure by the person affected to comply with those terms.
> (6) For the purposes of this section, a determination or decision is final if no appeal lies from it under this Part or if the time for bringing an appeal has expired and either:
> (a) no appeal has been brought, or
> (b) any appeal which was brought has been abandoned.
> (7) Without prejudice to the power of the Circuit Court to make an order for costs in favor of the complainant or the person affected, where an application is made by the Authority by virtue of *subsection (4)(b)*, the costs of the Authority may be awarded by the Circuit Court.

(8) The jurisdiction conferred on the Circuit Court by this section shall be exercised by the judge for the time being assigned to the circuit where the respondent ordinarily resides or carries on any profession, business or occupation.[82]

Equal Status Act

Important for equal rights, under the Equal Status Act (2000), discrimination is outlined in Section 3, and in particular Sections 3(2)(e) as to religion:

> 3(1) For the purposes of this Act, discrimination shall be taken to occur where:
> (*a*) on any of the grounds specified in *subsection (2)* (in this Act referred to as 'the discriminatory grounds') which exists at present or previously existed but no longer exists or may exist in the future, or which is imputed to the person concerned, a person is treated less favorably than another person is, has been or would be treated,
> (*b*) (i) a person who is associated with another person is treated, by virtue of that association, less favorably than a person who is not so associated is, has been or would be treated, and
> (ii) similar treatment of that person on any of the discriminatory grounds would, by virtue of *paragraph (a)*, constitute discrimination,
>
> or
>
> (*c*) (i) a person is in a category of persons who share a common characteristic by reason of which discrimination may, by virtue of *paragraph (a)*, occur in respect of those persons,
> (ii) the person is obliged by the provider of a service ... to comply with a condition (whether in the nature of a requirement, practice or otherwise) but is unable to do so,
> (iii) substantially more people outside the category than within it are able to comply with the condition, and
> (iv) the obligation to comply with the condition cannot be justified as being reasonable in all the circumstances of the case.
> (2) As between any two persons, the discriminatory grounds (and the descriptions of those grounds for the purposes of this Act) are:
> (*a*) that one is male and the other is female (the 'gender ground'),
> (*b*) that they are of different marital status (the 'marital status ground'),
> (*c*) that one has family status and the other does not or that one has a different family status from the other (the 'family status ground'),
> (*d*) that they are of different sexual orientation (the 'sexual orientation ground'),
> (*e*) that one has a different religious belief from the other, or that one has a religious belief and the other has not (the 'religion ground'),
> (*f*) ... that they are of different ages (the 'age ground'),

(*g*) that one is a person with a disability and the other either is not or is a person with a different disability (the 'disability ground'),
(*h*) that they are of different race, color, nationality or ethnic or national origins (the 'ground of race'),
(*i*) that one is a member of the Traveller community and the other is not (the 'Traveller community ground'),
(*j*) that one:
(i) has in good faith applied for any determination or redress provided for in *Part II or III*,
(ii) has attended as a witness before the Authority, the Director or a court in connection with any inquiry or proceedings under this Act,
(iii) has given evidence in any criminal proceedings under this Act,
(iv) has opposed by lawful means an act which is unlawful under this Act, or
(v) has given notice of an intention to take any of the actions specified in *subparagraphs (i) to (iv)*,
and the other has not (the 'victimization ground').[83]

Further, Section 5, specifically Section 5(2)(e), provides for non-discrimination as to religion in the disposal of goods and provision of services:

5(1) A person shall not discriminate in disposing of goods to the public generally or a section of the public or in providing a service, whether the disposal or provision is for consideration or otherwise and whether the service provided can be availed of only by a section of the public.
(2) *Subsection (1)* does not apply in respect of:
(*c*) differences in the treatment of persons on the gender ground in relation to services of an aesthetic, cosmetic or similar nature, where the services require physical contact between the service provider and the recipient,
(*d*) differences in the treatment of persons in relation to annuities, pensions, insurance policies or any other matters related to the assessment of risk where the treatment:
(i) is effected by reference to:
(I) actuarial or statistical data obtained from a source on which it is reasonable to rely, or
(II) other relevant underwriting or commercial factors,
and
(ii) is reasonable having regard to the data or other relevant factors,
(*e*) differences in the treatment of person on the religion ground in relation to goods or services provided for a religious purpose,
(*f*) differences in the treatment of persons on the gender, age or disability ground or on the basis of nationality or national origin in relation to the provision or organization of a sporting facility or sporting event to the extent that the differences are reasonably necessary having regard to the nature of the facility or event and are relevant to the purpose of the facility or event,

> (*h*) differences in the treatment of persons in a category of persons in respect of services that are provided for the principal purpose of promoting, for a *bona fide* purpose and in a *bona fide* manner, the special interests of persons in that category to the extent that the differences in treatment are reasonably necessary to promote those special interests,
> (*i*) differences in the treatment of persons on the gender, age or disability ground or on the ground of race, reasonably required for reasons of authenticity, aesthetics, tradition or custom in connection with a dramatic performance or other entertainment, or
> (*l*) differences, not otherwise specifically provided for in this section, in the treatment of persons in respect of the disposal of goods, or the provision of a service, which can reasonably be regarded as goods or a service suitable only to the needs of certain persons.[84]

Further, under Section 6(5), religious premises are protected from certain claims of religious discrimination:

> 6(5) Where any premises or accommodation are reserved for the use of persons in a particular category of persons for a religious purpose or as a refuge,…a refusal to dispose of the premises or provide the accommodation to a person who is not in that category does not, for that reason alone, constitute discrimination.[85]

In terms of educational establishments, exemptions from claims of discrimination are provided under Section 7:

> 7(1) In this section 'educational establishment' means a preschool service within the meaning of Part VII of the Child Care Act, 1991, a primary or post-primary school, an institution providing adult, continuing or further education, or a university or any other third-level or higher-level institution, whether or not supported by public funds.
> (2) An educational establishment shall not discriminate in relation to
>   (*a*) the admission or the terms or conditions of admission of a person as a student to the establishment,
>   (*b*) the access of a student to any course, facility or benefit provided by the establishment
>   (*c*) any other term or condition of participation in the establishment by a student, or
>   (*d*) the expulsion of a student from the establishment or any other sanction against the student.
> (3) An educational establishment does not discriminate under *subsection (2)* by reason only that
>   (*b*) where the establishment is an institution established for the purpose of providing training to ministers of religion and admits students of only one gender or religious belief, it refuses to admit as a student a person who is not of that gender or religious belief,

(c) where the establishment is a school providing primary or post-primary education to students and the objective of the school is to provide education in an environment which promotes certain religious values, it admits persons of a particular religious denomination in preference to others or it refuses to admit as a student a person who is not of that denomination and, in the case of a refusal, it is proved that the refusal is essential to maintain the ethos of the school.[86]

Further, religious clubs are given special treatment under Section 9:

9(1) …a club shall not be considered to be a discriminating club by reason only that
(a) if its principal purpose is to cater only for the needs of
(i) persons of a particular gender, marital status, family status, sexual orientation, religious belief, age, disability, nationality or ethnic or national origin,
(ii) persons who are members of the Traveller community, or
(iii) persons who have no religious belief,
(iv) it refuses membership to other persons.[87]

Certain measures are not prohibited under Section 14:

14. Nothing in this Act shall be construed as prohibiting:
(a) the taking of any action that is required by or under:
(i) any enactment or order of a court,
(ii) any act done or measure adopted by the European Union, by the European Communities or institutions thereof or by bodies competent under the Treaties establishing the European Communities, or
(iii) any convention or other instrument imposing an international obligation on the State,
or
(b) preferential treatment or the taking of positive measures which are *bona fide* intended to:
(i) promote equality of opportunity for persons who are, in relation to other persons, disadvantaged or who have been or are likely to be unable to avail themselves of the same opportunities as those other persons, or
(ii) cater for the special needs of persons, or a category of persons, who, because of their circumstances, may require facilities, arrangements, services or assistance not required by persons who do not have those special needs.[88]

Further, certain activities are not considered discrimination under Section 15:

15(1) For greater certainty, nothing in this Act prohibiting discrimination shall be construed as requiring a person to dispose of goods or premises, or to provide services or accommodation or services and amenities related to accommodation, to another person ('the customer') in circumstances which would lead a reasonable individual having the responsibility, knowledge and experience of the person to the belief, on grounds other than discriminatory grounds, that the disposal of the goods or premises or the provision of the services or accommodation or the services and amenities related to accommodation, as the case may be, to the customer would produce a substantial risk of criminal or disorderly conduct or behavior or damage to property at or in the vicinity of the place in which the goods or services are sought or the premises or accommodation are located.[89]

Importantly, redress in respect of prohibited grounds is covered under Section 21:

21(1) A person who claims that prohibited conduct has been directed against him or her may, subject to this section, seek redress by referring the case to the Director.
(2) Before seeking redress under this section the complainant:
    (*a*) shall, within 2 months after the prohibited conducted is alleged to have occurred, or, where more than one incident of prohibited conduct is alleged to have occurred, within 2 months after the last such occurrence, notify the respondent in writing of:
        (i) the nature of the allegation,
        (ii) the complainant's intention, if not satisfied with the respondent's response to the allegation, to seek redress by referring the case to the Director,
and
    (*b*) may in that notification, with a view to assisting the complainant in deciding whether to refer the case to the Director, question the respondent in writing so as to obtain material information and the respondent may, if the respondent so wishes, reply to any such questions.
(3) If, on application by the complainant, the Director is satisfied:
    (*a*) that exceptional circumstances prevented the complainant from notifying the respondent in accordance with *subsection (2)*, and
    (*b*) that it is just and equitable, having regard to the nature of the alleged conduct and to any other relevant circumstances, that the period for doing so should be extended beyond the period of 2 months provided for in that subsection,
the Director may direct that, in relation to that case, *subsection (2)* shall have effect as if for the reference to 2 months there were substituted a reference to such period not exceeding 4 months as is specified in the direction; and where such a direction is given, this Part shall have effect accordingly.
(4) The Director shall not investigate a case unless he or she is satisfied either that the respondent has replied to the notification or that at least one month has elapsed after it was sent to the respondent.
(5) The Minister may by regulations prescribe the form to be used by a complainant and respondent for the purposes of *subsection (2)*.
(6) Subject to *subsection (7)*, a claim for redress in respect of prohibited conduct may not be referred under this section after the end of the period of 6 months from the date of the occurrence of the prohibited conduct to which the case relates or, as the case may be, the date of its most recent occurrence.

(7) If, on application by the complainant, the Director is satisfied that exceptional circumstances prevented the complainant's case from being referred within the time limit specified in *subsection (6)*:
> (*a*) the Director may direct that, in relation to that case, *subsection (6)* shall have effect as if for the reference to a period of 6 months there were substituted a reference to such period not exceeding 12 months as is specified in the direction, and
> (*b*) where such a direction is given, this Part shall have effect accordingly.[90]

Finally, mediation is provided for under Section 24:

> 24(1) Subject to *subsection (2)*, if at any time after a case has been referred to the Director under section 21 it appears to the Director that the case is one which could be resolved by mediation, the Director shall refer the case for mediation to an equality mediation officer.
> (2) If the complainant or the respondent objects to a case being dealt with by way of mediation, the Director shall not exercise his or her powers under this section....
> (3) Mediation shall be conducted in private.
> (4) Where a case referred under section 21 is resolved by mediation
>> (*a*) the equality mediation officer concerned shall prepare a written record of the terms of the settlement,
>> (*b*) the written record of the terms of the settlement shall be signed by the complainant and the respondent,
>> (*c*) the equality mediation officer shall send a copy of the written record, as so signed, to the complainant and the respondent, and
>> (*d*) a copy of the written record shall be retained by the Director.
> (5) If, after a case has been referred to an equality mediation officer, it appears to the equality mediation officer that the case cannot be resolved by mediation, the officer shall issue a notice to that effect to the complainant and the respondent.[91]

Conclusion

Due to the overall legislation, employer behavior has changed in countries with antidiscrimination laws in that explicit discrimination, especially in recruitment, has reduced. However, society's and employers' attitudes to workers from religious minorities do not yet appear to have shifted as much as towards groups such as women and people from minority ethnic communities, where legislative protection has, generally, operated for longer. Discriminating against workers on the basis of their religion can be unfair to individuals and harmful to the economy.

Overall, more emphasis needs to be given to 'religious proofing' systems of promotion and higher-level recruitment, and to encouraging career development for any person in the United Kingdom and Ireland. As religious monitoring of posts, recruitment and promotion would be useful, action is needed both to encourage all people, including those belonging to religious minorities, to develop their careers and to remove obstacles in their paths. The principle is that redressing this inequality is a shared responsibility by all aspects of government stakeholders in religious analysis, planning and training. The State's accountability for violations committed by private actors has long been an important debate. This will be of critical relevance to Commonwealth governments and the Secretariat as part of their continuing priority work in the area of democracy, rule of law, and human rights. The increased participation of all, especially seniors at decision-making levels in conflict prevention, mediation and resolution is vital, in the pursuit of *Heaven Forbid*.

Notes

1 Commission for Racial Equality, *Code of Practice on the Duty to Promote Race Equality*, UK, 2002.
2 Race Relations Act, UK, at Section 71(1).
3 Race Relations Act (Statutory Duties) Order 2001, UK, at Section 5; Race Relations Act (Statutory Duties) Order 2003, UK, at Section 4.
4 *Mandla v. Dowell Lee* [1983] 2 AC 548.
5 *Seide v. Gillette Industries Ltd* [1980] IRLR 427.
6 *Mandla v. Dowell Lee* [1983] 2 AC 548.
7 *Commission for Racial Equality v. Dutton* [1989] IRLR 8.
8 *Tariq v. Young* Case 247738/88, EOR Discrimination Case Law Digest No. 2.
9 *Crown Suppliers (Property Services Agency) v. Dawkins* [1993] ICR 517.
10 *Lovell-Badge v. Norwich City College of Further and Higher Education*, Case no: 1502237/97, (Spring 1999).
11 *J H Walker Ltd v. Hussain* [1996] IRLR 11 EAT.
12 *Safouane & Bouterfas v. Joseph Ltd and Hannah* [1996] Case No. 12506/95/LS & 12569/95.
13 Sex Discrimination Act, UK, at Section 1.
14 *Ibid.*, at Section 6(2).
15 *Ibid.*, at Section 7.
16 *Ibid.*, at Section 19.
17 *Ibid.*, at Section 35.
18 *Sardar v. McDonalds* (1998), Muslim News, No. 115, 27th November 1998 – 8th Shaban 1419.
19 Equal Pay Act, UK, at Section 1(3).
20 *Ibid.*, at Section 2(1).
21 Equal Opportunities Commission, *Code of Practice on Equal Pay*, UK.
22 Human Rights Act, UK, 1998, at Section 13.
23 Hepple QC, Bob, Choudhury, Tufval, Home Office Research Study 221, *Tackling Religious Discrimination: Practical Implications for Policy-Makers and Legislators*, Home Office Research, Development and Statistics Directorate, 2001.
24 ACAS, *Religion or Belief and the Workplace, Putting the Employment Equality (Religion or Belief) Regulations 2003 into Practice.*

25 Employment Equality (Religion or Belief) Regulations, UK, 2003, at Regulation 3.
26 *Ibid.*, at Regulation 4.
27 *Ibid.*, at Regulation 5.
28 *Ibid.*, at Regulation 6.
29 *Ibid.*, at Regulation 7.
30 *Ibid.*, at Regulation 22.
31 *Ibid.*, at Regulation 25.
32 *Ibid.*, at Regulation 29.
33 *Ibid.*, at Regulation 30.
34 Equality Act, UK, 2006, at Section 3.
35 *Ibid.*, at Section 8.
36 *Ibid.*, at Section 9.
37 *Ibid.*, at Section 44.
38 *Ibid.*, at Section 45.
39 *Ibid.*, at Section 53.
40 *Ibid.*, at Section 54.
41 *Ibid.*, at Section 74.
42 *Saggers v. British Railways Board* [1977] IRLR 266 at 267.
43 Application for Registration as a charity by the Church of Scientology – Decision of the Charity Commissioners for England and Wales made on the 17th November 1999, at p. 19.
44 *Ibid.*, at p. 21.
45 *Ibid.*, at p. 25.
46 Employment Rights Act, UK, 1996.
47 *Ahmad v. Inner London Education Authority* [1978] 1 All ER 574 at 583.
48 School Standards and Framework Act, UK, 1998, at Section 59.
49 *Ibid.*, at Section 60.
50 Weller, Paul, Feldman, Alice and Purdam, Kingsley, Home Office Research Study 220, *Religious Discrimination in England and Wales*, Home Office Research, Development and Statistics Directorate, 2001.
51 *Ibid.*
52 Hepple QC, Bob, Choudhury, Tufval, Home Office Research Study 221, *Tackling Religious Discrimination: Practical Implications for Policy-Makers and Legislators*, Home Office Research, Development and Statistics Directorate, 2001.
53 Northern Ireland Act, 1998, at Article 76.
54 *Ibid.*, at Article 75.
55 Fair Employment and Treatment (Northern Ireland) Order 1998 (FETO) No. 3162 (N.I. 21).
56 *Ibid.*, at Article 55.
57 *Ibid.*, at Article 48.
58 *Ibid.*, at Article 52.
59 *Ibid.*, at Article 3.
60 *Ibid.*, at Article 19.
61 *Ibid.*, at Article 70.

62 *Ibid.*, at Article 4.
63 *Ibid.*, at Article 5(5).
64 *Ibid.*, at Article 7.
65 *Ibid.*, at Article 81.
66 Constitution of Ireland, Ireland, at the Preamble.
67 *Ibid.*, at Article 40.
68 *Ibid.*, at Article 44.
69 Employment Equality Act, Ireland, at Section 6.
70 *Ibid.*, at Section 28.
71 *Ibid.*, at Section 31.
72 *Ibid.*, at Section 8.
73 *Ibid.*, at Section 13.
74 *Ibid.*, at Section 7.
75 *Ibid.*, at Section 29.
76 *Ibid.*, at Section 30.
77 *Ibid.*, at Section 32.
78 *Ibid.*, at Section 33.
79 *Ibid.*, at Section 37.
80 *Ibid.*, at Section 39.
81 *Ibid.*, at Section 77.
82 *Ibid.*, at Section 91.
83 Equal Status Act, Ireland, at Section 3.
84 *Ibid.*, at Section 5.
85 *Ibid.*, at Section 6.(5)
86 *Ibid.*, at Section 7.
87 *Ibid.*, at Section 9.
88 *Ibid.*, at Section 14.
89 *Ibid.*, at Section 15.
90 *Ibid.*, at Section 21.
91 *Ibid.*, at Section 24.

References

ACAS, *Religion or Belief and the Workplace, Putting the Employment Equality (Religion or Belief) Regulations 2003 into Practice.*
Ahmad v. Inner London Education Authority [1978] 1 All ER 574 at 583.
Application for Registration as a charity by the Church of Scientology – Decision of the Charity Commissioners for England and Wales made on the 17th November 1999.
Commission for Racial Equality (2002), *Code of Practice on the Duty to Promote Race Equality*, UK.
Commission for Racial Equality v. Dutton [1989] IRLR 8.
Constitution of Ireland, Ireland, 1937.

Crown Suppliers (Property Services Agency) v. Dawkins [1993] ICR 517.
Employment Equality Act, Ireland, 1998.
Employment Equality (Age) Regulations, UK, 2006.
Employment Equality (Religion or Belief) Regulations, UK, 2003.
Employment Rights Act, UK, 1996.
Equal Opportunities Commission, *Code of Practice on Equal Pay*, UK.
Equal Pay Act, UK, 1970.
Equal Status Act, Ireland, 2000.
Equality Act, UK, 2006.
Fair Employment and Treatment (Northern Ireland) Order 1998 (FETO) No. 3162 (N.I. 21).
Health and Safety at Work Act, UK, 1974.
Hepple QC, Bob, Choudhury, Tufval (2001), Home Office Research Study 221, *Tackling Religious Discrimination: Practical Implications For Policy-Makers And Legislators*, Home Office Research, Development and Statistics Directorate.
Human Rights Act, UK, 1998.
J H Walker Ltd v. Hussain [1996] IRLR 11 EAT.
Lovell-Badge v. Norwich City College of Further and Higher Education, Case no: 1502237/97, (Spring 1999).
Mandla v. Dowell Lee [1983] 2 AC 548.
Northern Ireland Act, 1998.
Race Relations Act, UK, 1976.
Race Relations Act (Statutory Duties) Order 2001, 2003, 2004, UK.
Safouane & Bouterfas v. Joseph Ltd and Hannah [1996] Case No. 12506/95/LS & 12569/95.
Sardar v. McDonalds (1998), Muslim News, No. 115, 27th November 1998 – 8th Shaban 1419.
School Standards and Framework Act, UK, 1998.
Seide v. Gillette Industries Ltd [1980] IRLR 427.
Sex Discrimination Act, UK, 1975.
Tariq v. Young Case 247738/88, EOR Discrimination Case Law Digest No. 2.
Weller, Paul, Feldman, Alice, Purdam, Kingsley (2001), Home Office Research Study 220, *Religious Discrimination in England and Wales*, Home Office Research, Development and Statistics Directorate.

Chapter 9

Heaven Forbid in the European Union

Introduction

In the quest for religious tolerance in *Heaven Forbid*, this chapter will examine efforts against religious discrimination in the European Union (EU). As well as examining the European Court of Justice, it will review the European Union treaties from their inception, as well as other important legislation, namely the Treaty of Paris, the Treaty of Rome, the Maastricht Treaty, the Treaty of Amsterdam, the European Convention for the Protection of Human Rights and Fundamental Freedoms (ECHR), the European Social Charter, the Treaty Establishing a Constitution for Europe and the Treaty of Lisbon. Finally, important European Council legislation affecting equal rights will be analyzed, namely Council Directive 2000/78/EC Establishing a General Framework for Equal Treatment in Employment and Occupation, and Council Decision 2000/750/EC establishing a Community Action Program to Combat Discrimination (2001 to 2006).

The European Union's share of the world population is falling, and as such, it ranks third in the world population behind China and India. If current trends for fertility, mortality and migration continue, the European Union population will peak in the year 2025 and revert to its current level in the year 2050. Further, Europe has experienced an increased divorce rate, a falling birth rate, a longer life expectancy and a positive net balance of migration. Overall, legislation and education have proven to help overcome some discrimination. The European Union has provided important contributions to the ending of religious discrimination in the coming together of people of different nations, and equality in employment is a real commitment for the Member States.

Initially, many centuries ago, Europe was united within the Roman Empire. Throughout its history, the European continent has naturally been restless, fragile, contradictory, competitive and pluralistic, divided by language and religion. National ambitions and self-interest have been the predominant political forces throughout the twentieth century. However, with the two World Wars and the threat of the Cold War, European integration by peaceful methods was seriously reconsidered as an alternative to the independent and aggressive nation state. With democratic governments reinstated in liberated Europe in the post-war era, the restructuring of the region began. A Congress of Europe was held in the Hague in 1948, bringing together leading figures from France, Britain, the Netherlands, Belgium, Germany, Italy and elsewhere. Britain's Prime Minister Churchill referred to the idea of a setting up of 'a kind of United States of Europe', which made a powerful impact.[1] Political integration is the peaceful creation of a larger political unit out of several separate ones, which voluntarily give up some powers to a central authority and renounce the use of force toward the other units.[2] In Europe, a political structure at a supranational level exists. Only continental-wide superpowers can think of solving their major problems at the national level, but for smaller powers like Europe, it requires wider alliance decisions. It is a multitiered approach to government and decision making that is working.

There have been several important legislative instruments in Europe. The Treaty of Paris (1951) created the European Steel and Coal Community (ESCC). The Treaties of Rome (1957) established the European Economic Community (EEC) and the European Atomic Energy Community (EAEC). The Single European Act (1986) introduced measures aimed at achieving an internal market and greater political cooperation. The Maastricht Treaty (1992) established EU citizenship and the European Monetary Union (EMU). The Treaty of Amsterdam (1997) introduced measures to reinforce political union and prepare for enlargement toward Eastern Europe. The Nice Treaty (2001) defined the institutional changes necessary for enlargement. Finally, the Treaty Establishing a Constitution for Europe seeks to simplify and synthesize previous treaties within a single, clear, foundational document for the European Union.

Treaty of Paris

The advocates of integration sought to escape from national rivalries. Thus came the flagship of European integration, the European Communities. The first of these was the Coal and Steel Community, also known as the Treaty of Paris signed on 18 April 1951, which entered into force on 23 July 1952 and expired on 23 July 2002. It removed the coal and steel industries from full national control to a supranational stewardship. The High Authority, which it created, was presided over by Jean Monnet and comprised of delegates from the Member States, making decisions in consultation with the Assembly. The Treaty of Paris was regarded only as a starting point, with the success foreseen in this sector expected to spread to others. The Preamble of the Treaty of Paris wrote of safeguarding world peace, establishing an economic community, and substituting essential interests for age-old rivalries and conflicts.[3] Monnet, the most influential of the founding fathers of the European Economic Community, insisted on cooperation across national frontiers in a sector by sector approach at the Messina Conference held in 1955, with the foreign ministers of the six countries involved to meet at. They resolved that the moment had come to go a step further towards the construction of Europe by setting up a customs union with no internal tariff barriers, only a common external tariff.

Treaty of Rome

The Treaty of Rome was signed by France, Italy, West Germany, Luxembourg, the Netherlands and Belgium on 25 March 1957, and entered into force on 1 January 1958, creating the European Economic Community (EEC). The European Community was set up by the Treaty of Rome to maintain peace in Europe and to foster prosperity through cooperation. With the Treaty of Rome, the European Economic Community States transferred to the Community the power to conclude treaties with international organizations and with non-member countries.[4] Lord Denning, a leading constitutional expert, stated 'the Treaty of Rome is like an incoming tide. It flows into the estuaries and up the rivers. It cannot be held back'.[5] The Member States agreed to work together for an integrated multinational economy for the free movement of labor and capital in the Community, while having joint institutions and common policies toward underdeveloped regions of the Community and toward those outside the Community. The Treaty gave the community institutions power to take the necessary steps to adjust national legal rules through harmonization procedures. This was required in order to remove national legal arrangements inhibiting the free movement of products, people and resources. The larger market allowed for a more rational use of resources and provided for higher productivity. By 1 July 1968, all internal tariffs had been abolished among the Member States for a Community-wide production and distribution of products and services,[6] and with the abolition of tariffs encouraging mutual trade, intra-Community trade in manufactured products was about 50 percent higher than previously. The long-term implications of the Treaty of Rome were a system of majority voting among the representatives of the national governments in the Council, a supranational bureaucracy over which national governments would have little control, a directly elected European Parliament and a commitment by the Member States to work for a closer union.

In accordance with Article 3 of the Treaty of Rome, the activities of the Community include:

3(a) the elimination as between Member States, of customs duties and quantitative restrictions on the import and export of goods, and of all other measures having equivalent effect;
(b) a common commercial policy;
(c) an internal market characterized by the abolition, as between Member States, of obstacles to the free movement of goods, persons, services and capital;
(d) measures concerning the entry and movement of persons in the internal market ...;
(e) a common policy in the sphere of agriculture and fisheries;
(f) a common policy in the sphere of transport;
(g) a system ensuring that competition in the common market is not distorted;
(h) the approximation of the laws of the Member States to the extent required for the functioning of the common market;
(i) a policy in the social sphere comprising a European Social Fund;

(j) the strengthening of economic and social cohesion;
(k) a policy in the sphere of the environment;
(l) the strengthening of the competitiveness of Community industry;
(m) the promotion of research and technological development;
(n) encouragement for the establishment and development of trans-European networks;
(o) a contribution to the attainment of a high level of health protection;
(p) a contribution to education and training of quality and to the flowering of the cultures of the Member States;
(q) a policy in the sphere of development cooperation;
(r) the association of the overseas countries and territories in order to increase trade and promote jointly economic and social development;
(s) a contribution to the strengthening of consumer protection;
(t) measures in the spheres of energy, civil protection and tourism.[7]

Important for equal rights, although it does not specify religion, Article 6(a) prohibits discrimination:

6(a) Within the scope of application of this Treaty, and without prejudice to any special provisions contained therein, any discrimination on grounds of nationality shall be prohibited.[8]

Further, in terms of the free movement of persons, services and capital, in particular workers, Article 48 provides:

48. 1. Freedom of movement for workers shall be secured within the Community by the end of the transitional period at the latest.

2. Such freedom of movement shall entail the abolition of any discrimination based on nationality between workers of the Member States as regards employment, remuneration and other conditions of work and employment.

3. It shall entail the right, subject to limitations justified on grounds of public policy, public security or public health:

a. to accept offers of employment actually made;

b. to move freely within the territory of Member States for this purpose;

c. to stay in a Member State for the purpose of employment in accordance with the provisions governing the employment of nationals of that State laid down by law, regulation or administrative action;

d. to remain in the territory of a Member State after having been employed in that State, subject to conditions which shall be embodied in implementing regulations to be drawn up by the Commission.

4. The provisions of this Article shall not apply to employment in the public service.[9]

Important for religious women, in terms of equal pay, Article 119 states:

119. Each Member State shall during the first stage ensure and subsequently maintain the application of the principle that men and women should receive equal pay for equal work.
For the purpose of this Article, 'pay' means the ordinary basic or minimum wage or salary and any other consideration, whether in cash or in kind, which the worker receives, directly or indirectly, in respect of his employment from his employer.
Equal pay without discrimination based on sex means:
(a) that pay for the same work at piece rates shall be calculated on the basis of the same unit of measurement;
(b) that pay for work at time rates shall be the same for the same job.[10]

Maastricht Treaty

The Maastricht Treaty was signed on 7 February 1992 and entered into force on 1 November 1993, creating the European Union (EU). The EU became an internal market of over 340 million people providing for the free movement of goods, capital, services and citizens of Member States. The Maastricht Treaty affirms that it marks a new stage in the process of European integration undertaken with the establishment of the European Communities. It was designed to create a firm basis for the construction of the future of Europe, by deepening the solidarity between peoples while respecting the different histories, cultures and traditions. Further, the Maastricht Treaty espoused the desire to enhance the democracy and efficient functioning of the institutions so as to enable them to better carry out, within a single institutional framework, the tasks entrusted to them. The foundations for a united Europe were laid on fundamental values including peace, unity, equality, freedom, solidarity and security, through intergovernmental cooperation and the creation of the three pillars of EC society. By the Maastricht Treaty, the European Union confirms its 'attachment to the principles of liberty, democracy and respect for human rights and fundamental freedoms and of the rule of law'.

According to Article A of the Maastricht Treaty, the Treaty 'marks a new stage in the process of creating an ever closer union among the peoples of Europe, in which decisions are taken as closely as possible to the citizen'.[11] Further, Article B states:

B. The Union shall set itself the following objectives:

to promote economic and social progress which is balanced and sustainable, in particular through the creation of an area without internal frontiers, through the strengthening of economic and social cohesion and through the establishment of economic and monetary union, ultimately including a single currency in accordance with the provisions of this Treaty;
to assert its identity on the international scene, in particular through the implementation of a common foreign and security policy including the eventual framing of a common defence policy, which might in time lead to a common defence;
to strengthen the protection of the rights and interests of the nationals of its Member States through the introduction of a citizenship of the Union;
to develop close cooperation on justice and home affairs;
to maintain in full the 'acquis communautaire' and build on it with ... the aim of ensuring the effectiveness of the mechanisms and the institutions of the Community.[12]

Treaty of Amsterdam

The Treaty of Amsterdam, the treaty establishing the European Community, amending previous treaties, was signed on 2 October 1997 and entered into force on 1 May 1999.[13] Important for all people, in order to combat religious discrimination, Article 13, amending Article 6(a) of the Treaty of Rome for specificity, provides specifically for religion:

> 13. Without prejudice to the other provisions of this Treaty and within the limits of the powers conferred by it upon the Community, the Council, acting unanimously on a proposal from the Commission and after consulting the European Parliament, may take appropriate action to combat discrimination based on sex, racial or ethnic origin, religion or belief, disability, age or sexual orientation.[14]

Further, in terms of the free movement of persons, services and capital, in particular workers, Article 39, amending Article 48 of the Treaty of Rome, states:

> 39. 1. Freedom of movement for workers shall be secured within the Community.
> 2. Such freedom of movement shall entail the abolition of any discrimination based on nationality between workers of the Member States as regards employment, remuneration and other conditions of work and employment.
> 3. It shall entail the right, subject to limitations justified on grounds of public policy, public security or public health:
> (a) to accept offers of employment actually made;
> (b) to move freely within the territory of Member States for this purpose;
> (c) to stay in a Member State for the purpose of employment in accordance with the provisions governing the employment of nationals of that State laid down by law, regulation or administrative action;

(d) to remain in the territory of a Member State after having been employed in that State, subject to conditions which shall be embodied in implementing regulations to be drawn up by the Commission.

4. The provisions of this Article shall not apply to employment in the public service.[15]

Important for religious women, in terms of equal pay, Article 141, amending Article 119 of the Treaty of Rome, states:

141. 1. Each Member State shall ensure that the principle of equal pay for male and female workers for equal work or work of equal value is applied.

2. For the purpose of this Article, 'pay' means the ordinary basic or minimum wage or salary and any other consideration, whether in cash or in kind, which the worker receives directly or indirectly, in respect of his employment, from his employer.

Equal pay without discrimination based on sex means:

(a) that pay for the same work at piece rates shall be calculated on the basis of the same unit of measurement;

(b) that pay for work at time rates shall be the same for the same job.

3. The Council, acting in accordance with the procedure referred to in Article 251, and after consulting the Economic and Social Committee, shall adopt measures to ensure the application of the principle of equal opportunities and equal treatment of men and women in matters of employment and occupation, including the principle of equal pay for equal work or work of equal value.

4. With a view to ensuring full equality in practice between men and women in working life, the principle of equal treatment shall not prevent any Member State from maintaining or adopting measures providing for specific advantages in order to make it easier for the under-represented sex to pursue a vocational activity or to prevent or compensate for disadvantages in professional careers.[16]

European Law and the European Court of Justice

The extension of civil rights marks another step toward European integration. The concept of citizenship is based on the principle that nationals of Member States have certain rights to move freely across national borders in the common market. Freedom of movement, under the Treaty of Rome, applied only to certain economic categories of workers, the self-employed and service providers. This, however, was expanded by the Treaty of Amsterdam and the European Court of Justice, which had a profound impact on employment.

Where European Union law has direct effect, it will take precedence over domestic law in such cases as equality in employment. Under national law, the national court of the Member State is within its limits of discretion, when interpreting domestic law. However, domestic law must be in accord with the requirements of European Union law, and if this is not possible, then domestic law is inapplicable. This, therefore, is a strong incentive for national courts to rule against religious discrimination. European Union legislation establishes that a citizen of the European Union should not be discriminated against in the workplace on the basis of religion. In employment, discrimination can occur in two ways: direct discrimination when people are treated differently, solely on the basis of their religion; and indirect discrimination when people are treated differently because of an apparently neutral provision, criterion or practice determining recruitment, pay, working conditions, dismissal, and social security in practice disadvantaging a substantially higher proportion of the members of one group. Such provisions, criteria or practices are prohibited under European Union law, unless it is proven that they are justified by objective reasons in no way related to religious discrimination. In examining positive action, European Union law allows European Union countries and companies to undertake several initiatives to counter religious discrimination. While there is no official definition of positive action, it does include all measures which are designed to counter the effects of past disadvantages and existing discrimination, and to promote equality of opportunity in the field of employment. Historically, there have been discriminatory policies directly on their face or indirectly, applied to different groups. Positive action is needed not only to help guarantee equality, but also to combat the perpetuation of traditional discriminatory attitudes so as to ensure access to equal opportunities for all regardless of religion.

In terms of the burden of proof, in the European Court of Justice, the plaintiff has the burden of showing, in indirect cases, that a neutral policy has a disproportionate impact (*Teuling v. Bredrijfsverenigìng*, [1987] ECR 2497).[17] The burden is then shifted to the defendant who must justify this by objective reasons other than discrimination. The plaintiff must then show that the explanation is not effective for the purpose, or that there is an alternative provision to accomplish it in a manner that has a less discriminatory impact. Otherwise, if there is a difference in treatment, it must be justified by objective factors other than discrimination. If a provision is neutral on its terms, but factually disadvantages a particular group, an employer bears the burden of justification. The European Court of Justice requires a showing of objective justification as a defense to discrimination.

There are five European Union (EU) institutions, each playing a specific role, namely the European Parliament, which is elected by the citizens of the Member States; the Council of the European Union, which represents the governments of the Member States; the European Commission, which is the executive body; the European Court of Justice, which ensures compliance with the law; and the Court of Auditors, which controls sound and lawful management of the European Union budget. There are five other important bodies, namely the European Economic and Social Committee, which expresses the opinions of organized civil society on economic and social issues; the Committee of the Regions, which expresses the opinions of regional and local authorities; the European Central Bank, which is responsible for monetary policy and managing the Euro; the European Ombudsman, who deals with citizens' complaints about maladministration by any European Union institution or body; and the European Investment Bank, which helps achieve European Union objectives by financing investment projects. A number of agencies and other bodies complete the system.

Specifically, the Commission is responsible for making legislative proposals, executing policies and monitoring the compliance of Member States with their obligations. It is the driving force behind European integration by its right of initiative. It is also the guardian of the Treaties by its right to intervene with Member States and to demand compliance with their obligations. If Member States breach their Treaty obligations, they will face Commission action and possible legal proceedings in the European Court of Justice. As assistance to the European Court of Justice, the Commission is the European Union watchdog for the observance of the Treaties, as it originates and administers European Union law. The Council of Ministers is composed of representatives of Member State governments, and decides on Commission proposals. It is the Union's legislator, with all decisions involving new policies requiring unanimity. The Assembly is charged with proposing, to the Council, arrangements for universal direct elections. In addition, the Council, in turn, commends them to the Member States for adoption under constitutional procedures. The Assembly is consultative and can, if it has a sufficient majority, express its nonconfidence in the commission by dismissing it.

The European Union can legislate directly through regulations, which are binding in law and are automatically incorporated into the national legal systems of Member States, without the need for specific individual ratification. It can also work through the legal systems of the Member States, by the use of the Commission, which implements directives with broad objectives. Although directives require some legal action, such as legislation, by the Member States before they become national law, they are laws transposed into Member States' legislation to enforce Treaty principles. Importantly, decisions by the European Court of Justice are binding as force of law, whereas recommendations and opinions by the Council of Ministers or the Commission are not.

The European Court of Justice (ECJ) is the European Union's supreme constitutional authority. It renders judgments on the obligations of the institutions, Member States and citizens. The very existence of the European Union is conditional on the recognition of the binding nature of its rules, by the Member States, by the institutions, and by individuals. European Union law has successfully embedded itself thoroughly in the legal life of the Member States through the supervision of the European Court of Justice. The founding European Treaties are the primary source of European Union law, and therein is found the central jurisdiction of the European Court of Justice. European Union law involves primary law, namely Treaties, and secondary law, namely legislative acts, both of which are binding on national governments and take precedence over national law. The nature of the European Union, its existence and its functions, demand a consistent application of European Union law between Member States.

The ECJ was to provide the legal sanctions for the carrying out of the Treaties. Before the European Community and the European Union, courts operating beyond national boundaries were constrained by international agreement, such as the International Court of Justice. In essence, European Union citizens are affected by two legal systems, national and European Union law. The courts of law must apply both systems of law where relevant, and if there is a conflict, the European Union law takes precedence. The supremacy of European Union law is implicit in the nature of the European Union, since its existence and functioning require its application. European Union law is directly applicable to Member States, and there is no requirement that it be passed into national law for its validity, since the rights and obligations accrue directly to European Union citizens.[18]

The primacy of European Union law and its direct applicability are distinctive features of the European Union, turning freedoms into rights. It is a system of laws, which is directly applicable to people and institutions in Member States, and is invoked in national courts. European Union law touches on many aspects of national life, including immigration, control of foreign workers, and matters relating to equality. Thus, national law has been challenged or influenced by European Union law, which is enforced and overseen by the European Court of Justice. This surrender of sovereignty cannot be reversed by measures taken by national authorities in conflict with European Union law, relinquishing far-reaching powers to an independent legal order, which binds Member States. Points of law and the interpretation of Treaties are decided by the European Court of Justice, the European Union's judicial institution having jurisdiction over disputes concerning the Member States. Often, the national court is faced with issues, such as the interpretation of a Treaty, the validity of acts or the lack of a judicial remedy under national law. If a Nation State's court decides that a question of European Union law needs to be answered before it can render a judgment, it can go before the European Court of Justice for a ruling. The European Union Treaties are part of the domestic law of the State, and as such, they impinge on the finality of national court decisions.

The European Court of Justice is at the heart of the legal system, and ensures that European Union law is observed in the interpretation and application of the Treaties. Its judgments are binding on Member States. The court reviews the lawfulness of acts of Council, the Commission, the Member State's governments and citizens. National laws in conflict with European Union law may be declared invalid by the European Court of Justice. Appeals against acts of an institution or a Member State can be lodged by any other institution, government, firm or individual citizen directly affected.

Two types of cases may be brought before the European Court of Justice, namely direct actions, brought directly before the Court by the Commission, other European Union institutions or a Member State, or preliminary rulings, requested by courts or tribunals in the Member States on a question of European Union law. The European Court of Justice may hear a variety of cases involving: annulment of binding legal acts; failure to act; infringement of the European Union Treaties under Article 33, in order to have Commission decisions or recommendations declared void for lack of competence, infringement of an essential procedural requirement, the Treaty or any rule of law relating to its application, or misuse of powers; preliminary rulings, in which national courts petition the Court of Justice for a ruling on a point of European Union law, binding in the case; damages; and application of staff regulations. The Treaties state that the European Union's legal system, which must not be impeded by any State, applies throughout the European Union.

The legal order is called the 'originality' of the European Union, which is the jurisdiction of the constitutional court, the European Court of Justice. The Court's decisions are made by majority vote, presented in open court. The judgments are directly applicable to Member States and are enforceable through the national courts. The Court of Justice located in Luxembourg may sit in plenary session, when a Member State or a European Union institution is a party to the proceeding and so requests or when a case is considered complex and important, or may sit in chamber. Since all the official languages of the European Union are used at some point, the Court provides for a large translation and interpretation service. The Court is also assisted by an Advocate General, as *amicus curiae* acting as an independent judicial observer representing the public interest, who makes a reasoned presentation of the case before the Court, gives a summary of the submissions of the parties, puts forth observations of oral hearings, statute law and previous cases, and offers an opinion, which although published is not binding on the Court. In order to enable the Court of Justice to concentrate its activities on the fundamental task of ensuring uniform interpretation of European Union law, a Court of First Instance was established in 1989, which has jurisdiction over actions brought by individuals and companies against decisions of the European Union institutions and agencies, and these judgments are in turn subject to appeal before the European Court of Justice on a point of law.

As the arbiter of European Union law, the European Court of Justice, with its power, has strengthened the European Union as a political system, and defiance of its rulings has been exceptional. By creating a body of independent European Union law, the European Union has promoted its survival, by requiring harmonization of the laws of the Member States. The national courts are, therefore, responsible for aligning national law with European Union law. The Treaties are a comprehensive code of law, which set out the rights and duties of governments and individuals, and from which rights and remedies can be deduced. Interestingly, for the European Court of Justice, the European Union's common aims count more than a literal construction of legal texts, and in turn, the legal character of the European Union is concerned with influencing, shaping and controlling the legislative output of the European Union. Fundamental rights are part of the bedrock of the European Union's legal order. The European Court of Justice held that the protection of such rights, while inspired by the constitutional traditions common to Member States, must be ensured within the framework of the structure and objectives of the European Union (*Internationale Handelsgesellschaft* [1970] ECR 1125, [1972] CMLR 255).[19] Importantly, in a seminal case, the European Court of Justice stated:

The integration into the laws of each Member State of provisions which derive from the Community, and more generally the terms and the spirit of the Treaty, make it impossible for the States, as a corollary, to accord precedence to a unilateral and subsequent measure over a legal system accepted by them on a basis of reciprocity . The executive force of Community law cannot vary from one State to another . without jeopardising the attainment of the object of the Treaty.It follows from all these observations that the law stemming from the treaty, an independent source of law, could not, because of its special and original nature, be overridden by domestic legal provisions, however framed, without being deprived of its character as Community law and without the legal basis of the Community itself being called into question (*Costa v. ENEL* [1964] CMLR 425).[20]

Until recently, the prevalence of a predominantly secular culture throughout most of the European Union negated the role of religion as an element in determining identity and social interaction between European citizens and settlers in Europe, as the settler communities were perceived almost entirely in terms of their ethnicity, nationality or race, and it was expected that they would follow a course characterized by the privatization of religion. Prior to the Treaty of Amsterdam, there was no express power for the Community to deal with racial or religious discrimination. However, in *Prais v. EC Council* (130/75 (1976) ECR 1589), the European Court of Justice stated that the right to nondiscrimination on religious grounds is a fundamental right to be protected by Community law. Article 13 of the Treaty of Amsterdam puts an end to the long debate about Community competence on antidiscrimination matters by providing a legal basis for the Council, acting unanimously, on a proposal from the Commission and after consultation with the European Parliament, to take 'appropriate action' to combat discrimination based on religion or belief.[21]

In terms of religious discrimination, in the cases of *Valsamis v. Greece*[22] and *Efstratiou v. Greece*,[23] when the applicants, who were Jehovah's Witnesses, complained that a rule allowing schools to require pupils, under threat of a disciplinary penalty, to take part in the National Day Parade, was in violation of their freedom to manifest their pacifist beliefs. The Court and Commission rejected their applications, the European Court of Human Rights rejected their application, holding that it could 'discern nothing, either in the purpose of the parade or in the arrangements for it, which could offend the applicants' pacifist conviction'.

European Convention for the Protection of Human Rights and Fundamental Freedoms (ECHR)

Crucially, for human rights, the European Convention for the Protection of Human Rights and Fundamental Freedoms came into being on 4 November 1950, which affords protection against discrimination. In the Preamble of the European Convention for the Protection of Human Rights and Fundamental Freedoms, the Governments signatory hereto, being Members of the Council of Europe, undertake the agreement:

> Considering the Universal Declaration of Human Rights proclaimed by the General Assembly of the United Nations on 10th December 1948;
>
> Considering that this Declaration aims at securing the universal and effective recognition and observance of the Rights therein declared;
>
> Considering that the aim of the Council of Europe is the achievement of greater unity between its Members and that one of the methods by which the aim is to be pursued is the maintenance and further realisation of Human Rights and Fundamental Freedoms;
>
> Reaffirming their profound belief in those Fundamental Freedoms which are the foundation of justice and peace in the world and are best maintained on the one hand by an effective political democracy and on the other by a common understanding and observance of the Human Rights upon which they depend;
>
> Being resolved, as the Governments of European countries which are like-minded and have a common heritage of political traditions, ideals, freedom and the rule of law to take the first steps for the collective enforcement of certain of the Rights stated in the Universal Declaration.[24]

Article 1 guarantees:

> 1. The High Contracting Parties shall secure to everyone within their jurisdiction the rights and freedoms defined.[25]

Importantly, the freedom of thought, conscience and religion is guaranteed under Article 9:

> 9.1. Everyone has the right to freedom of thought, conscience and religion; this right includes freedom to change his religion or belief and freedom, either alone or in community with others and in public or private, to manifest his religion or belief, in worship, teaching, practice and observance.
>
> 2. Freedom to manifest one's religion or beliefs shall be subject only to such limitations as are prescribed by law and are necessary in a democratic society in the interests of public safety, for the protection of public order, health or morals, or for the protection of the rights and freedoms of others.[26]

Article 9 requires, firstly, negative protection from interference by the State unless the interference falls within Article 9(2), and secondly, a positive obligation on the State to ensure the peaceful enjoyment of the rights under Article 9. Article 9(2) effectively allows for limitations on the manifestation of beliefs to be prescribed by law provided that the test of necessity is met, meaning that although an employee could not be dismissed simply for holding extreme beliefs, dismissal or other discriminatory treatment for the manifestation of those beliefs, such as by proselytizing other employees or engaging in disruptive behavior, could be justified if this could be shown to be necessary for the protection of public order or health or morals or to protect 'the rights and freedoms of others'.

The European Court of Human Rights has decided that there is no obligation on the State to protect citizens from offence to their beliefs caused by other private individuals. However, in *Otto Preminger Institute v. Austria* (1994) 19 European Human Rights Reports 34, the Court has recognized that 'in extreme cases the effect of particular methods of opposing or denying religious beliefs can be such as to inhibit those who hold such beliefs from exercising their freedom to hold and express them'.[27]

The European Court of Human Rights has said that Article 9 is a 'precious asset for atheists, agnostics, sceptics and the unconcerned'.[28] However, to come within the protection of this article the views must attain a certain level of cogency, seriousness, cohesion and importance.[29] In *McFeely v. UK*, the Commission said that 'belief' in Article 9 'means more than just 'mere opinions or deeply held feelings'; there must be a holding of spiritual or philosophical convictions which have an identifiable formal content'.[30] A duty on employers, public authorities or schools to accommodate religious practices requires some method of determining whether an act constitutes a religious practice. Further, the European Commission for Human Rights has taken an objective approach, determining for itself whether an act is a manifestation of a person's belief rather than accepting a declaration by the person concerned that their conduct is a manifestation of their belief. In *Arrowsmith v. UK* (1978) 19 DR 5; (1978) 3 EHRR 110, the applicant argued that under Article 9 she had a right to hand out leaflets to soldiers advocating that they should not serve in Northern Ireland, because this was a manifestation of her pacifist beliefs; the Commission held that 'when actions of individuals do not actually express the belief concerned they cannot be considered to be as such protected by Article 9(1), even when they are motivated by it'.[31] In *C. v. the United Kingdom*, D&R 37 (1984), the Commission also rejected attempts by conscientious objectors to prevent payment of taxes that may be used on military expenditure, holding that only acts 'which are aspects of the practice of a religion or belief in a generally recognised form are protected by Article 9'.[32]

The prohibition of discrimination is guaranteed under Article 14, which specifically mentions religion:

> 14. The enjoyment of the rights and freedoms set forth in this Convention shall be secured without discrimination on any ground such as sex, race, color, language, religion, political or other opinion, national or social origin, association with a national minority, property, birth or other status.[33]

The right to an effective remedy is secured by Article 13:

> 13. Everyone whose rights and freedoms as set forth in this Convention are violated shall have an effective remedy before a national authority notwithstanding that the violation has been committed by persons acting in an official capacity.[34]

Further, Article 17 provides for the prohibition of abuse of rights:

> 17. Nothing in this Convention may be interpreted as implying for any State, group or person any right to engage in any activity or perform any act aimed at the destruction of any of the rights and freedoms set forth herein or at their limitation to a greater extent than is provided for in the Convention.[35]

Importantly, the European Court of Human Rights is established under Article 19:

> 19. To ensure the observance of the engagements undertaken by the High Contracting Parties in the Convention and the Protocols thereto, there shall be set up a European Court of Human Rights, hereinafter referred to as 'the Court'. It shall function on a permanent basis.[36]

Article 32 outlines the jurisdiction of the Court:

> 32. 1. The jurisdiction of the Court shall extend to all matters concerning the interpretation and application of the Convention and the protocols thereto which are referred to it as provided in Articles 33, 34 and 47.
>
> 2. In the event of dispute as to whether the Court has jurisdiction, the Court shall decide.[37]

Article 27 outlines the structure of the Committees, the Chambers and the Grand Chamber:

> 27. 1. To consider cases brought before it, the Court shall sit in committees of three judges, in Chambers of seven judges and in a Grand Chamber of seventeen judges. The Court's Chambers shall set up committees for a fixed period of time.
> 2. There shall sit as an *ex officio* member of the Chamber and the Grand Chamber the judge elected in respect of the State Party concerned or, if there is none or if he is unable to sit, a person of its choice who shall sit in the capacity of judge.
> 3. The Grand Chamber shall also include the President of the Court, the Vice-Presidents, the Presidents of the Chambers and other judges chosen in accordance with the rules of the Court. When a case is referred to the Grand Chamber under Article 43, no judge from the Chamber which rendered the judgment shall sit in the Grand Chamber, with the exception of the President of the Chamber and the judge who sat in respect of the State Party concerned.[38]

Inter-State cases are provided for under Article 33:

> 33. Any High Contracting Party may refer to the Court any alleged breach of the provisions of the Convention and the protocols thereto by another High Contracting Party.[39]

Individual applications are provided for under Article 34:

> 34. The Court may receive applications from any person, non-governmental organization or group of individuals claiming to be the victim of a violation by one of the High Contracting Parties of the rights set forth in the Convention or the protocols thereto. The High Contracting Parties undertake not to hinder in any way the effective exercise of this right.[40]

Further, third party intervention is provided for under Article 36:

> 36. 1. In all cases before a Chamber or the Grand Chamber, a High Contracting Party one of whose nationals is an applicant shall have the right to submit written comments and to take part in hearings.
>
> 2. The President of the Court may, in the interest of the proper administration of justice, invite any High Contracting Party which is not a party to the proceedings or any person concerned who is not the applicant to submit written comments or take part in hearings.[41]

Article 35 contains the admissibility of evidence criteria:

> 35. 1. The Court may only deal with the matter after all domestic remedies have been exhausted, according to the generally recognized rules of international law, and within a period of six months from the date on which the final decision was taken.
> 2. The Court shall not deal with any application submitted under Article 34 that:
> (a) is anonymous; or
> (b) is substantially the same as a matter that has already been examined by the Court or has already been submitted to another procedure of international investigation or settlement and contains no relevant new information.
> 3. The Court shall declare inadmissible any individual application submitted under Article 34 which it considers incompatible with the provisions of the Convention or the protocols thereto, manifestly ill-founded, or an abuse of the right of application.
> 4. The Court shall reject any application which it considers inadmissible under this Article. It may do so at any stage of the proceedings.[42]

Further, Article 37 contains the striking out of applications:

37. 1. The Court may at any stage of the proceedings decide to strike an application out of its list of cases where the circumstances lead to the conclusion that:
(a) the applicant does not intend to pursue his application; or
(b) the matter has been resolved; or
(c) for any other reason established by the Court, it is no longer justified to continue the examination of the application.
However, the Court shall continue the examination of the application if respect for human rights as defined in the Convention and the protocols thereto so requires.
2. The Court may decide to restore an application to its list of cases if it considers that the circumstances justify such a course.[43]

Article 38 outlines the examination of the case and friendly settlement proceedings:

38. 1. If the Court declares the application admissible, it shall:
(a) pursue the examination of the case, together with the representatives of the parties, and if need be, undertake an investigation, for the effective conduct of which the States concerned shall furnish all necessary facilities;
(b) place itself at the disposal of the parties concerned with a view to securing a friendly settlement of the matter on the basis of respect for human rights as defined in the Convention and the protocols thereto.
2. Proceedings conducted under paragraph 1.b shall be confidential.[44]

Further, Article 39 outlines the finding of a friendly settlement:

39. If a friendly settlement is effected, the Court shall strike the case out of its list by means of a decision which shall be confined to a brief statement of the facts and of the solution reached.[45]

Public hearings and access to documents are provided for under Article 40:

40. 1. Hearings shall be in public unless the Court in exceptional circumstances decides otherwise.
2. Documents deposited with the Registrar shall be accessible to the public unless the President of the Court decides otherwise.[46]

Further, Article 41 provides for just satisfaction:

41. If the Court finds that there has been a violation of the Convention or the protocols thereto, and if the internal law of the High Contracting Party concerned allows only partial reparation to be made, the Court shall, if necessary, afford just satisfaction to the injured party.[47]

Importantly, final judgments are contained in Article 44:

44. 1. The judgment of the Grand Chamber shall be final.

2. The judgment of a Chamber shall become final:
(a) when the parties declare that they will not request that the case be referred to the Grand Chamber; or
(b) three months after the date of the judgment, if reference of the case to the Grand Chamber has not been requested; or
(c) when the panel of the Grand Chamber rejects the request to refer under Article 43.
3. The final judgment shall be published.[48]

Further, reasons for judgments and decisions are contained in Article 45:

45. 1. Reasons shall be given for judgments as well as for decisions declaring applications admissible or inadmissible.
2. If a judgment does not represent, in whole or in part, the unanimous opinion of the judges, any judge shall be entitled to deliver a separate opinion.[49]

In addition, binding force and execution of judgments are contained in Article 46:

46. 1. The High Contracting Parties undertake to abide by the final judgment of the Court in any case to which they are parties.
2. The final judgment of the Court shall be transmitted to the Committee of Ministers, which shall supervise its execution.[50]

Finally, Article 47 provides for advisory opinions:

47. 1. The Court may, at the request of the Committee of Ministers, give advisory opinions on legal questions concerning the interpretation of the Convention and the protocols thereto.
2. Such opinions shall not deal with any question relating to the content or scope of the rights or freedoms defined in Section I of the Convention and the protocols thereto, or with any other question which the Court or the Committee of Ministers might have to consider in consequence of any such proceedings as could be instituted in accordance with the Convention.
3. Decisions of the Committee of Ministers to request an advisory opinion of the Court shall require a majority vote of the representatives entitled to sit on the Committee.[51]

In addition, the Preamble of Protocol No.1, entitled Enforcement of Certain Rights and Freedoms not included in Section I of the Convention, states that:

The Governments signatory hereto, being Members of the Council of Europe,
Being resolved to take steps to ensure the collective enforcement of certain rights and freedoms other than those already included in Section I of the Convention for

the Protection of Human Rights and Fundamental Freedoms signed at Rome on 4th November, 1950 (hereinafter referred to as 'the Convention'),
Have agreed as follows.[52]

Important for religious freedom, Article 2 states:

> 2. No person shall be denied the right to education. In exercise of any functions which it assumes in relation to education and to teaching, the State shall respect the right of parents to ensure such education and teaching in conformity with their own religious and philosophical convictions.[53]

Further, important for equal rights, in the Preamble of the Protocol No. 12 to the European Convention for the Protection of Human Rights and Fundamental Freedoms opened for signature on 11 April 2000, the Member States of the Council of Europe signatory hereto, undertake the agreement:

> Having regard to the fundamental principle according to which all persons are equal before the law and are entitled to the equal protection of the law;
> Being resolved to take further steps to promote the equality of all persons through the collective enforcement of a general prohibition of discrimination by means of the Convention for the Protection of Human Rights and Fundamental Freedoms signed at Rome on 4 November 1950 (hereinafter referred to as 'the Convention');
> Reaffirming that the principle of non-discrimination does not prevent States Parties from taking measures in order to promote full and effective equality, provided that there is an objective and reasonable justification for those measures.[54]

Article 1, which specifically mentions religion, outlines the general prohibition against discrimination:

> 1(1) The enjoyment of any right set forth by law shall be secured without discrimination on any ground such as sex, race, color, language, religion, political or other opinion, national or social origin, association with a national minority, property, birth or other status.
> (2) No one shall be discriminated against by any public authority on any ground such as those mentioned in paragraph 1.[55]

It is noteworthy that the words 'other status' includes religion, and such a specific inclusion was considered unnecessary from a legal point of view, since the list of nondiscrimination grounds is not exhaustive, and since inclusion of any particular additional ground might give rise to unwarranted *a contrario* interpretations as regards discrimination based on grounds not so included. According to the Explanatory Memorandum prepared by the Council of Europe, the expression 'any right set forth by law', is meant to cover (i) the enjoyment of any right specifically granted to an individual by national law; (ii) the enjoyment of a right which may be inferred from a clear obligation of a public authority under national law, such as where a public authority is obliged under national law to behave in a particular manner; (iii) the exercise of a discretionary power by a public authority; and (iv) any other act or omission by a public authority. The prime objective of Article 1 is to embody a negative obligation on public authorities not to discriminate; it does not impose a general positive obligation to take measures to prevent or prohibit all instances of discrimination between private persons. On the other hand, the duty to 'secure' might entail a positive obligation where there is a clear gap in protection from discrimination under domestic law, and would oblige a ratifying State to secure protection against discrimination on all the proscribed grounds, including religion.

European Social Charter

The European Social Charter promotes the right of workers to equal opportunities and equal treatment in matters of employment and occupation without discrimination. It espouses the notion of 'equal pay for work of equal value', and also provides for the equal treatment with regard to access to employment, vocational training, promotion and working conditions, aimed at eliminating all discrimination, both direct and indirect, in the world of work, providing for opportunities for positive measures. In the Preamble to the European Social Charter of 18 October 1961, the governments signatory hereto, being members of the Council of Europe, undertake the agreement, specifically mentioning religion:

> Considering that the aim of the Council of Europe is the achievement of greater unity between its members for the purpose of safeguarding and realising the ideals and principles which are their common heritage and of facilitating their economic and social progress, in particular by the maintenance and further realisation of human rights and fundamental freedoms;

> Considering that in the Convention for the Protection of Human Rights and Fundamental Freedoms signed at Rome on 4th November 1950, and the Protocol thereto signed at Paris on 20th March 1952, the member States of the Council of Europe agreed to secure to their populations the civil and political rights and freedoms therein specified;

> Considering that the enjoyment of social rights should be secured without discrimination on grounds of race, color, sex, religion, political opinion, national extraction or social origin;

> Being resolved to make every effort in common to improve the standard of living and to promote the social well-being of both their urban and rural populations by means of appropriate institutions and action.[56]

In the Preamble to the European Social Charter (revised) of 3 May 1996, the governments signatory thereto, being members of the Council of Europe, undertake the agreement:

... Considering that in the European Social Charter opened for signature in Turin on 18 October 1961 and the Protocols thereto, the member States of the Council of Europe agreed to secure to their populations the social rights specified therein in order to improve their standard of living and their social well-being;

Recalling that the Ministerial Conference on Human Rights held in Rome on 5 November 1990 stressed the need, on the one hand, to preserve the indivisible nature of all human rights, be they civil, political, economic, social or cultural and, on the other hand, to give the European Social Charter fresh impetus.[57]

Important for equal rights and religious tolerance, Article E, which specifically mentions religion, defines nondiscrimination:

E. The enjoyment of the rights set forth in this Charter shall be secured without discrimination on any ground such as race, color, sex, language, religion, political or other opinion, national extraction or social origin, health, association with a national minority, birth or other status.[58]

Important for all workers, including those from religious minorities, under Part I, and in particular I(23), several rights and principles are espoused:

The Parties accept as the aim of their policy, to be pursued by all appropriate means both national and international in character, the attainment of conditions in which the following rights and principles may be effectively realized:

1. Everyone shall have the opportunity to earn his living in an occupation freely entered upon.
2. All workers have the right to just conditions of work.
3. All workers have the right to safe and healthy working conditions.
4. All workers have the right to a fair remuneration sufficient for a decent standard of living for themselves and their families.
5. All workers and employers have the right to freedom of association in national or international organizations for the protection of their economic and social interests.
6. All workers and employers have the right to bargain collectively.
7. Children and young persons have the right to a special protection against the physical and moral hazards to which they are exposed.
8. Employed women, in case of maternity, have the right to a special protection.
9. Everyone has the right to appropriate facilities for vocational guidance with a view to helping him choose an occupation suited to his personal aptitude and interests.
10. Everyone has the right to appropriate facilities for vocational training.

11. Everyone has the right to benefit from any measures enabling him to enjoy the highest possible standard of health attainable.
12. All workers and their dependents have the right to social security.
13. Anyone without adequate resources has the right to social and medical assistance.
14. Everyone has the right to benefit from social welfare services.
15. Disabled persons have the right to independence, social integration and participation in the life of the community.
16. The family as a fundamental unit of society has the right to appropriate social, legal and economic protection to ensure its full development.
17. Children and young persons have the right to appropriate social, legal and economic protection.
18. The nationals of any one of the Parties have the right to engage in any gainful occupation in the territory of any one of the others on a footing of equality with the nationals of the latter, subject to restrictions based on cogent economic or social reasons.
19. Migrant workers who are nationals of a Party and their families have the right to protection and assistance in the territory of any other Party.
20. All workers have the right to equal opportunities and equal treatment in matters of employment and occupation without discrimination on the grounds of sex.
21. Workers have the right to be informed and to be consulted within the undertaking.
22. Workers have the right to take part in the determination and improvement of the working conditions and working environment in the undertaking.
23. Every elderly person has the right to social protection.
24. All workers have the right to protection in cases of termination of employment.
25. All workers have the right to protection of their claims in the event of the insolvency of their employer.
26. All workers have the right to dignity at work.
27. All persons with family responsibilities and who are engaged or wish to engage in employment have a right to do so without being subject to discrimination and as far as possible without conflict between their employment and family responsibilities.
28. Workers' representatives in undertakings have the right to protection against acts prejudicial to them and should be afforded appropriate facilities to carry out their functions.
29. All workers have the right to be informed and consulted in collective redundancy procedures.
30. Everyone has the right to protection against poverty and social exclusion.
31. Everyone has the right to housing.[59]

Under Part II, the right to work is provided for in Article 1:

1. With a view to ensuring the effective exercise of the right to work, the Parties undertake:

1. to accept as one of their primary aims and responsibilities the achievement and maintenance of as high and stable a level of employment as possible, with a view to the attainment of full employment;
2. to protect effectively the right of the worker to earn his living in an occupation freely entered upon;
to establish or maintain free employment services for all workers;
to provide or promote appropriate vocational guidance, training and rehabilitation.[60]

Further, Article 4 guarantees the right to a fair remuneration and equal pay:

4. With a view to ensuring the effective exercise of the right to a fair remuneration, the Parties undertake:
1. to recognize the right of workers to a remuneration such as will give them and their families a decent standard of living;
2. to recognize the right of workers to an increased rate of remuneration for overtime work, subject to exceptions in particular cases;
3. to recognize the right of men and women workers to equal pay for work of equal value;
4. to recognize the right of all workers to a reasonable period of notice for termination of employment;
5. to permit deductions from wages only under conditions and to the extent prescribed by national laws or regulations or fixed by collective agreements or arbitration awards. The exercise of these rights shall be achieved by freely concluded collective agreements, by statutory wage-fixing machinery, or by other means appropriate to national conditions.[61]

In addition, Article 24 provides for termination of employment under appropriate means:

24. It is understood that for the purposes of this article the terms 'termination of employment' and 'terminated' mean termination of employment at the initiative of the employer.
1. It is understood that this article covers all workers but that a Party may exclude from some or all of its protection the following categories of employed persons:
   a. workers engaged under a contract of employment for a specified period of time or a specified task;
   b. workers undergoing a period of probation or a qualifying period of employment, provided that this is determined in advance and is of a reasonable duration;
   c. workers engaged on a casual basis for a short period.
2. For the purpose of this article the following, in particular, shall not constitute valid reasons for termination of employment:
   a. trade union membership or participation in union activities outside working hours, or, with the consent of the employer, within working hours;

b. seeking office as, acting or having acted in the capacity of a workers' representative;
   c. the filing of a complaint or the participation in proceedings against an employer involving alleged violation of laws or regulations or recourse to competent administrative authorities;
   d. race, color, sex, marital status, family responsibilities, pregnancy, religion, political opinion, national extraction or social origin;
   e. maternity or parental leave;
   f. temporary absence from work due to illness or injury.

> 3. It is understood that compensation or other appropriate relief in case of termination of employment without valid reasons shall be determined by national laws or regulations, collective agreements or other means appropriate to national conditions.[62]

Pursuant to Article 22, the Parties undertake to adopt or encourage measures enabling all workers, in accordance with national legislation and practice, to contribute to the determination and the improvement of the working conditions, work organization and working environment; to the protection of health and safety within the undertaking; to the organization of social and sociocultural services and facilities within the undertaking; and to the supervision of the observance of regulations on these matters.[63]

Finally, importantly, under Part V, Article E is a provision on nondiscrimination, which specifically mentions religion:

> The enjoyment of the rights set forth in this Charter shall be secured without discrimination on any ground such as race, colour, sex, language, religion, political or other opinion, national extraction or social origin, health, association with a national minority, birth or other status.[64]

The right of all individuals to equality before the law and to protection from discrimination is a fundamental right which is essential in order to allow any democratic society to function properly, since it helps to achieve the objectives of promoting economic and social progress, and a high level of employment by increasing economic and social cohesion. Two key instruments were adopted which were intended to prevent and combat discrimination based on racial or ethnic origin, religion or belief, age, disability, or sexual orientation: Directive 2000/78/EC prohibiting discrimination in employment and excluding all discrimination based on religion or belief, disability, age or sexual orientation; and Council Decision 2000/750/EC the Community action program to combat discrimination, supporting and supplementing efforts at the Community level and in the Member States to promote measures to prevent and to combat direct or indirect discrimination based on religion or belief, racial or ethnic origin, disability, age, or sexual orientation, whether based on one or on multiple factors, aiming at promoting greater public consensus on the extent and impact of discrimination.

Treaty Establishing a Constitution for Europe

The Heads of State or Government of the 25 Member States and the candidate countries signed the Treaty establishing a Constitution for Europe on 29 October 2004, which need to be *ratified* by all Member States of the enlarged Union, in order for it to come into effect, and in order to enable the European Union to ensure the well-being of citizens, and the defense of values and interests; to assume responsibilities as a leading international player; to fight unemployment and social exclusion more effectively; to promote sustainable economic growth; to respond to the challenges of globalization; to safeguard internal and external security; and to protect the environment. The Charter of Fundamental Rights of the European Union, part of the intended Constitution of Europe, has to be seen in the wider context of the European Union's long-lasting commitment to human rights and fundamental freedoms and of its policy in the areas of justice, freedom, security and social rights.

The Preamble of the Treaty 2004/C 310/01, establishing a Constitution for Europe states:

> DRAWING INSPIRATION from the cultural, religious and humanist inheritance of Europe, from which have developed the universal values of the inviolable and inalienable rights of the human person, freedom, democracy, equality and the rule of law,
>
> CONVINCED that, while remaining proud of their own national identities and history, the peoples of Europe are determined to transcend their former divisions and, united ever more closely, to forge a common destiny,
>
> CONVINCED that, thus 'United in diversity', Europe offers them the best chance of pursuing, with due regard for the rights of each individual and in awareness of their responsibilities towards future generations and the Earth, the great venture which makes of it a special area of human hope,
>
> DETERMINED to continue the work accomplished within the framework of the Treaties establishing the European Communities and the Treaty on European Union, by ensuring the continuity of the Community *acquis*,
>
> WHO, having exchanged their full powers, found in good and due form. [65]

Article I-1 on the establishment of the Union states:

> I-1. 1. Reflecting the will of the citizens and States of Europe to build a common future, this Constitution establishes the European Union, on which the Member States confer competences to attain objectives they have in common. The Union shall coordinate the policies by which the Member States aim to achieve these objectives, and shall exercise in the Community way the competences they confer on it.

2. The Union shall be open to all European States which respect its values and are committed to promoting them together.[66]

The Union's values are outlined in Article I-2:

> I-2. The Union is founded on the values of respect for human dignity, liberty, democracy, equality, the rule of law and respect for human rights, including the rights of persons belonging to minorities. These values are common to the Member States in a society in which pluralism, non-discrimination, tolerance, justice, solidarity and equality between women and men prevail.[67]

Those beliefs which are essential to the dignity and integrity of the individual are likely to be protected as an aspect of freedom of belief.

Further, the Union's objectives are outlined in Article I-3:

> I-3. 1. The Union's aim is to promote peace, its values and the well-being of its peoples.
> 2. The Union shall offer its citizens an area of freedom, security and justice without internal frontiers, and an internal market where competition is free and undistorted.
> 3. The Union shall work for the sustainable development of Europe based on balanced economic growth and price stability, a highly competitive social market economy, aiming at full employment and social progress, and a high level of protection and improvement of the quality of the environment. It shall promote scientific and technological advance.
> It shall combat social exclusion and discrimination, and shall promote social justice and protection, equality between women and men, solidarity between generations and protection of the rights of the child.
> It shall promote economic, social and territorial cohesion, and solidarity among Member States.
> It shall respect its rich cultural and linguistic diversity, and shall ensure that Europe's cultural heritage is safeguarded and enhanced.
> 4. In its relations with the wider world, the Union shall uphold and promote its values and interests. It shall contribute to peace, security, the sustainable development of the Earth, solidarity and mutual respect among peoples, free and fair trade, eradication of poverty and the protection of human rights, in particular the rights of the child, as well as to the strict observance and the development of international law, including respect for the principles of the United Nations Charter.
> 5. The Union shall pursue its objectives by appropriate means commensurate with the competences which are conferred upon it in the Constitution.[68]

Important for equal rights, fundamental freedoms and nondiscrimination are upheld in Article I-4:

I-4. 1. The free movement of persons, services, goods and capital, and freedom of establishment shall be guaranteed within and by the Union, in accordance with the Constitution.

2. Within the scope of the Constitution, and without prejudice to any of its specific provisions, any discrimination on grounds of nationality shall be prohibited.[69]

The primacy of Union law is emphasized in Article I-6:

I-6. The Constitution and law adopted by the institutions of the Union in exercising competences conferred on it shall have primacy over the law of the Member States.[70]

Further, relations between the Union and Member States are contained in Article I-5:

I-5. 1. The Union shall respect the equality of Member States before the Constitution as well as their national identities, inherent in their fundamental structures, political and constitutional, inclusive of regional and local self-government. It shall respect their essential State functions, including ensuring the territorial integrity of the State, maintaining law and order and safeguarding national security.

2. Pursuant to the principle of sincere cooperation, the Union and the Member States shall, in full mutual respect, assist each other in carrying out tasks which flow from the Constitution.

The Member States shall take any appropriate measure, general or particular, to ensure fulfillment of the obligations arising out of the Constitution or resulting from the acts of the institutions of the Union.

The Member States shall facilitate the achievement of the Union's tasks and refrain from any measure which could jeopardize the attainment of the Union's objectives.[71]

The Preamble of the Charter of Fundamental Rights, part of the Constitution of Europe, states:

The peoples of Europe, in creating an ever closer union among them, are resolved to share a peaceful future based on common values.

Conscious of its spiritual and moral heritage, the Union is founded on the indivisible, universal values of human dignity, freedom, equality and solidarity; it is based on the principles of democracy and the rule of law. It places the individual at the heart of its activities, by establishing the citizenship of the Union and by creating an area of freedom, security and justice.

The Union contributes to the preservation and to the development of these common values while respecting the diversity of the cultures and traditions of the peoples of Europe as well as the national identities of the Member States and the organization of their public authorities at national, regional and local levels; it seeks to promote balanced and sustainable development and ensures free movement of persons, goods, services and capital, and the freedom of establishment.

To this end, it is necessary to strengthen the protection of fundamental rights in the light of changes in society, social progress and scientific and technological developments by making those rights more visible in a Charter.

This Charter reaffirms, with due regard for the powers and tasks of the Community and the Union and the principle of subsidiarity, the rights as they result, in particular, from the constitutional traditions and international obligations common to the Member States, the Treaty on European Union, the Community Treaties, the European Convention for the Protection of Human Rights and Fundamental Freedoms, the Social Charters adopted by the Community and by the Council of Europe and the case law of the Court of Justice of the European Communities and of the European Court of Human Rights.

Enjoyment of these rights entails responsibilities and duties with regard to other persons, to the human community and to future generations.

The Union therefore recognizes the rights, freedoms and principles set out hereafter.[72]

Importantly, in terms of freedom of thought, conscience and religion, Article II-70 states:

II-70. 1. Everyone has the right to freedom of thought, conscience and religion. This right includes freedom to change religion or belief and freedom, either alone or in community with others and in public or in private, to manifest religion or belief, in worship, teaching, practice and observance.
2. The right to conscientious objection is recognised, in accordance with the national laws governing the exercise of this right.[73]

Equality before the law is contained in Article II-80:

II-80. Everyone is equal before the law.[74]

Important for equal rights, Article II-81, which specifically mentions religion, deals with nondiscrimination:

II-81. 1. Any discrimination based on any ground such as sex, race, color, ethnic or social origin, genetic features, language, religion or belief, political or any other opinion, membership of a national minority, property, birth, disability, age or sexual orientation shall be prohibited.
2. Within the scope of application of the Treaty establishing the European Community and of the Treaty on European Union, and without prejudice to the special provisions of those Treaties, any discrimination on grounds of nationality shall be prohibited.[75]

Further, Article III-118 states:

> III-118. In defining and implementing the policies and activities referred to in this Part, the Union shall aim to combat discrimination based on sex, racial or ethnic origin, religion or belief, disability, age or sexual orientation.[76]

Importantly, Article III-124 provides for measures for combating discrimination:

> III-124. 1. Without prejudice to the other provisions of the Constitution and within the limits of the powers assigned by it to the Union, a European law or framework law of the Council may establish the measures needed to combat discrimination based on sex, racial or ethnic origin, religion or belief, disability, age or sexual orientation. The Council shall act unanimously after obtaining the consent of the European Parliament.
>
> 2. By way of derogation from paragraph 1, European laws or framework laws may establish basic principles for Union incentive measures and define such measures, to support action taken by Member States in order to contribute to the achievement of the objectives referred to in paragraph 1, excluding any harmonisation of their laws and regulations.[77]

Finally, in terms of social security and social assistance, Article II-94 provides:

> II-94. 1. The Union recognises and respects the entitlement to social security benefits and social services providing protection in cases such as maternity, illness, industrial accidents, dependency or old age, and in the case of loss of employment, in accordance with the rules laid down by Union law and national laws and practices.[78]

Treaty of Lisbon

Finally, the Treaty of Lisbon amending the Treaty on European Union and the Treaty establishing the European Community was signed at Lisbon on 13 December 2007, after the rejection of the Constitution for Europe, in order to enhance the efficiency of the decision-making process and democratic participation in a Union of 27 Member States. The target date for ratification set by member governments is 1 January 2009. The Preamble of the Treaty of Lisbon states:

> DRAWING INSPIRATION from the cultural, religious and humanist inheritance of Europe, from which have developed the universal values of the inviolable and inalienable rights of the human person, freedom, democracy, equality and the rule of law.[79]

Specifically, Article 5(b) notes:

5(b) In defining and implementing its policies and activities, the Union shall aim to combat discrimination based on sex, racial or ethnic origin, religion or belief, disability, age or sexual orientation.[80]

The Treaty of Lisbon hopes to provide for: A more democratic and transparent Europe, with a strengthened role for the European Parliament and national parliaments, more opportunities for citizens to have their voices heard and a clearer sense of who does what at European and national level; a more efficient Europe, with simplified working methods and voting rules, streamlined and modern institutions for a Europe Union of 27 members and an improved ability to act in areas of major priority for today's Union; a Europe of rights and values, freedom, solidarity and security, promoting the Union's values, introducing the Charter of Fundamental Rights into European primary law, providing for new solidarity mechanisms and ensuring better protection of European citizens; and Europe as an actor on the global stage by bringing together Europe's external policy tools, both when developing and deciding new policies, harnessing Europe's economic, humanitarian, political and diplomatic strengths to promote European interests and values worldwide, while respecting the particular interests of the Member States in Foreign Affairs.

Council Directive 2000/78/EC Establishing a General Framework for Equal Treatment In Employment and Occupation

Important for equal rights, the Preamble of Council Directive 2000/78/EC of 27 November 2000, Establishing a General Framework for Equal Treatment in Employment and Occupation, which specifically mentions religion in Sections 11, 12, 23, 26, 29 and 31, states:

THE COUNCIL OF THE EUROPEAN UNION,

Having regard to the Treaty establishing the European Community, and in particular Article 13 thereof,

Having regard to the proposal from the Commission,

Having regard to the Opinion of the European Parliament,

Having regard to the Opinion of the Economic and Social Committee,

Having regard to the Opinion of the Committee of the Regions,

Whereas:

1. In accordance with Article 6 of the Treaty on European Union, the European Union is founded on the principles of liberty, democracy, respect for human rights and fundamental freedoms, and the rule of law, principles which are common to all Member States and it respects fundamental rights, as guaranteed by the European Convention for the Protection of Human Rights and Fundamental Freedoms and as they result from the constitutional traditions common to the Member States, as general principles of Community law.

4. The right of all persons to equality before the law and protection against discrimination constitutes a universal right recognised by the Universal Declaration of Human Rights, the United Nations Convention on the Elimination of All Forms of Discrimination against Women, United Nations Covenants on Civil and Political Rights and on Economic, Social and Cultural Rights and by the European Convention for the Protection of Human Rights and Fundamental Freedoms, to which all Member States are signatories. Convention No 111 of the International Labor Organisation (ILO) prohibits discrimination in the field of employment and occupation.

6. The Community Charter of the Fundamental Social Rights of Workers recognises the importance of combating every form of discrimination, including the need to take appropriate action for the social and economic integration of elderly and disabled people.

7. The EC Treaty includes among its objectives the promotion of coordination between employment policies of the Member States. To this end, a new employment chapter was incorporated in the EC Treaty as a means of developing a coordinated European strategy for employment to promote a skilled, trained and adaptable workforce.

8. The Employment Guidelines for 2000 agreed by the European Council at Helsinki on 10 and 11 December 1999 stress the need to foster a labor market favourable to social integration by formulating a coherent set of policies aimed at combating discrimination against groups such as persons with disability. They also emphasise the need to pay particular attention to supporting older workers, in order to increase their participation in the labor force.

9. Employment and occupation are key elements in guaranteeing equal opportunities for all and contribute strongly to the full participation of citizens in economic, cultural and social life and to realising their potential.

11. Discrimination based on religion or belief, disability, age or sexual orientation may undermine the achievement of the objectives of the EC Treaty, in particular the attainment of a high level of employment and social protection, raising the standard of living and the quality of life, economic and social cohesion and solidarity, and the free movement of persons.

12. To this end, any direct or indirect discrimination based on religion or belief, disability, age or sexual orientation as regards the areas covered by this Directive should be prohibited throughout the Community. This prohibition of discrimination should also apply to nationals of third countries but does not cover differences of treatment based on nationality and is without prejudice to provisions governing the entry and residence of third-country nationals and their access to employment and occupation.

14. This Directive shall be without prejudice to national provisions laying down retirement ages.

15. The appreciation of the facts from which it may be inferred that there has been direct or indirect discrimination is a matter for national judicial or other competent bodies, in accordance with rules of national law or practice. Such rules may provide, in particular, for indirect discrimination to be established by any means including on the basis of statistical evidence.

16. The provision of measures to accommodate the needs of disabled people at the workplace plays an important role in combating discrimination on grounds of disability.

17. This Directive does not require the recruitment, promotion, maintenance in employment or training of an individual who is not competent, capable and available to perform the essential functions of the post concerned or to undergo the relevant training, without prejudice to the obligation to provide reasonable accommodation for people with disabilities.

21. To determine whether the measures in question give rise to a disproportionate burden, account should be taken in particular of the financial and other costs entailed, the scale and financial resources of the organisation or undertaking and the possibility of obtaining public funding or any other assistance.

23. In very limited circumstances, a difference of treatment may be justified where a characteristic related to religion or belief, disability, age or sexual orientation constitutes a genuine and determining occupational requirement, when the objective is legitimate and the requirement is proportionate. Such circumstances should be included in the information provided by the Member States to the Commission.

25. The prohibition of age discrimination is an essential part of meeting the aims set out in the Employment Guidelines and encouraging diversity in the workforce .... It is therefore essential to distinguish between differences in treatment which are justified, in particular by legitimate employment policy, labor market and vocational training objectives, and discrimination which must be prohibited.

26. The prohibition of discrimination should be without prejudice to the maintenance or adoption of measures intended to prevent or compensate for disadvantages suffered by a group of persons of a particular religion or belief, disability, age or sexual orientation, and such measures may permit organisations of persons of a particular religion or belief, disability, age or sexual orientation where their main object is the promotion of the special needs of those persons.

28. This Directive lays down minimum requirements, thus giving the Member States the option of introducing or maintaining more favourable provisions. The implementation of this Directive should not serve to justify any regression in relation to the situation which already prevails in each Member State.

29. Persons who have been subject to discrimination based on religion or belief, disability, age or sexual orientation should have adequate means of legal protection. To provide a more effective level of protection, associations or legal entities should also be empowered to engage in proceedings, as the Member States so determine, either on behalf or in support of any victim, without prejudice to national rules of procedure concerning representation and defence before the courts.

30. The effective implementation of the principle of equality requires adequate judicial protection against victimisation.

31. The rules on the burden of proof must be adapted when there is a prima facie case of discrimination and, for the principle of equal treatment to be applied effectively, the burden of proof must shift back to the respondent when evidence of such discrimination is brought. However, it is not for the respondent to prove that the plaintiff adheres to a particular religion or belief, has a particular disability, is of a particular age or has a particular sexual orientation.

32. Member States need not apply the rules on the burden of proof to proceedings in which it is for the court or other competent body to investigate the facts of the case. The procedures thus referred to are those in which the plaintiff is not required to prove the facts, which it is for the court or competent body to investigate.

33. Member States should promote dialogue between the social partners and, within the framework of national practice, with non-governmental organisations to address different forms of discrimination at the workplace and to combat them.

35. Member States should provide for effective, proportionate and dissuasive sanctions in case of breaches of the obligations under this Directive.

36. Member States may entrust the social partners, at their joint request, with the implementation of this Directive, as regards the provisions concerning collective

agreements, provided they take any necessary steps to ensure that they are at all times able to guarantee the results required by this Directive.

37. In accordance with the principle of subsidiarity set out in Article 5 of the EC Treaty, the objective of this Directive, namely the creation within the Community of a level playing-field as regards equality in employment and occupation, cannot be sufficiently achieved by the Member States and can therefore, by reason of the scale and impact of the action, be better achieved at Community level. In accordance with the principle of proportionality, as set out in that Article, this Directive does not go beyond what is necessary in order to achieve that objective,

HAS ADOPTED THIS DIRECTIVE.[81]

Article 1 outlines the Purpose of the Council Directive, which includes protection against religious discrimination:

1. The purpose of this Directive is to lay down a general framework for combating discrimination on the grounds of religion or belief, disability, age or sexual orientation as regards employment and occupation, with a view to putting into effect in the Member States the principle of equal treatment.[82]

Further, the scope of the Directive is outlined in Article 3:

3(1) Within the limits of the areas of competence conferred on the Community, this Directive shall apply to all persons, as regards both the public and private sectors, including public bodies, in relation to:
   a. conditions for access to employment, to self-employment or to occupation, including selection criteria and recruitment conditions, whatever the branch of activity and at all levels of the professional hierarchy, including promotion;
   b. access to all types and to all levels of vocational guidance, vocational training, advanced vocational training and retraining, including practical work experience;
   c. employment and working conditions, including dismissals and pay;
   d. membership of, and involvement in, an organisation of workers or employers, or any organisation whose members carry on a particular profession, including the benefits provided for by such organisations.

(2) This Directive does not cover differences of treatment based on nationality and is without prejudice to provisions and conditions relating to the entry into and residence of third-country nationals and stateless persons in the territory of Member States, and to any treatment which arises from the legal status of the third-country nationals and stateless persons concerned.

(3) This Directive does not apply to payments of any kind made by state schemes or similar, including state social security or social protection schemes.[83]

Importantly, the concept of discrimination and in particular religious discrimination is defined under Article 2(2)(b):

2(1) For the purposes of this Directive, the 'principle of equal treatment' shall mean that there shall be no direct or indirect discrimination whatsoever on any of the grounds referred to in Article 1.

(2) For the purposes of paragraph 1:
    a. direct discrimination shall be taken to occur where one person is treated less favourably than another is, has been or would be treated in a comparable situation, on any of the grounds referred to in Article 1;
    b. indirect discrimination shall be taken to occur where an apparently neutral provision, criterion or practice would put persons having a particular religion or belief, a particular disability, a particular age, or a particular sexual orientation at a particular disadvantage compared with other persons unless:
        i. that provision, criterion or practice is objectively justified by a legitimate aim and the means of achieving that aim are appropriate and necessary, or
        ii. as regards persons with a particular disability, the employer or any person or organisation to whom this Directive applies, is obliged, under national legislation, to take appropriate measures in line with the principles contained in Article 5 in order to eliminate disadvantages entailed by such provision, criterion or practice.

(3) Harassment shall be deemed to be a form of discrimination within the meaning of paragraph 1, when unwanted conduct related to any of the grounds referred to in Article 1 takes place with the purpose or effect of violating the dignity of a person and of creating an intimidating, hostile, degrading, humiliating or offensive environment. In this context, the concept of harassment may be defined in accordance with the national laws and practice of the Member States.

(4) An instruction to discriminate against persons on any of the grounds referred to in Article 1 shall be deemed to be discrimination within the meaning of paragraph 1.

(5) This Directive shall be without prejudice to measures laid down by national law which, in a democratic society, are necessary for public security, for the maintenance of public order and the prevention of criminal offences, for the protection of health and for the protection of the rights and freedoms of others.[84]

However, Article 11 guards against victimization:

11. Member States shall introduce into their national legal systems such measures as are necessary to protect employees against dismissal or other adverse treatment by the employer as a reaction to a complaint within the undertaking or to any legal proceedings aimed at enforcing compliance with the principle of equal treatment.[85]

Article 4, which specifically mentions religion in Article 4(2), contains genuine occupational requirements:

4(1) Notwithstanding Article 2(1) and (2), Member States may provide that a difference of treatment which is based on a characteristic related to any of the grounds referred to in Article 1 shall not constitute discrimination where, by reason of the nature of the particular occupational activities concerned or of the context in which they are carried out, such a characteristic constitutes a genuine and determining occupational requirement, provided that the objective is legitimate and the requirement is proportionate.

(2) Member States may maintain national legislation in force at the date of adoption of this Directive or provide for future legislation incorporating national practices existing at the date of adoption of this Directive pursuant to which, in the case of occupational activities within churches and other public or private organisations the ethos of which is based on religion or belief, a difference of treatment based on a person's religion or belief shall not constitute discrimination where, by reason of the nature of these activities or of the context in which they are carried out, a person's religion or belief constitute a genuine, legitimate and justified occupational requirement, having regard to the organisation's ethos. This difference of treatment shall be implemented taking account of Member States' constitutional provisions and principles, as well as the general principles of Community law, and should not justify discrimination on another ground

Provided that its provisions are otherwise complied with, this Directive shall thus not prejudice the right of churches and other public or private organizations, the ethos of which is based on religion or belief, acting in conformity with national constitutions and laws, to require individuals working for them to act in good faith and with loyalty to the organization's ethos.[86]

Further, Article 8 provides for minimum requirements:

8(1) Member States may introduce or maintain provisions which are more favourable to the protection of the principle of equal treatment than those laid down in this Directive.

(2) The implementation of this Directive shall under no circumstances constitute grounds for a reduction in the level of protection against discrimination already afforded by Member States in the fields covered by this Directive.[87]

Positive action is provided for under Article 7:

> 7(1) With a view to ensuring full equality in practice, the principle of equal treatment shall not prevent any Member State from maintaining or adopting specific measures to prevent or compensate for disadvantages linked to any of the grounds referred to in Article 1.[88]

Importantly, in terms of remedies and enforcement, Article 9 provides for defense of rights:

> 9(1) Member States shall ensure that judicial and/or administrative procedures, including where they deem it appropriate conciliation procedures, for the enforcement of obligations under this Directive are available to all persons who consider themselves wronged by failure to apply the principle of equal treatment to them, even after the relationship in which the discrimination is alleged to have occurred has ended.
>
> (2) Member States shall ensure that associations, organisations or other legal entities which have, in accordance with the criteria laid down by their national law, a legitimate interest in ensuring that the provisions of this Directive are complied with, may engage, either on behalf or in support of the complainant, with his or her approval, in any judicial and/or administrative procedure provided for the enforcement of obligations under this Directive.[89]

The burden of proof is detailed in Article 10:

> 10(1) Member States shall take such measures as are necessary, in accordance with their national judicial systems, to ensure that, when persons who consider themselves wronged because the principle of equal treatment has not been applied to them establish, before a court or other competent authority, facts from which it may be presumed that there has been direct or indirect discrimination, it shall be for the respondent to prove that there has been no breach of the principle of equal treatment.[90]

Article 16 provides for compliance:

> 16. Member States shall take the necessary measures to ensure that:
>
> any laws, regulations and administrative provisions contrary to the principle of equal treatment are abolished;
>
> any provisions contrary to the principle of equal treatment which are included in contracts or collective agreements, internal rules of undertakings or rules governing the independent occupations and professions and workers' and employers' organisations are, or may be, declared null and void or are amended.[91]

The religious strife in Northern Ireland is specifically provided for under Article 15.2:

15.2. In order to maintain a balance of opportunity in employment for teachers in Northern Ireland while furthering the reconciliation of historical divisions between the major religious communities there, the provisions on religion or belief in this Directive shall not apply to the recruitment of teachers in schools in Northern Ireland in so far as this is expressly authorised by national legislation.[92]

Finally, Article 17 deals with sanctions:

17. Member States shall lay down the rules on sanctions applicable to infringements of the national provisions adopted pursuant to this Directive and shall take all measures necessary to ensure that they are applied. The sanctions, which may comprise the payment of compensation to the victim, must be effective, proportionate and dissuasive. Member States shall notify those provisions to the Commission by 2 December 2003 at the latest and shall notify it without delay of any subsequent amendment affecting them.[93]

Council Decision 2000/750/EC Establishing a Community Action Program to Combat Discrimination (2001 to 2006)

Important for equal rights, the Preamble of Council Decision 2000/750/EC of 27 November 2000, Establishing a Community Action Program to Combat Discrimination states:

(1) The European Union is founded on the principles of liberty, democracy, respect for human rights and fundamental freedoms, and the rule of law, principles which are common to all Member States. In accordance with Article 6(2) of the Treaty on European Union, the Union should respect fundamental rights as guaranteed by the European Convention for the Protection of Human Rights and Fundamental Freedoms and as derived from the shared constitutional traditions common to the Member States, as general principles of Community law.

(2) The European Parliament has strongly and repeatedly urged the European Union to develop and strengthen its policy in the field of equal treatment and equal opportunities across all grounds of discrimination.

(5) The different forms of discrimination cannot be ranked: all are equally intolerable. The program is intended both to exchange existing good practice in the Member States and to develop new practice and policy for combating discrimination, including multiple discrimination. This Decision may help to put in place a comprehensive strategy for combating all forms of discrimination on different grounds, a strategy which should henceforward be developed in parallel.

(8) Access to the program should be open to all public and/or private bodies and institutions involved in the fight against discrimination. In this connection account must be taken of the experience and abilities of both local and national non-governmental organizations.

(9) Many non-governmental organizations at European level have experience and expertise in fighting discrimination, as well as acting at European level as the advocates of people who are exposed to discrimination. They can therefore make an important contribution towards a better understanding of the diverse forms and effects of discrimination and to ensuring that the design, implementation and follow-up of the program take account of the experience of people exposed to discrimination.

(11) It is necessary, in order to reinforce the added value of Community action, that the Commission, in cooperation with the Member States, should ensure, at all levels, the coherence and complementarity of actions implemented in the framework of this Decision and other relevant Community policies, instruments and actions, in particular those in the fields of education and training and equal opportunities between men and women under the European Social Fund and those to promote social inclusion. Consistency and complementarity with the relevant activities of the European Monitoring Centre on Racism and Xenophobia should also be ensured.[94]

Important for equal rights and religious discrimination cases, Article 1, which specifically mentions religion, enunciates the establishment of the program:

1. This Decision establishes a Community action program, hereinafter referred to as 'the program', to promote measures to combat direct or indirect discrimination based on racial or ethnic origin, religion or belief, disability, age or sexual orientation, for the period from 1 January 2001 to 31 December 2006.[95]

Objectives of the program are outlined in Article 2:

2. Within the limits of the Community's powers, the program shall support and supplement the efforts at Community level and in the Member States to promote measures to prevent and combat discrimination whether based on one or on multiple factors, taking account, where appropriate, of future legislative developments. It shall have the following objectives:
(a) to improve the understanding of issues related to discrimination through improved knowledge of this phenomenon and through evaluation of the effectiveness of policies and practice;
(b) to develop the capacity to prevent and address discrimination effectively, in particular by strengthening organizations' means of action and through support for the exchange of information and good practice and networking at European level, while taking into account the specific characteristics of the different forms of discrimination;

(c) to promote and disseminate the values and practices underlying the fight against discrimination, including through the use of awareness-raising campaigns.[96]

Article 3 stipulates the Community actions to be undertaken:

3. 1. With a view to achieving the objectives set out in Article 2, the following actions may be implemented within a transnational framework:
(a) analysis of factors related to discrimination, including through studies and the development of qualitative and quantitative indicators and benchmarks, in accordance with national law and practices, and the evaluation of anti-discrimination legislation and practice, with a view to assessing its effectiveness and impact, with effective dissemination of the results;
(b) transnational cooperation and the promotion of networking at European level between partners active in the prevention of, and the fight against, discrimination, including non-governmental organizations;
(c) awareness-raising, in particular to emphasize the European dimension of the fight against discrimination and to publicize the results of the program, in particular through communications, publications, campaigns and events.[97]

Finally, in terms of the implementation of the program and cooperation with the Member States, Article 4 states:

4. 1. The Commission shall:

(a) ensure the implementation of the Community actions covered by the program in conformity with the Annex;
(b) have a regular exchange of views with representatives of non-governmental organizations and the social partners at European level on the design, implementation and follow-up of the program and on related policy orientations. To that end the Commission shall make the relevant information available to the non-governmental organizations and the social partners. The Commission shall inform the committee established under Article 6 of their exchange of views.
2. The Commission, in cooperation with the Member States, shall take the necessary steps to:
(a) promote the involvement in the program of all the parties concerned, including non-governmental organizations of all sizes;
(b) promote active partnership and dialogue between all the partners involved in the program, inter alia to encourage an integrated and coordinated approach to the fight against discrimination;
(c) ensure the dissemination of the results of the actions undertaken within the framework of the program;
(d) provide accessible information and appropriate publicity and follow-up with regard to actions supported by the program.[98]

The European Union Member States are still looking to formulate a Constitution for Europe. Currently, the Member States of the European Union are: Austria, Belgium, Denmark, Finland, France, Germany, Greece, Ireland, Italy, Luxembourg, the Netherlands, Portugal, Spain, Sweden and the United Kingdom, and since 1 May 2004, Cyprus (Greek part), the Czech Republic, Estonia, Hungary, Latvia, Lithuania, Malta, Poland, Slovakia and Slovenia, expanded it from 15 to 25 Member States, and since 1 January 2007, Bulgaria and Romania bringing the number to 27 Member States. Candidate countries are Croatia, the Former Yugoslav Republic of Macedonia, and Turkey. The remaining European Countries which are not Member States of the European Union are Albania, Andorra, Belarus, Bosnia-Herzegovina, Iceland, Liechtenstein, Moldova, Monaco, Montenegro, Norway, Russia, San Marino, Serbia, Switzerland, Ukraine and Vatican City. The European Union is at a crossroads challenged to adapt the vision of the 'founding fathers' that was first designed for six Member States to a future union of over twenty States. In essence, Europe is now the biggest frontier-free market in the world. The single market removed three types of barriers to free movement, namely physical, technical and fiscal. The four freedoms of the Union, for goods, services, people and capital, have become a reality. Further, the new single currency, the euro was introduced as legal tender on 1 January 1999, and replaced the currencies of those Member States in agreement on 1 January 2002. The criteria used for a nation to secure membership in the ever-growing European Union are: (1) democratic institutions and the rule of law, with respect for human rights and minorities within the borders; (2) a functioning market economy capable of competing within the union's single market; and (3) the acceptance of obligations of membership, signing onto the union's body of rules. The latter is perhaps the most important criterion for equal rights and their enforcement.

European enlargement has increased the population of the European Union by almost 20 percent, to more than 453 million inhabitants, the third most-populated political entity in the world after China and India.[99] However, the trend towards ageing of the European population, a major challenge for the EU-15, is present in the EU-25. Immigration, the other driving force behind European Union demographic change, has grown considerably over the last decade. At present, it accounts for three-quarters of the net growth of the EU-15 population. The situation in the new Member States, on the other hand, has changed very little. In some of the Baltic republics, the population has even declined as a result of emigration. With the accession of the ten new Member States in 2004, migratory movements from acceding countries to EU-15 countries, historically classified as immigration flows, have become internal mobility. Previous experience and recent estimates suggest that labour mobility from new to old Member States will be moderate, with specific situations in the border regions. Furthermore, in the light of cultural and historical links, new Member States could become host countries for people emigrating to the European Union from countries of other countries.

The socioeconomic conditions in the EU-15 countries have been marked by steady improvements in employment and real income since 1995. Furthermore, significant progress has been recorded in reducing disparities both among countries and among regions within the countries. By contrast, eight of the ten new Member States, Estonia, Hungary, Latvia, Lithuania, Poland, the Czech Republic, Slovakia and Slovenia, experienced an economic crisis as they emerged from a long period of economic stagnation under the old regime and started on the road towards a market economy. However, the great majority of them have already made up the ground lost during the initial transition period. Moreover, the new Member States are well-placed for pursuing faster economic growth after enlargement, thereby making progress in achieving real convergence.

In the area of social cohesion, the differences between the EU-15 countries and the new Member States are particularly pronounced. With enlargement, income disparities increased considerably. Whereas income differentials between the EU-15 countries and regions diminished significantly, they rose among the new Member States, and so the European Union must therefore address the new east-west divide resulting from enlargement. Employment levels in the EU-15 countries, a major determining factor of economic and social inclusion, still show a north-south divide, which has significant implications for the social situation. With enlargement, the lower employment rates in several regions of the south will be mirrored in the east due to the effects of restructuring and job losses in agriculture and industry. This substantial reduction of jobs in these sectors has not yet been compensated for by the growth of services.

As for investing in education, the new Member States are outperforming the majority of the EU-15 countries in upper secondary education. However, the EU-15 countries produce better results when it comes to tertiary education. Disparities as regards lifelong learning and familiarity with information and communication technologies (ICT), more current in the EU-15 countries, also exist. Satisfaction with life also differs considerably between the EU-15 countries and the ten new Member States, the latter being significantly less satisfied with their personal safety and social life. The instruments of social protection aim to reduce poverty, promote social and civil dialogue, create jobs and tackle regional and social disparities in a strategic fashion.

As for minimum income and social assistance, almost all the EU-15 Member States provide all legal residents with some form of minimum income guarantee, supplemented by various benefits and allowances in the form of cash or services, which help to reduce the risk of poverty and promote effective integration in the labor market. The impact of social assistance programs in the countries of central and eastern Europe show poor targeting, widespread undercoverage and low levels of benefits. Some countries have reinforced schemes intended to ensure adequate minimum levels of income through guaranteed minimum income schemes, social pensions or universal social assistance guarantees.

European societies are witnessing a growing trend towards ethnic, cultural and religious diversity that continues post enlargement due to a combination of factors such as the ageing of the population, labour shortages in certain sectors, and political instability and poverty. Measures to promote the inclusion and participation of ethnic minorities are therefore needed. In the new Member States, immigration is a fairly recent phenomenon and the main focus is on the situation of the historical minorities, including the Roma, who often have lower levels of training and are more likely to live in low-income households. It will be necessary to tackle these problems by combining measures for employment, social inclusion and the fight against discrimination.

Importantly, the extent of civic mindedness, trust and participation of the population forms the basis of a civil society that influences the economic, social and political performance of a country. In most of the new Member States of central and eastern Europe, civil society is marked by sparse participation in public life and distrust of public institutions, a legacy of the previous centralized regimes. Even if civic participation has improved since the beginning of the transition period, it is still lower than in the EU-15 countries. Collective bargaining at bipartite and tripartite level is fairly limited in the new Member States. Despite sustained efforts to develop industrial relations and social dialogue in the ten new Member States, their social partners still face challenges with a view to fully participating in economic and social governance.

Developments in coordination on policies and employment at the European Union level have broadened the scope of the European Social Agenda. The situation in several acceding countries calls for political efforts to be intensified to prevent disparities in living conditions, and to fight against poverty and social exclusion. To achieve these objectives, it will be important to draw on mutually reinforcing synergies between social and employment policies. The new Member States have a number of achievements and advantages in their favour, such as a relatively high level of training, an ability to tackle difficult reform issues and a good level of social cohesion. With the support of European Union policies, these advantages will become the basis of a powerful driving force of economic growth and social progress within the enlarged Union.[100]

The right of all individuals to equality before the law and to protection from discrimination is a fundamental principle of all democratic societies.[101] Establishing an effective set of laws against discrimination is an essential part of stamping out unfair treatment, but laws themselves are not enough. If discrimination is to be eliminated, attitudes and behaviour must also change. A European Union-wide action program against discrimination was developed, with its purpose to support activities which combat discrimination and to raise awareness as to measures being taken across the Union to tackle it.

The 57th Eurobarometer survey on discrimination was carried out in 2002 in all of the previous 15 European Union countries.[102] Few respondents reported personally experiencing discrimination on any of the six grounds explored, but the most often cited ground for discrimination was age (5 percent), followed by race or ethnicity (3 percent), religion or beliefs (2 percent), physical disability, learning difficulties or mental illness (2 percent), and sexual orientation (less than 1 percent). Young people, the better educated and those on the Left of the political spectrum were more likely to report having experienced discrimination. In terms of religious discrimination, in Ireland, Spain, Denmark, Italy and Portugal, about 1 percent of respondents said they suffered discrimination because of their religion; however, compared with most other countries, discrimination on grounds of religion was reported by about twice as many respondents in the UK, in Luxembourg and France (4 percent).

In terms of equal opportunities in employment, thirty seven percent of respondents believed that a person with minority religious or other beliefs, with the same skills or qualifications, would have less chance than everyone else of getting a job, training or promotion. While 22 percent in Italy and Ireland thought that membership of a religious minority would reduce their chances of employment, 61 percent in Sweden and 52 percent in Denmark thought so. Five percent in Greece and 4 percent in the UK thought that a person with minority religious or other beliefs would have more chance. Professional and managerial employees recorded antidiscrimination scores slightly higher than other workers but the gap between them and manual workers was still only about two points. This gap was larger in Italy, Belgium and the former East Germany, exceeding five points in each case, and reversed in Luxembourg (86.9 compared with 88.6).

Further, those who personally experienced discrimination, young people and respondents with leftist political views were significantly more likely to report witnessing discrimination. The most often cited ground for witnessed discrimination was race or ethnicity (22 percent), followed by learning difficulties or mental illness (12 percent), physical disability (11 percent), religion or beliefs (9 percent), age (6 percent) and sexual orientation (6 percent). The rates of witnessed discrimination are considerably higher than the rates of discrimination experienced, and in general, the longer the time spent in full-time education, the more likely a respondent was to report having witnessed discrimination. Professionals and managers and the service sector employees were more likely than the other respondents to report witnessing discrimination on all grounds; compared with manual workers and the self-employed, twice as many professional and managerial employees reported witnessing discrimination on grounds of religion.

Interestingly, the majority of European citizens oppose discrimination on all six grounds, with their antidiscrimination scores averaging an 80 percent of the ideal score they would achieve if they said 'always wrong' to discrimination in all sites. The young, better-educated and non-manually-employed women are more likely to oppose discrimination, older male manual workers with little education less so, but there is no clear evidence that the tendency to believe discrimination right or wrong, or to attribute such views to others, is socially determined to any great degree.[103]

Overall, the Union is convinced of the usefulness of international cooperation so that countries can learn and profit from each other's experience. In the European Employment Strategy, the European Union has set out to combat unemployment and significantly increase the employment rate of Europe on a lasting basis. Flexicurity strategies imply political choices between various aspects of flexibility and security. The flexicurity model remains in line with the central elements of the

European Union strategy for sustainable economic growth with more jobs, better jobs and greater social cohesion. Policy measures must focus on making the labor market more open to all workers, rather than putting the blame for their exclusion from employment on them. Seen as an integral part of the macroeconomic policy-mix, flexicurity should be an additional tool strengthening the European social model, which promotes strong social protection, gender equalities, high living standards and quality of life, social cohesion, and measures to combat exclusion, both from the labor market and within society. The effects of policies related to flexicurity on vulnerable groups, such as religious minorities, must be adequately considered as should the interconnected dimensions of social cohesion, nondiscrimination and equality. The flexicurity approach must draw on a high level of workforce training.

Assuring a flexible approach towards employees not only attracts the best workers, but it also contributes to achieving employment targets and reducing barriers to the labor market by making employment accessible to more people. Flexible and short-term contracts should not lead to increased discrimination in employment by providing a rationale to terminate employment and becoming a substitute for discrimination. Flexicurity policies must make it attractive for employers to employ workers from minority religions, and attractive for religious workers to remain or re-enter employment. A two-fold responsibility exists: on the employer side, this responsibility lies in the provision of suitable working conditions accommodating religious practices, of adequate early warning systems, and of the availability of training and support to workers to find future employment; on employee side, there is an individual responsibility to remain continuously employable.[104] Thus, it will be necessary to develop incentives to change people's behaviour with regard to people who belong to religious minorities and to combat discrimination.

Conclusion

It is important that equality be achieved in securing access to jobs that are commensurate with skill levels. Some groups, namely those from religious minorities, are still lagging behind due to horizontal segregation, and vertical segregation, with difficulty acceding to higher positions in the occupational hierarchy. The system has failed to reward skills, and even provides guises for discrimination. The demographic changes on the horizon will bring about a further need for qualified workers. However, some remain underutilized, considered as reserve labor. This attitude is a barrier to progressive legislation. Although European laws have gone a long way to improving the plight of many in the European Union, in reality, some have yet to enjoy the equality they are entitled to in theory. The European Union is a political structure, which emerged out of a general act of will of heterogeneous States. It is ultimately dependent on statements of general principle. Therefore, European Union law is the motor to enable the European Union to move toward its ultimate aim, the 'ever closer union'.

In terms of religious tolerance, the European Union's action programme has several main components, namely a fair deal in rights at work involving equality legislation and court cases; better opportunities to earn a living involving the promotion of jobs, education and entrepreneurship; getting minorities in positions of power involving equal opportunities in employment; and European Union-wide networks involving training, expanding subjects in school and reinforcing a positive image of all religions.[105] Relations between the institutions of the European Union are based on partnership, cooperation and mutual dependence. The concern is to enhance the social, economic and cultural welfare of all citizens in an atmosphere of peace. This, thereby, advances the cause for religious freedom in stamping out discrimination of any kind, including religious discrimination, through the effective use of laws and the courts, in the pursuit of *Heaven Forbid*.

Notes

1 Nicoll, William and Salmon, Trevor, *Understanding the New European Community*, Prentice Hall, Exeter, 1994, p. 11.
2 Daltrop, Anne (1982), *Political Realities, Politics and the European Community*, Longman, London, 1982, p. 2.
3 Nicoll, William and Salmon, Trevor, *Understanding the New European Community*, Prentice Hall, Exeter, 1994, at p. 13.
4 *Ibid.*, at p. 20.
5 *Ibid.*, at p. 99.
6 Daltrop, Anne (1982), *Political Realities, Politics and the European Community*, Longman, London, 1982, p. 18.
7 Treaty of Rome, at Article 3.
8 *Ibid.*, at Article 6(a).
9 *Ibid.*, at Article 48.
10 *Ibid.*, at Article 119.
11 Maastricht Treaty, at Article A.
12 *Ibid.*, at Article B.
13 Treaty of Amsterdam, at Article 141.
14 *Ibid.*, at Article 13.
15 *Ibid.*, at Article 39.
16 *Ibid.*, at Article 141.
17 *Teuling v. Bredrijfsvereniging* [1987] ECR 2497.
18 Nicoll, William and Salmon, Trevor, *Understanding the New European Community*, Prentice Hall, Exeter, 1994, p. 97.
19 *Internationale Handelsgesellschaft* [1970] ECR 1125, [1972] CMLR 255.
20 *Costa v. ENEL* [1964] CMLR 425.
21 Hepple QC, Bob, Choudhury, Tufyal, Home Office Research Study 221, *Tackling*

Religious Discrimination: Practical Implications for Policy-Makers and Legislators, Home Office Research, Development and Statistics Directorate, 2001.
22 *Valsamis v. Greece*, Judgement of 18 December 1996; Comm. report, 6.7.95.
23 *Efstratiou v. Greece*, Judgement of 18 December 1996; Comm. report, 11.4.96.
24 European Convention for the Protection of Human Rights and Fundamental Freedoms (ECHR), at the Preamble.
25 *Ibid.*, at Article 1.
26 *Ibid.*, at Article 9.
27 *Otto Preminger Institute v. Austria* (1994) 19 European Human Rights Reports 34 at para.47; cf. *Choudhury v. United Kingdom* (1991) 12 Human Rights Law Journal 172.
28 *Kokkinakis v. Greece* (1994) 17 EHRR 397 at para 31.
29 *Campbell and Cosans v. UK* (1982) 4 EHRR 293.
30 *McFeely v. UK*, [1981] 3 EHRR 161.
31 *Arrowsmith v. UK* (1978) 19 DR 5; (1978) 3 EHRR 110.
32 *C. v. the United Kingdom*, D&R 37 (1984), p. 142.
33 European Convention for the Protection of Human Rights and Fundamental Freedoms (ECHR), at Article 14.
34 *Ibid.*, at Article 13.
35 *Ibid.*, at Article 17.
36 *Ibid.*, at Article 19.
37 *Ibid.*, at Article 32.
38 *Ibid.*, at Article 27.
39 *Ibid.*, at Article 3.
40 *Ibid.*, at Article 34.
41 *Ibid.*, at Article 36.
42 *Ibid.*, at Article 35.
43 *Ibid.*, at Article 37.
44 *Ibid.*, at Article 38.
45 *Ibid.*, at Article 39.
46 *Ibid.*, at Article 40.
47 *Ibid.*, at Article 41.
48 *Ibid.*, at Article 44.
49 *Ibid.*, at Article 45.
50 *Ibid.*, at Article 46.
51 *Ibid.*, at Article 47.
52 European Convention for the Protection of Human Rights and Fundamental Freedoms as amended by Protocol No. 1, at the Preamble.
53 *Ibid.*, at Article 2.
54 European Convention for the Protection of Human Rights and Fundamental Freedoms as amended by Protocol No. 12, at the Preamble.
55 *Ibid.*, at Article 1.
56 European Social Charter, 1961, at the Preamble.
57 European Social Charter (revised), 1996, at the Preamble.
58 *Ibid.*, at Article E.

59 *Ibid.*, at Part I.
60 *Ibid*, at Part II, Article 1.
61 *Ibid.*, at Article 4.
62 *Ibid.*, at Article 24.
63 *Ibid.*, at Article 22.
64 *Ibid.*, at Part V, Article E.
65 Treaty establishing a Constitution for Europe, at the Preamble.
66 *Ibid.*, at Article I-1.
67 *Ibid.*, at Article I-2.
68 *Ibid.*, at Article I-3.
69 *Ibid.*, at Article I-4.
70 *Ibid.*, at Article I-6.
71 *Ibid.*, at Article I-5.
72 Treaty establishing a Constitution for Europe, the Charter of Fundamental Rights, at the Preamble.
73 *Ibid.*, at II-70.
74 *Ibid.*, at Article II-80.
75 *Ibid.*, at Article II-81.
76 *Ibid.*, at Article III-118.
77 *Ibid.*, at Article III-124.
78 *Ibid.*, at Article II-94.
79 Treaty of Lisbon, at the Preamble.
80 *Ibid.*, at Article 5(b).
81 Council Directive 2000/78/EC Establishing a General Framework for Equal Treatment in Employment and Occupation, at the Preamble.
82 *Ibid.*, at Article 1.
83 *Ibid.*, at Article 3.
84 *Ibid.*, at Article 2.
85 *Ibid.*, at Article 11.
86 *Ibid.*, at Article 4.
87 *Ibid.*, at Article 8.
88 *Ibid.*, at Article 7.
89 *Ibid.*, at Article 9.
90 *Ibid.*, at Article 10.
91 *Ibid.*, at Article 16.
92 *Ibid.*, at Article 15.2
93 *Ibid.*, at Article 17.
94 Council Decision 2000/750/EC of 27 November 2000 Establishing a Community Action Program to Combat Discrimination (2001 to 2006) [OJ L 303, 02/12/2000 P. 0023 – 0028], at the Preamble.
95 *Ibid.*, at Article 1.
96 *Ibid.*, at Article 2.
97 *Ibid.*, at Article 3.
98 *Ibid.*, at Article 4.

99 Commission Report on the social situation in the European Union, Report on social protection in Europe 2004, [Not published in the Official Journal].
100 *Ibid.*
101 Eurobarometer 57, Discrimination in Europe, For Diversity Against Discrimination, 2003, Alan Marsh and Melahat Sahin-Dikmen, The European Opinion Research Group (EEIG) for the European Commission Directorate General Employment and Social Affairs.
102 Alan Marsh, Melahat Sahin-Dikmen, *Discrimination in Europe*, Policy Studies Institute, London, 2002.
103 *Ibid.*
104 *Ibid.*
105 Commission of the European Communities, *Equal Opportunity for Women and Men*, Brussels, p. 5.

References

Arrowsmith v. UK (1978) 19 DR 5; (1978) 3 EHRR 110.
C. v. the United Kingdom, D&R 37 (1984).
Campbell and Cosans v. UK (1982) 4 EHRR 293.
Commission Report on the social situation in the European Union, Report on social protection in Europe 2004, [Not published in the Official Journal].
Costa v. ENEL [1964] CMLR 425.
Council Decision 2000/750/EC of 27 November 2000 Establishing a Community Action Program to Combat Discrimination (2001 to 2006) [OJ L 303, 02/12/2000 P. 0023 – 0028].
Council Directive 2000/78/EC Establishing a General Framework for Equal Treatment in Employment and Occupation.
Daltrop, Anne (1982), *Political Realities, Politics and the European Community*, Longman, London.
Efstratiou v. Greece, Judgement of 18 December 1996; Comm. report, 11.4.96.
Eurobarometer 57, Discrimination in Europe, For Diversity Against Discrimination, 2003, Alan Marsh and Melahat Sahin-Dikmen, The European Opinion Research Group (EEIG) for the European Commission Directorate General Employment and Social Affairs.
European Convention for the Protection of Human Rights and Fundamental Freedoms, 1950.
European Convention for the Protection of Human Rights and Fundamental Freedoms as amended by Protocol No. 12, 2000.
European Social Charter, 1961.
European Social Charter (revised), 1996.
Hepple QC, Bob, Choudhury, Tufyal (2001), Home Office Research Study 221, *Tackling Religious Discrimination: Practical Implications for Policy-*

Makers and Legislators, Home Office Research, Development and Statistics Directorate.
Internationale Handelsgesellschaft, [1970] ECR 1125, [1972] CMLR 255.
Kokkinakis v. Greece (1994) 17 EHRR 397.
Maastricht Treaty, 1992.
Marsh Alan, Sahin-Dikmen, Mehalat (2002), *Discrimination in Europe*, Policy Studies Institute, London.
McFeely v. UK, [1981] 3 EHRR 161.
Nicoll, William and Salmon, Trevor (1994), *Understanding the New European Community*, Prentice Hall, Exeter.
Otto Preminger Institute v. Austria (1994) 19 European Human Rights Reports 34.
Teuling v. Bredrijfsvereniging [1987] ECR 2497.
Treaty establishing a Constitution for Europe, 2004.
Treaty of Amsterdam, 1997.
Treaty of Lisbon, 2007.
Treaty of Paris, 1951.
Treaty of Rome, 1957.
Valsamis v. Greece, Judgement of 18 December 1996; Comm. report, 6.7.95.

Chapter 10
Conclusion to Heaven Forbid

In the quest for religious freedom in *Heaven Forbid*, a deep embedded patriarchal authority is still keeping society on the designated track, as *de jure* discrimination has given way to *de facto* discrimination; and in essence, inequality, once obvious and accepted, is now hidden and protected in a most dangerous way. Since within society there is an *a-priori* assumption of freedom and impartiality, the burden is high on the attackers of this universal opinion. Human inequality both encompasses religious discrimination and conceals it, and although other types of discrimination exist apart from religious inequality, discrimination which is so blatant and open as to focus on one's religion is most persistent and threatening to society. Therefore, seeking out inequality and bringing it to the forefront of microscopic debate can only serve to advance all quests for equality.

Both legislation and the court system have made inroads into religious discrimination. It is important to have adequate legislation to influence conduct and outcomes, as well as an appropriate legal system to achieve favorable and enforceable results. By cooperating and learning from other similarly disadvantaged groups in the fight for equality of opportunity, more advances can be made in the fight for religious equality. We will never totally correct the injustices of the past or of the present. However, with a greater appreciation of religious freedom and the pursuit of religious tolerance, as well as a better understanding of the importance of adequate legislation, future endeavors in the field will help to improve the situation for all people.

Countries around the world have made important progress in the development of equal rights. Equality rights legislation and court challenges are required, in order to improve the situation of all in the workplace. The desire is for equal human rights for all. Religious discrimination is an equal opportunity discrimination as it cuts across race, language, gender, age and disability. Therefore, the law needs to be enforced by way of the courts to achieve greater equality in an effort to modify historical attitudes, so that nations conform to certain standards. There should be real freedom to choose one's amount of participation in the work force, in the pursuit of flexibility as to a just remuneration and access to employment.

Further, taking into account the fact that continuing inequalities and noticeable progress coexist, rethinking employment policies is necessary in order to integrate the religious neutral perspective, not only to address any negative implications of current patterns of work and employment, but also to draw attention to a wider range of opportunities. Governments and other actors need to promote an active and visible policy of mainstreaming the *Heaven Forbid* perspective into all policies and programs.

The central importance of equality legislation in order to bring about change is evident and indeed critical. Our very rights as human beings emanate from the word of the law and the interpretation given by the highest courts in the land. Therefore, it is imperative that the struggle for religious equality encompass the legal system. The concept of total equality has never truly existed, nor was it ever meant to be anything more than empty promises of change. Absolute equality is not sought in this book, nor is it realistic. However, in a feeling of mutual respect for individual differences, a better equality among humans is possible and desirable through society's laws and legal institutions.

The keys to the future are the implementation and development of the law, the deepening in understanding of specific legal issues relating to employment discrimination, and the raising of the level of awareness of legal rights and obligations. In addition, a continuing exchange of experience and expertise needs to occur on the international front for mutual benefit among all groups in order to best serve the fight for religious equality. We must all strive to promote and improve the situation of all humans through networks of awareness, in the raising of initiatives, the dissemination of information and the provision of support for equality. In addition, there needs to be a full employment policy for the integration of all humans into the labor market, the reduction of barriers to access and participation in employment, the improvement in the quality of employment through education, training and management of resources, and the improvement in the status of all in society for a change of attitudes and a lasting progress.[1]

Further, we must learn from other groups' experiences in the fight for equality. As such, like the civil rights' movement, the women's liberation movement and the disability movement, in examining legislation, we should take into account the religious movement, and specifically its advancements in religious rights in general and tolerance for those of all faiths. Therefore, in the struggle to secure equal rights for all, the consultation process must include input from other groups for strategic purposes in order to strengthen the cause. The process must be one of inclusion not exclusion.

It is realistic to say that inequality in general exists, but especially inequality of opportunity within the labor force. This is to be expected, since not all humans have occupied a major role in the employment sphere. In addition to this, laws have been enacted and courts have enforced them in a traditionally younger white male non-disability dominant way. However, all humans too need to be a rallying symbol of political and economic force, so that equality can become a reality. The impact of equality legislation will depend on the legislative provisions as well as the effectiveness of the legislation's enforcement.

The full and equal enjoyment of all human rights and fundamental freedoms should be a priority for all and is essential for the advancement of all. Equal rights are explicitly mentioned in the Preamble to the Charter of the United Nations, and all the major international human rights instruments include or should include religion as one of the grounds upon which States may not discriminate. Unless the human rights of all are fully recognized and effectively protected, applied, implemented and enforced in national and international law as well as in national practice in family, civil, penal, labor and commercial codes and administrative rules and regulations, they will exist in name only.[2]

It is evident that we are moving in the right direction, since some change has taken place. However, further change is necessary and plausible. Only by working on the very thing that controls and defines all of our lives, the law, can further progress be made.

Once again, the memorable words of the Rev. Martin Luther King Jr. in his struggle for civil rights are most relevant today in the struggle for equality of religion and religious tolerance, in the pursuit of *Heaven Forbid*:

> I have a dream that one day every valley shall be exalted, every hill and mountain shall be made low, the rough places shall be made plain, and the crooked places shall be made straight and the glory of the Lord will be revealed and all flesh shall see it together. This is our hope . And when we allow freedom to ring, when we let it ring from every village and hamlet, from every state and city, we will be able to speed up that day when all of God's children will be able to join hands and to sing in the words of the old Negro spiritual, 'Free at last, free at last; thank God Almighty, we are free at last'.[3]

Notes

1 Commission of the European Communities, *Promotion of Positive Action*, Brussels, p. 4.
2 United Nations, *Beijing Declaration and Platform for Action*, 1995.
3 King Jr., Martin Luther, *March on Washington*, 1963.

References

Commission of the European Communities, *Promotion of Positive Action*, Brussels.
King Jr., Martin Luther (1963), *March on Washington*.
United Nations (1995), *Beijing Declaration and Platform for Action*.

Bibliography

ACAS, *Religion or Belief and the Workplace, Putting the Employment Equality (Religion or Belief) Regulations 2003 into Practice.*
African Charter on Human and Peoples' Rights, 1981.
Ahmad v. Inner London Education Authority [1978] 1 All ER 574 at 583.
American Convention on Human Rights, 1978.
American Declaration of the Rights and Duties of Man, 1948.
American Federation of State, County and Municipal Employees v. Washington, 770 F.2d. 1401 (1985).
American Nurses Association v. State of Illinois, 783 F.2d. 716 (1985).
Amor, A., Implementation of the Declaration on the Elimination of All Forms of Intolerance and Discrimination Based on Religion or Belief, UN doc E/CN.4/1998/6/Add.2.
Anti-Discrimination Act, Australia, 1991.
Application for Registration as a Charity by the Church of Scientology – Decision of the Charity Commissioners for England and Wales made on the 17th November 1999.
Arrowsmith v. UK (1978) 19 DR 5; (1978) 3 EHRR 110.
Australia's Beijing Plus Five Action Plan 2001–2005.
Axworthy, Lloyd (1988), 'Free Trade, The Costs for Canada', in A.R. Riggs and Tom Velk, *Canadian-American Free Trade: (The Sequel) Historical, Political and Economic Dimensions*, The Institute for Research on Public Policy, Montreal.
Basi v. Canadian National Railway (1984), 9 CHRR 4. D/5029 (CHRTribunal).
Bill of Rights Act, New Zealand, 1990.
Blake v. Ministry of Correctional Services and Mimico Correctional Institute (1984), 5 CHRR D/2417 (Ontario).
Board of Trustees of Keene State College v. Sweeney, 439 US 24 (1978).
Boyle, K. and Sheen, J. (1997), *Freedom of Religion and Belief - A World Report*, Routledge, London.
Braunfeld v. Brown, 366 U.S. 599 (1961).
Brecher, Irving (1987), 'The Free Trade Initiative, On Course or Off', in A.R. Riggs and Tom Velk, *Canadian-American Free Trade: Historical, Political and Economic Dimensions*, The Institute for Research in Public Policy, Montreal.
Brennan v. City Stores, 479 F.2d. 235 (1973).
British North America Act, Canada, 1867.
Canada Employment Equity Act, Canada, 1995.

Bureau of Democracy, Human Rights and Labor (2006), *International Religious Freedom Report*.

C. v. the United Kingdom, D&R 37 (1984).

Campbell and Cosans v. UK (1982) 4 EHRR 293.

Campbell, Bruce (1993), *Free Trade, Destroyer of Jobs*, Canadian Centre for Policy Alternatives, Ottawa.

Canada–United States Free Trade Agreement, 1989.

Canadian Advisory Council on the Status of Women (1992), *Feminist Guide to the Canadian Constitution*, Ottawa.

Canadian Bill of Rights, Canada, 1960.

Canadian Constitution, Canada, 1982.

Canadian Constitution, Canadian Charter of Rights and Freedoms, Canada, 1982.

Canadian Human Rights Act, Canada, 1978.

Cantwell v. State of Connecticut, 310 U.S. 296 (1940).

Cassin, René (1969), From the Ten Commandments to the Rights of Man, France.

Charter of the Organization of African Unity, 1963.

Church of the New Faith v. Commissioner for Pay-Roll Tax (Vic) (1983) 154 CLR 120.

Civil Rights Act, United States, 1964.

Coleman, Frank (1977), *Hobbes and America*, University of Toronto, Toronto.

Constitución Política de los Estados Unidos Mexicanos, Mexico.

Commission for Racial Equality (2002), Code of Practice on the Duty to Promote Race Equality, UK.

Commission for Racial Equality v. Dutton [1989] IRLR 8.

Commission of the European Communities, *Promotion of Positive Action*, Brussels.

Commission Report on the Social Situation in the European Union, Report on Social Protection in Europe 2004, [Not published in the Official Journal].

Constitution of Ireland, Ireland, 1937.

Constitution of South Africa, 1996.

Corning Glass Works v. Brennan, 417 US 188 (1974).

Costa v. ENEL [1964] CMLR 425.

Council Decision 2000/750/EC of 27 November 2000 Establishing a Community Action Program to Combat Discrimination (2001 to 2006) [OJ L 303, 02/12/2000 P. 0023-0028].

Council Directive 2000/78/EC Establishing a General Framework for Equal Treatment in Employment and Occupation.

County of Allegheny v. American Civil Liberties Union Greater Pittsburgh Chapter, 492 U.S. 573 (1989).

Cox, Archibald (1967), *Civil Rights, The Constitution and the Court*, Harvard University Press, Cambridge.

Cox, Archibald (1976), *The Role of the Supreme Court in American Government*, New York: Oxford University Press, New York.

Crown Suppliers (Property Services Agency) v. Dawkins [1993] ICR 517.

d'Aquino, Thomas (1987), 'Truck and Trade with the Yankees, The Case for a Canada-U.S. Comprehensive Trade Agreement', in A.R. Riggs and Tom Velk, *Canadian-American Free Trade: Historical, Political and Economic Dimensions*, The Institute for Research on Public Policy, Montreal.

Daltrop, Anne (1982), *Political Realities, Politics and the European Community*, Longman, London.

Davis v. Passman, 442 US 228 (1979).

Declaration of Independence, United States, 1776.

Ely, J. (1980), *Democracy and Distrust*, Harvard University Press, Cambridge.

Equal Pay Act, United States, 1963.

Discrimination Act, Australia, 1991.

Durkheim, E. (1975), *The Elementary Forms of Religious Life,* 1915, trans. J.W. Swain, Free Press, New York.

Easterbrook, W.T. and Aitken, Hugh (1976), *Canadian Economic History*, Macmillan, Toronto.

Economic Commission for Africa (2002), *Economic Report on Africa*.

Efstratiou v. Greece, Judgement of 18 December 1996; Comm. report, 11.4.96.

Employment Contracts Act, New Zealand, 1991.

Employment Equality (Age) Regulations, UK, 2006.

Employment Equality (Religion or Belief) Regulations, UK, 2003.

Employment Equality Act, Ireland, 1998.

Employment Equity Act, South Africa, 1998.

Employment Relations Act, New Zealand, 2000.

Employment Rights Act, UK, 1996.

Equal Opportunities Commission, *Code of Practice on Equal Pay*, UK.

Equal Pay Act, UK, 1970.

Equal Status Act, Ireland, 2000.

Equality Act, UK, 2006.

Estate of Thornton v. Caldor, Inc., 472 U.S. 703 (1985).

Eurobarometer 57, Discrimination in Europe, For Diversity Against Discrimination, 2003, Alan Marsh and Melahat Sahin-Dikmen, The European Opinion Research Group (EEIG) for the European Commission Directorate General Employment and Social Affairs.

European Convention for the Protection of Human Rights and Fundamental Freedoms, 1950.

European Convention for the Protection of Human Rights and Fundamental Freedoms as amended by Protocol No. 12, 2000.

European Social Charter, 1961.

European Social Charter (revised), 1996.

Everson v. Board of Education of Ewing, 330 U.S. 1 (1947).

Fair Employment and Treatment (Northern Ireland) Order 1998 (FETO) No. 3162 (N.I. 21).

Federal Task Force on Disability Issues, Equal Citizenship for Canadians with Disabilities: The Will to Act, 1996.

Federalist Papers, United States, 1787-1788.
Frazee v. Illinois Department of Employment Security, 489 U.S. 829 (1989).
Fried, Morton (1967), *The Evolution of Political Society*, Random House, New York.
Fry, Earl (1987), 'Trends in Canada-U.S. Free Trade Discussions', in A.R. Riggs and Tom Welk, *Canadian-American Free Trade: Historical, Political and Economic Dimensions*, The Institute for Research in Public Policy, Montreal.
General Agreement on Tariffs and Trade, 1947.
Gething L. (1999), *We're Growing Old Too: Quality of Life and Service Provision Issues for People with Long Standing Disabilities Who Are Ageing*, Community Disability and Ageing Program, The University of Sydney.
Gillette v. United States, 401 U.S. 437 (1971).
Goldman v. Weinberger, 475 U.S. 503 (1986).
Government of Canada (1993), *The North American Free Trade Agreement at a Glance*, Ottawa.
Government of Canada (2002), *NAFTA at Eight*, Ottawa.
Grant, Hugh M.K. and Gretta Wong Grant, Gretta, *Age Discrimination and the Employment Rights of Elderly Canadian Immigrants*, 2002.
Greenwalt, K. (1999), *Diverse Perspectives and the Religion Clause: An Examination of Justification and Qualifying Beliefs*, 74(5) Notre Dame Law Review 1433.
Griffin Cohen, Marjorie (1987), *Free Trade and the Future of Women's Work, Manufacturing and Service Industries*, Garamond Press, Toronto.
Griggs v. Duke Power Co., 401 US 424 (1971).
Habermas, Jurgen (1998), *Between Facts and Norms*, MIT Press, Massachusetts.
Hamelin, Jean (1976), *Histoire du Québec*, Edisem, St. Hyacinthe.
Harris, Diana K. (2005), 'Age Norms', in Erdman B. Palmore, Laurence Branch, Diana K. Harris, *Encyclopedia of Ageism*, The Haworth Press, Inc, New York.
Harris, Richard (1988), 'Some Observations on the Canada-U.S. Free Trade Deal', in A.R. Riggs and Tom Velk, *Canadian-American Free Trade: (The Sequel) Historical, Political and Economic Dimensions*, The Institute for Research on Public Policy, Montreal.
Health and Safety at Work Act, UK, 1974.
Hepple QC, Bob, Choudhury, Tufval (2001), Home Office Research Study 221, *Tackling Religious Discrimination: Practical Implications for Policy-Makers and Legislators*, Home Office Research, Development and Statistics Directorate.
Higher Education Amendments, United States, 1998.
Hobbie v. Unemployment Appeals Compensation Commission of Florida, 480 U.S. 136 (1987).
Hornstein, Zmira, *Outlawing Age Discrimination: Foreign Lessons, UK Choices*, The Policy Press.
Human Resources and Social Development Canada.

Human Rights Act, New Zealand, 1993.
Human Rights Act, UK, 1998.
Human Rights and Equal Opportunity Commission (1998), *Article 18 – Freedom of Religion and Belief.*
Human Rights and Equal Opportunity Commission Act, Australia, 1986.
Hurtig, Mel (1991), *The Betrayal of Canada*, Stoddart Publishing, Toronto.
Inter-American Democratic Charter, 2001.
Interim Constitution of South Africa, Schedule 4.
Internationale Handelsgesellschaft, [1970] ECR 1125, [1972] CMLR 255.
J.H. Walker Ltd v. Hussain [1996] IRLR 11 EAT.
Kimel v. Florida Board of Regents, 528 U.S. 62 (2000).
King Jr., Dr. Martin Luther (1963), *March on Washington*, United States.
Kokkinakis v. Greece (1994) 17 EHRR 397.
Labor Canada (1986), *Equal Pay for Work of Equal Value*, Ottawa.
Lemon v. Kurtzman, 403 U.S. 602 (1971).
Laun, Louis (1987), 'U.S.-Canada Free Trade Negotiations: Historical Opportunities', in A.R. Riggs and Tom Velk, *Canadian-American Free Trade: Historical, Political and Economic Dimensions*, The Institute for Research in Public Policy, Montreal.
Layton, Robert (1987), 'Why Canada Needs Free Trade', in A.R. Riggs and Tom Velk, *Canadian-American Free Trade: Historical, Political and Economic Dimensions*, The Institute for Research in Public Policy, Montreal.
Ley del Seguro Social, Mexico.
Ley Federal de Trabajo, Mexico.
Lipsey, Richard (1987), 'Canada's Trade Options', in A.R. Riggs and Tom Velk, *Canadian-American Free Trade: Historical, Political and Economic Dimensions*, The Institute for Research in Public Policy, Montreal.
Lovell-Badge v. Norwich City College of Further and Higher Education, Case no: 1502237/97, (Spring 1999).
Lynch v. Donnelly, 465 U.S. 668 (1984).
Lyng v. Northwest Indian Cemetery Protection Association, 485 U.S. 439 (1988).
M.A.B.; W.A.T. and A.Y.T. v. Canada, Communication No. 570/1993, Inadmissibility Decision of April 8 1994, cited in *Article 18-Freedom of Religion and Belief,* (Human Rights and Equal Opportunities Commission, 1998), at p. 11.
Maastricht Treaty, 1992.
Magna Carta, Great Britain, 1215.
Mandel, Michael (1989), *The Charter of Rights and the Legalization of Politics in Canada*, Wall & Thompson, Toronto.
Mandla v. Dowell Lee [1983] 2 AC 548.
Marbury v. Madison, 1 Cranch 137 (1803).
Marsh Alan, Sahin-Dikmen, Mehalat (2002), *Discrimination in Europe*, Policy Studies Institute, London.
McCullough v. Maryland, 4 Wheaton 415 (1819).
McDonnell Douglas Corp. v. Green, 411 US 792 (1973).

McFeely v. UK, [1981] 3 EHRR 161.
McGowan v. Maryland, 366 U.S. 420 (1961).
McPhail, Brenda (1985), *NAFTA Now*, University Press of America, Lanham.
Merrett, Christopher (1996), *Free Trade, Neither Free Nor About Trade*, Black Rose Books, New York.
Mexican Investment Board (1994), *Mexico Your Partner for Growth, Regulatory Reform and Competition Policy, Setting the Incentives for an Efficient Economy*, Mexico.
Murphy v. Miller Brewer Co., 307 F.Supp. 829 (1969).
Nader, Ralph (1993), *The Case Against Free Trade*, Earth Island Press, San Francisco.
Neufeld, E.P. (1987), 'Financial and Economic Dimensions of Free Trade', in A.R. Riggs and Tom Velk, *Canadian-American Free Trade: Historical, Political and Economic Dimensions*, The Institute for Research on Public Policy, Montreal.
New Zealand Bureau of Democracy, Human Rights, and Labor, *International Religious Freedom Report*, 2007.
Nicoll, William and Salmon, Trevor (1994), *Understanding the New European Community*, Prentice Hall, Exeter.
North American Agreement on Labor Cooperation, 1993.
North American Free Trade Agreement, 1994.
North, Arthur (1964), *The Supreme Court, Judicial Process and Judicial Politics*, Appleton Century Crofts, New York.
Northern Ireland Act, 1998.
Ontario Human Rights Commission v. Simpsons-Sears Ltd. [1985] SCR 536.
Otto Preminger Institute v. Austria (1994) 19 European Human Rights Reports 34.
Oxford English Dictionary.
Pew Forum on Religion and Public Life, 2008.
Pope John Paul II (1981), *Laborem Exercens*, Rome.
Pope John XXIII (1963), *Pacem in Terris*, Rome.
President John F. Kennedy.
Promotion of Equality and Prevention of Unfair Discrimination Act, South Africa, South Africa, 2000.
Protocol on the Rights of Women in Africa, 2003.
Protocol to the African Charter on Human and Peoples' Rights on the Establishment of an African Court on Human and Peoples' Rights, 2003.
Public Employees Retirement System of Ohio v. Betts, 492 U.S. 158 (1989).
Race Relations Act (Statutory Duties) Order 2001, 2003, 2004, UK.
Race Relations Act, New Zealand, 1971.
Race Relations Act, UK, 1976.
Racial Discrimination Act, Australia, 1975.
Racial Hatred Act, Australia, 1995.

Raynauld, Andre (1987), 'Looking Outward Again', in A.R. Riggs and Tom Velk, *Canadian-American Free Trade: Historical, Political and Economic Dimensions*, The Institute for Research on Public Policy, Montreal.
Regina v. Oakes, [1986] 1 S.C.R. 103.
Reynolds v. United States, 98 U.S. 145 (1878).
Safouane & Bouterfas v. Joseph Ltd and Hannah [1996] Case No. 12506/95/LS & 12569/95.
Sardar v. McDonalds (1998), Muslim News, No. 115, 27th November 1998 – 8th Shaban 1419.
School Standards and Framework Act, UK, 1998.
Seide v. Gillette Industries Ltd [1980] IRLR 427.
Sex Discrimination Act, Australia, 1984.
Sex Discrimination Act, UK, 1975.
Shakes v. Rex Pak Ltd. (1982), 3 CHRR D/1001.
Sherbert v. Verner, 374 U.S. 398 (1963).
Soldatos, P (1988), 'Canada's Foreign Policy in Search of a Fourth Option: Continuity and Change in Orientation Towards the U.S.', in A.R. Riggs and Tom Velk, *Canadian-American Free Trade: (The Sequel) Historical, Political and Economic Dimensions*, The Institute for Research on Public Policy, Montreal.
Spaulding v. University of Washington, 740 F.2d. 686 (1984).
Statute of the Inter-American Court on Human Rights, 1980.
Stone, Frank (1987), 'Removing Barriers to Canada', in A.R. Riggs and Tom Velk, *Canadian-American Free Trade: Historical, Political and Economic Dimensions*, The Institute for Research on Public Policy, Montreal.
Tariq v. Young Case 247738/88, EOR Discrimination Case Law Digest No. 2.
Teuling v. Bredrijfsvereniging [1987] ECR 2497.
Thomas v. Review Board of the Indiana Employment Security Division, 450 U.S. 7 (1981).
Torcaso v. Watkins, 367 U.S. 488 (1961).
Treaty establishing a Constitution for Europe, 2004.
Treaty of Amsterdam, 1997.
Treaty of Lisbon, 2007.
Treaty of Paris, 1951.
Treaty of Rome, 1957.
Treaty of Waitangi, New Zealand, 1840.
United Nations (1945), Charter of the United Nations.
United Nations (1945), Statute of the International Court of Justice.
United Nations (1948), Universal Declaration of Human Rights.
United Nations (1951), Equal Remuneration Convention (ILO No. 100).
United Nations (1958), Discrimination (Employment and Occupation) Convention (ILO No. 111).
United Nations (1964), Employment Policy Convention (ILO No. 122).

United Nations (1965), International Convention on the Elimination of All Forms of Racial Discrimination.
United Nations (1966), International Covenant on Civil and Political Rights.
United Nations (1966), International Covenant on Economic, Social and Cultural Rights.
United Nations (1966), Optional Protocol to the International Covenant on Civil and Political Rights.
United Nations (1979), Convention on the Elimination of all Forms of Discrimination Against Women.
United Nations (1981), Declaration on the Elimination of All Forms of Intolerance and of Discrimination Based on Religion or Belief.
United Nations (1989), Convention on the Rights of the Child.
United Nations (1991), Principles for Older Persons.
United Nations (1993), Resolution on the Elimination of All Forms of Religious Intolerance 48/128.
United Nations (1995), Beijing Declaration and Platform for Action.
United Nations (1999), Optional Protocol to the Convention on the Elimination of All Forms of Discrimination against Women.
United Nations (2002), Second World Assembly on Ageism.
United Nations (2005), *The Fight Against Racism, Racial Discrimination, Xenophobia and Related Intolerance and the Comprehensive Implementation of and Follow-Up to the Durban Declaration and Programme of Action*, (F/CN.4/2005/18).
United Nations Development Program (1994), *Human Development Report*, Oxford University Press, Oxford.
United States Constitution, United States, 1776.
United States v. Ballard, 322 U.S. 78 (1944).
United States v. Seeger, 380 U.S. 163 (1965).
Universal Military Training and Armed Services Act, United States, 50 USC (1958 ed.), s.456(j).
Valsamis v. Greece, Judgement of 18 December 1996; Comm. report, 6.7.95.
Velk, Tom and Riggs, A.R. (1987), 'The Ongoing Debate Over Free Trade', in A.R. Riggs and Tom Velk, *Canadian-American Free Trade: Historical, Political and Economic Dimensions*, The Institute for Research on Public Policy, Montreal.
Wallace v. Jaffree, 472 U.S. 38 (1985).
Watkins, Mel (1989), 'The Political Economy of Growth', in Wallace Clement and Glen Williams, *The New Canadian Political Economy*, McGill-Queen's University Press, Kingston.
Weller, Paul, Feldman, Alice, Purdam, Kingsley (2001), Home Office Research Study 220, *Religious Discrimination in England and Wales*, Home Office Research, Development and Statistics Directorate.
Welsh v. United States, 398 U.S. 333 (1970).
West Virginia State Board of Education v. Barnette, 319 U.S. 624 (1943).

Wigle, Randall (1987), 'The Received Wisdom of the Canada-U.S. Free Trade Qualifications', in A.R. Riggs and Tom Welk, *Canadian-American Free Trade: Historical, Political and Economic Dimensions*, The Institute for Research in Public Policy, Montreal.

Wirth, L. (1945), 'The Problem of Minority Groups', in R. Linton (Ed.), *The Science of Man in the World Crisis* (pp. 347-372), Columbia University Press, New York.

Wisconsin v. Yoder, 406 U.S. 205 (1972).

Workplace Relations Act, Australia, 1996.

Index

Africa 93-110
    African Charter on Human Peoples'
        Rights 98-104
    Charter of the Organization of African
        Unity 95-97
    Protocol to the African Charter on
        Human and Peoples' Rights 104-107
    Protocol on Rights of Women in
        Africa 107-110

Australia 65-77
    Discrimination Act and Anti-
        Discrimination Act 66-69
    Human Rights and Equal Opportunity
        Commission Act 69-71
    Race Discrimination Act and Racial
        Hatred Act 72-74
    Sex Discrimination Act 74-76
    Workplace Relations Act 71-72

Canada 131-144
    Canada Employment Equity Act 138-140
    Canadian Bill of Rights 134
    Canadian Constitution 131-134
    Canadian Human Rights Act 135-138

European Union 265-309
    Council Decision 2000/750/EC
        Establishing a Community
        Action Program to Combat
        Discrimination 302-304
    Council Directive 2000/78/EC
        Establishing a General
        Framework for Equal
        Treatment in Employment and
        Occupations 294-302
    European Convention for the
        Protection of Human Rights and
        Fundamental Freedoms 276-284
    European Social Charter 284-288
    European Law and the European Court
        of Justice 271-276
    Maastricht Treaty 269-270
    Treaty Establishing a
        Constitution 289-293
    Treaty of Amsterdam 270-271
    Treaty of Lisbon 293-294
    Treaty of Paris 266
    Treaty of Rome 267-269

Ireland 243-259
    Constitution 243-246
    Employment Equality Act 246-254
    Equal Status Act 254-259

Mexico 145-146
    Constitución Política de los Estados
        Unidos Mexicanos 145
    Ley Federal de Trabajo 145
    Ley del Seguro Social 146-146

New Zealand 78-89
    Bill of Rights Act 82-83
    Employment Contracts Act and
        Employment Relations Act 87
    Human Rights Act and Human Rights
        Amendment Act 83-89
    Race Relations Act 88-89
    Treaty of Waitangi 80-82

North American Free Trade
    Agreement 169-214
    American Convention on Human
        Rights 204-210
    American Declaration of the Rights
        and Duties of Man 201-203
    basis for 169-174
    Inter-American Democratic
        Charter 211-213

North American Agreement on Labor
    Cooperation 188-196
North American Free Trade
    Agreement 174-188
Statute of the Inter-American Court on
    Human Rights 209-211

South Africa 110-126
    Constitution 113-118
    Employment Equity Act 118-122
    Interim Constitution Schedule 4 112-113
    Promotion of Equality and Prevention
        of Unfair Discrimination
        Act 122-126

United Kingdom 221-243
    Employment Equality (Religion or
        Belief) Regulations 229-233
    Equal Pay Act, Equal Opportunities
        Commission and code of
        practice 226-227
    Equality Act 234-236
    Human Rights Act 227-228
    Race Relations Act 222-224
    Sex Discrimination Act 224-226

United Nations 19-59
    Charter 20-21
    Convention on the Elimination of All
        Forms of Discrimination against
        Women 35-38
    Optional Protocol to the Convention on
        the Elimination of All Forms
        of Discrimination against
        Women 38-39
    Convention on the Rights of the
        Child 41-43

Declaration on the Elimination of
    All Forms of Intolerance and of
    Discrimination Based on Religion
    or Belief 47-50
Discrimination (Employment and
    Occupation) Convention (ILO
    No.111) 44-46
Employment Policy Convention
    (ILO No. 122) 46-47
Equal Remuneration Convention
    (ILO No. 100) 43-44
International Convention on the
    Elimination of All Forms of Racial
    Discrimination 31-35
International Covenant on Civil and
    Political Rights 24-27
Optional Protocol to the International
    Covenant on Civil and Political
    Rights 28
International Covenant on
    Economic, Social and Cultural
    Rights 28-31
Resolution on the Elimination
    of All Forms of Religious
    Intolerance 51-54
Statute of the International Court of
    Justice 21-22
United Nations Principles for Older
    Persons 39-40
Universal Declaration of Human
    Rights 22-24

United States of America 146-161
    Civil Rights Act 152-157
    Constitution 148-151
    Declaration of Independence 147
    Equal Pay Act 151-152
    Federalist Papers 147-148

For Product Safety Concerns and Information please contact our EU
representative GPSR@taylorandfrancis.com
Taylor & Francis Verlag GmbH, Kaufingerstraße 24, 80331 München, Germany

www.ingramcontent.com/pod-product-compliance
Lightning Source LLC
Chambersburg PA
CBHW071800300426
44116CB00009B/1152